JOHN NORDEN'S MS. MAP OF ESSEX. 1594

ELIZABETHAN LIFE:

DISORDER

Standard Book No. 900360 10 0

To

COLONEL SIR JOHN RUGGLES-BRISE
Bt., C.B., O.B.E., T.D., J.P.

Her Majesty's Lieutenant and Custos Rotulorum of the County of Essex
and
the Justices of the Peace and Members of the County Council of Essex
in the same spirit as the words of a young American historian with which
this book ends

Essex Record Office Publications No. 56

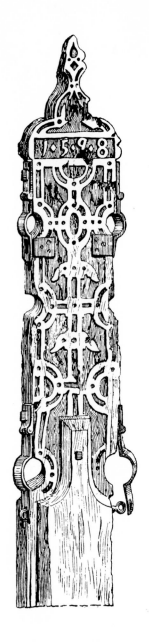

1   WHIPPING-POST AND STOCKS, WALTHAM ABBEY

Height 5 ft. 9 ins. General width 13 ins.

ELIZABETHAN LIFE: *DISORDER*

Mainly from Essex Sessions and Assize Records

F. G. EMMISON

Chelmsford
Essex County Council
1970

Printed by
Cullingford and Co. Ltd., Colchester, Essex, England

Contents

Introduction

Much of the Essex documentary material of the Elizabethan period about to be summarized may rightly be termed unique: especially the Quarter Sessions records because of their abnormal completeness; the Assize and Queen's Bench records because of their exceptional availability; and the Wills because the great series proved in the local courts have all been examined. I hope below to justify this sweeping statement. The material is, therefore, of much wider than county interest.

My commission from the Essex County Council, briefly, is to include as much information as possible from the original records, within the limits of three volumes each of about 300 pages, selecting what appears to be of value to the specialist and of interest to the general reader from the Sessions, Assize, Queen's Bench, Archidiaconal, Manorial, Municipal, Probate and Parochial archives for 1558–1603. The volumes are therefore primarily source books. Owing to the immense number of documents, it was imperative to restrict editorial comment to a minimum. Only a tiny fraction of the material has previously appeared in print, so that the reader is presented with a big corpus of new evidence. Much of this is taken from classes of records of which relatively little has been published for any other county for the period.

My position accordingly is not unlike that of Professor Asa Briggs, who, in his address to the Standing Conference for Local History in 1969, said of his *History of Birmingham*, 'I knew that the proper and better treatment would be series of monographs.' The fresh Essex evidence should provide some of the foundation for other books, articles and theses by writers in their own fields. It may perhaps partly meet the needs of a few of those referred to in *The Place and Purpose of History*, prepared for this year's Historical Association Conference. 'How difficult it is', the pamphlet states, 'to supply satisfactory evidence to endorse general statements which impute common motives to or purport to describe the general condition of large groups of people, and how inconclusive such statements may be without satisfactory evidence; for this difficulty is one of the historian's most serious problems.' I hope, for example, to furnish ample support to the recently revised but still tentative view that the manor, as a significant influence on agriculture and as a social unit of self-government in the Midlands and some other areas, had not virtually ceased to exist by 1500: so far from being dead, a clear picture of the renewed vigour of some Essex manors will emerge from the extracts to be given in the next volume.

My terms of reference preclude evaluation of the evidence now published. It is not my task, for instance, to enter into the wider concepts of Protestantism or Religious Toleration, or of other Elizabethan controversial subjects. Comments may occasionally be made on the factual information, but assessment and opinion will be eschewed. Two examples may serve to illustrate the point: one, political and general; the other economic and local. In his classic *Queen Elizabeth* (1934), Sir John Neale refers to scandalous rumours about intimate relations between Elizabeth and Dudley, while at the same time he mentions the Imperial ambassador's report that her virtue was unbesmirched. Professor Neale quotes the two known records of seditious talk in Essex and Hertfordshire of the Queen being pregnant by Dudley in the summer of 1560. The Essex Sessions rolls yield three more tales: according to them, by 1580 the Queen had had two children by Leicester; by 1590, when two apparently unassociated persons were charged, the offspring was alleged to have been four, of whom one or two had been burned by Leicester! But no such gossip is on record from other counties. Of more importance is the fact that the Essex records disclose no less than fifty-five further indictments for seditious speech against the Queen, the Council, its leaders, or the Established Church, some of it highly treasonable and two of the charges revealing plans for rebellion in Essex. Again, indictments for sedition generally, so far from being matched in the surviving Sessions records of other counties, are almost non-existent, apart from six Middlesex charges in the whole reign. Some of the Essex cases were, of course, merely the result of tongues loosened in the alehouse, but it is for historians, not myself, to assess the degree of disorder manifested by this persistent pestilence of treasonable talk. On the other hand, to take a purely local example, brief editorial attention will be drawn in a later volume dealing with the Wills to the clear evidence that 'the great fields of saffron in Essex' alluded to in Trevelyan's *English Social History* were in fact very small fields, rarely more than two acres and usually only garden plots of one or two roods; the reason being that the plant demanded intensive and laborious cultivation to secure the high potential profit.

The preservation, almost intact, of the great series of Quarter Sessions rolls of Essex from as early as 1556 is little short of miraculous, when one reflects on the dangers and vicissitudes through which county records have passed during four centuries. The small number of sixteenth-century series possessed by other counties date from the 1580s or 1590s or are incomplete, with only a few exceptions, and for some counties they are extant only from the eighteenth century.[1] The tragic loss of so many Sessions records is partially qualified by the survival of a large number, from 1549, for Middlesex though the series is very deficient owing to many documents having been

[1] For the date of the earliest Quarter Sessions records in each county, see F. G. Emmison and I. Gray, *County Records* (Historical Association, revd. edn., 1967), Appendix II.

destroyed by damp, and of a unique minute-book, 1563 and 1574–92, for Wiltshire.[1] Most of the counties for which Elizabethan Sessions records have survived have zealously published them in full calendar form.[2] But continually rising costs since World War II have virtually stopped further publication of calendars. Essex had never begun to print its calendar. The County Council over a period of twenty years had engaged several outside editors to prepare a calendar, using the annual allocation to press on in typescript rather than to divide the available funds between compilation and publication. When the calendar reached 1714, the Council authorised expenditure on similar calendars of the Assize files and the Queen's Bench indictments in the Public Record Office : both pioneer tasks, and still unattempted for any other county. Elizabethan Assize files, in fact, exist only for the Home circuit, which comprised Essex, Hertfordshire, Kent, Surrey and Sussex.

The Essex Sessions rolls, 1556–1603, number about 10,000 documents. Many of these, especially the presentments by the juries for the hundreds, each contain a large number of individual and independent entries, perhaps as many as 6,000. When the newly calendared material in the Assize and Queen's Bench records was added (about 3,500 and 500 documents respectively), it became all too clear that the cost of printing in the usual format would be quite prohibitive. It was necessary therefore to consider ways of publishing it in a highly condensed form. The writs, jury lists, and recognizances to keep the peace are of little value. Many of the indictments for theft are of minor interest, and the majority of the articles stolen appear time after time. Drastic elimination of such documents would reduce the length and present the reader with the important and more detailed remainder, including, in particular, the real treasures of the Essex Sessions rolls—the depositions, petitions and letters, and much of the unique hundredal high constables' petty sessions presentments.[3]

The Assize records, comprising mostly indictments and other formal documents, were obviously much simpler to deal with. Their chief value and that of the Queen's Bench indictments is in chronicling the graver crimes which mainly lay outside the county justices' jurisdiction and in being complementary in other ways to the Sessions rolls. Many offences, tried at the Assizes, first came before the Quarter Sessions, and dovetailing of documents relating to the same case is sometimes highly informative both on points of procedure and in details of the charges. The inter-relationship between the three series of records has been explained elsewhere.[4]

[1] *Middlesex County Records* (ed. J. C. Jeaffreson), vol. i [1549–1603] (1886) ; *Wiltshire County Records* (ed. H. C. Johnson, Wilts. Archl. Soc., Records Branch, vol. iv, 1949).
[2] *County Records*, Appendix I. The exception is Norfolk, for which incomplete Sessions records from 1532 have survived. For Kent, see *Kentish Sources*, vols. i–vi (Kent C.C.).
[3] Kent has even more depositions, although only from 1595.
[4] Emmison, 'The Elizabethan Assize Files, with particular reference to the County of Essex' (*Bulletin of Society of Local Archivists*, no. 13, 1954) and 'Calendars of Essex Assize Files, 1559–1714, and King's Bench Indictments, 1558–1675' (*Essex Journal*, i, 126–30).

Sometimes it is the Queen's Bench series which supplements the others. The extraordinary libel charge against the Chelmsford barber in 1602 is recorded in an indictment of abnormal length owing to its incorporating the 76-line scandalous verse : the Assize document has several holes eaten away by a rodent ; but that in the Bench records fortunately is perfect.

There was however a new factor which created a difficult problem. At the time when most of the printed calendars appeared elsewhere, the county authorities, with rare exceptions, had in their custody Sessions records only. But the more recent county record offices were created for the reception of many additional classes of official, ecclesiastical, private and other archives. With the arrival of those of the church and manor courts, the county justices' records lost their isolated dignity, but their importance increased with the companionship of these new deposits. The latter were not blood relations, but a different form of relationship existed which called for investigation. Historians already knew that much of the business with which the justices were concerned was also the affair of other local institutions—parish vestries, for example, as well as the ecclesiastical and manorial courts. When all their archives could be studied side by side with the Sessions and Assize records, a further mass of complementary material was revealed, for some of the functions and many of the offences were common to more than one local body. The overlapping nature of their business was even more marked than previously realised : recusancy, witchcraft, alehouse disorders, poor relief, roads and bridges are among those more generally known, but there are others which the series will disclose. Finally, private archives uncovered fresh and exciting aspects of the work not only of the J.P.s but also of the church and parochial officials.

Confronted with this vast quantity of interlocking information, I tried to meet the challenge of getting the salient sections into print by estimating the amount of money which the Council might be willing to spend, hoping to equate it with the minimum length which would allow reasonably full treatment, beginning at any rate with the Elizabethan period—that in which Essex excels. Such a new venture had little chance of being approved if it could not be printed in three or four volumes (about 1,000 pages in all). Such a task, in any case, could not be absorbed by the Essex Record Office staff. Indeed, no county archivist working under heavy pressure on their primary (and multitudinous) duties had been able to undertake the publication of Quarter Sessions records, except for single volumes for Caernarvonshire, 1541–58, and Sussex, 1642–49, let alone the other major classes of records such as manor court rolls. The only hope lay in the appointment of an outside editor, a precedent for which existed with some other County Records—an editor thoroughly familiar with the county, its topography, families and peculiar features.

A happy solution was found. It was arranged that I should retire as County Archivist three years before the normal age and be commissioned to undertake the preparation of the books.

The task involved only material in the Essex Record Office, though this included the sole copies of the typescript calendars of Assize and Queen's Bench records : there was little question of embracing records housed elsewhere. But in one respect it may be that my original terms of reference will be extended to embrace the more substantial testators' wills proved in the Prerogative Court of Canterbury, because the intimate picture of Elizabethan Life would otherwise lack much important detail. In anticipation of this, the Friends of Historic Essex decided to bear the heavy cost of obtaining photostats—a most valuable contribution.

A very rough estimate of the main groups in addition to County records may be given. The 74 volumes of the court records (acts, visitations and depositions) of the two archdeaconries (those of the Middlesex (Essex and Herts. jurisdiction) court are lost for Elizabeth I's time) and the two other ecclesiastical courts in Essex contain approximately 25,000 entries, though there are numerous repetitions where the persons cited failed to appear. Some thousands of extracts have been card-indexed by myself as a preliminary task. There are now in the Essex Record Office court rolls for 200 manors for Elizabeth. They may contain up to 100,000 entries. Many of these rolls have been similarly extracted, but it seems unlikely that all will be gone through, as most offences are common to nearly all manors, though some courts are remarkable for their own diversity or peculiarities. All the 10,000 Elizabethan Wills housed in the Essex Record Office have also been read and indexed. Parish records have been deposited for nearly all parishes, and churchwardens' accounts and some other Elizabethan records will be used, but it is doubtful whether the large number of surviving Elizabethan parish registers can be examined.

The borough records of Maldon, deposited in the Essex Record Office, will be used to some extent, but those of the other Essex boroughs, still in municipal custody, can only be referred to briefly. Finally, there is the enormous quantity of private archives in addition to manorial records. Through public spirit and local patriotism, the ancient archives of virtually all the large Essex estates and of scores of the smaller estates have been entrusted to the County Council. These are not included in my commission, but certain outstanding documents will be quoted. My *Tudor Food and Pastimes* (1964) was filled in describing only one very small section—the household accounts of Sir William Petre of Ingatestone Hall—of one series of private archives, so it is clear that most of the private archives apart from manor court rolls are beyond the scope of the *Elizabethan Life* series.

These volumes were intended to follow generally the form of Mr. A. C. Edwards's *English History from Essex Sources, 1550–1750* (Essex Record Office Publications no. 17, 1952), but with less editorial annotation as the number of documents quoted would be very much larger. It soon became evident, however, that although hundreds of extracts would be fairly long there would be thousands of short extracts, giving some pages a patchy appearance with much wasted space, for the context would often require citation of a few lines or only a few words. I felt obliged therefore to alter the form into a narrative one : this is of course more time-consuming, but allows further condensation without any loss of detail, and it is hoped that this format is preferable to readers.

Essex is also fortunate in having been the home of three renowned Elizabethan authors, two of whom drew much from the conditions which they observed locally. William Harrison's *Description of England* (revised in 1587), the astonishingly detailed contemporary account of social life, is of course of paramount importance as a source book.[1] *Elizabethan Life* will serve as a criterion of the accuracy of many of his generalisations : suffice it to say at this stage that the new material is a tribute to Harrison's shrewd comments, most of which seem to be borne out.[2] Harrison and Sir Thomas Smith, author of *De Republica Anglorum* (1583), borrowed from each other's works ; Smith's, however, deals far more with constitutional matters than with social conditions. Thomas Tusser's *Five Hundreth Pointes of Good Husbandrie, Huswiferie and Gardening* (1573) will be used in later volumes.

As originally envisaged, the three books were to be called *Life in Elizabethan Essex*. It is hoped that the alternative adoption of the present, more general, title is justified because so few Elizabethan criminal court records have survived elsewhere and because relatively few of the other classes of local archives have been published for the same period.Owing to the change in title of the series, it was decided to end most chapters in this first volume by drawing briefly from the relevant printed calendars of Quarter Sessions records of other counties by way of comparison.

This volume is confined in the main, though by no means wholly, to felonies. Some of the lesser offences, broadly speaking, are excluded, chiefly because there is parallel material in other archives. The secular and church courts had a quasi-concurrent jurisdiction in recusancy and witchcraft cases, which will be narrated largely from the major source— the archdeacons' court books—in the next volume. Overlapping with the functions of the manor courts and parish vestries are offences such as neglect of roads, bridges and ditches, which will also appear in the next volume. In a later volume, perhaps with the title *Home and Work* (which will bring in the treasures from the wills), we shall look at the various trade offences, including apprenticeship, wages, weights and measures, licensing and purveyance, also the illuminating material about vagrants and the poor.

---

[1] Now available in Dr. G. Edelen's invaluable and scholarly edition (Cornell Univ. Press, 1968).
[2] An exception is some Essex evidence of disparking for conversion to arable (p. 233).

One of the chief problems was to decide into which category some cases fall. For example, with Assault and its kindred offences it is often difficult to know whether the case should appear under Riot, Disseisin, Barratry, Trespass, or Common Assault, but cross-references are given.

The first two chapters describe the contents of the very early records as far as 1561, including the three oldest Quarter Sessions rolls which precede 1558. From 1562 to 1568 the contents of the presentments are similarly treated, because the two series of reports by the juries for the hundreds, especially those of the Essex high constables' petty sessions, are the sole survival for the period. With this important exception, the arrangement of the Elizabethan material is by subject, according to the type of felony or misdemeanour. No completely logical order could be worked out. The final result will be apparent from the list of contents.

What are the chief omissions from the vast number of entries? Jury lists and writs, which are virtually confined to personal names, are completely ignored. No mention is made of the hundreds of recognizances and indictments for larceny where the personal names are those of humble people or the articles are of common use. Many personal names are omitted, to save space, where their being quoted would add little or nothing to the context; but they are included where identification, for instance, in a long deposition, facilitates narration. Documents referring to esquires, gentlemen, or persons with important or unusual occupations, are among those selected for citation. The early presentments by the hundreds contain hundreds of names of those who had failed to appear or failed to scour their ditches or so forth: only typical entries or those of interest in other ways are extracted. The great majority of documents relating to persons or parishes are of interest mainly to family historians and genealogists and to parish historians. For them the Essex Record Office has compiled not only full indices to the calendars of the criminal court records but also what is probably the biggest index of personal names for any county; this now includes all names in the official typescript calendars of deeds, etc. Similar remarks apply to the comprehensive index of parish references in the Office. Those interested in individual families or particular towns and villages will still need to visit the Office or to employ a professional record searcher. The County Council has spent large sums of money in providing these indices—as well as detailed indices of subjects to all classes—which save the searcher an immense amount of time and trouble.

There still remained, however, three important aspects: the justices of of the peace, verdicts and punishments, and the judicial procedure and administrative business of Quarter Sessions and Assizes. None of these aspects was included in my terms of reference, which, as already stated, were limited to an attempt to condense into about 300 pages the more interesting of the 14,000 Sessions, Assizes and Queen's Bench documents, without my undertaking research, compiling analyses, or writing a long introduction on the general background of the courts. As it is, I have done considerably more work than anticipated, and, partly in consequence, the volume has exceeded my authorized length. Fortunately, however, I have been privileged to be given valuable contributions on the first two subjects, which appear as Appendices E and F. After attending a short seminar on Elizabethan local records which I was invited to conduct at Northwestern University, Illinois, U.S.A., in 1968, Mr. J. Samaha, M.A., J.D., a postgraduate member of the history department with a legal qualification, decided to visit Essex to carry out a year's research on Crime and Punishment in Elizabethan Essex. Dr. Samaha has most generously offered to the County Council and myself these two appendices, containing a number of analytical tables compiled in the course of his examination of the material. While these represent only a part of the two subjects they go some way to filling the gap, and it is hoped that his completed thesis will be published in the fairly near future. The subject of Crime and Punishment (1595–1866) has also been dealt with recently in extracts from Kent records, prefaced by a useful 34-page introduction.[1]

On the judicial and administrative functions of the courts there are scholarly accounts of Quarter Sessions[2] in the Elizabethan period and of Assizes[3] in the Stuart period written by Mr. H. C. Johnson and Professor T. Barnes respectively. Mr. Johnson, formerly Keeper of Public Records, is well known as an authority on Sessions procedure, having previously edited the series of Warwickshire Quarter Sessions records from 1625 onwards. His Wiltshire and Warwickshire volumes have invaluable introductions. Dr. Barnes's research was a pioneer task, and his book and those of Mr. Johnson are complementary. The volume containing an edited transcript of the abnormally early Caernarvonshire Sessions records, 1541–58, has another comprehensive introduction by the late W. Ogwen Williams, and most of the other printed calendars of Sessions records possess good accounts of the general background.[4] For further information readers are referred to Professor C. Bridenbaugh's narrative account, which in many ways continues the theme of Disorder for the next half century.[5] The author chose 1590 as his *terminus a quo* because so few Sessions records before that date were in print when he wrote his book.

Ingatestone Hall, September, 1970 F.G.E.

---

[1] *Kentish Sources: VI, Crime and Punishment* (ed. E. Melling, Kent County Council, 1969).
[2] *Wiltshire County Records: Minutes of Proceedings in Sessions, 1563, 1574–92* (ed. H. C. Johnson, Wilts. Archl. Soc., Records Branch, iv, 1949); the records also refer to twelve Assizes, 1576–85. There is an exceptionally good index of subjects.
[3] *Somerset Assize Orders, 1629–40*, ed. T. G. Barnes (Som. Rec. Soc., lxv, 1959).
[4] *Caernarvonshire Quarter Sessions Records, 1541–58* (ed. W. O. Williams, Caerns. Hist. Soc., 1956). *County Records*, Appendix I.
[5] C. Bridenbaugh, *Vexed and Troubled Englishmen, 1590–1642* (Oxford, 1968).

ACKNOWLEDGEMENTS

The circumstances which led to the inauguration of an entirely new work on Elizabethan Life have been explained in the Introduction, and it is my pleasant duty to thank my former Authority, the Essex County Council, for sponsoring its publication. I am especially grateful to the Library and Records Committee for entrusting their County Archivist, when nearing his retirement, with this challenging project, and to Mr. J. S. Mills, M.C., LL.B. (who will become Clerk of the County Council shortly after publication of this volume) for his personal support, as on so many previous occasions. The Friends of Historic Essex, whose funds assist the Essex Record Office, have given generous contributions, not only in bearing the whole cost of the illustrations but in several other respects. I also wish to thank the Leverhulme Research Trustees for a grant towards my personal expenses. Several friends, expert in their own fields, who have so kindly helped me, are thanked in the relevant chapters; and Dr. J. Samaha's valuable contribution of Appendices E and F is acknowledged in the Introduction. Mr. K. C. Newton, M.A., F.R.HIST.S., County Archivist, and my wife have given me constant help during the preparation of the book. I am grateful to Miss Olwen Hall for typing my much-altered drafts, for initial proof-reading, and for compiling the draft Index of Persons and Places; also to Mr. Alan Sorrell for drawing the dust-jacket from my very rough sketch. Lord Petre most generously offered me the use of his Queen Anne Room at Ingatestone Hall.

For allowing reproduction of originals in their possession, grateful thanks are due to the Incumbents and Churchwardens of Wickham St. Paul's and Margaret Roothing, and especially to Mr. T. C. Gepp, Churchwarden of the latter parish, in respect of their communion cups (No. 24), to Lord Petre (Nos. 4, 8, 16, 20), to Miss M. Majendie, C.B.E. (No. 21), Mr. J. H. L. Arkwright (No. 15), the Director of the Cleveland Museum, Ohio, and Mr. Colket Jr., the Director of the Western Reserve Historical Society (No. 7); also, for lending blocks, to Messrs. Faber and Faber, publishers of Mr. Norman Scarfe's *Shell Guide to Essex* (No. 14), the Friends of Historic Essex, as owners of the remaining stock of the *Essex Review* (Nos. 1, 9, 10, 19, 23, 25), and to the Essex Archaeological Society for permission to reproduce No. 13. The remaining illustrations are from blocks belonging to the Essex Record Office, or from photographs made by Mr. N. Hammond, the office photographer.

Plates

NOTE ON EDITORIAL METHOD

All *dates* between 1 January and 24 March are expressed in modern style.

The general principle regarding *omission of material* such as jury lists is referred to in the Introduction (p. xiii). The following table indicates, for each chapter, whether all cases, nearly all cases, or only select cases have been incorporated in the book. 'Cases' normally implies indictments : nearly *all* presentment and *all* depositions, petitions and letters are used.

> *All cases quoted :* chapters 1–7, 13–17, 25, 27, 28.
>
> *Nearly all cases quoted :* chapters 8, 9, 12, 18–20
>
> *Selection only* (i.e. omitting cases of a repetitive nature or very minor interest) : chapters 10, 11, 21–23, 24 (but *all* in Appendix A), 26 (but *all* cloth and leather goods stolen in Appendices B, C).

References have been omitted to avoid cluttering the book with several thousand figures : the year or names should enable students in the Essex Record Office to trace entries in the indexed typescript calendars without difficulty.

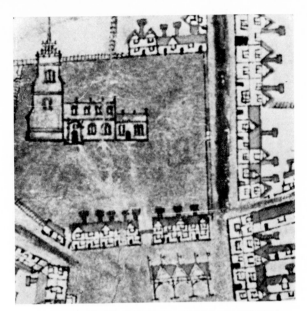

2 SESSIONS HOUSE, CHELMSFORD

Quarter Sessions and sometimes Assizes were held in the upper
rooms of the Market Cross.
(From John Walker's map of Chelmsford, 1591.)

3 ASSIZE HOUSE, BRENTWOOD

Demolished *circa* 1860. (From an engraving, *circa* 1830.)

4   SIR JOHN PETRE, *circa* 1590

One of the most active Essex justices of the peace.
(Created 1st Baron Petre, 1603.)   Artist unknown.
(On view in the Long Gallery, Ingatestone Hall.)

1

Preview

The earliest Sessions Rolls, 1556–57

The Essex Quarter Sessions rolls are fairly complete from 1562 and the Assize files from 1563, in each case from the beginning of the year. Some earlier records have also survived. There are three Sessions rolls from Michaelmas 1556 to Epiphany 1557, which include a few indictments from 1554, and five Assize files from Lent 1559 to Lent 1561. Very few Marian and early Elizabethan Sessions and Assize records are extant for other counties, and only the Essex Record Office has prepared calendars of the Elizabethan Assize files and the Queen's Bench indictments. A summary of the early documents in the three series will therefore be given as a preliminary review. In the main part of the book the great mass of information is presented, by synthesis, under each crime and offence, and the statutory background will be explained. Between this preview chapter and the later chapters a full account is given of the presentments by the ordinary and the high constables' juries of the hundreds for 1562–68.

Among the most interesting documents preserved in Quarter Sessions records are depositions. These give lively phrases and many details that are mostly omitted from the more formal documents. In 1556 a certain Thomas Jordan, late of Hungerford (Wiltshire), who describes himself as a cook, is brought before Lord Rich, one-time Lord Chancellor, whose treacherous perjury at Sir Thomas More's trial earned him unforgivable notoriety. In his capacity as an Essex justice of the peace he examines Jordan, whose deposition is written out in Rich's own handwriting. Jordan says that he had been Sir John Eath's man, on whose death he dwelt with Anthony Styrley at Greenwich for a year, then with Richard Lukener, prisoner in the Counter (a London gaol), and since Midsummer he has lived in London 'as a cook and dressed dinners'. Intending to go to Surrey he left London on the previous Sunday at 4 or 5 a.m. for Ilford and there apparently got drunk, thence proceeding to Chelmsford and Braintree (certainly not the route into Surrey). He adds that he owns two chests at a poor widow's house in Peacock Alley in the Fleet, and he delivers the key of the great chest to Lord Rich. Attached is a note of receipt of the key as well as of a knit purse with 23s. 9½d. in money, a testern and a piece of 2d., both counterfeit, with a further note that 2s. is given to Jordan on his going to Colchester and 3s. 4d. to the constables of Braintree, 'and so remains 18s. 5½d.' This is clearly an examination under the vagrancy laws.

On 13 August of the same year three men of Cottenham (Cambridge-shire) are examined and affirm that a horse claimed at Thremhall Green by Thomas Brewer, a Felsted husbandman, and now in his custody, being a dark grey gelding with a jointed tail, was bred by one of them 'and is now of the age of five years at last grass'. The alleged horse thief is a labourer of Brent Pelham, a Hertfordshire parish adjoining Stansted Mountfitchet. The clue to this short deposition is Thremhall Green, on the boundary of Hatfield Broad Oak and Stansted, lying next to Stane Street and only two miles from Bishop's Stortford on the London–Cam-bridge road. On this accessible site St. James's Fair, belonging to Lord Rich's manor of Hatfield, was held on St. James's Day (25 July) each year.

The scene of the next incident is the adjacent parish of Takeley. A boy of only ten vividly describes a burglary with threatened violence. His name is Tom Hornesby, son of a butcher of Elsenham, the next village, and he is examined by John Wiseman of Great Canfield Park nearby, one of the richest landowners in Essex, whose estates marched with those of Lord Rich : a man with a character almost as unsavoury as Rich's. Young Tom, for reasons unstated, was in the company of one Henry Woodford, a woman called Dodd's wife, and another man and two women unknown to him, in a barn belonging to John Thorpe's manor house of Colchester Hall in Takeley. An hour or so after midnight they compelled the lad to go with them to the cottage of Henry Peter, a Takeley labourer. Woodford broke down a wall by the hall door, crept through the hole and opened the hall door to let the others in. Lighting a candle they entered Peter's chamber. He was not at home. Woodford willed Dodd's wife to hold his knife over Peter's wife, telling her that if she stirred she would be killed. In the meantime Woodford broke open a chest with his dagger, taking out 20s. in 'white' money and two pieces of gold (one, a half angel, the other, a French crown) belonging to Joyce Peter widow, also a coat, a kirtle, a petticoat and a sheet of Henry Peter's and a petticoat cloth of Margaret Peter's. Woodford had promised Tom a doublet and a pair of slops (wide baggy breeches), and afterwards threatened to kill him if he should betray them. They all returned to the barn, but Tom got nothing from the haul, which was all hidden in Bushey Leas near Takeley windmill. But no goods had been found there after a search. The justice thereupon took recognizances, binding Peter and another labourer to prosecute the burglars and Tom's father to secure the lad's appearance to give evidence. The formal indictment names Henry Woodford as a labourer of Hatfield Regis (Broad Oak), Joan Dodd as a spinster of the same, and Elizabeth Tomson as a spinster of Takeley, also gives Joan Peter as the victim's name, and as usual gives the value of each article stolen. The defendants were found not guilty.

It is sheer luck that many more of these informative depositions have been preserved in the later Essex rolls, but even so they concern only a small proportion of the cases which came before the justices, and some of the crimes and offences are chronicled only in the indictments drawn up in the orthodox legal form. In the three Marian rolls there are forty-five indictments, including that for the Takeley burglary. The majority are for theft, preceded in most cases by unlawful or forcible entry into the victim's house or field ('close' is the medieval and Tudor term, hence closebreaking).

A typical entry reads : John Screvener of Liston labourer in 1556 broke into the house of William Fyrmyn of Borley called Borley Hall and stole 17lb. wool (found guilty). Three men of Yarmouth and Ipswich forcibly entered the house of Thomas Plomer of Dunton and stole two silver rings (worth 14d.), two silver hooks (3s.), a woman's robe (20s.), a gold angel (10s.), a gold French crown (value 6s. 8d.), 40s. in numbered money, and other (unspecified) goods. A Great Baddow man broke into the house of James Drylande there and stole two old gold ryals (value 30s.), a gold double ducat (13s. 4d.), a gold half angel (5s.), four gold angels (40s.), two gold crowns (10s.), two gold crusadoes (13s. 4d.), three gold French crowns (19s. 4d.), and four gold sovereigns (40s.). Thomas Otes of Debden smith stole from the dwelling of James Bourdells at Newport four pieces of holland cloth (worth £3) and two shirts of holland cloth (5s.) ('died in prison'). Most larceny cases are however in the Assize files.

Indictments for closebreaking follow much the same form, stock and crops replacing household goods and money. Two Great Waltham labourers forcibly entered the close of Stephen Collyn in Berners Roothing and stole two pigs (16s. 3d.) ; a West Thurrock man stole a boar (13s. 4d.) and three barrow hogs (10s. each) at Great Warley ; a Dagenham wheelwright stole a bay horse (26s. 8d.) at the manor of Corbets Tye in Upminster ; two High Roothing men cut down and stole two cartloads of firewood from a close called Great More there (fined 16d. each) ; two Braintree labourers drove away two pigs (13s. 4d.) from a wood at Notley (pleaded not guilty, verdict not given). The first case of a butcher stealing farm stock, of which some rather startling evidence occurs in later years, records that Thomas Stebbyng of Belchamp Walter broke into and took a wether (3s.) from the close of Robert Lawsell in Bulmer (acquitted).

Brought before the Michaelmas Sessions 1556 was Edward Torrell, the rector of Mount Bures, for stealing on three days in July and August 1555, in company with several labourers of his parish, a total of five cartloads of corn, barley and rye in sheaves (each load worth 20s.) and a cartload of 'pease pulse' (10s.) from Fen Field and Jenors Field in Bures St. Mary belonging to William Sidey the elder, gentleman. The rector and the others were fined 20d. on each count. This is possibly a case of illegal tithe-snatching.

The only cases of simple larceny were thefts by a labourer at Alresford of two wether sheep (5s.), eight lambs (16s.), a silver-gilt ivory whistle with a 'flue' (6s. 8d.), and £4 in money, and by a Lavenham (Suffolk) labourer at Braintree of a mare (33s. 6d.). A flue was a mouth-pipe, as opposed to a reed-pipe, and this is the earliest known reference to the word.

An important element in our theme of Disorder is that of insecure tenure of landed property. The three Marian rolls abound with indictments for forcible dispossession and these are perhaps the outstanding feature. Their place in the chronicle of gradually increasing security in the later Tudor period is of importance, so details are deferred for discussion under Disseisin (pp. 117–31).

Both constables of Alresford were charged with suffering a man to escape from their custody after he had been arrested for felony on the warrant of Edmund Tyrell esquire, justice, and ordered to be conveyed to Colchester Castle Gaol (each fined 3s. 4d.).

Unusually early evidence of the justices' administrative control by judicial means over alehouses is found in two block indictments dated January 1555, which did not however come before the Court until Midsummer 1556. Charged with being unlicensed are ten of West Ham, six of Brentwood, five each of Epping and Prittlewell, four of Leigh, and twelve of other places. Except for a single alewife, all are termed labourers or husbandmen.

The division between the jurisdictions of the ecclesiastical and the secular courts was far from clear in the case of various offences involving the Church or the clergy. The records of the Archdeacons' courts will be the main source in the next volume of *Elizabethan Life*. Four cases occur in the Marian rolls. A Quendon yeoman was charged with violently assaulting a woman in Takeley church with a dagger, intending to kill her. (The bill was found true only in part, in that he acted in self-defence.) There was trouble, too, in Mashbury church, when Thomas Eve clerk (the rector) was called by William Lukyn yeoman, one of his parishioners, 'a crying rascal' because he 'prepared for the celebration of the blessing of the Lamb contrary to the Statute of 1 Mary.' Joan Kent *alias* Austin and Agnes Stanley, both spinsters of Leigh, were charged with heresy for saying, 'In the sacrament of the Eucharist after the consecration thereof there is nothing other than bread and wine only,' thus denying the Real Presence. The doctrine of transubstantiation was thus again enforced under Mary. They were 'committed to the Ordinary' (bishop or archdeacon).

Of wider interest is the case involving a mysterious figure who stumped through Tendring Hundred sowing heresy. He appears in an indictment dated 25 July 1556 against John Geffrye the elder of West Mersea husbandman and Thomas Toose of Dedham clothier for assembling with twenty others unnamed at both these places and many other places unspecified, where they 'received abetted and maintained George Egle *alias* Trudy of Moze tailor in his heresies and schismatic sermons and preachings.' The clothier was fined 5s. but the husbandman had died before the Michaelmas Sessions. The case of Egle *alias* Trudgeover was before the Privy Council throughout July and August. It was the fear of rebellion, rather than Trudgeover's 'conventicles and readings', which gave the Council anxiety. Lord Darcy of St. Osyth's Priory was enjoined to search for him and to arrest this 'runagate'. A 'conspiracy' was being hatched. Darcy apprehended the man, and he was specially thanked by the Council.[1] 'Eagles *alias* Trudgeover' has an honourable place in Foxe's *Book of Martyrs*. He was tried for treason at Chelmsford, found guilty, and sentenced to be hanged, drawn and quartered, but was first taken to the 'Crown' inn, a room in which served as the Sheriff's temporary prison. The 'Crown', in the High Street at the Springfield Road corner, was shortly afterwards pulled down and was replaced by the well-known 'Black Boy' inn.[2]

A crime or offence might also be recorded indirectly in a recognizance, which is a pecuniary bond taken before one or more justices of the peace to perform some act such as keeping the peace, or to appear at Quarter Sessions or Assizes. There is a group of recognizances in almost every Sessions roll. They were taken to secure the attendance not only of defendants but also of prosecutors and witnesses. The three earliest (1556) are examples of the single and double type: a Felsted man is bound to prosecute for felony at the next Sessions; a London haberdasher and a Kelvedon husbandman are bound as sureties for the prosecution by a citizen of London (a doctor of civil law) of Anthony Lukyn, aged 14 years, taken at High Roothing for stealing £7 from the citizen, his master, and for the boy's appearance at the next Sessions or Assizes; eight men living in villages on the Suffolk–Essex border bind themselves for the attendance of a Melford (Suffolk) man at the Assizes, and he is to keep the peace in the meantime (endorsed to the effect that he was committed). Two Orsett men are bound for the appearance of one of them to answer for refusing to aid the constables in carrying a prisoner to Colchester Castle Gaol 'at the commandment of the justices'. The earliest Essex alehouse recognizance concerns one at Milton, a hamlet in Prittlewell. Having been licensed by Roger Appleton and Edmund Tyrell, two local justices, the alehousekeeper binds himself with two other Milton men as his sureties, not to 'suffer any suspicious persons, vagabonds, barrators, quarrellers or thieves' to be maintained in his alehouse nor any unlawful game 'as bowls, tennis, dice, cards, tables' (backgammon) nor 'any company eating, drinking or playing in the time of any sermon or service in the parish church.'

[1] *Acts of the Privy Council*, v. [2] *Essex Review*, vi, 167.

As in all Sessions rolls there are also several writs and precepts to summon defendants. One of them is at the petition of a man who alleged in 1556 that he had suffered 'mutilation of his body' by Thomas Nottak clerk (rector of Debden 1544–60), but no other document mentions the charge.

Two of the three rolls include a memorandum beginning with a list of the justices present at the Sessions (six or seven names), followed by a few short notes. Among them is the bare statement that each juror is bound in the large sum of £5 for appearance before the Privy Council in the Star Chamber on the following Wednesday, and an order to place a woman in the pillory at Rayleigh for an unnamed offence.

The almost wholesale loss of Quarter Sessions records of other counties for the Marian–Elizabethan period would in any case have enhanced the importance of the Essex series, but their significance is further increased by the presence of a very rare type of record – the presentments of the juries for the hundreds, at the two Sessions held in 1556. There are nine of them. Their importance generally is explained in the next chapter, which describes the presentments for 1562–68.

The foreman of the Barstable hundred jury presents 'with all his company' that Robert More of Orsett 'ought to make Skynners Bridge the which he is owner of both sides and is in sore decay'; and that Francis Clopton 'hath not made Bellow Bridge which was presented at the last Sessions, the which is in decay and a great nuisance to the King's and Queen's liege people'; Clopton 'is lord (of the manor of Ramsden Bellhouse) on both sides and ought to make it.' They also present that Thomas Howe of Ramsden Bellhouse 'is a singleman wearing a cognizance whom he said is Sir Henry Parker knight, the which we do not know' (apparently against Henry VII's laws of livery and maintenance, known to every schoolchild because of the vast fine imposed on the Earl of Oxford at Hedingham Castle). The hundred of Becontree 'say that all things are well and quiet as far as they know, nor have they anything whereof enquiry should be made.' John Stokes the foreman and the 'questmen' of Ongar hundred and Harlow half hundred present a bridge at North Weald Bassett 'that doth greatly annoy the country' (the contemporary term for the district or county), 'the which Aweker of the same town did give 40s. to the same bridge' (probably by his will), 'and we do not know who should make it'; also 'a bridge at Halls Ford' (evidently the bridge of that name over the Roding on the Stondon–Ongar road). There are two presentments for Chafford hundred. Richard Watkyn of Rainham Ferry keeps an alehouse without surety; Stifford Bridge is 'sore decayed'; Laurence Lewes has kept in his house at Grays Thurrock a young woman since the Feast of Hallowmas last and came not to the church; and the butts in Childerditch are out of repair. In Chelmsford hundred the bridge in Mountnessing is in decay; also two in Sandon which were 'made' by 'Mr. Tamworthe esquire within these twenty years', and yet another there 'is fallen in decay but we know not who shall make it'. Three more bridges are reported, all in north-west Essex : one in Great Dunmow 'in Chelmsford highway, and the Queen's Majesty ought to repair it'; another in Walden 'in the highway towards the bridge at the end of the town to the windmillward (towards the windmill) is decayed with water and the inhabitants of Walden do (i.e. must) make the same before Michaelmas next under a penalty of £10'; and the third in Debden 'leading from Smythe Green called Sheepwashers Bridge leading to (? Thaxted) market and the inhabitants do make it before the Feast of St. John the Baptist under a penalty of 40s.'

There is a tenth presentment. Judging from the places mentioned, which are at opposite ends of the county, this must be that of the grand jury, though not specifically so termed. It has only two items : 'A bridge in Much (Great) Oakley is in decay and the inhabitants of Much Oakley ought to repair it; also one John Nuland of Orsett doth buy certain wheat and rye on the ground and sold it again to divers persons unknown' (the first reference to engrossing – one of the trade offences which will be dealt with probably in the third volume of *Elizabethan Life*.

The three Marian rolls also contain twenty-one jury lists for the various hundreds. The juries were largely made up of the petty constables of each township. There is also a single grand jury list and a single list of bailiffs of the hundreds. The three rolls thus briefly described comprise a total of 101 documents.

The earliest Assize Files, 1559–61

In the days of Elizabeth I, as in those of Elizabeth II, the records of Her Majesty's Assize judges reveal more of the violent and vicious aspects of life than those of Her Majesty's justices of the peace, but some of the cases originated in Quarter Sessions, whence they were transmitted to Assizes. The five earliest Essex Assize files are fortunately a complete series from February 1559 to March 1561. There are none for Mary's reign, but several of the cases had arisen in 1557–58 and one in 1555. These files tell of death and theft in its numerous forms and of the ways in which little-changing human cruelty and greed, lust and despair manifested themselves in the broad picture of Elizabethan Disorder. The judges held two Assizes, Lent and Summer, each year.

The great majority of the documents are indictments. The files also contain many coroners' inquisitions some of which led to indictments. There are seven cases of murder in 1559–61. A labourer assaulted a boy of five years, broke his neck and murdered him (not guilty). A spinster put her six-year-old son into a 'fiery furnace' (probably an oven) and

violently held him there so that he languished from suffocation and died
a fortnight later (guilty, but remanded because she was pregnant).
A Stratford Langthorne cordwainer (shoemaker), in a wood called
Hallewell Grove in Leytonstone, struck a woman on the head with a
hedging bill, killing her instantly and then cut off both her arms and
legs. Anthony Bugges, a gentleman of Harlow, first struck one of his male
servants with a hedging bill in his outer courtyard, then with a pole in
one hand and a 'shackfork' (threshers' pitchfork) in the other, wounded
his right arm, cutting off a piece three inches long and 2½ inches deep,
from which he died some days later. The accused was found guilty of
homicide, not of murder; he read as a clerk and was delivered to the
Bishop. Bugges was lord of the manor of Moor Hall in Harlow. A
Wickham St. Paul's spinster killed a four-year-old boy then in her house
by striking him with her fist under his left ear. She was found not guilty
and acquitted. Two St. Osyth men burgled a house at Great Clacton,
stealing 40s. One mortally wounded the occupant with his sword; the
other aided him. Both were found not guilty.

Two witchcraft indictments came before the Assizes, both in 1560.
The first defendant was one of the few males accused. A Danbury beerbrewer, being a 'common wizard', bewitched a man and a woman, who
thereupon languished, the former for three weeks, the latter for three
months, when they died. The case was transmitted to the Assizes, but in
neither record are his plea and the verdict given. A Witham woman was a
'common witch', but hers was not an indictment for murder. On divers days
she had bewitched a wife and a man and divers others, and fraudulently
received various sums of money from them. She was pardoned.

The three alleged victims of rape were all servants, assaulted in their
masters' houses, in two of the cases, by their masters. All three verdicts:
guilty. Burglary (19 cases), housebreaking (10) and closebreaking (17)
and other versions of grand larceny account for nearly all the other cases.
A few were acquitted. Of those found guilty, more than one is noted as
'clerk', that is, he read the 'neck verse' and was delivered to the bishop;
the others were hanged.

A typical indictment is that of a Good Easter shoemaker who burgled
a widow's house there and stole a black frizado (good quality frieze)
frock worth 4s., two red petticoats each worth 4s., a pair of flaxen sheets
(8s.), a double rail (20d.), a headkercher (20d.), five linen neckerchers
(5s.), a pair of silver gilt buckles (4s.), a high-collared neckercher (8d.),
and 9s. in her purse.

John Hakyn of Braintree, who apparently kept a haberdasher's shop,
was burgled by Richard Letch of Ridgewell, a mercer, whose haul
involved 66 yards of lace (13s. 4d.), 7 dozen silk 'points' (laced tags)
(12d.), 3,000 pins (18d.), 3 oz. 'saunge silk' (3s.), 1 oz. Spanish silk (18d.),
17 skeins of thread (9d.), 7 dozen shirt strings (10d.), 7 dozen coloured

thread (3s. 6d.), 8 napkins (2s. 8d.), 2 'byggers' (?biggins, or night-caps) (12d.), 12 neckerchers (4s.), 3 shirt bands (2s.), and thread and silk lace (20s.).

Late one evening in November 1555 Kitchen Hall in the parish of Harlow was broken into by seven local men, all described as yeomen. This small manor house lay on the edge of the three-mile long Harlow Bush Common, and Kinge, who lived there, was a tenant farmer. He lost the substantial sum of £30. It was not until 1559–60 that two of the gang were tried, when both were found guilty ; the others were not caught. As much as £56 was stolen from a chest in the house of John Brown at Debden by a Middlesex hackneyman and a parishioner in 1560. The first was found guilty, the local man acquitted.

Two Stisted men burgled the house of John Fyssher clerk (rector, died 1564[1]) and went off with 5 pairs of linen shirts (40s.), a diaper tablecloth (6s. 8d.), a jerkin (10s.), and 2 ells of white damask (13s. 3d.) (guilty ; read). A Horndon-on-the-Hill house was burgled after midnight by John Mongomerie of the same place, clerk (an otherwise unrecorded vicar, or the curate) and Alice his wife, who stole £6 13s. 4d. (not guilty). Both these burglaries occurred in Mary's last months.

A few weeks after Elizabeth's accession, five men of Colchester district burgled Layer Marney rectory (then surrounded by a moat[2]), assaulted Richard Gyle clerk (the rector, 1554–77), put him in fear of his life, and stole from him a sarcenet tippet (20s.), three gold rings (£3), a coif (5s.), 6 old ryals of gold (15s. each), 2 gold double ducats (13s. 4d. each), 2 gold crusadoes (6s. 8d. each), 26 gold angels (10s. each), 2 gold half-angels (5s. each), 2 gold double sovereigns (20s. each), 36 gold half sovereigns (10s. each), 42 gold French crowns (6s. 4d. each), 12 gold Spanish crowns (6s. 4d.), 4 gold English h . . . (illegible, probably half-angels) (5s. each), 3 gold crusadoes (6s. 4d.), and £7 'in money' (pre-sumably coins of less value). All the men were condemned to the gallows : perhaps worth the risk for a haul valued at £68 6s. Other indictments charged defendants with terrorising the victim without actual assault.

Housebreaking, of which there are several cases, differs from burglary only in being committed by day, not night, and calls for no comment. Closebreaking, with no distinction between day and night, embraces most of the livestock thefts, and such indictments, nearly all for cattle-stealing, range from the taking of a single animal to a planned raid. Yet the lightest of such crimes, as in the typical case of an Earls Colne man who broke into a White Colne man's field and stole a horse worth 20s., led to his being hanged, if the verdict was guilty ; while a Tolleshunt man, who on a November day, perhaps under cover of fog on the heath, stole 36 sheep at Great Birch belonging to five owners, fared likewise.

[1] *Trans. Essex Archaeological Society*, vii, 171.
[2] Newcourt, *Repertorium* (1710), ii, 372.

A Tollesbury miller, William Okeley, accused of stealing five wethers (20s.) from a parishioner's field, was acquitted, but a Romford miller, John Gynkes, who stole four oxen (20s. each) from a field in Layer-de-la-Haye, many miles from his home, was found guilty, read, and was delivered to the Ordinary.

A few men connected with the meat trade succumbed to stealing beasts ready for slaughter.[1] A butcher of Newport stole three wethers (3s. 4d. each) out of 'Fannes Crofte' belonging to George Medley esquire, lord of the manor of Tilty; a London butcher took four oxen from Cow Ham in the West Ham marshes; and a Woodham Ferrers drover stole four cows (£8) and four heifers (46s. 8d.) belonging to three different owners on the same day. In all three cases the men were found guilty and claimed benefit of clergy. Two labourers of the little Suffolk town of Brandon Ferry carried off 42 wethers (5s. each) from a Felsted man. What looks like a little scheme of two 'gentlemen', one of London, the other of Harwich, quietly to ship away 14 stolen cows, evidently went awry.

Not all these livestock cases (thirty in all) involved closebreaking. Some of the animals may have been straying. In two cases they were taken while grazing on commons: five ewes and a lamb from a common (heath) at Wix; and a mare and a foal from 'the common waste of the King and Queen called Fayermeade' in the parish of Loughton (the wide glade of Fairmead is well known to lovers of Epping Forest, then part of the Forest of Waltham). Only once, at Little Bentley, when eight sheep were taken, is there a record of night-stealing. Once, too, a closebreaker was not after livestock but stole two bushels of wheat in the granary of John Tomworth of Waltham Holy Cross, esquire.

Simple larceny accounts for a number of indictments, usually of clothes or money. For example, two labourers of Great Chishall stole a man's doublet of 'marble' (variegated) colour and a red petticoat (then occasionally a male garment). A Wethersfield woman lifted £5 13s. 4d. from a leathern pouch on the victim's person. She may have been a pickpocket. Two men from Braintree and Ipswich were accused of receiving and 'comforting' her. A very large sum of money, £50, was stolen by a Willingdale Doe cleaver (wood-splitter) from a chest in John Levington's house at Latton.

In these opening years of the reign there is one indictment for seditious speech. Robert Taylor of Chelmsford labourer on 8 August 1560, was alleged to have publicly said, 'The service that the Queen did use in her Chapel was but paltry' (acquitted).

Nearly every Assize file has a 'calendar' (the ancient name for a list) of the county officers (the justices of the peace, the two coroners, and the

---

[1] For the high number of cattle-stealings by butchers, see p. 286.

bailiffs of the hundreds and liberties) and a calendar of the prisoners, giving the parish where arrested.

Early Elizabethan Queen's Bench Indictments, 1558–61

To the Court of Queen's Bench for trial at the Assizes were removed a few Quarter Sessions cases. This was effected by a writ of *certiorari* under which the inferior court 'certified' the record of the proceedings. To the same court were certified the verdicts of coroners' juries by similar transmission of the inquest records. The majority returned verdicts of suicide or misadventure (which will appear in the third volume of *Elizabethan Life*), but there are some verdicts of murder and homicide. Both types of documents are preserved in the Public Record Office among the so-called 'King's Bench Indictments (Ancient)', and they help to fill in the picture.

In the slightly incomplete Queen's Bench records for 1558–61 (years for which the Sessions rolls are lost), there is a small miscellany of Essex cases, including that of the Danbury wizard; also one of riotous disseisin by Robert Chadwycke gentleman, two husbandmen, five labourers and twenty unnamed persons, all of Great Waltham, of a meadow belonging to Lord Rich; one against William Beryff of Colchester gentleman (apparently the Town Clerk) for being a common barrator (disturber of the peace); and one of rape. From Quarter Sessions came a case of attempted murder, the victim having died three months later of a rapier wound. Two servants of Thomas Herne of Woodford gentleman were assaulted in his close called Milkwell by three local husbandmen. Two Colchester yeomen trespassed in a close called 'Castle land' belonging to Henry Mackwilliam esquire and trampled down the hay.

Of much wider significance are two documents submitted by the Attorney General himself to the Court in Trinity term 1561. He sought stern proceedings against two Catholic magnates for being present at mass in their homes—Sir Edward Waldegrave at Borley and Sir Thomas Wharton at New Hall, Boreham; their cases being due to come before the next Assizes and Sessions respectively. Wharton was the first person to be prosecuted under Elizabeth for having mass said in his house.[1]

One case (probably a rare instance) was removed by *certiorari* from the Sheriff's tourn (his half-yearly tour of the hundredal courts) held in April 1560, when the jury declared that a 'lane or common horse way' called Spakeman's Lane in Upminster, leading to Aveley, had recently been stopped up illegally.

---

[1] *Essex Review*, xvii, 121–5, quoting *State Papers Domestic*; and *Essex Recusant*, ii.

2
Presentments, 1562-68

Presentments by the ordinary Hundredal Juries

The presentments by the juries of the hundreds about specific disorders in response to the 'charges' or 'articles of enquiry' given to them, or about other matters on their own initiative, afforded the rulers of the county a partial picture of the prevailing social and economic conditions in their areas. Every quarter they learned of the state of the roads and bridges, and almost as often one or more hundreds reported on alehouses, unlawful games, vagrants and other idle persons. They were also informed about the observance of trade regulations, and, after the passing of the Statute of Artificers in 1563, of its enforcement with regard to the hiring of servants, apprenticeship and wages. But frequently 'Omnia bene' or 'All is well' is the statement put in for the whole hundred or for some of the parishes within the hundred, although occasionally they declare they have made 'diligent enquiry.' Disobedience in these and other ways, by parishes or individuals, gave rise to a multitude of offences and 'nuisances' which were presented under various Acts of Parliament, ancient and recent.

In their primary capacity as keepers of the peace, the justices were thus cognisant of all crimes except the gravest (which were tried by the Assize judges) and of all offences, either through hundredal presentment or private prosecution. The main part of this book is devoted to these crimes and offences, each of which is dealt with in subsequent chapters. To this treatment by subject we have felt it desirable to make two exceptions: the detailed preview of the earliest Essex Quarter Sessions and Assize records for 1556–61 in the previous chapter, and a similar account of the presentments by the hundredal and grand juries for 1562–68 which now follows.

The range of matters on which the juries for the hundreds reported is fairly well known from the presentments for several counties, such as Hertfordshire from 1589, which have been printed. Impassible roads, unscoured roadside ditches, defective and dangerous bridges, and disorderly or unlicensed alehouses were the most common subjects of such presentment.

Essex possesses by far the largest number of these hundredal reports, and they are among the earliest in England. The only presentments extant before 1562, the nine made in 1556, pp. 6–7, all concern bridges, and indeed the great majority of the disorders admitted during Elizabeth's time relate to bridges and roads. For the first decade (in effect, only 1562–68) we shall try to give nearly all the references to roads and to bridges, the alleged liabilities for their repair, and the action, if any, taken. The overall picture for the remaining thirty-five years is very similar, but there is no space in this volume for continuing such a detailed description of the bridges. Persons interested in a given parish or bridge will need to consult the very full indices to the seventeen typescript volumes of the calendar of Quarter Sessions rolls for 1556–1603 in the Essex Record Office.[1] Decayed bridges were occasionally presented at manor courts. The archives of these courts will be a chief source used in the next volume, and the various aspects of certain overlapping functions of Quarter Sessions and manor courts, including roads and bridges, will then be discussed.

As in Hertfordshire, it was not uncommon for two or three hundreds to submit a joint presentment, but such groupings appear to have been a matter of scribal convenience – perhaps the readiness of the foreman of one hundred jury to include items for another hundred in his own document – rather than conformity with the traditional local groupings of the Essex hundreds in twos, threes or fours.[2]

A fairly full description of the roads, compiled from the Quarter Sessions records for the whole Elizabethan period, has already been published, to which the reader is referred.[3]

Roads

In the sixteenth and in each succeeding century people have complained of the state of the roads and of the difficulties of travel. 'Travail' and 'travel', in Elizabethan times, were still undifferentiated spellings of a single word having much the same meaning. But despite the troubles, obstacles and dangers encountered, a great deal of journeying was undertaken, some involving long distances. In our own context we can watch hosts of country gentlemen, yeomen and humbler folk attending Quarter Sessions and Assizes as justices, jurors, defendants, sureties and witnesses. Many were obliged to appear at the hundredal or archidiaconal courts. Others, including the many litigious-minded landowners, appeared in the courts at Westminster. The royal court frequently left the capital, accompanying Elizabeth with a large mounted retinue and a long procession of clumsy waggons from palace to palace, or striving to keep up

---

1 All the more important items about bridges and roads in the Quarter Sessions records will eventually appear in the introductory section to each parish in the *Victoria History of Essex*.

2 For the usual groups of hundreds, see F. G. Emmison, *Guide to the Essex Record Office* (1969), 1.

3 F. G. Emmison, four articles in *Essex Review*, vol. lxiv (1955).

with her annual summer progresses. Witness, for example, the astonishing amount of travel revealed in the account-books of Sir William Petre of Ingatestone Hall.[1] Young men travelled to and from the universities. Visits to relations and friends many miles away were common. Trade was thriving. The general picture shows that the roads were carrying a good deal of traffic and it is now well established that carts and waggons, except on clayey roads in winter, as well as packhorses, were used.

The word 'road' has already been used twice – not anachronistically, as will be seen. Shakespeare is usually cited (*1 Henry IV*, II, i, 16) for its first appearance (1596) in the modern sense, as opposed to its earlier meaning of 'riding on horseback.' In referring to travel the Elizabethan lawyers used only 'highway' (or 'way') or 'lane' (a way enclosed on both sides). But the Essex Session rolls disclose three instances of the use of 'road' beginning to assume its current sense a generation before Shakespeare's time. The two earliest occur in presentments of 1567–68 : 'the highway between Stratford Langthorne and Bow Bridge in West Ham being the road way to London, much decayed to the great annoyance of all that do travel that way', and 'a bridge in North Weald that is a very noyable way and is unmade and being a road way to London.'[2]

Elizabeth's long reign has captured the imagination of modern writers. But the historian of the highways is not among them. The sixteenth century was a transitional period in the history of travel. The age of the pilgrim and the mendicant friar is vivid to us through Chaucer and one historian.[3] The turnpike and coaching eras have been described by many authors. Of Tudor roads, ' 'twixt these times', there is however little in print. Yet the period is one of great interest. It saw the real start of the vast outpouring of legislation affecting roads.

In 1555 the highways were 'both very noisome and tedious to travel in, and dangerous to all passengers and carriages'. This brief preamble was deemed adequate to explain the need for the 'Statute for Mending of Highways' (2 & 3 Philip and Mary, c.8), the Act which introduced a novel method of road maintenance that was destined to last in the main for nearly three centuries.

It enjoined the constables and churchwardens of every parish yearly in Easter week to 'call together a number of the parishioners' in order to 'elect and chuse two honest persons of the parish to be surveyors and orderers of the works for amendment of the highways of their parish leading to any market town.' The constables and churchwardens were to appoint four days of compulsory 'work and travel' (here, as explained, 'travail' and 'travel' were still synonymous). The Act then proceeded to

---

[1] F. G. Emmison, *Tudor Secretary: Sir William Petre at Court and Home* (1961).
[2] The Shakespeare quotation is in the *New English Dictionary*, which also gives 1600 as the first known reference to 'roadway' and suggests that it equals 'riding way' in origin.
[3] J. J. Jusserand, *English Wayfaring Life in the Middle Ages* (1888, translated 1950).

impose a personal liability, distinguishing between the upper and lower grades of society.

> Every person for every plow-land in tillage or pasture that he or she shall occupy in the same parish, and every other person keeping a draught or plough, shall send . . . one wain or cart furnished after the custom of the country with oxen, horses or other cattle . . . also two able men, upon pain of every draught making default, ten shillings; and every other householder, and also every cottager and labourer of that parish, able to labour, and being no hired servant by the year, shall by themselves or one sufficient labourer for every of them, . . . work and travel in the amendment of the highways, upon pain of every person making default, to lose every day twelve pence.

The practical Tudor parliamentarians enjoined that 'every person and carriage shall bring with them such shovels, spades, picks, mattocks, and other tools and instruments, as they do make their own ditches and fences withal'.

The Chelmsford hundred jury's presentment to Epiphany Sessions 1562 includes this entry: 'The parish of Sandon hath done little in mending of the Queen's highways, being the common trade (ways) to the market (towns) (n)ever since the Statute made for the same.' (What a mouse has eaten away is replaced in parentheses.) The parishioners were fined 20s. The fine on Sandon for neglecting its highways may be the sole surviving record in the whole country of the action taken under the Marian Act.[1] It was only a seven-year measure. The plan met with a qualified success. Its provisions were continued and developed by several Elizabethan statutes. The preamble to that of 1562 (5 Elizabeth, c.13) declares that the Act of 1555 'is very beneficial, and most necessary to be continued for the eaze and common-weal of the people', and it was extended for a further twenty years. The four days a year were increased to six, and so 'statty duty', as it came to be known colloquially, remained, apart from money compositions, for nearly three centuries. The 'surveyors' were empowered to take what we should call road material – 'the rubbish or smallest broken stones of any quarry, gravel, sand or cinders, and likewise to gather stones' anywhere in the parish except from gardens and meadows.

Another clause enjoined the cutting down of trees and bushes in the highway and the scouring of ditches 'next adjoining on either side to any high or common fairing way',[2] in all cases by the owners. Tree clearance was a re-enactment of the Statute of Winchester, 1285 (13 Edward I, st. ii, c.5), which is the first Act to refer to roads. This enjoined that 'highways leading from one market town to another shall be enlarged where bushes, woods, or dykes be, so that there by neither dyke nor bush whereby

---

[1] *Middlesex County Records*, vol. i (1886), has nothing bearing on the operation of the Act. No other sessions rolls of this decade are in print. *Caernarvonshire Quarter Sessions Records, 1541–48* (ed. W. Ogwen Williams, 1956) has no reference.
[2] 'Fairing way', i.e. the modern roadway or carriageway in contrast to the unmetalled or green verges.

a man may lurk to do hurt within two hundred feet of the one side and two hundred feet of the other side of the way'. A remarkable instance of action recommended under this statute has been found in an Ingatestone manor roll. At a court held in 1468 it was presented that a tenant should cut and clear his pasture near 'Heybregge' by the king's highway 'for that robbers lurk there by day and night to despoil passers-by.'[1]

To cleanse roadside ditches was a duty which the adjacent landholders had to discharge under the common law, reinforced by early Tudor legislation. Hundreds of such unscoured roadside ditches occur as presented nuisances in surviving Essex manor court rolls of pre-Elizabethan date.[2] Several were presented to Quarter Sessions a year before the Act of 5 Elizabeth and scores in later years. By 1618, when the first edition of Michael Dalton's *Country Justice* appeared, the statutory clearance width was regarded as excessive : 'now it seemeth that if . . . all the hedges . . . be kept low, the trees and bushes cut down, and the ditches scoured, it sufficeth, though the ways be not two hundred foot wide on each side.'

Enforcement of the 1562 statute was the duty of the 'surveyors', who were to present every 'default or offence to the next justice of peace' under pain of 40s., and he in turn was to certify the presentment at the next 'general session'; the justices were also to 'enquire of any such default or offence . . . at every their quarter sessions', and to assess fines. A justice could present 'upon his own knowledge' any highway not well repaired, and his independent action had the same effect in law 'as if the same had been presented, found and adjudged by the oath of twelve men', i.e. by a formal indictment.

Affecting every able-bodied householder as it did, it is astonishing that this perennial and ubiquitous duty has left so little mark in contemporary literature. Neither prose (with one exception, the renowned Essex author quoted later) nor poetry, diary or correspondence, affords a picture of the parishioners at their simple road-mending. Official archives, however, ought to help, because road work was imposed by Act of Parliament and its neglect was punishable in the courts : again, with a notable exception, they fail. The public (i.e. national) records apparently yield nothing : the watchfulness of the Privy Council over local government was to arise a little later. Parish surveyors' records for the pre-1600 period have very rarely survived. Although there is an abundance of Elizabethan manor court rolls very few indeed have been printed. Apart from two Middlesex indictments in the 1570s for refusal to furnish carts and a solitary Hertfordshire list of defaulters in one parish, 1598, the early Highways Acts have left a clear mark only in the county records of Essex and Wiltshire.[3]

In 1566 there are two indictments of defaulters in the parishes of

---

[1] Essex Record Office, D/DP M53.
[2] See also C. T. Flower, *Public Works in Medieval Law* (Selden Soc., 1915), 67.
[3] *Wiltshire County Records: Minutes, 1563, 1574–92* (ed. C. H. Johnson, 1949).

Feering and Coggeshall, which are adjacent on the (Roman) Colchester–
Braintree road. Each refers to an attached schedule; these are lists of the
defaulters certified by the parish surveyors, writing in rustic English. The
Feering indictment has William Merler gentleman, four husbandmen and
five labourers, all parishioners; the other has eight husbandmen, two
weavers, a fuller, a tiler, a wheelwright and forty labourers, all of Coggeshall, and two Feering husbandmen, one of whom held 140 acres in
Coggeshall. Merler and the husbandmen were all 'offenders for want of
their help with carriages or carts', the rest 'for want of the six days work
in labour in the highways'. Fines are noted on the Coggeshall list: all the
husbandmen including the one who had done two days' work were fined
40s. except for the man owing only two days who had to pay 20s.; the
labourers were fined 6s. each. These are stiff fines, at the rates laid down by
the Marian Act. Three Sessions afterwards another long list was put in by
the surveyors of Coggeshall – William Turnor of Coggeshall Hall and four
others who ought to have sent in their carts, together with twenty-three
labourers. The names of two husbandmen and thirteen labourers are struck
through in the presentment paper, having no doubt done their work
under threat of prosecution, so that the formal indictment names eleven
defaulters. The cart-owners were fined between 60s. and 35s. each, accord-
ding to the number of days due, and the labourers, all of whom owed the
whole duty, 6s. each, totalling £19 13s. Two offenders in the previous list
appear again in 1567.

The Coggeshall and Feering lists are quite exceptional in the early
Sessions rolls of Essex. There are no similar lists until 1575. Only two
other parishes presented any defaulters: one in Brentwood (1566) and
one in Ardleigh (1568). The latter was evidently an obstreperous fellow,
as the jurors also complain that he 'dismantles' an ancient church footpath.

So much for the degree of disobedience actually reported to Quarter
Sessions. It seems probable, however, that other delinquents (and this
may have applied to disorderly alehousekeepers and similar offenders)
who were reported by their parishes to the hundred received a warning
through the petty constables without their names being submitted to the
Court. Certainly there was more neglect than the Bench was formally
told about, if we read the scathing comments made by Harrison. 'The
rich,' he wrote, 'do so cancel their portions, and the poor so loiter in their
labours, that of all the six, scarcely two good days' work are well per-
formed and accomplished in a parish on these so necessary affairs.' And
he enlarges on this theme in a long account in which he also condemns
those who neglect to cleanse their roadside ditches. This passage has been
printed in full more than once.[1]

---

[1] Harrison, *Description of England*, 443–44. Also extracted by J. Dover Wilson in *Life
in Shakespeare's England* (1911 and later reprints) and by F. G. Emmison in *Essex Review*,
lxiv, 24–5.

C

The contemporary Sessions records of Harrison's own county fully
bear out what he wrote. In the same year (1562) as the Sandon presentment already quoted, Hinckford hundred jurors admit no defects, but
quite exceptionally go beyond their own jurisdiction. 'Please that your
right honourable lords and worshipful justices to understand', they write,
'that there is a certain lane at Panfield (that) goeth through Mistress
Cotten's ground to Braintree ward which doth annoy the Queen's
Majesty's liege people so that they cannot pass with their horse nor pack,
but it is without our hundred and our hundred is annoyed. Therefore
we desire to have a redress therein.' Another jury 'find that Mr. Langley
doth stop the watercourse against Thomas Sander of Takeley and doth
annoy the Queen's Majesty's liege people in a certain lane to Stansted
Mountfitchet ward because he maketh a hedge where the water should
have his course and doth not scour the right watercourse.'

In 1564 the Chelmsford hundred jurors present that the way between
the maple against 'Chenfeldes and Stistedes' lieth between the parishes
of Writtle and Widford and is not mended, neither are the ditches scoured
nor the wood felled off. Next year and again in 1566 it is still 'very
noisome' between a farm called 'Stystydes and the mill hill in the parishes
of Writtle, Widford and Margareting'. Shenfields is the moated Tudor
house, now called Killigrews, a quarter of a mile south-east of the Great
Essex Road. Stisteds lay close to it on the opposite side; it was pulled
down when Hylands Park was enlarged but its ancient kitchen-garden
wall still stands by the now-closed London gate of the park. Roads along
the middle of which parish boundaries ran were a continual source of
trouble for three centuries after the passing of the Marian Highways Act,
and this stretch was notoriously bad. Also in a bad condition in 1566 are
100 yards of the highway between the Lazar House (in Chelmsford) and
'the high cross to Stock ward' (probably Stump Cross). Barstable hundred
reports a widow for not amending two sloughs and for not cutting down
the trees in Fallytes Lane in Doddinghurst leading from Brentwood to
Bentley Common.

The remaining cases belong to 1566–68. Furnoll Lane in Broxted,
Chickney and Henham, being the highway from Thaxted and Broxted
church towards Stortford, is in decay through the default of five named
yeomen 'who with other inhabitants' of these parishes 'have used and
ought to repair it.' The Braintree road in Great Dunmow is 'so noisome
that no man can pass without jeopardy of horse and man.' The last bit of
the Great Essex Road before the Middlesex boundary between Stratford
in West Ham and Bow Bridge is twice presented; 'it is in such decay that
the Queen's subjects cannot pass at divers times without danger to their
lives.' The Witham length of the road to Hatfield Peverel is also twice
reported as 'very noisome'. A 'piece of highway, very foul', lying against
Lea Wood and leading from Crooked Causey to the foot of Laindon Hills,

'ought to be repaired' by Little Burstead. Dunmow jurors think that
Great Canfield and High Roothing ought to amend a noisome slough
between 'Royshemead' and the river in a chaseway leading from my
Lady Josselyne's mill to Great Canfield mill. (A chaseway was usually
a private access-way.)

From medieval times roads have been subject to various forms of
encroachment, obstruction and closure. Four cases appear between 1562
and 1568. Mr. Wood of Stanford Rivers has dug a sandpit in the highway ;
a Lamarsh man is to remove his hedge at the three-way leet (meeting of
three roads) ; Harry Munke farmer has shut up a highway in Laindon
Hills leading from Stanford-le-Hope to Billericay; and a Twinstead man
has encroached on Twinstead Tye (the Essex name for a small common
or green).

Bridges

The Bridges Act of 1530 (22 Henry VIII, c.5) provided what appears
at first sight to be a simple remedy for dealing with 'decayed' bridges. If
it could not be proved that one or more persons or a local body or certain
lands were liable for the repair of such a bridge, four J.P.s after summoning
the constables and two other parishioners to attend on them were empowered to levy a rate for its repair and three hundred feet of the highway
at each end. The justices were to appoint two 'collectors' for the hundred
in which the bridge lay and two 'surveyors' to arrange for the work to be
done. All were to render their account to the justices. But a primary and
overriding problem was to ascertain who was responsible, by ancient
prescription or evidence of earlier repair : generally by reason of tenure
of lands adjoining the bridge. In this respect both the law and the evidence could be confusing, as Dalton in his *Country Justice* frankly admitted.
Essex had no charitable trust such as that for the great Rochester Bridge
nor any chantry chapel like that on St. Ives Bridge from which funds or
alms were received for its maintenance.

The Essex presentments disclose only one reference to this procedure,
and that is puzzling. In 1566 Uttesford and Freshwell hundreds 'find all
things well, saving the mending of the ways, but we have collectors
appointed, and with as much speed as may be they shall be mended.'
This would seem to refer to bridges and their approach roads, because
of the reference to collectors, rather than to parish roads, which were
repaired through labour, unless 'collectors' is used in error for 'surveyors'.

The usual terms for presented bridges are 'ruinous', 'in (great) decay',
'sore decayed', or 'very noisome'. Sometimes the jurors are more specific :
it is 'ruinously decayed for the default of timber work', 'not fit to bear
horse or cart', 'the timber so rotten that no footman nor horseman can
pass without danger' (or 'without great peril' or 'jeopardy'), 'they go in

danger of their lives', 'so that no man can go thereby', or 'no man can travel that way in winter.' In even stronger language, the jurors in 1562 twice declare of a bridge in Stansted Mountfitchet (on the road to Stortford) that travellers going to market 'are like to be drowned' or 'are as like to be drowned at every flood'. This probably refers to the bridge in Stansted Street over Palmers Brook running into the Stort. Stebbing Ford Bridge on the Dunmow–Braintree road is the only one actually reported as 'broke and gone', but it only crossed a stream and the ancient ford could normally be used. Clap Bridge between Rayne and Dunmow, a few miles along the same highway, is 'broken of a long time', but this does not imply its being completely down, as later presentments refer to it as only 'decayed'.

The jurors are expected to help the Court in expressing their opinion about liability for repair. The charge given to them at every Sessions includes an injunction not only to present every decayed bridge but to give their view on 'what hundred, city, town, parish, or person certain, or body politic' (Statute of Bridges) is liable for its repair. By common law the county was responsible for the upkeep of public bridges, which were therefore known as 'county bridges': a duty originating in the Saxon *trinoda necessitas*. By usage, prescription, or ancient tenure, however, the liability for a particular bridge might fall on a smaller area, body, or one or more individuals. As many streams are boundaries between parishes, manors or smaller estates, the lord of the manor or the landholder (who might be the same person) on each side of the stream is usually named, whether known to be liable or not, unless responsibility could be otherwise ascribed.

In 1562 Lord Rich (of Leighs Priory) and the owner of Braintree Parsonage are given as the landholders on each side of the bridge on the parish boundary between Braintree and Rayne on the old Roman road towards Dunmow. In the same year a jury presents one of the two bridges in the county town – the timbered Springfield Bridge over the Chelmer, a little to the east of Chelmsford High Street on the Colchester road, linking the parishes of Chelmsford and Springfield; it ought to be made by the Queen and Sir Harry Tyrell (owners of the manors). The same bridge, 'at Chelmsford town's end', again presented in 1565, 'lies between Sir Henry Tyrell and Master Mildmay' (Thomas Mildmay had been granted the manor of Chelmsford *alias* Bishop's Hall by the Crown in 1563).

In 1563 the jurors present Sheldon Bridge in Stisted, on the lane joining the village with the Braintree–Colchester highway, adding, 'Mr. Fabian lord on the one side and Mr. Wiseman on the other'; they owned the two manors of Jenkins and Stisted Hall. 'And who should maintain it we cannot certify you the truth by enquiry or otherwise.' Likewise Clap Bridge, already mentioned, 'Master Capel's land on one side and Master Wiseman on the other' ; and Stansted Bridge, 'betwixt the honourable Lord the Earl of Oxford, the Lord Bishop of London, and the Warden of Oxford (New College), the lord (of the manor) of Birchanger'. Sometimes a single owner is named as having land on each side, for example, the Earl of Oxford at Ford Bridge between Tilbury-juxta-Clare and Great Yeldham. Many juries plead ignorance. For instance, at Stewards Bridge in Stanford Rivers (presumably that on the Roding) 'Mr. Steward hath land lying on both sides and Edward Fuller is fermor (lessee) but who should make it we know not.'

Repair in former years is often referred to or implied ('made it' usually means only 'repaired'). A bridge at Little Dunmow (probably Priory Bridge between that parish and Felsted) 'hath heretofore been made by my Lord Rich'. Another 'under Dunmow Park' (on the Braintree road) is 'decayed and will be worse and it ought to be made by the Queen as far as we know' is one of several references to Crown ownership of adjacent land. In Great Dunmow there are two more dangerous bridges. One, at Church End, is to be repaired by the landholders of the Parsonage; the other, Langeholdes Bridge, is to be 'redressed' by Mr. Jenninges and William Longe, both parishioners. (Jenninges was lord of the manor of Shingle Hall *alias* Olives.) 'Mr. Gyver and one Cowyld in default for not making Embridge Mill bridge' in Little Easton (on the Cambridge road). This bridge is presented again two Sessions later, when the second man is alleged to be liable, 'to amend the great part thereof by reason he is a miller there and payeth for the stream.' Shelley Bridge should be made by 'the parson of Shelley and hath made it in times past.' Similarly, a bridge in High Roothing 'my Lady Josselyn should mend.' Cawsey Bridge between Aveley and West Thurrock (over the Mardyke) the lord of West Thurrock, Mr. Sadler and Mr. Merydyth ought to repair (Roger Sadler and William Meredith had married the co-heirs of the previous lord of the manor). 'Fulbrook Bridge in Danbury near Studley Green ought to be made by the lord of the manor of Bicknacre, who is Sir Walter Mildmay'. Shanes Bridge on the Witham–Maldon road 'should be made by the town of Witham'; but an earlier presentment in which it is called Salles Bridge has 'Who should make it we cannot find.' Of Joys Bridge in Great Baddow the jurors state that 'the father of Master Notynghyrst did make the same and John Bridges and Edward Hurste hold the lands on both sides.' Next year they say that Josse Bridge ought to be made by William Lucken dwelling at Sir Hewes in Much Baddow' and that it 'leadeth to Rayleigh ward.' 'The predecessor of Mr. Harvey, lord of Langford, hath made it' is reported about Langford Bridge. A bridge in 'Gynge Mountneye' (Mountnessing) is decayed 'for lack of gravel and the lord hath made it, Mr. Wilforde.' Woodford Bridge is ruinous, 'the lord of Woodford to make it, Robert Browne esquire.' After declaring that the landholders on each side of Broad Bridge in Aythorpe Roothing are Lady Bourchier and Lady Josselyn, the

presentment adds that 'Mr. John Josselyn about forty years past did give
a plank toward the making thereof.' (A plank meant a piece of sawn
timber eight feet or more in length.) In 1562 Boreham Bridge and
Plomsted Bridge, both in Sandon, 'ought to be made by the lord of
Sandon Hall', and both are presented again as Borams and Plomton
Bridges, 'which Mr. Tamworthe ought to make, the lord of the town, and
he hath made them heretofore.' Another bridge in Sandon, 'Knight
Bridge with the calcey (causeway) continueth in great decay and ruin,
which beforetime was repaired by the devotion of the country'. It appears
next as 'Knight Bridge Watering hath been made by a play that was
made in Sandon, also there was given to it a tree by Sir Thomas Darcy.' In
this century religious plays were produced by many Essex parishes and
some yielded profits.

Once only, at Easter Sessions 1568, a hundred jury definitely puts the
liability on the county: 'Pyssingforde Bridge is ruinously in decay in
default of timber work and Master Pyllysdon as executor to Mr. Smythe
did give a certain sum of money to the making of the same, and there were
certain men had licence to gather for making the same bridge, so we find
the country should make it.' In the previous year this bridge, lying between the two Staplefords on the London–Ongar road, was referred to as
having been presented 'beforetime'.

The lessee of a manor is held liable in the case of Witham (or Newland)
Bridge (on the Colchester road); 'at the last making it was made by Sir
John Smyth farmer of this manor, also afore that time it was repaired by
one Mr. Edmondes likewise farmer'; and 'John Sames farmer of the
manor of Langford did make it the last time.'

Of Loxford Bridge in Barking, over a small but tidal stream running
into the Roding, the jurors 'cannot tell justly by whom it should be made,
but this we know that one Master Pownsytt gave a certain sum of money
to the repairing.' William Pownsett had been the receiver-general of
Barking Abbey.[1] Ramsey Bridge is declared to have 'first been made and
kept by the gifts of the country and always by the Abbess of Ramsey and
be now taken away by the Queen's Majesty's laws.' Henry VIII's dissolution seems to have been temporarily forgotten by the jurors, who
add, 'since repaired by certain of the parish that be departed out of this
world, which bridge is in length at least six score yards.' A further instance
of earlier work refers to pre-Dissolution days: 'A stone bridge called
Dagenham Beam in the Queen's highway from Dagenham to Rainham
as we do understand by the knowledge of the country hath been made by
the Abbess of Barking' (1564); it is presented again in 1567 in similar
language. In 1568 an ingenuous opinion is submitted: 'Dagenham Beam
Bridge near Dagenham dividing the manor of Dagenham and the liberty
of Havering should be repaired by the whole inhabitants of Dagenham

[1] Emmison, *Tudor Secretary*, 9.

for that it beareth the name of Dagenham Beam.' The earliest mention of this bridge occurs in 1299 and the name is derived from 'beam', a Saxon word for tree used in the sense of 'plank bridge'.[1] It lay over the Mardyke, later known, by process of 'back-formation', as the River Beam.

Some bridges lie at the point where three parishes meet. One, between Great Yeldham, Tilbury and Ridgewell is 'supposed that it hath been made by the foresaid parishes.' This is clearly the bridge over the infant Colne on the Colchester–Cambridge road. But who should repair Blackwater Bridge, at the junction of Stisted, Pattiswick and Bradwell-juxta-Coggeshall on the Roman road, 'which is mightily in decay that no cart can pass over it we know not.' Partial liability for Golden Bridge between Orsett and Horndon is thus expressed : 'The tenants do confess that the lord of the manor doth find the timber but who should make it we do not know ; Mr. John Broughton did make it last time, being the tenant of the manor.' Of Paynes Bridge in Romford 'in London highway' the jurors state that Thomas Leggatt gentleman and Richard Lake hold land on each side, but do not know who is liable. 'Mr. Colle parson of High Ongar' (Thomas Cole, rector 1559–72) and Mr. James Morris of Chipping Ongar are named as the owners on each side of High Ongar Bridge (this rectory ranked as a manor), but the jury do not know who should repair it.

'Who should make it', 'We know not', or some such phrase, is indeed given in the majority of bridge presentments. The Essex records show that, in the sixteenth century, liability *ratione tenurae* is being asserted only when the juries feel safe in doing so. Public liability is advanced in only one other case, apart from Witham : 'We have learned by our evidence, which be John Deyer and Hugh Polle which be sworn and of the age of 60 years and upward, which saith for the space of this 40 or 50 years it hath not been repaired but by the hamlet of Bures.' Whether this refers to the county boundary bridge (the Stour divides the hamlet of Bures, which lies in Essex from Bures proper in Suffolk) or one over a smaller stream is not clear.

Presentments of the other bridges out of repair yield no further points of interest ; except for words in parentheses, they are named as follows : Holeyn Bridge between Horndon and Orsett ; Wethin Bridge in Orsett on the highway to Brentwood ; Ashford Bridge in Halstead (now Blue Bridge, on the Colchester road) ; Down Bridge in Hatfield Broad Oak on the way between Brentwood and Bishop's Stortford ; Gullet Bridge in North Weald Bassett on the way between London and Hatfield Broad Oak ; Stand Bridge in High Laver ; Watersworth Bridge between Birdbrook and (Steeple) Bumpstead (in later maps, Watsey or Watsoe Bridge) ; Bourne Bridge in Stapleford Abbots (on the tiny Bourne, before it becomes Mardyke) ; Navestock Mill Bridge ; Typhanes Bridge in North Benfleet ; Wastells Bridge in Takeley ; and Tanners Bridge in Broomfield.

[1] *Place-Names of Essex* (1935), 92.

Also five unnamed bridges: in Rainham on the Upminster road; in Sible Hedingham on the Braintree–Sudbury road; (? between) Stisted and Gosfield on the Braintree–Halstead road; in Great Easton; and in Little Baddow between Barowe and Little Baddow mill.

There is still no proper history of the ancient stone Bow Bridge over the Middlesex–Essex boundary, but as little is known about its condition in Elizabethan times mention may be made of its being on the Council agenda in 1579–80. Towards 'the building of a timber frame to serve the necessity of the passengers until the stone bridge may be built', meaning no doubt extensive repairs as 'mending' is also referred to, money was then being raised not only by tolls on carts, cattle and horsemen but also by rates on several counties benefiting from the restoration, including Essex and Suffolk. In 1580 passengers were beginning to refuse to pay toll because the two counties had also been rated. The Council therefore instructed the sheriffs urgently to pay over any rate arrears to 'Mr. Fanshawe' (Thomas Fanshawe of Jenkins in Barking, J.P., an Exchequer official) in order to free the bridge from toll as soon as possible.[1]

It is of course impossible to estimate the total number of bridges in Essex in the sixteenth century, partly because the smallest structures could scarcely be termed bridges. Many of the normally fordable streams were to remain unbridged until much later. But one may hazard that between four and six hundred bridges, if minor ones are included, existed in Elizabeth's time in the public roads of Essex. There were thousands of little culverts on the private farmtracks – many of them planks over hollowed tree trunks, called 'wholves' in Essex – and doubtless this rudimentary method served also for bridging the smallest streams on the highways.

Nevertheless, the evidence is fairly clear about the dangerous condition of the road bridges, affecting almost every thoroughfare in the county, and on some routes several bridges are unsafe, especially after heavy rain. It amounts to a disordered state of affairs. The jurors of the hundreds are not merely obeying the statute and the charge in presenting these defects. Many of them have to travel to market or further afield, and they are anxious about their business being disrupted by dangerous or almost impassible bridges. When they declare that a bridge 'doth greatly annoy the country', they use the word in its legal sense applying to the area and people represented by the jurors, that is, the hundred. If a grand jury refers to 'the country', the whole county is inferred in a loose sense. Their lives are led mostly within the area of their own hundred and the nearest market-towns, and nuisance to 'the country', to them, is a major public nuisance.

The outstanding feature is that little action is taken to remedy it. There is no doubt that several bridges, in addition to Clap Bridge, have been

[1] *Acts of the Privy Council*, xi, 287–8; xii, 108.

'broken of a long time'. The earliest Sessions rolls reveal that a few bridges, including two of those in Sandon, had been presented in the previous decade. Of the bridges in a bad state during 1562–68 at least six appear between three and eight times, and nearly all of these are on through routes. The bridge most frequently reported is Broad Bridge in Aythorpe Roothing. The hundred presentments more than once from 1563 onwards name Lady Bourchier and Lady Josselyn as adjacent owners. At Epiphany 1568 the hundred's patience is exhausted: 'The lack of repair hath been divers times declared and no redress had, wherefore we commit the judgement of the penalty due for the same default to be fixed by your honours' (and three other unrepaired bridges the same jury deem 'worthy of penalty'). So they bluntly add that it is to be repaired by the landholders of Aythorpe Hall. Yet by Easter Sessions nothing has been done. 'Lady Bourchier ought for to make it, which hath been presented oft times before; whereof we crave aid, and it is decayed more than ever it was'; and much the same language is recorded next Michaelmas. And so it continues, session after session, until at Easter 1574 the jury 'do find the bridge is now substantially mended by the lord of the manor, which is Matthew Barnard of Aythorpe Roothing.' When the Stansted Mountfitchet bridge is presented for the second time, the jurors 'desire to see a redress, for it hath been oft times put up and no remedy found.' In 1568 Springfield Bridge, brought to the justices' notice for the third time, 'is like to fall down if it be not mended, and that shortly.'

Such was the picture for the first decade of the reign. It is with regret that we cannot paint similar canvases for the period 1569–1603. There is no decrease in the number of decayed bridges in the later presentments, and it would take many more pages to attempt even a condensed account. But we must stray beyond 1568 to mention what nearly befell one traveller, if only because it shows that the two prophesies in 1562 of likely drownings in times of flood at Stansted Bridge were not exaggerated. In his lesser known book on Britain (not that on England) Harrison refers to a bridge at the opposite side of the county. At the 'mill above Ramsey Bridge', he wrote, 'I was once almost drowned by reason of the ruinous bridge which leadeth over the stream, being there very great.' This bridge lay on the Manningtree–Colchester road near the head of the estuary running into the much wider Stour estuary.[1] Termed Ramsey otherwise Michaelstow Bridge, it was presented no less than four times in 1574–76 as 'broken and in great ruin'; in 1575 a writ was issued by Quarter Sessions to distrain the lord of the manor of Ramsey; but it was presented yet again in 1581.

The Sessions rolls also abound in presentments of ruinous footbridges and obstructed footpaths – matters which frequently came before the manor courts – and will be considered in the next volume.

[1] Quoted by Dr. G. Edelen in his edition of Harrison's *Description of England*, 444, n.9; it is of course in north-east Essex, not 'south-east' Essex.

Persons desirous of studying the condition of roads and bridges as revealed by the Sessions records of other counties will find the published calendars for Worcestershire and Hertfordshire among the best.[1]

Other Offences

Disorder in other respects is presented by the juries of the hundreds. Notes on the legislation concerning the offences is deferred until they are individually dealt with for the whole of the Elizabethan period.

Inadequate archery butts and stocks, and unlawful games, are reported, but there are only a few cases in this decade. The East Hanningfield stocks and butts have recently been broken; and, two years later, their stocks 'be not sufficient.'

The juries betray more concern about alehouses. At the Epiphany Sessions in 1567 the justices received a statement about certain unsavoury aspects of life in Chelmsford, the county town. Headed 'The names of all those houses that sell ale or beer without licence,' ten men and two women are listed, one living in New Street. Mother Bowden, Walter Baker and George Blacklocke each keep a 'brothel house' and a third man a 'disordered house'. There are no comments about the rest, except for two, of whom they furnish lively accounts.

> The above Henry Cooe liveth in great disorder with his wife, for that she reproveth him for his incontinent life and using of suspect houses, and on a time she went to the brothel house of Mother Bowden to see if her husband were there (which before was often denied). He slipped out of the house through the backside, and his wife beat both the old woman and the harlot her daughter, and pulled her about the house by the hair of the head, which daughter came running into the street and made 'anawtes' (announced) that Cooe his wife would kill her mother. This was in the evening as the people came from church being about the hour of 6 of the clock being dark. On 19 day of December last, being Friday, word came that Henry Cooe was at this said brothel house, and after 8 of the clock the house was beset to take him, and as they did knock at the door on the foreside of the house he went out at the backside. He feared that some were at the back gate and leaped over the pale into another man's yard thinking so to escape, but he was taken before he could get any further and was carried to the constables to use their office upon him. Also George Blacklocke besides his brothel house keeping doth keep common play both at dice and cards and doth 'howster' (allow in his house) men's servants and their children to play all that they may get and come by, and that at all hours of the night, to the great hurt of their masters and breaking of the good laws of this realm. Also he doth keep victualling during the time of divine service and will not be reformed by any gentle persuasion.

Two other charges of immorality are brought during this decade (p. 197).

In 1567 and 1568 two Fyfield men are presented, both for unlicensed alehouses and for harbouring 'a great resort of rogues and other naughty persons'; and in 1566 a Kelvedon man for keeping a tippling house

---

[1] *Worcestershire County Records, 1591–1643* (1900), esp. pp. clxxix–clxxxi.

'without (outside) the town' and lodging 'guests without the consent of the constable.' In addition to these disorderly houses, twenty-nine unlicensed victuallers, tipplers and alehouse keepers are reported during 1562–68, of whom one is also presented for not 'setting out his sign'; together with eight more for keeping alehouses, 'but whether they be bound or not we know not', of whom two in fact declare that they have been licensed by Mr. Anthony Cooke and Mr. Franke, J.P.s, respectively. Two bricklayers and two tapsters of Brentwood, with others unknown of Brentwood, Hutton and Shenfield, on Passion Sunday 'played at football' in Shenfield. Thirteen men, all of Good Easter and mostly labourers, unlawfully played football there. A London chandler with another tapster and an ostler servant of Robert Salmon of Brentwood in the Christmas holidays 'went a-mumming' to Ralph Whitlocke's of Great Warley. Two Brentwood men are 'great players at dice and cards'; William Aukyn of the 'White Hart', Brentwood, and an Aveley man 'keep unlawful gaming'; and a bowling pair are reported at Stansted Mountfitchet.

Buying and selling calves, lambs, and chickens, cheese, butter, and other victuals without the licence of two justices is presented four times, each involving one or more men. Clarke the Orsett beerbrewer sells beer by the 'kinderkin' (kilderkin, 18 gallons) at 2s. By the Act of 8 Elizabeth, c.9. (1566), Quarter Sessions fixed the price annually; it was usually 1d. a quart. The only other trade offence found by the jurors is against Robert Corney of Great Bardfield, who 'doth ingrate wheat to the number of 30 quarters and hath kept it so long that it is not meet or wholesome for men's sustenance, whereof 10 seam is not good, and hath sold of the same 15 quarters contrary to the statute.' This occurs immediately after the disastrous harvest of 1565. Two further echoes are heard in the following year. In April an Aveley man is discovered to be hoarding in his loft eight seam of wheat and rye 'and selleth none of it' (a seam contained eight bushels); in June 'one William Scott of Pebmarsh did lay in in Halstead in the cellar of one Thomas Batman 8 or 9 seam of wheat and kept it there for a year and was required of divers that would buy of the same corn and would neither sell or bring any of it to the market, and this we made certificate of to the high constables and they to Sir Thomas Goldyng'. The same jurors explain that they have also certified this offence to 'the Queen's commissioners regarding engrossers, forestallers and regrators'.

There is a solitary presentment (by Tendring hundred) of larceny: 'Hugh Sheppheard lately dwelling in Mistley hath stolen from Richard Reede a brazen kettle price 16d., a sack from Mr. Philip Wolverstone gentleman price 20d., another brasen kettle from Middle John Anger of Mistley, and two sheep from John Wyng in the same parish, and he is gone, so we know not where he is now.' It was not uncommon at this period for two children or even three, as in this instance, to be successively christened with the same name, especially if the earlier infants had died. Three accusations of witchcraft are copied in full :

> There was a witch in Boreham, and upon her confession before Mr. Archdeacon Cole she fled and went away. Joan Cocke of Kelvedon did lay her hands upon the knees of Richard Sherman, clapping her hand, upon which it is by common report come to our knowledge that he was presently (i.e. instantly) lamed and yet halteth. Noble's wife of Kelvedon (Joan Cocke's daughter) is suspected, by reason that she could not have butter according as she was wont to be served by Belfield's wife of Inworth, to have by the craft of witchcraft slain and killed one milch neat, and two other to have caused to give milk of all colours, being the beasts of Belfield's wife.

Witchcraft will be considered in the next volume of *Elizabethan Life*.

Presentments by the Petty Sessions or High Constables' Hundred Juries, 1562–68

While very few hundredal juries' presentments for Elizabeth and especially her first decade have survived in other counties, Essex possesses an even greater treasure in the presentments of the hundredal petty sessions or high constables' sessions or juries. For Elizabeth's early years they are believed to be unique.[1] In our documents they are variously termed 'petty sessions', 'petty juries', 'inquests', or 'inquisitions'; occasionally 'special sessions', 'petty sessions otherwise called statute sessions', or 'statute sessions called petty sessions'; once 'the court or leet called petty sessions'. These presentments mostly differ in form and content from the more normal presentments of the juries for the hundreds which have just been described, but a few offences reported are common to both.

Who were present at each hundredal petty sessions? It seems clear that the two high (or chief) constables were generally in charge. Summonde to attend from each township[2] were the (one or two) constables or petty constables, occasionallly called sub- or under-constables, and from one to four other 'jurors'. A total of seventy men may thus have attended for each of the larger hundreds; some of the lists give the townships which they represented. 'The Half Hundred of Witham : the certificate of the petty sessions holden at Witham before John Stonard and John Choppyn high constables of the half hundred by the oaths of the petty constables' is perhaps the best description of the personnel. On four occasions, somewhat surprisingly, one or two justices were present, their names of course preceding those of the high constables.

---

[1] This statement was first made by Margaret Gay Davies in *The Enforcement of English Apprenticeship, 1563–1642* (Harvard Univ. Press, 1956), 189, who adds that some incomplete pre-Elizabethan presentments are extant for Norfolk.

[2] The territorial unit was the vill or township, not the parish; but the distinction matters only in the five parishes which lay in two hundreds. In these cases constables were appointed for each part, as they owed attendance at their respective hundreds (or half hundreds).

Petty sessions were held to receive the reports of the constables of each township based on certain articles of enquiry. These articles could be deduced from various presentments, but they are clearly set out in that for Chafford hundred, Easter 1566.

ARTICLES FOR THE PETTY SESSIONS

To enquire of all those that be breakers of the Queen's peace
  for the punishment of vagabonds
  of servants both men and women, for excess wages
  for alehouse keeping
  for engrossers
  for butts
  for unlawful games
  for false rumours or sowers of sedition.

Here, in brief epitome, is a contemporary statement of what the Tudor government deemed to be among the main local weaknesses in the social, economic, military and political structure of the country. Defence depended partly on archery practice at the butts, which must be kept in repair. Excessive drinking and gambling not only affected people's moral fibre but also prejudiced archery or their masters' work. Control of vagrancy had been the subject of many earlier statutes. Masterless men and excessive wages were economic problems which the Act of 1563 had attempted to deal with. Not unrelated was engrossing, or cornering a commodity by wholesale buying.

The record handed in at Easter Quarter Sessions 1562 of the 'Petty Sessions held for the Half Hundred of Harlow according to the form of the statutes of late made and provided' based itself, however, on legislation rather than articles of equity, though actually 'all well' was reported by every township except one.

We shall interrupt this brief general survey of the Essex petty sessions presentments for 1562–68 with only occasional remarks about the earlier statutes.

An Ongar hundred petty sessions presentment of 1562 reveals that fines could be exacted.

Presentments at a Petty Sessions, before Robert Thurgood and John Grene, chief constables.

William Naylar, one of the constables of Little Laver, has not appeared according to the warning given to him; thereupon he is amerced 6s. 8d. (Six jurors of six parishes also make default and each is fined 2s.)

Stephen Howe of Magdalen Laver garment-maker made large stockings with worsted, contrary to divers warnings; therefore he is in mercy (fined) 20d.

William Tynge of Stanford Rivers is ordered that he shall not further frequent the society of Joan Palmer widow of Chipping Ongar, because they are suspected persons and of dishonest conversation, under a penalty to forfeit as often as they are found associating, to wit, William 13s. 4d., Joan 6s. 8d.

Robert Cheston of Bobbingworth, Richard Towse of North Weald, John Elderton of Lambourne and Roger Benton of Chigwell are bachelors and not in service.

The 'certificate' of the Clavering hundred high constables is also in the same Easter Sessions roll, but an unlicensed tippling-house (alehouse) is the only item. These are the earliest petty sessions records surviving for Essex, apart from the original presentments of the previous year, evidently made by two villages to the hundredal meeting.

Other petty sessions presentments show that absentees were also fined (usually 12d. each); as, for example, twelve defaulters for Chafford hundred in 1566. But, apart from fines for non-attendance, few later notes of fines at the high constables' sessions are found.

The next presentment is another by the same Clavering hundred officers at Midsummer 1563, and again only alehouses are referred to. Langley had one and six other townships including that of Bentfield in the parish of Stansted Mountfitchet each had one, all licensed, and two had none. 'All other things are in good order' in this small hundred.

Another function of petty sessions, and an important one, is revealed in what is evidently the complete return from the Rochford hundred petty constables to the Midsummer Sessions 1564 of their anti-vagrancy activities. The Hadleigh constables, for example, reported, 'On 30 May was punished and whipped John Barber of Sudbury (Suffolk) and sent to the constable of Thundersley. On 3 June punished and whipped Mary Fearne and Agnes Fearne, sisters, of Painswick (Glos.) and sent to the parish of South Benfleet.'

A long series of detailed vagrants' returns from petty sessions has been preserved for 1566–68. These and many later vagrancy items throw a flood of light on this dark and dismal feature of early Elizabethan life and will be described in a later volume under Vagrancy.

With the exception of the Rochford vagrants' papers, no petty sessions documents exist for most of 1564–65, but they are numerous from Michaelmas 1565. Sometimes, as in the first entry, the jurors indulged in a multiple complaint against a disreputable individual: 'John Gosnall of Chigwell is an unlicensed vendor of ale, a common player at cards, common disturber of his neighbours, and a keeper of bawdy house (fined 12d.); and Richard Bett of Stanford Rivers tailor uses his hose with great slops contrary to the proclamation and form of the statute (fined 4d.)'. Hose with great slops refers to the absurdly wide, baggy breeches of the period. The wearing of extravagant dress by the lower classes, inveighed against by Harrison[1] and satirized by Shakespeare, was forbidden by the sumptuary laws. At the same Quarter Sessions the adjacent hundred presents another man for wearing hose with great slops, also one of the constables of Roydon for not executing his office (fined 12d. in each case). One presentment is endorsed to the effect that a Great Bardfield man, reported as unlicensed, 'desireth to be admitted to sell ale and to keep a tippling house and bringeth in two sureties for his good

[1] Harrison, *Description of England*, ch. 7, 'Of Their Apparel'.

behaviour to be bound according to the statute.' Three men are to cleanse
their roadside ditches before Whitsuntide under penalty of 4d. for each
rod.

The presentment at Chafford hundred 'inquisition' held at Horndon-
on-the-Hill in 1566 is a long one. Mucking and Stanford each report one
unlicensed buyer and seller of butter, eggs, calves, lambs and chickens
(i.e. two 'badgers'). Little Burstead, Hutton and Shenfield each name an
unlicensed victualler. Two Great Burstead men have each received and
taken into service a man who has not produced his certificate or testimonial. Orsett presents a man for working with a tailor contrary to the
statute (of 1563), also two singlemen out of service, and Downham a
similar offender. At Shenfield John Atkynson of Brentwood has felled the
parsonage spring (small wood) and at Little Thurrock Master Josselyng
has sold two acres of woodland, and neither has left any staddles (young
trees). Bowers Gifford and Thundersley admit that their archery butts
are in disrepair. Little Thurrock states that 'there is no bill made for the
collection towards the relief of the poor' (the first of the Tudor poor relief
statutes in 1563 had introduced a compulsory parish rate). Great Warley
presents a bachelor for working out of service. Two Aveley parishioners
play tables (backgammon) and cards 'by day as well as by night' at the
'Harrow'. Childerditch and Grays Thurrock are each to be 'pained' (fined)
10s. if their pairs of butts are not in order by Whitsuntide. Grays Thurrock
cucking-stool is to be repaired by the Feast of St. John the Baptist. All is
well elsewhere in the hundred.

In 1566 appears the first complaint against purveyance – the system
under which the royal household bought its own provisions at low prices.
The Barstable jury present that 'Gregory Middleton, purveyor for
veals (calves) for the Queen's Majesty, came with the constable of Pitsea
to the 'coop' of Edward Bailiff of the same parish and there marked four
'veals' (calves), the which were as many as were there able to serve the
Queen, and also came within five days and drew the said four veals, and
at the present time drew one other veal that was but ten days old, the
which veals be yet unpaid for ; whether he might do this or not we defer
unto your worships' discretions.' In the following year Witham hundred
reports that on 6 August Robert Woodmansey's man 'did take up' in
Terling, Fairstead, White Notley and Chatley hamlet 5½ dozen chickens,
and on 13 August another 4 dozen chickens and a capon, in each case by
the appointment of the high constables. On three days in November
and December there are delivered to Middleton 11 hogs price 40s., to
Woodmansey 2 dozen and 2 capons at 6d. apiece and 1 dozen and 5
geese at 4d. apiece, and to Ralph Keable 7 dozen hens at 2d. apiece and
6 capons and 3 geese, all at 4d. apiece. In February there are deliveries
to the purveyor for wheat of 30 quarters and 6 bushels, and to William
Sewardde 'for the Queen's own mouth' (so they like to think) 6½ dozen

hens at 4d. each and 2 capons at 6d. each, with 9 flitches of bacon price 13s. 10d.

The royal privilege of purveyance was extremely unpopular, largely because it was open to abuse by the peripatetic officers, who not only pursued their business by summoning the petty constables and handing them a list of food and so forth which they were obliged to collect from unwilling victims, but could also purchase goods in local markets and even stop farmers on their way to market. The system was however subject to control by Quarter Sessions, which was empowered to imprison offending purveyors and in flagrant cases to sentence them to hanging. The Privy Council also investigated serious complaints against them. In August 1565 the councillors had written to thank Sir Thomas Throckmorton and Sir Nicholas Poyntz, Essex J.P.s, for their 'diligence in searching out of disorders' by purveyors' servants, such as those named above, and the culprits were to be punished.[1] The subject has been discussed in a long article dealing with the whole country, though not using the Essex Sessions records.[2] We may have an opportunity of drawing on them in a later volume.

In 1568 the rolls afford the first references to the hiring of servants and their wages. From this date onwards there are scores of presentments from the hundredal sessions : a most valuable corpus of material on the administration of those sections of the Statute of Artificers governing apprenticeship and service by yearly contracts. Servants' hiring sessions or hiring fairs survived in some parts of England well into the nineteenth century, as will be remembered from the colourful description of the hiring of agricultural labourers in Hardy's *Far from the Madding Crowd*. We hope to illustrate the enforcement of the regulations in Elizabethan Essex when dealing with Work and Trade in a later volume.[3]

The presentments for 1568 name twenty men and thirteen women who 'are not retained in anyone's service for a year but are free to give service to those who ask it ; therefore proclamation is made.' The document then records no less than nineteen contracts. Here are three typical entries.

> Thomas Radley of Dedham, butcher, agreed to serve John Sperlinge of the same, butcher, from the day of this sessions until the end and term of one whole year, taking therefor for his wages 40s. and 6s. 8d. for his livery (clothes).
>
> John Holdinge agreed to serve Henry Moysse of Feering for one year for sufficient victuals and clothing.
>
> Joan Smyth agreed to serve Anthony Pulleyn from 8 March until the end of one whole year, taking for her wages 16s. and one petticoat cloth of household cloth.

A man is also presented for assaulting the petty constables, and seven men of Wivenhoe and Stanway for selling bread, beer and other victuals

[1] *Acts of the Privy Council*, vii, 241.
[2] Allegra Woodworth, 'Purveyance for the Royal Household (under) Elizàbeth' (*Trans. Am. Phil. Soc.*, N.S., xxxv, 1946).
[3] Apprenticeship has been dealt with thoroughly by Margaret Gay Davies (see p. 28, n. 1), who drew copiously from the Essex Sessions records.

without licence, one of whom also 'keeps unlawful games, viz. (bowling) alleys, cards and slidethrift (shove-ha'penny).'

From the petty constables of Dunmow hundred in the same year come charges against three Great Dunmow singlemen, tailors by occupation, who refuse to serve by the year (as covenanted servants) and 'use great excess in their apparel for their hosen contrary to the statute'. One singlewoman and five singlemen of several parishes are out of service, one of whom 'works about by the day', that is, instead of being hired for a whole year.

It is obvious that presentments made to Quarter Sessions by the hundreds were based on reports given in by the individual parishes or townships. Many of their representatives who were unable to write presumably put in their statements orally. By good fortune three original documents, all no doubt handed in at the Hinckford petty sessions, are preserved. Two of them are in the oldest Elizabethan roll, for Epiphany 1562. The first document, given in modernised spelling, came from Great Maplestead.

> The presentments of Richard Grene and John Payne, constables, and John Parker and Robert Bryaunte, parishioners.
>
> Upon Christmas eve last we the said constables with divers other of the parish willing to see things well ordered according to our oath, because a little before we did hear of matters much needful and worth to be amended, we did search divers houses being suspect, among which we came unto one who nameth himself Newcome, other name we know not, and when we came to his house he nor his wife was not at home. And then we went into one Smethe's house and there we met the said Newcome at Smythe's gate, unto whom we said, 'Newcome, we have been at your house as we have been at others to see what order or rule you do keep.' And then he made us this answer, 'What have you to do to search my house? You shall not come there. I am as honest as the best of you all. For you are all churls and that is the alms that you do give.' Moreover about Michaelmas last this Newcome's wife did dwell in Sible Hedingham with her husband to our knowledges, and as we have understand while she was there this Newcome chanced where this woman was and claimed her for his wife, upon which the man that came with her to Hedingham suddenly was gone and none could tell where he became. And so since that time this Newcome and she have continued together and still do. Whether she be his wife or no we cannot tell. Very suspect persons they both and how they live we cannot tell. And therefore we desire your good counsel or order in this behalf and remedy for the same.

Both are in painfully penned writing in north Essex crude, vernacular language. The second, put in by Wickham St. Paul's, is best read first in the literal transcript given below the reproduction (plate 6). If the reader has done this and looked at the photograph, he may be glad to re-read it in modern form!

> These be the words that John Northe of Wickham constable and Thomas Edwardes of the same town (i.e. village) did hear Elizabeth Fettes say, coming thither to examine them for their apparel as they were commanded by the Queen's commissioner. First they asked him whose servant he was, and he said, 'My Lord Robert's man'. And they did ask him whether he was of household or a retainer, and he

said of household but he was not in wages, but said he might, and if he would then
they said to him, 'You have held out at the court well.' And he said, 'I came from
thence, I came yesterday and thither I will again by and by' (at once). And they
did say, 'Master Fettes, we did hear say Her Grace was wassail received at my
Lord Rich's and great resort'. And he said, 'No, not us the resort, that was at Sir
John Wentworth's, for they might not be suffered.' And then she said thus, 'He is
a very villain and as rank a papist as one is wit (aware of, known) in the realm of
England.'

While 'wossarwante' (whose servant) and 'were fellen' (very villain) are
easy, though precious examples of local pronunciation, the one problematical word is, if correctly understood, the most interesting in this remarkable document. 'Worccelle' at first sight would seem to be 'worsely', an
unrecorded word though possible enough in vernacular language. It does
not, however, make sense because it fails to fit in with 'great resort',
whereas wassail, the salutation used in drinking another's health, had
acquired the further meaning of riotous festivity or revelling. Admittedly,
this sense is not recorded before *Hamlet* (I, iv, 9).

To explain this obscure presentment is more difficult than to struggle
with the script and spelling. The royal commissioner, through the petty
constables, was evidently investigating obedience to any abuses of the law
of livery and maintenance, the signal abuse of which by the Earl of Oxford
at Hedingham Castle in 1489 must still have been common talk (p. 6).
'Mr. Fettes' and his wife have not been identified: it is possible that
the surname is Fitch, an old-established family with various branches
in North Essex. 'My Lord Robert' must refer to Sir Robert Rich, son
and heir apparent of Richard Lord Rich. As a household servant ('Mr'
denotes that he was not a menial servant) the wearing of his master's
livery was not illegal. Of more significance is the allusion to two of the
Queen's hosts during her recent progress. On leaving Hedingham Castle,
a short stage brought her to Gosfield Hall, where she stayed for two days
with Wentworth, moving on to Leighs Priory, where Rich entertained
her for four or five days. The royal train left his roof on 25 August. 'Her
stay with Rich cost him £389, that with Oxford £273', and Sir William
Petre at Ingatestone Hall spent £136 for a visit of three or four days.[1] The
implications of popish leanings on the part of Wentworth must await the
next volume of *Elizabethan Life*, when we shall deal with Recusancy.

The third document is dated two day before the Epiphany Sessions
1567.

John Turner, Cuthbert Gasckyn, John Lawrence, Edward Parmenter, Richard
Page and John Parmenter of Little Maplestead do present unto the jury that one
Richard Strutt of Little Maplestead who keepeth an alehouse against the statute
and being forbidden by the justice and constables maintaineth evil rule and
receiveth vagabonds, so that there was of late a robbery committed by one that
was a vagabond and harboured in the house of the said Richard Strut, and also
upon Saint Stephen's day last there was a bloodshed drawn in his house, viz. of
one which had a broken head.

[1] Emmison, *Tudor Secretary*, 243–5.

In the ordinary presentment for Hinckford hundred occurs the resulting entry: 'We find in the parish of Little Maplestead that Richard Strut keepeth a tippling house and disorder.'

Mention of petty sessions in the *ordinary* hundredal presentments, though uncommon, points to the complementary nature of their functions. In 1564 one such presentment adds: 'We find that all other things be reformed at the petty sessions and be in good order within the whole hundred.' Hinckford jury declare in 1566 that they have given certificates to the high constables about vagrants, forestallers and regrators, and in 1568 that 'as for our alehouses and apparel we had the petty sessions of late and all is in good order as far as we know.' Two sessions afterwards the same hundred report a broken contract. John Coo of Belchamp St. Paul's had been ordered by the constables to find a master. When 'the high constables did hold the statute sessions called petty sessions' Anthony Thurrold of the same 'did avow' Coo to be his covenant servant; but within a short time Coo 'was again at his liberty', and Thurrold 'did not retain him after, but only to colour (excuse) him, contrary to the law and good order'. The normal reports from several hundreds finish with 'all other things that were amiss we presented at our last petty sessions' or a similar phrase.

These brief allusions to 'our petty sessions' illustrate the administrative co-ordination between the two bodies. The ancient hundreds were thus acting in a dual capacity. On the whole each jury understood its terms of reference: roads and bridges were the sole concern of the ordinary juries; servants and vagrants were the responsibility of the constables' juries. But disorderly alehouses and unlawful games and broken butts could come within the purview of either, and both seemed to regard themselves as liable for reporting breaches of the provisions of the Statute of Artificers.

Presentments by the Grand Juries, 1562–68

All bills for indictment had first to be submitted to the grand jury. If it found *Ignoramus* (we do not know) or 'No true bill' there were no further proceedings on such an indictment. On its returning *Billa vera* or 'A true bill' the accused was then tried before a petty jury.

The grand jury emerged as a body which would throw out any indictments that seemed to be based on an unfounded charge. It also served as the mouthpiece for the county in presenting offences on its own initiative. In this respect its function was complementary to that of the hundredal juries in reporting decayed bridges, disorderly alehouses, and so forth. Occasionally, however, it drew the Court's attention to abuses of a general nature, such as purveyance. In this decade the only example is the presentment of a trading offence. The term 'Grand Jury' first appears in the Essex Rolls in 1566; 'Grand Inquest' is used in 1568; in all the other documents it is a presentment 'for the body of the County', or it is un-named, in which case its being a grand jury presentment is deduced from the fact that offences are reported from parishes in various parts of the county.

The earliest grand jury presentment was made at Easter Sessions 1562. 'On Midlent Sunday there was football play at Agnes Grene widow, the parish of Stondon against the parish of Kelvedon, and play at the cards all the night'; Thomas her son also played at bowls on the following day; three men keep common alehouses in Terling but are not bound; a Chelmsford widow keeps a common house of bawdery and has been commanded by a justice not to receive any more 'guests' nor to 'draw so much as a pot of beer', but disobeys it (is this Mother Bowden's brothel of 1567?); Machins Mill Bridge in the highway to Maldon is decayed and had been made by the farmer (lessee) of 'Benyngtons' (the manor of Bennington Hall in Witham).

In the same year Springfield Bridge is presented as being out of repair, in language identical with that of the Chelmsford hundred jury at the previous Sessions (p. 20). Its important position on the Colchester road may well have led the grand jurors, some of whom had perhaps crossed it to attend the Court, to report its condition.

Also in 1562 occurs the first reference to a bridge which was probably about to collapse, and was never to be replaced: 'Hull Bridge in the highway in the parish of Hockley within the hundred of Rochford is in great decay and it is not possible to find out or prove what hundred, riding, wapentake, city, borough or parish, or what person or what lands and tenements or what body politic by right or custom ought to repair the same, so that it remains unrepaired to the great peril of all travellers, and it is presented that it is outside any city and corporate town and is a common highway in the said parish.' Clearly, one of the jurors knew the Statute of Bridges (p. 20). The interesting story of the gradual disappearance of Hull Bridge will be traced from later rolls in a subsequent volume.

A long grand jury presentment for 1564 deals solely with unlicensed buyers and sellers of butter. West Ham offenders account for eight, Steeple Bumpstead for two, and Dagenham, Barking and Great Baddow for one each.

In 1566 the grand jury present a Brentwood man as a common dicer and carder and two north Essex men as idle and masterless; none of them will obey the Queen's officers, and one has been ordered by the high constables to appear at Quarter Sessions but has defaulted. Next year a Shenfield butcher 'keepeth an alehouse and doth daily hospitate and succour vagabonds and idle persons and suffer them to play at cards;' and the jury even present so mild a nuisance as fourteen perches of a fleam ditch (an artificial drain) in Frythes Mead in Takeley which a woman of an adjacent parish ought to scour.

The remaining grand jury presentments, all belonging to 1566–68, deal solely with the ever-present problem of unrepaired bridges. At Michaelmas 1567 they name two bridges – Broad Bridge in Aythorpe Roothing, 'which has many times been presented but not amended' (true enough, as we have seen), and Langford Bridge (its first appearance in the rolls), Mr. Harvey having the land on both sides, but they do not know who is liable. Both bridges are dutifully but ineffectively included in their appropriate hundred reports at the following Sessions, at which the grand jury present four further bridges. Of these, Paynes Bridge in Romford, the one between Hatfield Peverel and Witham, and High Ongar Bridge have previously been before the Court through the hundredal presentments. 'The highway in Romford from Paynes Bridge to Goossis Gate in Romford containing 60 rod is in great ruin in London highway' is the sole instance of both bridge and adjacent road being reported at the same time. This 1,000 foot length of the Great Essex Road between Gooshays Manor avenue and the bridge is seen on Chapman and André's map of 1777. The fourth bridge, at which three parishes meet (p. 23), was to be constantly presented in the future but here occurs for the first time : 'Blackwater Bridge in Bradwell is in great decay and no cart can pass over, in the highway between Coggeshall and Braintree, and Mr. Fabyan, Mr. Maxy and Mrs. Wyseman hath land of both sides.'

At Midsummer 1568 the 'verdict of the Great Inquest' concerns four bridges. 'Touching the examination and depositions of the ruinous and decayed bridge called Pissingforth Bridge, we see no matter or cause apparent whereby to charge any particular person for the repair thereof but that the country ought to do the same.' So the grand jury endorses the view of the hundred jury (p. 22) that this bridge should be treated as a county bridge. Unfortunately, the recorded evidence, probably from some of the oldest inhabitants, has not survived.

The other bridges presented are very minor ones. A broken bridge at Studley Green in Danbury 'which heretofore hath been repaired by the lord or owner of the manor or late priory of Bicknacre' has appeared earlier as Fulbrook Bridge. Radwinter Bridge 'they know not who is liable', but 'a little decayed bridge called a wholve in the highway from Sampford to Walden in the parish of Hempstead hath heretofore been repaired by Mr. Robert Mordaunt of Hempstead.' It may be that one of the grand jurors had recently experienced difficulty in riding in the Radwinter area, but in any case it is evident that the grand jury do not regard such trifling obstructions as beneath their dignity to present.

We have given as briefly as possible a fairly comprehensive survey of the heterogeneous crimes and offences and other forms of disorder such as dangerous bridges presented at Quarter Sessions during 1562–68 as well those found in the earlier Sessions and Assize records for 1556–61.

It seems unnecessary to trace their activities in this way any further. We shall now try to examine for the whole of our period the somewhat more numerous crimes and offences according to their own categories – in so far as they fall into categories. Information about disobedience to the laws of the realm came before the Courts by way of charges brought by individual justices or pairs of justices or by other prosecutors, by way of recognizances to keep the peace in which the offence is specified, through coroners' inquests, or through informations and petitions. Serious disorders occasionally went to the Privy Council or were referred by that body to the county justices. The depositions taken down by the examining J.P.s give infinitely more detail than the formal indictments, and it is very fortunate that the Essex Sessions rolls contain an abnormally large number of such documents covering almost the entire range. These are very precious to both the social and the local historian. The Assize and Queen's Bench records are not so detailed, but they supplement those of Quarter Sessions in various ways. We have so far only examined a little of the documentary treasure.

3

Sedition

Although sedition is scarcely mentioned either in Lambarde's *Eirenarcha* or Dalton's *Country Justice*, it was cognisable at Quarter Sessions as well as at Assizes.[1] Indeed, sedition was one of the nine matters about which the Essex hundredal petty sessions were ordered to enquire in 1566 according to their 'articles', and any case was to be reported to the county justices. 'As concerning matters of our Prince', one hundredal jury returned in 1583, 'we find nothing to present'; actually, only one petty sessions during her reign brought a seditious charge to the court. The number of Essex persons alleged to have committed the crime is however surprisingly large, and no period in Elizabeth's time is entirely free from it. Indictments for sedition were preferred mostly at the Assizes, but a few of the cases had originated in Quarter Sessions. Charges of sedition occasionally came also before the Privy Council, and the firm hand which the councillors kept over the local courts, especially the justices of the peace, is well illustrated in a number of cases involving Essex people. There are some borderline cases. Slanderous speeches against privy councillors or other magnates were regarded as sedition rather than the lesser offence of slander, as they might prejudice the government; and disturbances in church which savoured of leanings towards Rome tended to be treated in the same way.

Sedition, or the inciting of people to disaffection towards the Crown, could be perpetrated by violent action or by spoken or written words. Nearly all our cases are confined to speech, except the written doggerel which appeared at Walthamstow (p. 60). But it is not always easy to differentiate between slander and sedition. In its most dangerous form sedition was high treason, for which the convicted culprit was generally drawn, hanged and quartered. For petty treason he was pilloried and lost both ears. At the lower end of the scale, it was little more than idle talk against the Queen or Privy Council, sometimes when tongues were loosened by strong beer, good cheer and an alehouse audience, for whose benefit the drunken braggart started or magnified a scandalous rumour. Englishmen have ever been prone at the slightest provocation to complain against the government. The cases we shall consider are therefore a strange mixture of major and minor seditious speech.

[1] I am grateful to Professor J. Hurstfield for his comments on this chapter.

Essex was not directly involved in rebellion against the government. But there is found some evidence in our records (and apparently unrecorded elsewhere) of an abortive attempt at insurrection in the cloth-manufacturing towns in the north-east of the county in 1566; and subversive comments, which could also have led to a rising, were overheard during famine years in the last decade of the reign (pp. 61–65). Apart from the usual crop of seditious talk at every sovereign's accession, the Assize files regularly echo the cries of discontented subjects, sober or drunken, and ears were strained in later years to listen for any whisper which seemed to come from the twin menaces of Spanish power and Catholic treason. Specific indictments of high treason are relatively few, but they include the notoriously false charge against John Payne of Ingatestone Hall, Catholic martyr, who was hanged (p. 52). Rarely is the sentence given – a common defect of criminal court records of the period – but where the verdict was guilty it may be assumed that the law took its course.

At the Winter Assizes, 1576, Mary Cleere of Ingatestone was charged with having traitorously declared there a few months earlier that the Queen was 'baseborn and not born to the Crown, but that another Lady was the right inheritor.' She added, somewhat irrelevantly, that it did not become a woman to make knights, which she would justify. Found guilty, she was sentenced to be drawn and burnt (*trahatur et comburatur*). Burning was rightly deemed to be a more severe punishment than hanging : a criterion of the gravity of her crime and the sole instance actually recorded in our Elizabethan records.

A Catholic impostor impersonating the dead Queen Mary would have been less surprising to a Protestant government than one alleging that he was Edward. (Two Essex men had been arrested in the middle of Mary's reign for reporting that Edward was still alive.[1]) This late Tudor pretender, emulating Perkin Warbeck's attempt against Henry VII, first appeared in May 1578, when the Council ordered that 'one Blosse *alias* Mantell' be removed from the Tower to the Marshalsea prison, also in London, to await his trial by the Assize judges in Essex.[2] The indictment at the following Midsummer Assizes states that Robert Mantell *alias* Bloys of London, at Maldon and many other places, 'gave out and said that King Edward was alive, that he (meaning the said Robert) was King Edward the Sixth, and that if he would find one that was trusty he could disclose that which should rejoice them all; howbeit he could never find such an one.' He was found guilty, but he escaped from the Castle gaol a year later. So Lord Darcy and Sir Thomas Lucas were enjoined by the Council to visit the gaol and interrogate the prisoners. Lucas reported that widow Symonds, a prisoner, had probably helped

---

[1] *Acts of the Privy Council*, v, 126.   [2] *Ibid.*, x, 223; also xii, 29, 353–4.

him to escape. At the Midsummer Assizes 1579 Richard King, the gaoler (deputy of Henry Mackwilliam esquire, Keeper of the Castle gaol) was charged. The impostor had been sent thither by the Council on 1 June 1578, 'on suspicion of high treason', had been re-committed after conviction by the Assize judges for further trial, but on the Assize day King 'treacherously allowed him to escape'. King pleaded not guilty of treason but guilty of negligence, and he exchanged his gaoler's house for a cell in his own prison, where he remained until released by Council order in January 1580. Re-captured and thrown into Newgate prison, Mantell was sent under secure guard to Brentwood, where he was before the judges again at the Lent Assizes 1581, this time pleading guilty. Judgement: 'To be drawn from prison to the gallows and there hanged and afterwards whilst still living cut down, etc.'

Edward, no longer young, was still living in 1587, according to another rumour. For spreading it, Walter Mildmay had committed William Francis, a smith of Hatfield Peverel, who, being asked what news was at London, had said, 'There is one in the Tower which saith he is King Edward'; then a bystander remarked, 'I dare say that King Edward is dead', which Francis denied, 'I dare not say so', adding 'I know the man that carried King Edward in a red mantle into Germany in a ship called the Harry'. When it was pointed out that he was buried where they used to bury kings, Francis declared that 'there was a piece of lead buried that was hollow but there was nothing in it and that it was but a monument', on which he was told, 'These are naughty words which ought not to be spoken.' He was found guilty of treason.

Rumours of a highly treasonable and scandalous nature were being bruited in Essex and Hertfordshire in the summer of 1560. Thomas Holland, who had become rector of Little Burstead on the death of his predecessor in the same month as Mary's death, was charged by the Privy Council, after their receiving a letter from the Earl of Oxford (written at Hedingham Castle), with 'uttering malicious words against the Queen.' Holland confessed that he heard the vicar of Stortford (Herts.) say that one had been sent to the Tower for reporting that the Queen was with child.[1] He resigned his benefice very soon afterwards. About the same time Lord Rich and Thomas Mildmay, J.P.s, wrote to Cecil enclosing depositions of certain Essex folk about similar reports, adding that they had committed Anne Dowe of Brentwood, the chief offender, to gaol. Mother Dowe was alleged to have openly asserted that the Queen was pregnant by Dudley.[2]

By 1580 fertile rumour in Essex had credited such a liaison with two children, a story not matched in reports to the Council from elsewhere.

[1] *Cal. State Papers Domestic, 1547–80*, 154.
[2] *Ibid.*, 157. She was not of 'Brentford' (J. Neale, *Queen Elizabeth*, 86), who cites both these cases as the only known gossip that the Queen had borne a bastard by Dudley.

They were so informed by the Maldon bailiffs (the borough's two chief officers) about Thomas Playfere (or Playfair), a labourer of their town. The Council referred the matter to the Essex Assize judges, ordering him to be transferred from the London prison (the Tower or the Marshalsea) to Colchester Castle prison.[1] Two separate indictments were laid against him for seditious speeches, both on 29 January and in the presence of two witnesses. 'Let the parliament begin when it will', he had declared, 'there will one stand up for heir apparent, beat him down who will'. Asked whom he meant, he said, 'The Earl of Shrewsbury; there were others if they were known who would make a black day.' Again asked whom he meant, he replied, 'The Queen had two children by my Lord Robert, the Earl of Leicester'; he had seen them where they were shipped at Rye in two of the Queen's best ships. Found guilty on each charge, he was committed to prison for five months, then to stand in the pillory, and afterwards to return to prison for three years. This intermediate punishment between gallows and pillory shows that the judges exercised discretionary powers in varying the statutory penalties for high and petty treason.

The climax was reached ten years later, when two persons, independently as it seems, came out with fantastic stories about the Queen's progeny. Dionisia Deryck of Chipping Hill in Witham, a widow, declared there that Elizabeth 'hath already had as many children as I, and that two of them were yet alive, one a man child and the other a maiden child, and the others were burned.' Questioned about paternity, she said that 'my Lord of Leicester (Dudley) was the father and wrapped them up in the embers in the chimney which was in the chamber where they were born.' Two months afterwards, in June 1590, Robert Gardner of Coopersale in Epping produced a somewhat similar account, to the effect that Leicester 'had four children by the Queen's Majesty, whereof three were daughters and alive, and the fourth a son that was burnt.' Both indictments were tried at the Summer Assizes; both the accused, who were convicted, received identical sentences: 'to be set upon the pillory on some market day in market time with a paper on his (her) head for slanderous words against her Majesty.' This extreme clemency suggests that the Assize judges decided that their proper course was to discount such highly treasonable sayings as those of irresponsible rustics. But the two charges originated in places twenty-five miles apart, which at least suggests that the gossip was widespread, at any rate, in Essex.

Not unconnected with this traitorous theme is an indictment of the previous year. Thomas Wenden of Aldham yeoman at Colchester said, 'God's wounds, I will keep it no longer, Parson Wylton spake openly in the church of Aldham that the Queen's Majesty was an arrant whore' (which Wylton did not say, according to the indictment). John Weste,

[1] *Acts of the Privy Council*, x, 405.

a tailor, was stupified by the horrid and diabolical words spoken to him, yet Wendon repeated them, exclaiming, 'Why, the Queen is a dancer, and Wylton said that all dancers are whores.' The verdict is not given. Wenden, described as a husbandman, had joined with Robert Page, the Aldham miller, as surety for a licensed alehouse-keeper in the previous year. John Wylton, the rector, has been convicted at the Summer Assizes in 1586 for 'defacing' the Book of Common Prayer.[1]

The seditious preaching of George Egle *alias* Trudy *alias* Trudgeover in Mary's time has already been mentioned (p. 5). The Marian rector of St. Leonard's, Colchester, was accused by the Council four months after Elizabeth's accession: 'Peter Walker, priest, for uttering lewd and untrue reports.' In great letters, 'For false seditious tales', was to appear in a label on his head while he was in Colchester market pillory; then, if he could find sureties for good behaviour, he was to be freed, otherwise to go to the Castle dungeons.[2] He conformed, and died in his rectory in 1570. In the same year (1559), 'one Clybburne' was prosecuted by Dr. George Wythers (Archdeacon of Colchester) for having uttered unseemly words of the Queen, calling her a rascal, but nothing is known of this man;[3] and in the next it was the Queen's service that was 'paltry' (p. 10).

Seditious speeches by alleged papists came before the Essex courts in 1574, when John Rypton of East Tilbury smith was indicted, but found not guilty, for publicly declaring that he 'trusted to have the plucking of twenty such knaves as the vicar of East Tilbury was out of their houses by the heads, and that a parson gone to Rome should come from thence and have his benefice again, and that ere it was long he would have him out of his benefice.' The patronage had been in the hands of the Crown since the Dissolution. This must refer to Christopher Eaton, vicar from 1560 to 1575. He had been presented by the Queen on the death of Thomas Martyn, to whom Mary had given the benefice six months before her own death, so the smith's prophetic declaration seems nonsensical.

It is from 1574 onwards that various charges of seditious talk became frequent. Some of the men were indicted for speaking against the Queen, or the Council, or the Church. Some denounced both the Church and the Crown or government, for it was one and the same where religion was concerned. The cases cannot be grouped by themes, so they will be presented more or less in order of date.

A charge of seditious language of more than ordinary interest was made in 1574: interesting because it uses the word 'Puritan'. Before narrating

[1] Davids, *Annals*, 110, quotes from the 1584 report of the Council to the Archbishop of Canterbury, 1584: 'Mr. Wilton, parson of Aldham, indicted at the Assizes for omitting the surplice and cross in baptism', adding that the parish register gives him as rector, 1563–99 (he is not in Newcourt).

[2] *Acts of the Privy Council*, vii, 71.

[3] *State Papers Domestic, 1547–80*, 127.

the incident, something of the immediate background events must be told, because Thomas Cartwright, one of the leading early Puritans, was mentioned.[1] A Cambridge man, who became a Fellow of Trinity in 1562, he had attacked the use of the surplice and more recently had preached against the Church, which led to deprivation of his fellowship in 1571, when he left for Geneva. Returning the next year he departed again for the continent soon afterwards, having written his *Replye* to Bishop Whitgift's *Answere to the Admonition*. The *Replye* had been printed secretly by one Lacy at 'Hempsteade' (the town of Hemel Hempstead, Herts., rather than Hempstead, Essex, a mere village). The emergence of 'puritans' although well-known to historians, is so relevant to the indictment that it may be told again here. The word had first[2] appeared in the *Admonition* (1572) : 'They lincke in togither and slaunderously charge pore men . . . with greeuous faults, calling them Puritanes', which brought forth Whitgift's retort in his *Answere* (1572) : 'This name Puritane is very aptely giuen to these men, not bicause they be pure . . . but bicause they think themselves to be . . . more pure than others, and separate them selves from all other Churches and congregations as spotted and defyled.' To which Cartwright in his *Replye* had written : 'If you meane that those are puritanes which do set forth a true and perfect patern of reforming the church, then the marke of thys heresie reachethe unto those which made the booke of common prayer.'

The person charged at Quarter Sessions was Thomas Bedell of Writtle esquire. He came of a very ancient landed Writtle family, and had inherited the manors of Bedell's Hall and Shakstons in that parish in 1535 at the age of eight.[3] In 1539 he had sold some land to William Pynchon of Writtle,[4] who was the ancestor of William Pynchon, the founder (1636) of Springfield, Massachusetts. He had been bailiff of the Essex liberties of the Duchy of Lancaster in 1565, for that year only, an office thereafterwards held for many years by George Deane. The important manor of Writtle, which included Roxwell, was a liberty. It had been granted by Queen Mary to Sir William Petre in 1554, and claimed certain exemptions, for example, the right to have its own coroner. The indictment against Bedell is abnormally long and has a sanctimonious preamble. Then, after a reference to the 'salutary laws' governing the Church of England, it recites that a sermon was preached in Writtle church on the preceding 18 April by Michael Mayshort (or Mayshott), the vicar, in which he inveighed against the malice of papists towards the clergy. Enlarging on this theme, the vicar declared that the papists vexed the ministers of the Word of God 'with their suits and quarrels'. Immediately after the service James Chapman, bailiff of the hundred of Chelmsford,

---

[1] The best account is in P. Collinson, *The Elizabethan Puritan Movement* (1967).
[2] Professor Hurstfield points out that the word is found in the previous decade.
[3] Morant, *History of Essex*, ii, 67.
[4] Essex Record Office, Q/RDb 52.

delivered to the vicar a writ of *subpoena* (evidently the result of the disturbance in the church earlier in the year, p. 185). But, going out through the churchyard, the bailiff was accosted by Bedell, who vehemently accused him of infringing the Liberty of Writtle. The bailiff replied that the writ had been demanded by the Queen, upon which Bedell said to the bailiff, 'What, is the Queen become a papist now?'

Bedell was later strictly questioned at the Assizes held on 20 July 1574 concerning his 'speech of scandalous words about the Queen indecently and irreverently spoken'. In full Court Bedell again repeated, 'They are not papists who say that the Queen is a papist, but rather divers others who are called Puritans'. Interrogated as to which 'puritans' he himself knew who said the Queen was a papist, Bedell answered, 'Master Cartwright (meaning Thomas Cartwright) affirmed this in a certain book that he wrote'. But Bedell 'did not produce any proof, nor show any other sufficient matter to prove that the said Cartwright had written any such scandalous and seditious words in his book.' The jury's verdict was that Bedell 'of malice and his own imagination spoke of the Queen the said false, scandalous and seditious words, news and rumours'. He was found guilty, 'and judgement is delivered according to the statute'.

The Assize judges then made a rare decision – they asked the county justices to hold a special Sessions to deal further with Bedell. This took place at Braintree on 12 August, and two lists of twenty-four men juries to try Bedell, as well as that of the grand jury, are preserved. Some of the county's leading gentlemen who were not justices appear in these lists. Bedell was accordingly brought to Court by the Sheriff, having apparently been in prison. Rich presided. The verdict again was that Bedell 'did speak the said words against the Queen maliciously.' The justices then ordered their clerk to prepare a special memorandum, which they all signed—Lord Rich, Lord Darcy, Henry Grey, Sir Thomas Mildmay, Francis Harvey, Thomas Meade, Robert Mounson, George Nycolls, James Morrice and Thomas Gent. Their note adds a few very minor points: merely emphasising that they 'reproved' Bedell, while at the same time questioning him about puritans.

The matter was then reported to the Council. At their meeting on 16 August, the councillors decided to send a letter to Lord Rich and Lord Darcy. 'In consideration of his repentance', they wrote, 'they do accept the fine of C li. and so discharge him from the pillory and the loss of his ears; and (on payment) to set him at liberty, but first to make his submission in writing and to put in bonds for good behaviour.' Bedell had stoutly defended his remark in the churchyard. His crushing fine of £100 is a criterion of the Council's attitude towards seditious speech.[1]

In 1575 George Dibney of St. Giles, Colchester, was summoned before the Council for seditious libels 'thrown abroad' in the town and was

[1] *Acts of the Privy Council*, viii, 283.

imprisoned at Woodstock but set at liberty three months later under a bond of £100 to appear in the Star Chamber, which fined him £20.[1] His house had been searched by one of the borough bailiffs, Sir Thomas Lucas the recorder, and others; and the case of 'the Colchester libels' was a concern of the Council for some months. Next year they were apparently still dealing with the same libels and thanked Lord Darcy, Lucas and Henry Golding for their pains. Whether seditious words spoken by Richard Southwell at Berechurch on Easter Eve 1576 (see p. 105) were linked with the Dibney case is not clear, but the Southwell charge was considered by the Council at the same time as they were worried about an abortive insurrection in the Colchester area (p. 105).[2] Dibney, borough serjeant-at-mace, had been involved in some trouble in 1567 with William Cole, the town preacher.[3]

George Binkes and William Binkes, both tailors of Finchingfield, were far too outspoken about the Old Faith in 1577, and no less than six Finchingfield and four Wethersfield villagers testified before Henry Medeley, J.P. (of Tilty Abbey), about their popish sayings. While at William Cooke's house at Finchingfield, 'reasoning very earnestly' with one of Cooke's servants about matters of religion, William Binkes said that 'after the bread and wine was by the priest consecrated it was the very body, flesh and blood of Christ'. 'Why', said Cooke, 'then we are wrong taught'. 'Marry, so you are', quoth Binkes, 'and that I will prove by good authors, for the true religion is at Rome.' Another Finchingfield man confirmed the last statement, adding that Binkes declared, 'What manner of religion we have here in England I know not, for the preachers now do preach their own inventions and fantasies, and therefore I will not believe any of them'. A Finchingfield wife said that, through the persuasions of the two Binkes, 'by certain books which they have read' to her husband, he would no longer go to sermons nor suffer her to go, to her great grief. A Wethersfield man averred that George Binkes told him that 'God made but one commandment and that was that we should love our neighbour as ourself, secondarily that the mass is good and confiteor (confession) is good, and that he will believe as long as he liveth, also that the images are good and ought to stand in the church to put men in remembrance that such saints there were and that the crosses in the churches and in the highways ought to stand to put men in remembrance that Christ died upon the cross; and he desired and would be called by the name of a Papist.' All this originated from the presentment of Hinckford hundred, which not only stated that these two men 'are Papists and enemies to the Gospel' but that they are singlemen and keep a shop, working as tailors although under the age of thirty (an offence

[1] Essex Record Office, D/DP O58, f. 10v.
[2] *Acts of the Privy Council*, ix, 25, 31, 43, 50, 61, 105, 112, 117, 125; Essex Record Office, D/Y 2 (Morant MSS., *Catalogue of Essex Archaeological Society Library*, 31).
[3] D/Y 2 (*Catalogue*, 40).

against the trade laws). The Binkes brothers evidently came to blows with their neighbours, as mutual recognizances to keep the peace by and towards them were put in at the same Sessions. In 1592 George was before the Assize judges on a more serious charge of treason (p. 58) and in 1585 William was involved in a riotous assault (p. 109).

In the same year (1577) careless talk of a Suffolk man in Essex also smacked of sedition. John Howard, a petticoat-maker of Bury, was examined by Henry Capel, a Suffolk J.P. While Howard was working at Mr. Wentworth's at Bocking, so it was alleged, a sermon led his master's men to discuss it at dinner, when the defendant said, 'It was never merry in England sithence the scriptures were so commonly preached and talked upon among such persons as they were.' Four men, presumably those so addressed, not unnaturally bore witness against him. Bound to appear at the Essex Sessions next Easter, he defaulted. No more is heard of him. But it is interesting to read the retort made by one of his listeners to the effect that 'he hoped he would never live to see no other time but when the Gospel should be preached in England'. Bocking and its neighbour Braintree were soon to become Puritan strongholds. Our time-honoured 'Merry England' meant pleasant, not joyful (p. 65).

In 1578 John Williams *alias* Floud, vicar of Grays Thurrock, was alleged to have preached some very strange themes : 'Balaam being touched with covetousness said to him, "Thou shall cause all the fair damsels within thy regions to be set before the faces of all the children of Israel and they shall fall in lust with them and commit fornication with the damsels and displease their God. And then God shall cast them off, and so shall thou overcome them. And God being displeased with them called the chief rulers of the people to be called together and to be hanged up against the Son".' And, to make matters far worse, the preacher added, 'Even so, if Elizabeth with the Council and other magistrates were hanged up against the Son, there would not be such wickedness done as there was.' Williams had been charged before Edward Barrett and Edward Rich, J.P.s, with seditious speech at the instigation of Thomas Kightle (usually spelt Kighley), junior (lord of the manor of Grays Thurrock) and found not guilty ; but a John Williams was in Colchester Castle gaol a year later. He was instituted as vicar in the same month as he was charged, and held the benefice apparently only for a few months, which is hardly surprising. No more is heard about this curious case.

The Northern Earls' Revolt (1571) and the Ridolfi Plot (1572) which resulted in the executions of the Earl of Northumberland and the Duke of Norfolk were still on people's lips, Protestant and Catholic, for many years afterwards. Overheard at Dedham in March 1579 were remarks which soon reached the local justices, who committed the accused to the next Sessions. They were Gregory Clover of Colchester and Thomas Wixsted of Dedham saltpetreman. 'My Lord of Warwick and my Lord of

Leicester', Clover said, 'are traitors and come of a traitor's blood, and if they had right they had lost their heads so well as others for making away of King Edward'; spoken, so the indictment reads, to procure contention between them and the Earl of Oxford. The Dedham man, out of malice to Oxford, had retorted that he 'would go to the Lord of Oxford's town in spite of the Lord of Oxford, who was not worthy to wipe my Lord of Warwick's shoes, and the Earl of Oxford was confederate with the Duke of Norfolk and was as well worthy to lose his head as he, meaning the Duke.' The saltpetreman's taunt doubtless refers to the claim by the de Veres, Earls of Oxford, of Hedingham Castle, for exemption of their manors from searches for saltpetre, essential to the making of gunpowder. Wixsted was evidently in the service of the Earl of Warwick, Master of the Ordnance,[1] which explains the insulting comparison of the two earls. Both men were sentenced to the pillory in Colchester on market-day, each to have one of his ears nailed to the pillory.

In 1581 anti-Protestant talk was heard again in East Tilbury. David Brown husbandman made two seditious statements. Firstly, 'It was a merry world when the service was used in the Latin tongue, and now we are in an evil way and going to the devil and have all nations in our necks, for there is no Christian prince that hath such cruel laws as to burn men through their ears, which are now used in this Realm.' Secondly, 'The late Earls of Northumberland and Westmorland, who were accounted traitors, the one is dead and the other is alive and intendeth to come again into England and to possess his lands again; he is in Ireland with a great army of soldiers and the King of Spain hath given him a great dukedom for his good service, and a great part of his soldiers are such as have been burned through the ears already.' Questioned whether he would help Westmorland if he came back, Brown answered that he would do the best he could. Found guilty, he was in the list of Colchester Castle prisoners ('remanded, because it was doubtful') until 1582, after which his name does not recur. An earlier echo of the Westmorland treason had been heard in 1577. Two 'Dutchmen' of Colchester were committed to gaol for speaking 'lewd words of the Earl of Oxford which they were sorry for', alleging that they mistook him for the Earl of Westmorland. The Council advised the bailiffs of Colchester to set them at liberty.[2]

'Jesus – Jesuits'. So thought William Shepherd (rector, 1541–86), apparently forgetful for the moment of its sinister meaning in the late 1570s, while preaching in his church at Heydon on the Cambridgeshire border. He had only exhorted his hearers to be 'true Jesuits' in what appears to have been a spiritually inspired sermon on New Year's Day, 1580. During his preaching he drew a simple analogy between *Christiani*

---

[1] *Cal. State Papers Domestic, 1547–80*, 461.
[2] *Acts of the Privy Council*, ix, 292.

5 HIGH CONSTABLES' PETTY SESSIONS, FRESHWELL HUNDRED, 1573

Presentments for Hadstock, Ashdon and Radwinter.

(For full transcript, see *Guide to the Essex Record Office*, Part I (1st edition, 1946), p. 100.)

6 HIGH CONSTABLES' PETTY SESSIONS, HINCKFORD HUNDRED, 1562

Thes bethe worde[s] that John Northe of Wyckame Constabell & Thomas Edwarde[s] of the same town ded here ellesabette fettes say Commyng thether to examyne theme for ther a parell as thay whar commanded by the quennes komessionner ferst they acced hem wossarwante he wase and he sayde my lorde Roberd[es] man and they ded acce hem wotter he war of howshold or a rettayner and he sayd ofhowsholld butt he wase notte In wage[s] butt he sayed he mytte & yf he wollde then they sayd to heme you have holld owtte att the coorte well and he sayd I kame frome thence I kame yester daye & thether I well akayne bey & bey & then ded saye master fettes we ded her say here grace wase worccelle recaywed att my llord Recces and grette resorte & he sayed no nott huse the resortte thatt wase att sore Jhon Wenforde[s] for they mytte notte be sofvered & then she sayred thwse he ys a were fellen & asc Ranke a papeste as onne ys wette In the Reme of Yngellond.

Original presentment for Wickham St. Paul's (p. 33).

a Christe and *Jesuite a Jesu*, or more fully *a Christo dicimus Christiani sic in celesti gloria ab ipso Jesu dicemus Jesuite*. But the name Jesuits got the rector into 'great trouble', for he added, 'Let us study to be true Christians, true Jesuits.' Unfortunately for him, 'it fortuned my ill-willers to be present, viz. John Shr(i)ve, John Reade and William Dixon, who taking occasion to accuse me, which long before had lain in wait to take me in my words, hearing me speak of Jesuits, supposing I had met of those Jesuits that were lately entered into this land from beyond the seas, that I had commended them for the austerity and holiness of their lives, not noting well my words.'

John Sherif reported Shepherd to the Privy Council for preaching 'very corrupt and dangerous doctrine, especially tending to the commendation of the Jesuits (a very seditious sort of Popish priests)'.[1] The rector was also alleged to stand by his doctrine and to have 'procured malice towards the complainant'. So the councillors asked Lord North, Lord Lieutenant of Cambridgeshire, when next at his country home, to summon the rector and to examine him. If unsatisfactory, he was to be sent to the bishop and to be deprived of his benefice or otherwise punished. Shepherd's three adversaries testified against him, but apparently no friendly parishioners were allowed to speak. North's instructions were severe. The rector was forbidden to preach in the future, merely confining himself to reading homilies, under the penalty of forfeiting £40; and to recant his speech about the Jesuits; to pay his three accusers £3 10s. (in addition to which his own expenses had amounted to over £20); and the churchwardens were ordered to record the matter in the parish register. What the rector did, however, was to write his own version (quoted above) following the 'official' one. His register is enriched with other memoranda, including copies of his letters, 1577–8, against the abuse of holding fairs on holy days at Walden and at Foxton (Cambs.) and an 'epitome' of his 'beneficial good deeds' for the parish. The rector was undoubtedly a pious cleric, in contrast to some of the disorderly ministers. He resigned his benefice in 1586 at the age of 84.

In the same year (1580) John Pullyver of Writtle clerk (apparently not the vicar) said that 'the mass was up in Lincolnshire very brim and some did say that we had no Queen.' He also was assigned to the pillory. Another outspoken priest, John Malvill of South Benfleet clerk (not the vicar), declared in 1582 that the Book of Common Prayer was an English mass and that the surplice was a rag of Rome – an extreme puritan view which could not be tolerated by Government or Church.

Robert Colman, a bricklayer of Langham, had said in 1581 that it was lawful for a minister to pray publicly in the congregation because many of them might be outcasts, that warfare was not lawful though commanded by a prince, and that being a queen Elizabeth was therefore

[1] *Acts of the Privy Council*, xiii, 56.

E

no Christian. He also denied the Three Persons in the Godhead and asserted that baptism of infants was unlawful (he was an anabaptist).

The Assize calendar of prisoners in Colchester Castle gaol, put in at the Lent Assizes 1582, is made up of three lists, 'felons', 'witches' and 'rogues'. There are 38 felons; the eighth name, John Payne. The key words in the first of the 29 indictments on the file reads: 'John Payne of Ingatestone clerk, on 7 January 1579 at Ingatestone falsely, maliciously, wickedly and traitorously conspired to kill the Queen and traitorously incited George Elliot to assist him. Pleaded not guilty; guilty'. The general calendar, in the usual gaol delivery section, has 'Guilty, to be hanged by the neck.' Thus the Assize file laconically records the death of an undoubted Catholic martyr, executed as a result of a foul and false charge by a former member of Lady Petre's staff. (Of the others who were hanged, four were convicted as felons (two cutpurses, one horse-stealer, one burglar) and two as witches. The remaining 57 persons tried received lesser sentences.)

John Payne was born at Peterborough, entered Douai College in 1574, was ordained priest, and returned to England two years later. He lived for a while under the roof of Lady Petre, widow of Sir William, the former Secretary of State. There, at Ingatestone Hall, in February 1577 he was arrested as a Catholic priest and imprisoned, but soon released. Back again at Douai for a few months, he had returned to Ingatestone by June 1578, when he was one of the witnesses to Lady Petre's will, in which was included a legacy of £10 to her 'servant' John Payne. He was in fact her private chaplain, serving in the guise of household steward. Nothing is known of his movements during the next three years. In July 1581 he was again arrested in Warwickshire, on the information of George Elliot, for having said mass at Haddon in Oxfordshire and was sent to the Tower.

This specious scoundrel then produced a grave charge against Payne, who was to refute it at his trial as a complete fabrication by the informer. According to this, Payne had propounded to Elliot that it was no offence to God to kill the Queen and had urged him to join in an assassination plot to be put into effect during a royal progress by a party of fifty persons, to be led by the Earl of Westmorland and to include Robert Tamistie and Philip Lowes, servants of Sir John Petre and old Lady Petre. Lord Burghley endorsed a memorandum about it, 'Payne to be examined'. Sir Francis Walsingham wrote to Burghley on 14 July immediately after examining Payne, 'I think it will prove nothing.' But he was violently tortured on the rack in a vain attempt to persuade him to confess. Elliot received £100 reward for his betrayal.

At last, in March 1582, the Privy Council decided on his trial. It was to be held at the Essex Assizes. Payne and Elliot were both sent to Chelmsford. No official depositions have been preserved, but more is known about the trial than of any other in Elizabethan Essex because a full account was printed later in 1582 at Rheims.[1] This was written by a Catholic and is of course a partisan statement; but it bears the stamp of truth and throws some interesting light on the actions of the judge, sheriff, counsel and others. Payne's indictment makes no reference to any conspiracy involving many others. The printed version states that Payne's indictment gave the date of the alleged conversation as Christmas, and took place in Payne's chamber at Ingatestone Hall. ('John Payne's lodge' in the inventory of Ingatestone Hall, 1608, commemorated his room.[2]) The indictment gives 7 January: the previous day, Twelfth Day, was the end of Christmastide.

Payne denied the charges, protesting his complete loyalty to the Queen. There was some argument with 'Mr. Morrice, the Queen's Counsellor', who would seem to be James Morrice of Chipping Ongar, the well-known Essex J.P., usually described in the Assize files as 'Attorney of the Court of Wards'. Payne then not only averred that he had never had traitorous speech with Elliot but strove to show that he was a discreditable witness. 'For a rape and other manifest lewd acts with women, for breach of contract, for cozening (cheating) the Lady Petre of money, for being attached (arrested) of murder and such like acts'. These are the words in the Catholic pamphlet, but there is no confirmation from other sources of Elliot's alleged crimes. The account thus continues. 'Hereupon a jury was impanelled, who upon Friday after dinner brought evidence that he was guilty. Upon Saturday a little before dinner, coming again to the bar, Judge Gaudy asked Mr. Paine what he should say for himself. Who answered that he had said sufficiently, alleging that it was against the law of God and man that he should be condemned for *one* man's witness notoriously infamous. Then the judge said that if he were not guilty, the country (i.e. the jury) would have found it. Mr. Paine answered that those men of the jury were but poor, simple men, nothing at all understanding what treason is, and that he had demanded a definition of conspiracy before Mr. Morrice and them, which they would not give.' The judge sentenced Payne, exhorting him to repent.

He was sent back to prison (probably in the 'Crown' inn, see p. 5). The high sheriff and others visited him with the same aim. 'All Sunday till 5 of the clock one Dr. Withers and Dr. Sone were with him, persuading him very earnestly to change his religion, the which (said they), if you will alter, we doubt not to procure mercy for you. This Mr. Paine told me himself, for nobody was suffered to come unto him, saying that the

---

[1] William Allen, *A Briefe Historie of the Glorious Martyrdom of Twelve Reverend Priestes* (1582), ed. J. H. Pollen (1908). A unique copy of this book is in the British Museum. Dr. Allen had been Payne's Superior at Douai.

[2] Olwen Hall, *Inventories of Ingatestone Hall and Thorndon Hall, 1572–1613* (Friends of Historic Essex, 1968), 7.

ministers by their foolish brabbling did much vex and trouble him.' Dr. Withers was Archdeacon of Colchester and rector of Danbury, but Dr. Sone has not been identified. Next morning, 2 April, at 8 a.m. he was laid on a hurdle and brought to the place of execution, where Lord Rich bade him to confess that he died a traitor. Argument about their religious tenets ensued. Of this and the execution, details are given in the pamphlet.[1]

A slight aftermath quickly sprang up. John Gaye, a Blackmore yeoman, was examined before the end of the month by Eustace Clovile, J.P., because James Haptin, a Chelmsford tailor, had overheard him refer to Payne. Gaye deposed how he remembered that on Sunday before Easter in widow Wade's victualling house at Writtle, where Haptin was present, he had chanced to speak of 'Payne the traitor that was executed', saying he heard that Payne was once in the service of one Master Shelley. No more is heard of this, but Haptin, who seems to have been an informer, had also accused others. The Council on 2 May ordered that Edward Bell and John Chalke of Writtle yeomen should appear at the Essex Assizes, Bell to stand trial because of speech in defence of Payne. The councillors were not convinced about Bell's denial because of his violent reaction when charged by Haptin. Bell, however, had declared that their quarrel had originated 'upon some falling out at a foot ball play' at Writtle about the beginning of Lent.[2] The Assize file gives nothing. The defendant was apparently the second son of Edward Bell, Sir William Petre's house steward, whose very detailed account-books have been preserved.[3] He held a Writtle farm on lease from Petre and was coroner of Petre's Liberty of Writtle. The father and son founded a grammar school at Coleford in the Forest of Dean, Gloucestershire.[4]

Depositions taken at Chelmsford in 1582 by Thomas Gent, J.P., throw light on a dispute between a puritan preacher and a fellow incumbent. From the examination of Roger Nowell, vicar of Heybridge, it appears that George Gifford, 'preacher licensed by the Bishop of London' (who had just been instituted vicar of All Saints with St. Peter, Maldon), had warned Nowell that he was determined to preach in his church one afternoon, whereupon Nowell told one of the churchwardens that if he suffered Gifford to preach he was 'foresworn'. A parishioner then told the vicar that he thus showed himself an enemy to the preached Word. Nowell retorted, 'If I am an enemy to the Word preached, the Queen is

---

[1] An extremely full transcript of all the documents in the case, written by the Right Rev. B. C. Foley, Bishop of Lancaster, recently appeared in *Causes of the Canonization of Blessed Martyrs* [13 including Payne] . . . *1535–82* (Vatican Polyglot Press, 1968), 179–228. *See also* long accounts in *Essex Review*, xix (1910), 21–33, and *Essex Recusant*, ii (1960), 48–75.

[2] *Acts of the Privy Council*, xiii, 417–8.

[3] F. G. Emmison, *Tudor Food and Pastimes* (1964).

[4] B. S. Smith, 'Edward Bell of Newland' (*Trans. Bristol and Gloucester Archaeological Society*, 1966, 147–55).

an enemy to the Word preached.' Being reproved he repeated the seditious statement. The churchwarden, the parishioner and two others were witnesses against him. (Gifford was deposed for nonconformity in 1584, but managed to remain in the town as a lecturer. He was to become a noted author of works on religious controversies and in 1593 his *Dialogue concerning Witches and Witchcraft* was published.)

Next year (1583) a warrant was issued by Lord Rich, Sir Thomas Lucas and Sir John Petre to the constables of Heybridge to arrest Nowell and bring him before them by 6 p.m. that day or 8 a.m. next day. Nothing more can be gathered about the quarrel, but in 1588 Mark Wiersdale, then vicar of All Saints and another puritan, was in trouble for offering to lay a wager with Nowell that her Majesty had no claim to be styled Queen of France or Ireland. He was indicted at the Midsummer Assizes for this seditious statement. Depositions preserved in the State Papers yield a good deal about the case. The most damning witness was probably the first to be examined – William Lee, servant to Dr. Walker (Archdeacon of Essex). He said that he was writing a 'bill' (presentment) for the North Fambridge churchwardens 'this present day' (29 April) and in the course of his duties questioned them on (Archdeacon's) visitation articles, one of which was whether the minister prayed for her Majesty. The churchwardens replied, 'Yea', whereupon Wiersdale, who was standing by, said he thought all prayed thus. On this Nowell remarked that there were preachers in Essex who would not give the Queen her right style, refusing to call her Queen of France and Ireland. But, exclaimed Wiersdale, she was not Queen of France, at which the deponent rebuked him, saying that France and Ireland were united by marriage in Edward III's time and that his statement tended to high treason. It was at this moment that the vicar of All Saints repeated his denial and offered to lay a wager on it. A Burnham sailor and two North Fambridge husbandmen, all overhearing this in the church porch of All Saints, confirmed that the vicar offered the wager. Nowell, when examined, added a few points. Some ministers, he said to Wiersdale, prayed very coldly that God would preserve the Queen whom he had placed over them ; and on hearing Wiersdale's denial of her full title exclaimed, 'Have you not read the statute of Edward the Third?', to which the retort was, 'No, are you so good a lawyer?', and Wiersdale still insisted that she was not Queen of France. Finally, one of the borough serjeants testified to the same effect. Wiersdale, examined on the same day, stressed that when he made his first comment he added that any ministers who did not pray for the Queen were traitors, but Nowell affirmed that the best preachers in Essex were guilty of treason and had been convicted 'and twelve men had passed on them' (presumably a jury's verdict), and that Mr. Gifford was one of them. This had led the defendant to swear 'on his death' that Gifford prayed as heartily for the Queen as her truest subject, but Nowell, while admitting that he, Wiersdale, prayed for her, asserted that he did not say 'Queen of England, France and Ireland.' Wiersdale confessed with all his heart that he had spoken in ignorance and he acknowledged all her Majesty's title and authority in matters ecclesiastical and civil, desiring to be further instructed. These depositions were taken before the two borough bailiffs and Richard Pellet gentleman, a J.P. for the borough.[1]

Arthur Wright of Stebbing tailor was bound over in 1583 to give evidence about a sermon preached there by George Tuke, 'preacher of Birch', on which no indictment was apparently preferred, but may refer to seditious speech. Tuke may possibly have been rector of Little Birch ;[2] he was a member of the family owning Layer Marney Tower. The offence of John Hull, another Stebbing tailor five months later, was that he had remarked there, 'The preachers' licences are taken away, the more the pity is, and there were two hanged of late which suffered wrongfully.' He was found not guilty. It is perhaps to the credit of the judges at the same Assizes that they influenced the jurors to bring in the same verdict against John Tusser of Tolleshunt D'Arcy gentleman, who had published there in writing 'fanatical and false prophecies' which must have raised a snigger in court. 'Seek a cross of stone between Gloucester and the Forest but they shall not find it', he declared. 'Then shall they go to London and there shall the lion do great harm and destruction, and then he shall go into Norfolk and there shall be slain of an elephant. And then the poor commonalty shall take the white horse for their captain and rejoice because there shall come into England one that was dead, and with him shall come the royal E. and the dead men shall set the crowns of England upon his head. And then the laws shall turn and then the people shall rejoice the dead man's coming because sorrow and care shall be then almost past. And then shall the royal E., which is the blood in all the world, root out all heresies clean out of this realm, restoring the Church and the Catholic Faith. A lion, a horse, a leopard shall crown E. by the help of the great eagle.' Such incoherent meanderings might otherwise have been overlooked, had it not been for the one specific anti-Protestant statement. But even that was disregarded.

In yet another curious clerical utterance, in 1586, Edward Burges, 'minister of the Word of God in Wivenhoe parish church', declared, 'Let us also commend in our prayers my right reverend sister Elizabeth, by the grace of God of England, France and Ireland Queen, Defender of the Faith.' Asked what he meant, he replied that he was King Henry's son and that she was his sister both by father and mother. Burges was vicar of Fingringhoe as well as rector of Wivenhoe from 1572 to his death in 1589.

[1] Public Record Office, S.P. 12/178/27.
[2] George Tuke is in the index to Newcourt's *Repertorium*, but without page reference.

In the latter half of the 1580s there was a spate of indictments of men with grievances against the Queen and her government. Stephen Slater of Smithfield in the suburbs of London weaver said publicly at Pleshey in 1585 that 'King Philip was a father to England and did better love an Englishman than the Queen's Majesty did, for he would give them meat, drink and clothes, and he thought her Majesty was not Queen and Supreme Head of England, and would say so before the best in England, for he was pressed to serve as a soldier in Flanders by commission and had not those things which he was promised, and that if her Majesty were Queen she had villains under her.' Two years later Richard Daye of Wendon yeoman said there that 'the Queen did poll the country' (the offending verb meant to plunder, by excessive taxation). At the Easter Sessions 1587 Isaac Felsted of Laindon husbandman was charged with speaking against the Council in market-time. He was bound to good behaviour and to appear at each Sessions, but defaulted at Easter 1588, after which no more is heard of him. At the same Sessions the Court considered an indictment against Edward Tabor, innkeeper of Fryerning, for speaking very lewd and seditious words against the Queen and the Divine Service. Sir Thomas Mildmay had certified Quarter Sessions under the Act of 23 Eliz., but the Court referred the charge to the Assizes because of doubt whether it should be based on this Act or on that of 10 Eliz. In the meantime he was discharged from his office of constable. He remained in Colchester Castle until the following year, when he was released, 'because no wrong found against him.' Later in 1587 John Ashley of Goldhanger husbandman was indicted at Quarter Sessions on the evidence of two Tollesbury men for opprobrious and slanderous language there against the Queen and the Council. The case went to the next Winter Assizes, when the judges learned that what he said was, 'Those ministers are dumb ministers and dunces that would pray for the Queen's Majesty, and there are some of the Council that are traitors.'

Northumberland had been beheaded, but Westmorland on being attainted went to the Low Countries. In 1586 William Medcalfe of Coggeshall labourer was charged with strangely false but seditious words there. 'The King of Spain with the noble Earl of Westmorland with Norton and six of his sons of noble birth are come into England with others and with 15,000 or else 20,000 Englishmen, whereof a great part are bored through the ears, of which the Queen hath a letter of their several names, which the King of Spain hath sent to her, and she may look on them to her shame, and that this world will be in better case shortly. The King of Denmark hath aided the Queen with 10,000 men, which power the King of Spain hath met withal and destroyed and overthrown. The Earl of Westmorland did put his trust in God to be at the Tower of London shortly and there to apprehend all such as he thought good, to be revenged of the death and blood of the late Duke of

Norfolk.' The verdict was 'judgement according to the statute': somewhat ambiguous but apparently denoting punishment for high treason.

Scarcely an Assize passed without such political or religious malcontents appearing. What they said seems and doubtless was nonsense, but
it represents what poor people were thinking – what the speakers had
heard as they went about and what their hearers, in their turn, might
repeat. Such was the case in 1586 when Edward Lynwood, a petty
chapman of Ongar, produced this story, on being examined by Henry
Appleton. On his way to Rochford fair on Easter Monday he had met
some men who declared that Lord Hunsdon had been captured at sea
by the Flemings, when he had 'not above half a score or half a dozen
men with him, for he went very suddenly to sea and would not return
until a good ransom had been paid.' The J.P. wrote to Hunsdon, who
replied from the Court at Greenwich that the story was completely false
and probably his own invention. He also recommended the justices to
commit him to gaol and then bind him over for good behaviour, for
'such a very bad fellow is belike a common spreader of news and false
rumours'.

In the year which followed the execution of Mary Queen of Scots and
saw the defeat of the Armada, the two Assize cases were evidently treated
by the judges as little more than idle boasting. During talk at Tollesbury
early in 1588 Roger Baker of Wethersfield husbandman exclaimed that
'the Earl of Leicester was a knave and a villain and it were a good deed
he were hanged, and that unless they did rise and cut him off they should
never have other laws.' For this he was given a spell in the pillory. Two
weeks after the threat of invasion had been removed David Ramsey of
Moulsham labourer declared, 'I am a Papist and I will pray for the Pope.
The Queen loves the Pope better than any.' Although found guilty on
the testimony of three witnesses he was soon discharged.

From the earliest surviving Hertfordshire Quarter Sessions roll of 1589
it is found that yet another Essex priest was indicted for a gravely seditious
statement. A prisoner in Hertford county gaol, drinking with a Hoddesdon
man in the gaoler's house, gathered that John Hopkyns, vicar of Nazeing,
had said to Henry Taylor, who dwelt with George Duckett, keeper of
Nazeing Wood, 'There is no supreme head under God but the minister'.
The vicar's remark had been made while catechizing in church. Hopkyns
was brought by the constable of Nazeing to the Court at Hertford, where
he utterly denied the allegation; but he was deprived of his benefice a
few months afterwards.[1]

There were extraordinarily violent scenes and scurrilous words in
Stanford-le-Hope church and churchyard in 1591. The trouble arose

[1] Newcourt, *Repertorium*, 432. I have to thank Mr. P. Walne, County Archivist of
Hertfordshire, for lending me an advance copy of the unpublished calendar (Herts.
County Record Office, HAT/SR 1, no. 190).

between Martin Clipsam the rector and Tristram Blaby the preacher. In his sermon at morning service on Sunday 8 August, Blaby said that 'there was never any so high or mighty in authority that could or might rule and govern both sorts of people, both the spirituality and the temporality, for the Bishop of Rome himself, being as mighty and in as great authority as he is, could never hitherto rule and govern both, neither can or may any other potentate whatsoever they be rule and govern both in any of their own dominions and jurisdictions.' Nine parishioners signed the statement which led to his being prosecuted. It is aptly summarized in a later note: 'Tristram Blaby, a rude preacher, spoke divers seditious words in his sermon against authority and the parson there.' A much longer deposition vividly describes the whole affair, but the rest of the story will be told under Church Disturbances (p. 190).

'Let us pray for a father, for we have a mother already', exclaimed a labourer of Great Wenden in 1591. Asked why, John Feltwell *alias* Jon answered, 'Let us pray for a king.' The retort was a loyal one, 'We have a gracious queen already, wherefore would you pray for a king?' The would-be social reformer expatiated, 'The Queen is but a woman and ruled by noblemen, and the noblemen and gentlemen are all one, and the gentlemen and farmers will hold together so that the poor can get nothing.' Waxing to his theme, he added, 'Therefore we shall never have a merry world while the Queen liveth, and had we but one that would rise I would be the next, or else I would the Spaniards would come in that we may have some sport.' He was sentenced to two hours in the pillory on market-day, doubtless at Walden. This man, who was often before the justices for various assaults, was the subject of a letter sent by the Council on 30 April in the following year to the Essex Assize judges. A petition from many inhabitants of Great Wenden, it appears, had reached the Council complaining that Feltwell was 'a very troublesome and contentious person who prosecuteth divers frivolous suits against them to their great charge and vexation'. The charge had been confirmed by 'divers justices' and other local gentlemen, which had led the Council to instruct certain neighbouring justices to look into the matter, Feltwell having obstinately refused to submit or attend, to examine the parties concerned and to 'take some good order for the quiet of the inhabitants.'[1]

A small group of sailors 'who seemed to be newly come from the sea,' overtaken in December 1591 on the Great Essex Road at Springfield by three travellers, were asked if they had come over with Lord Thomas Howard (under whom they had apparently served, and if so in his attack on the Azores fleet). 'Hang him, villain, for he hath cast away a number of men better than himself' was the answer. Warned against using seditious language about a noble lord, the sailor retorted that he was a better man than Howard. But one of the witnesses said that the sailors

[1] *Acts of the Privy Council*, xxii, 413.

appeared to be drunk, for they were 'halloing, skipping and dancing.' They admitted this, having had cakes and beer at Chelmsford, but denied having spoken thus about the nobleman.

In April 1592 the Council considered a petition from Reginald Metcalfe, vicar of Elmstead, addressed to Sir Thomas Mildmay, Sir Thomas Lucas, Dr. Wythers (Archdeacon of Colchester), 'and others', complaining of 'very many injustices offered to him' by Mr. Pyrton, J.P., 'bearing him displeasure' because he with other parishioners had presented some of Pyrton's servants for certain speeches tending to sedition. 'Although we have a good opinion of the gentleman', the county justices commented, they were moved to ask the Council to examine him, 'and if just to cause Pyrton to surcease to trouble the suppliant.' No more is heard of the complaint.[1]

In the same year Randal Duckworth of Bradwell-by-the-Sea labourer, in the hearing of rector John Debanck and others, said there, 'The Earl of Derby keepeth the crown of England and the Earl of Shrewsbury hath had three children by the Queen of Scots in Stafford Castle, and this is no good government which we now live under, and it was merry England when there was better government, and if the Queen die there will be a change and all those that be of this religion now used will be pulled out.' His punishment was to stand in the pillory, labelled like other seditious offenders with a copy of his statement.

One of the Finchingfield papists who had been haled before the justices in 1577 was also brought before the Assize judges in 1592. George Bynckes, still described as a tailor of Finchingfield, had asserted that 'the Pope is Supreme Head over all Christendom and that King Philip is the right King of England, and that if he should be commanded to do any service in the Queen's behalf, the same would be against his conscience; and that Captain Drake and his soldiers when they have gone forth in the prince's service do rob and spoil the King of Spain of his goods.' He was acquitted of treason and remanded in prison until he found security for his good behaviour.

In the early 1590s Aveley must have been a hotbed of religious strife. In September 1592 Wilfred Lutie was accused by William Danvers clerk (not the vicar) and three parishioners of 'traitorous speeches and intended practices', but no details are given. Next year, then described as Wilfred Lutey of Aveley gentleman, he was charged with enticing Danvers to adhere to the Bishop of Rome, but was found not guilty. In 1594, now termed a scrivener, he was charged at the Assizes with publicly saying there in October 1591, 'All those that her Majesty sent over into the Low Countries were damned because the King of Spain is our anointed king and that Skynke and all the states of the Low Countries were drunkards and cobblers, and that all those that she sent over were rebels because

[1] *Acts of the Privy Council*, xxii, 399.

they fought against their anointed king.' From the fact that he was again acquitted one would have suspected that the charges were unfounded, and this apparently is proved by a letter which the Council had resolved to send to the Bishop of London before Lutey had been prosecuted. It was in August 1591 that they had received 'a grievous complaint' from Margaret Lewty on her husband's behalf against John Spencer, vicar of Aveley. The vicar, according to Margaret, was 'of a very corrupt disposition', and in revenge for an old grudge had recently procured Danvers, 'a man detected (presented) of bad behaviour', to accuse Lewty of papistical speeches to the prejudice of the State. He had been examined by Dr. Swale and Mr. Topclif, to whom it appeared that Spencer, for his own defence, had been moved by malice. But Lewty had been committed to Newgate gaol. The Council, however, had received credible reports of his good behaviour and conformity as well as a certificate of forty parishioners about the long-standing contention between them, and they therefore asked the bishop to bail Lewty for further examination by 'indifferent gentlemen' of the neighbourhood. That Lewty was the victim of persecution seems to be borne out by two charges against Spencer. The first was for seditious speech, which suggests that he was of unsound mind or in his dotage. In March 1592, scheming to disturb the rule of the Queen and to excite sedition, he announced, 'I will be lord and king of Aveley and I will make the best of you in the parish to stoop, and first I will begin with the little ones and then afterwards with the great men', in great derogation of the royal authority. At the following Sessions he was indicted as a common barrator (quarreller). He had held the living since 1589, and his resignation took place in September 1592.

A few pieces of vernacular verse have recently come to light in the Essex Assize files. Of these, one is wholly religious in tone, and it led to a charge of sedition; another, grossly scandalous, to one of libel (p. 71). In 1594 Thomas Hale of Walthamstow gentleman was indicted for writing a 'ballad or rhyme', alleged to have been devised in the presence and hearing of many. He pleaded not guilty. The verdict – unusually long and unorthodox – ran thus: 'We find that he did eight years past copy a slanderous and seditious libel but did neither devise or publish it maliciously, and that it was found by Edward Godfre in the house that was sometime the father's of the said Thomas Hale on the 9th day of February last.' The jury added that the defendant had been examined by Robert Wroth, J.P. (of Loughton Hall), and they concluded, 'If this be felony, then we find him guilty, if it be not felony, then not guilty.' A literal transcript follows.

Weepe, weepe, and still I weepe,
For who can chuse but weepe,
To thyncke how England styll
In synne and heresey doth sleepe.

The Christian faythe and Catholick
Is everyewhere detested,
The holy servyce, and such like
Of all degrees neglected.

The Sacramentes are taken awaye
The holy order all,
Religious men do begg astraye,
To ground their howses fall.

The Byshoppes and our pastors gone,
our Abbottes all be deade,
Deade (alas), alyve not one,
Nor other in their steede.

The Churches gaye defaced be,
Our alters are thrown downe,
The walles lefte bare, a greefe to see,
That once coste maney a Crowne.

The monementes and lefe of Sayntes
Are brent and torne by vyolence,
Some shedd the holye Sacramentes,
O Christe thy wondrous pacyence.

The memory of Christe his death ;
Is rootinge owte a pace,
The Joyes above the paynes beneathe,
In few mens hartes have place.

In steed of theis comethe tumblinge in,
A gosppell full of heresies,
Wyved goates their lyfe of synne,
Their mowth of blasphemies.

Nexte farewell virgynytie,
Let Venus have a place,
Come Bacchus banyshe modestie,
Say Epicurus grace.

For Sacramentes a loaf of bread,
Good baker make yt fyne,
And tapster with the drunken heade,
Take heede we want no wyne.

Nowe favour hyndreth equytie,
And ryches rule the roste,
In vayne the poore crye Cherytie,
God healpe you saye the moste.

Now pryde doth sytt the fasshion,
And flatterye can thryve,
Now truth dothe mysse the cusshion,
One foxe can cosen fyve.

O tyme of tymes that ever have bene,
The wickeddest I feare,
For lesse good frutes no age hathe seene,
Nor more synnes I dare sware.

O England once that wert alofte,
In favour highe with God,
Nowe hast thou neede a Jonas
Oft, to warne the of his rodd.

Thy victoryes, thy force in feilde,
Thy tryumphes in araye,
When crosse was badge, when vertue sheild,
When godlye men did praye.

Nowe poore and naked scant thy selfe
Defendest from thy foes,
For all thy truste in worldly pelfe,
Awaye thy glorye goes.

But troest thou still to scape thus cleer,
And daunce within a nett,
Naye God will make the buy this deer,
Thy synnes and heaven have mett.

God of his mercye graunt the grace,
Thy synnes for to deplore,
That none hereafter have my place,
In waylinge the so sore.

Weepe weepe and let us weepe,
And nothing elses but weepe,
To washe awaye thy synnes so deepe,
For ever thou must weepe.

The vergins chaste are shutt in Jayles,
To seas go modest dames,
And some are hoysed with the sayles
Of Venus fylthie games.

The plaint was probably written much more than 'eight years past' when it was discovered. The emphasis on the iconoclastic activities could have suggested an Edwardian date but for the second line of the last verse, which probably refers to the founding of schools for daughters of upper-class English Catholics during 1570–78 in Western Europe, especially Belgium.[1] In other verses the writer reveals humour even when bewailing

[1] I owe this comment to Professor J. Murphy (p. 77n.).

the loss of the mass as well as loyalty to his country for past martial victories.

As Hale was a convicted Catholic recusant, the jury had given a very fair, if cautious, verdict. His father (also Thomas) and mother had been frequently presented for recusancy since 1576, and their children, including the defendant, since 1589 (sometimes in company with Thomas More of Leyton, grandson of Sir Thomas More the martyr).[1] The family, old-established in Walthamstow, owned the mansion of Moons, which they had acquired from the well-known Monoux family. His mother's brass in the church (she had died in 1588) bears an openly Catholic inscription. In the year she died Thomas had been in trouble with the Council, to whom he made his humble submission and declaration of loyal allegiance, and he sought his freedom because of long illness while in the custody of William Rowe esquire (of Leyton), his guardian on their behalf. The Council granted him bail provided that he was 'forthcoming at all times within ten days' warning.[2] His name occurs among those in Bridewell prison in 1594, listed as 'dangerous recusants.' The general calendar, annotated immediately after the Assize, gives, 'Guilty – delivered to bail upon a special verdict and to be of good behaviour.' The Essex justices exercised good sense.[3]

Despite the general economic distress, the Essex courts were not disturbed by any more seditious acts in the last seven years of the reign, except for one case in 1595 which they probably dismissed with a light sentence, if any. The affair lay on the narrow borderline between seditious speech and drunken debate. It was indeed with reluctance that the examining magistrate, Arthur Herrys, reported the matter to the Bench, because the accused was retained in his own service as a farrier. He told the plaintiff to prefer the charge before another J.P., as he 'might haply be thought to favour' the farrier, but he was driven to act. The informer was far from consistent during his examination, so the justice enjoined him to set down the offending words in writing, which he did unwillingly. Then Herrys wrote his letter to the Court from his home at Woodham Mortimer, having bound two witnesses to appear with the plaintiff and the defendant, who were William Thrustell of Purleigh yeoman and Thomas Bynder of Danbury smith. The scene was Widow Glascock's alehouse at Runsell (in Danbury); the time, September 1595. The smith (Herrys's farrier) was alleged to have 'put forth speeches tending to sedition'. According to the alewife's customers, Richard Rolfe of Danbury, Thrustell's father-in-law, and John Sayer of Runsell, both tanners, the

---

[1] D. Shanahan, 'The Family of St. Thomas More in Essex, 1581–1640' (*Essex Recusant*, vols. i–iv).
[2] *Acts of the Privy Council*, xviii, 30.
[3] For a much fuller account of this recusant family, the Hales, see B. Foley (*Essex Recusant*, i, 17–24), who also published the verses, unfortunately with some copyist's slips.

company included two others, all drinking together, when Thrustell asked the smith if he had any horsenails. The price was too dear, to Thrustell's mind. Bynder pointed out that everything was dear, and if high prices continued and victuals did not 'grow better cheap' some who had 'made shift so long would be plucked out of their houses.' Thrustell demanded, 'Who should remedy it?' Bynder replied, 'Thou and such as thou art.' Quoth the other, 'Why, what am I?' Bynder said, 'I know well enough. Thou wast cock pudding Thrustell's son'. Angry words multiplied. Turning to the account written by Thrustell and borne out by Rolfe, Bynder was alleged at this stage to have declared that the poor, failing redress, would make 'such a stir before Christmas Day as they that had most corn, cheese and suchlike should have the least, and he would go with them.' He added that as he had neither wife nor children he did not care, and 'twenty of them, meaning the sellers of victuals, would be hanged at their gates before Christmas.' But according to the other witnesses Rolfe said that he perceived Bynder to be overcome with drink, and pulling his son-in-law by the sleeve he had departed. Sayer declared that the threat of revolt was not heard by him and thought that Thrustell had enlarged the words through choler and anger', and he gave his opinion that Bynder had always been an honest fellow without a seditious mind. The tailpiece is convincing enough. Thrustell had added to his deposition (and it is clearly in a different ink), 'But I think he were drunk when he spake these words.' And as the Court's verdict is not recorded, it is left to the reader's own judgement. But, even if the sinister part of the drunkard's curse was a figment of the informant's malice, he doubtless expressed vicariously the poorer folk's mutterings, echoes of the oft-repeated egalitarian views of John Ball, the Colchester priest, who had fomented Wat Tyler's rebellion more than two centuries earlier.

The Queen was now old by contemporary standards, and wishful thinking by some of her subjects gave birth to other rumours. William Stevens of Fyfield labourer was indicted in 1597 for a dangerous remark, that 'there was a change and he had heard that our Queen's Majesty is made away with and dead, and that the noblemen which were lately gone on this voyage were gone to fetch another prince.' But by the time the case reached Quarter Sessions it was he, not Elizabeth, who was dead.

Indictments for seditious talk of a more serious nature were brought before the courts on three occasions, one group in the first decade of the Queen's reign, the others in her last decade. All sowed seeds of insurrection against the government. That charges were laid against four men, all apparently of Colchester (three of them weavers), for public utterances there on separate days between 9 May and 16 June 1566 indicates discontent in the woollen industry. All were accused of endangering the public peace, and all were found guilty. The affair had

first reached the Privy Council on 17 February 1567, when it was referred
to the judges at the next Essex Assizes. The defendants at this date
numbered six: John Broke and Thomas Hunwicke were in the Tower,
Edward White and Nicholas Saye in the Marshalsea prison, and John
Lingwood and Roger Morrell in the Queen's Bench prison.[1] Against
their names in the calendar of prisoners in Colchester Castle at Midsummer 1566 is written, 'Taken for rebellion'. It gives the places where
they were arrested. This is of some importance as revealing that five of
them fled after their presumed attempts to raise revolt: Morrell taken at
Heybridge, White at Sible Hedingham, Hunwicke at Feering, Lingwood
at Kelvedon, and Broke at Colchester. But Hunwicke was evidently a
Feering man, as his name is among those who had not done their work in
repairing the parish roads in that year. In the same list of prisoners
Katherine Harryson is named as having been arrested at Southwark 'for
words against the Queen.'

Four of the six were independently charged at the Lent Assizes 1567.
Their alleged words are given as in the indictments. Thus, Saye of St.
Peter's parish, yeoman: 'Wool goeth over as fast as it did, it will cause the
people to go together by the ears. God help us, for we are beset both
within the realm and without, and if there come business it will come
about harvest and that will make as hot a harvest as ever it was.' Morrell
of Colchester, weaver: 'We be at a hard stay, Bocking and Braintree for
they are minded there to rise and to get a mad knave and set him on
horseback and to begin at Bocking town's end and so to Braintree and
Coggeshall and through this town, and to cry, "They are up! they are up!"
Then the people to get to the churches and to ring "Awake". If they do
rise, it will be a hard and a hot time.' Broke of Holy Trinity, woollenweaver: 'Weavers' occupation is a dead science nowadays, and it will
never be better before we make a rising. I will get a horse and ride into a
town in Suffolk and so come from thence to Bocking and Braintree and
Coggeshall, and so straight through Colchester, and cry cry "They are up,
they are up!" And Broke 'willed one Roger Morrell that he would give
knowledge of his coming thither to the end they may then be ready to
rise and to go to the church and ring the bells "Awake".' Broke further
said: 'When I have so done, I will slip off my horseback into a by lane
and so come among them and thus will I do at Midsummer next, for that
will be the best time, for at that time began the last commotion.' Finally,
White of Holy Trinity, woollenweaver: 'We can get no work nor we have
no money, and if we should steal we should be hanged, and if we should
ask, no man would give us, but we will have a remedy one of these days,
or else we will lose all, for the commons will rise, we know not how soon,
for we look for it every hour. Then will up two or three thousand in
Colchester and about Colchester, and we look for it every day, for there

[1] *Acts of the Privy Council*, vi, 330.

is no more to do but one to ride on a horse with a clap and cry, "They are up, they are up!", and another to ring "Awake", for ye shall see the hottest harvest that ever was in England.' All four were hanged.

The attitude of the poor, short of food through disastrous harvests and high prices in the 1590s, is illustrated by a case brought in 1594 against two Hatfield Peverel labourers for seditious speech at Ulting. Committed by Sir Thomas Mildmay, both confessed and were found guilty at the Summer Assizes three weeks afterwards. On 17 July William Barbor had said, 'Corn will be dear and there is one in the Tower that doth prophesy that wheat will be at 16s. a bushel shortly, and I know where there are four ships in the water laden with corn to carry it to the enemy, and I will be one of them that shall rise and gather a company of 8 or 9 score together and will go to fetch it out where it is to be had. I can bring them where corn enough is to be had. And if we were such a company gathered together, who can withstand us?' On the following day, similar speech by Peter Francis : 'Corn will be dear and rather than I will starve I will be one of them that shall rise and gather a company of 8 score or 9 score together and will go and fetch it out where it is to be had' ; finishing, so it was alleged, with words identical with Barbor's. Someone said, 'What can poor men do against rich men?', to which Francis answered, 'What can rich men do against poor men if poor men rise and hold together?'

The famine conditions continued and gave rise to another indictment at Quarter Sessions two years later. Henry Went, a weaver of Ardleigh near Colchester, was charged with these seditious words : 'It would never be better until men did rise and seek thereby an amendment, and he wished in his heart a hundred men would rise, and he would be their captain to cut the throats of the rich churls and the rich cornmongers, for he had served as a soldier divers times beyond the seas and could lead men.' The case went to the Assizes. He was found guilty, survived the terrible gaol fever which killed thirty-one prisoners in the following year, and escaped from prison in 1600.

The scarcity of corn and the excessive prices of food had led the Council after the bad harvest of 1595 to address a letter to the county justices referring to the poulterers and 'buttermen' who 'swarm in every market', forestalling the produce which ought to be freely bought, as a result of which Quarter Sessions issued a proclamation ordering them to be 'newly licensed.' This aspect, however, must await a later volume dealing with Work and Trade. The distress at Colchester and in several other counties troubled the Council again in the winter of 1597–8.

The rebellious speeches of 1566 and 1594–6 are of profound interest as indicative probably of smouldering discontent. Authority took on the whole, however, a lenient view of the scores of other utterances. Incautious men and women purged their fault in the pillory, or, at worst, lost their ears. The graver seditions went before the Privy Council. But

7   ELIZABETH HALF SOVEREIGN, *circa* 1560

A fine example of a rare piece, the first produced by milling instead of stamping (p. 81).

8   MANOR OF GYNG JOYBERD LAUNDRY HERTFORD STOCK, 1594

Heading of court roll of one of Sir John Petre's manors (p. 70).

9 (*above*)

Spains Hall, Finchingfield. Medieval-style plan, with central hall and cross-wings

10 (*left*)

Moyns Park, Steeple Bumpstead.   Elizabethan - style plan, nearly symmetrical façade

(For the dispute between the owners, see pp. 109–11.)

TWO NEWLY-BUILT MANSIONS, *circa* 1575

the mild ebullitions of popular fooling and fancy, if it were not for the
Assize files, would have perished without trace, like the folk who gave
voice to them.

When people mention 'Merrie England' Elizabeth's time is often in the
mind, which conjures up an actively joyful scene. The term, it will have
been noticed, occurs no less than four times in our records. But the
contemporary meaning was pleasant, or agreeable, and applied to the
country, not the people. Those convicted of sedition wanted to turn the
clock back. Elizabeth stood firmly against all forms of attack. The
outburst of treasonable sayings by Essex folk after the accession of James I
is a remarkable posthumous tribute. The Essex court records certainly
provide a mass of evidence of a kind that shows what some of the ordinary
people – both laity and clergy – were thinking and saying about the
Crown, the State and the Church. But we can never hope to assess with
any degree of accuracy what proportion of the people were disgruntled,
and these cases must not be allowed to create an exaggerated impression
of discontent or disorder. Disorder there certainly was in the eyes of the
Church, as will be seen when the thousands of cases brought before the
Archdeacons' courts are considered in the next volume. But, apart from
religious offences involving quasi-seditious elements, disturbances in
churches and assaults in churchyards, and witchcraft, all crimes and
offences dealt with at the Assizes and Quarter Sessions were essentially
secular in nature.

The sudden sprouting of seditious statements after Elizabeth's death
was much thicker than at any time during her life. Nevertheless, taking
her reign as a whole, the large number of indictments for sedition in Essex
has no parallel in the surviving records of any other county. Even the
big series for Middlesex discloses a mere half-dozen charges; and sedition
cases are rarely found elsewhere, whether political or religious utterings.
The frequency of the latter in the Essex records of course conforms with
what is well known about dissent in the county, though less established
perhaps for the sixteenth than the next century. The former confirm that
the medieval stirrings of radicalism in Essex were becoming rampant.
It was this sturdy, independent spirit that was to plant so many Essex
names on the early maps of New England – names taken from the towns
and villages which they had left behind.

F

4
Libel and Slander

While seditious or scandalous speech against the Queen or her councillors led to so many Essex people being prosecuted, scurrilous accusations against neighbours, a ubiquitous and everyday feature of Elizabethan life, resulted in relatively few indictments at Quarter Sessions and Assizes. Such non-traitorous denunciations were made orally (slander) or in writing (libel). In contrast, the act books of the Essex Archdeacons' courts, as elsewhere, abound in cases of slander against ministers or churchwardens, in churches or churchyards, or against parishioners alleged to have committed sexual offences, as will be seen probably in the next volume of this series. Libel and slander, for our purposes, scarcely need to be distinguished, for the scandalous writing, if in ballad form, was also meant to be sung. Dalton reminds us that libel might be committed not only in writing, in 'book, ballad, epigram or rhyme, either in metre or prose', or in 'words, scoffs, jests, taunts or songs, maliciously repeated or sung in the presence of others', but also by 'pictures or signs of shame, as pictures of the gallows, pillory, cucking-stool, horns or such like'.[1] The horns were the mark of the cuckolded husband, and the rowdy incident in which such 'ensigns' were put up to adorn a Burnham house is described under Riot (p. 108). Slanderous speech also occurs incidentally in other cases, particularly those related under Church Disturbances, Assaults on Officers, and Barratry. The presentment of a Wivenhoe man in 1576 that he 'is a common slanderer of his neighbours and bears himself evilly towards the constable', for which he was fined 3s. 4d., is a typical though not frequent dual charge.

The violent quarrels and assaults with dagger-thrusting and beard-pulling which broke out in Willingale churchyard in 1565 (p. 187) were evidently further incidents in an old family feud, for six months earlier the same Ellen Sampford and Thomas Cowlande, with Andrew Cowlande of Willingale Doe husbandman and Thomas Salinge of Chipping Ongar butcher, were indicted for conspiring to defame Thomas Sampford by a false slander : 'Thou art a thief and a common stealer of sheep, for thou hast stolen other men's sheep and some of them thou hast killed in the house and other some of them thou hast sold to butchers, and thou also

---

[1] A later ballad, with a sketch of the victim sentenced to both pillory and gallows, is illustrated in F. G. Emmison, *Archives and Local History* (1965), 83.

diddest give counsel to Richard Sampford to cut his wife's throat, and thou art also a perjured and a false crafty man.' In consequence of which Thomas Sampford was arrested, but the charge was found 'void'.

Abbess Roothing churchyard, a few miles away, was the scene of a similar slander in 1595. During an altercation about an alleged theft of wheat, Gilbert Aylett called goodman Poole 'lying churl and lying knave', which was varied somewhat by Henry Aylett denouncing him as 'old lying, peasantly knave'.

Calumny of a sharply-barbed but more refined kind was directed against an Essex magnate. William Rust, vicar of Felsted, 'moved by malice' towards Robert Lord Rich, was charged in 1582 with slanderous words : 'If Lord Rich might have his will to put men out of their bene-fices he would keep their livings and have some serve the cure for little or nothing.' Rust then went on to include the headmaster of Felsted School, founded by the first Baron, and the first Puritan lecturer at Wethersfield (p. 141). 'Greenwood being a schoolmaster and Rogers being a preacher', he declared, 'did mislike of the book of common prayer and therefore Greenwood refused to be a minister ; the book was not fine enough for them ; and there were none of Lord Rich's neighbours but would be glad if he were further from them' ; finishing with the insulting remark, 'Lord Rich was in the commission of the peace, but as a cipher in agree-ment, for he could do nothing.' Rust had been given the benefices of both Felsted and Rayleigh by the first Lord Rich in 1558–59, but had just been deprived of the latter by the young grandson.[1]

Ten years later Lord Rich was insulted in a different way. George and John, sons of Nicholas Raye of Stansted Mountfitchet, had been bound over to the Sessions but had produced in Court a Chancery writ of *supersedeas* discharging them from their bonds. The writ 'was accepted and reverently allowed by the Court'. The men then not only exhibited 'a very arrogant, inconsiderate and slanderous bill of complaint' to Lord Rich and the other justices present but also 'very unreverently demeaned themselves (especially the said George) in the face of the whole Court,' which accordingly fined George £10 with a month's imprisonment and John £5 with a week. Their father, too, was in trouble at the same Sessions. Nicholas Raynebeard, also of Stansted, had contemptuously torn up a warrant from Rich and other J.P.s for the arrest of one Barnard, and Nicholas Raye had abetted him. Both had been sent to gaol, but made their humble submission before the Bench. Because of his poverty, Raynebeard was discharged without fine, and Raye was fined only 20s. on account of his age. A cryptic note, 'About Thremnall Fair', suggests that the case is linked with a case before the Council in 1593 about the suppression of this fair at Thremhall Green on the boundary of Stansted and Hatfield Broad Oak.[2] In 1583 Nicholas Raye had purchased the

[1] M. Craze, *History of Felsted School* (1955), 39. [2] *Acts of the Privy Council*, xxiv, 394.

manor of Thremhall Priory, and in 1590 his two sons had acquired the rectory of Thremhall with Stansted.[1]

The records of any Elizabethan Archdeacon's court, popularly known as the 'Bawdy Court', show, as Shakespeare was to do a little later, that Englishmen were not prudish in expressing their views on sexual misbehaviour. What follows is a paper, without date or note, found in the Michaelmas Sessions roll, 1583.

> Here dwelleth an arrant bichant whore,
> Such one as deserves the cart.
> Her name is Margaret Townsend now.
> The horn shows her desert.
> Fie, of honesty, fie, fie,
> Your whore's head is full of jealousy.
> Therefore I pray your whore's tricks fly,
> And learn to live more honestly.
> Alack for woe. Why should I do so?
> It will cause a sorrowful hey-ho.
> Thus do I end my simple verse,
> He that meeteth her husband, a horned beast.

Its author is probably revealed in the roll for the following Sessions, when Stephen Bull of West Ham was bailed by two fellow parishioners and a Writtle man at the suit of Nicholas Townsend's wife. Adulterous folk were sometimes punished by being carted publicly (p. 178). The obscene libel may have been fastened by the accused (perhaps a rejected lover) outside her house, from which the enraged husband plucked it and thrust it into the hands of the constable who took it to the Sessions. An indictment against John Sewell the younger of Great Dunmow in 1585 lays only a general charge against him for being a barrator and a composer of scandalous libels and a public singer of the same libels. His defence was that the indictment was insufficient in law. A single but pithy obscene verse, written and recited at Earls Colne, came before the County Bench in 1588.

> Woe be unto Kendall that ever he was born.
> He keep his wife so lustily she makes him wear the horn.
> But what is he the better or what is he the worse?
> She keeps him like a cuckold with money in his purse.

Thomas Kendall lived at Earls Colne, and John Brande, a tailor of the same town, wrote the 'slanderous rhyme against Kendall and his wife'. Four men testified to having heard the words, and a fifth 'rebuked him (Brande) for them', adding that Kendall had beaten his wife on hearing the rhyme.

At the Epiphany Sessions 1585 some of the less puritan-minded justices must again have chuckled softly at a licentious libel. Obviously written to demonstrate that Lewis Madocke, rector of Fryerning (1550–87), who also had the living of Buttsbury, was a papist, it breaks into a multiple accusation.

[1] Morant, *History of Essex*, ii, 580.

Sir John Clarke of Ingatestone that serveth at Fryerning under Sir Lewis Madocke parson of Buttsbury hath hearty commendations unto you, Charles Whiskarde of Stock, trusting in God that you are of the same religion that he is, of a right papist, to love a whore with all your heart as well as he. Moreover he doth desire you to send an answer to this letter with all speed to his loving priest and friend Master Pinder cuckold, Master Garret cuckold, Nicholas Bush cuckold, Christopher Driver cuckold, John Tansye cuckold, Richard Hoper cuckold, Robert Newman of the Cock cuckold and cuckoldmaker, Master Braye cuckold, William Lynes the crocklegged smith cuckold, William Stonard cuckold, John James cuckold, Jeffrey Petecrue cuckold. This be delivered with speed. This is true, *per obictum est.*

'Cuckolds' Haven', the contemporary name of a spot on Thamesside below Greenwich, was outrivalled by Stock! Clarke was curate of Fryerning[1] ('Sir' was commonly used for any non-graduate priest) and Whiskarde was one of Stock's millers. But the letter first got into other hands, as is learned from the depositions of four uncuckolded villagers taken before Sir John Petre, Eustace Clovile and John Butler. Thomas Petchey, apparently an innkeeper,[2] said that 'on Friday was a fortnight he found in the porch of his house a writing which he read somewhat of it and laid it up, and upon Friday following he showed it to one Gillam, a stranger coming to his house with one Miller of the same town.' The constables came along, having heard about it. He first claimed ignorance, but afterwards admitted he had it. John Lynsell confessed that 'on Friday was sevennight' he received of his brother-in-law Petchey a slanderous libel against many of the inhabitants, and the same night a little before 8 o'clock he, with five other men, went to the 'Swan' door singing this song by the way:

> As I me-walked in a May morning
> I heard a bird sing, one, two, three, cuckoo.

They had come from Petchey's house, where there was another song but he did not remember it. Thomas Moncke's confession adds that Robert Tabor was among the singers, and that one song was sung at his father's door and another when passing from Petchey's house by Bush's house. Both 'were full of ribaldry and filthiness'. John son of Nicholas Bush of Stock said that 'on Tuesday was sevennight', going by Charles Whiskarde's door, he saw Thomas Ammott standing at his pale before the door. When he came near, Ammott went away 'into the common wards' (towards the common), all which Ammott 'utterly denieth.'

Nearly all the company of cuckolds appear in the Stock parish register and manor court rolls, and Newman is in the case against Agnes Sawen, the Stock witch, in 1576 (see next volume). Margery wife of John James had been presented at the manor court in 1574 for scolding the bailiff and assaulting him with firebrands, and on the same day John and she were ordered to clear out of Stock under threat of whipping; but perhaps they sneaked back, for Jeffrey Petycrewe in 1579 was to be put in the stocks if he allowed James to remain in his house.

[1] E. E. Wilde, *Ingatestone*, (1913), 111.
[2] F. W. Austen, *Rectors of Two Essex Parishes* (1943), 82.

The first derided husband, William Pinder, was the rector of Stock from 1580 to 1626. He was also rector of Mottisfont (Hants.) and on that account non-resident at Stock for the greater part of his long incumbency (not to be confused with that of his later namesake and successor, 1626–43). Pinder was far from being a gentle man, having been once found fighting in a Chelmsford inn with the rector of Leaden Roothing and on another occasion with a local man, and Charles Whiskarde and William Newman because of 'disagreements' between them and the rector were to be allowed in 1586 by the Archdeacon's court to attend a neighbouring church. Whiskarde was a man of some substance, having paid £180 for his windmill in 1581 ; he died in 1587. Perhaps Mistress Pinder had sought solace in another's arms. Except possibly for her the allegedly unfaithful wives were hardly in the bloom of their youth, for most of them were to die (according to the parish register) between 1588 and 1592.

And the choristers who sang about the cuckoo down the village street? Their names : William Heywood, Thomas Moncke, William Dyson, Thomas Stafforde, James Castle. The last had a tile kiln, and Moncke was again before Justice Clovile in 1588 for stealing rabbits in Sir John Petre's warren (p. 244). William Heywood was a nephew of John Heywood, singer and virginal-player in Henry VIII's time and favourite jester in Mary's court. In his *Play of the Weather* (1533), Merry Report claims to have been at many places :

> At Gravelyn, at Gravesend, and at Glastonbury,
> Ynge Gyngiang Jayberd the parish of Butsbury.
> The devil himself, without more leisure,
> Could not have gone half this much, I am sure.

The dramatist had evidently visited his brother William, and learned from him the curious contemporary name.[1] It is seen at the heading of the manor court roll of 1539, 'Ginge Joyberde Laundry Herford Stok in the parish of Buttysbury' (also plate 8). Our bawdy singer therefore had a strain of buffoonish blood in him, but as owner of the 'Swan', which he had bought in 1551 (it no longer exists), and as a member of the 'homage' or chief manorial tenants, he ought not to have joined the village rowdies. The old English buffoonery was deep-rooted.

Between 1588 and 1592 three further indictments for using 'scandalous' or 'pernicious' (but unrecorded) words earned two of the speakers an hour or more in the pillory. In 1602 a Halstead husbandman was presented by the jury of the hundred for reviling a fellow townsman with 'rascal, whoremaster and other words not fit to be used' : evidently a case of malicious slander. The same man had been charged at the previous Sessions with assaulting one of the constables. As William Harrison had remarked, the talk 'of the inferior sort is now and then such as savoureth of scurrility and drunkenness'.[2]

[1] F. W. Austen, *Rectors of Two Essex Parishes* (1943), 34, 41.
[2] Harrison, *Description of England*, 131.

The Chelmsford Ballads

At the turn of the century one of the chief subjects of conversation among Chelmsfordians must have been the slanderous tales about the morals (or lack of morals) of some of their number – tales which resulted in an extraordinary case of libel arising from a long stretch of highly scurrilous doggerel.

The affair first appears on record in the report of the Chelmsford hundred jury to the Epiphany Sessions 1602, which presented Hugh Barker of Chelmsford for being 'a very troublesome and dangerous fellow and a raiser of great seditions among his neighbours.' The juries of the hundreds rarely troubled to present such offenders; the fact that they did so on this occasion is evidence of the feelings aroused in the town. Recognizances for Barker's appearance at the Sessions had been taken in the previous October. Richard Tye blacksmith and George Knightbridge tailor, both of Chelmsford, had stood bail for Barker by one recognizance, and John Goose of Chelmsford saddler and Valentine Turner of Writtle yeoman by a separate bond had been additional sureties; very rarely was attendance thus doubly ensured. The appearance of Thomas Chitham of Boreham schoolmaster was secured by John Whale of Chelmsford tailor. Another unusual feature is that Chitham's recognizance refers to his having confessed to 'making the libel, but that Barker procured him thereunto and gave him the theme'.

The matter was adjourned to the next Sessions, from which the charges against Barker and Chitham were sent to the Assizes, and Barker's good behaviour in the meantime was secured by the bonds of two more Chelmsfordians, John Blanck grocer and Jonas Charney glover. The Court also received the recognizance, taken before Sir Thomas Mildmay, of John Whale and his wife Mary for keeping the peace towards Barker.

The case duly came up at the Midsummer Assizes in July 1602. Chitham admitted that he had made the libel in verse for Barker, who had 'given him the substance thereof in prose'.

On the file is a big sheet of parchment, very much larger than any other indictment in the whole reign. After the formal usual beginning – Hugh Barker of Chelmsford barber, on 10 December 1600, publicly 'said', showing that the Court had a charge of both slander and libel – comes the scandalous verse. Lawyers eschewed blank spaces, so the indictment is not written out in verse, but is now set out as the original must have been. By good fortune the indictment is preserved in duplicate, and the Queen's Bench copy, which differs from the Sessions original only in a few letters, is perfect, whereas the Sessions parchment has several holes: evidently a rat enjoyed bits of it as much as the reader may do. The significance of the two ballads (Barker's and Chitham's) is tentatively discussed at the end, together with a few notes about the libelled parties. Several points, however, remain obscure, such as 'W.P.', perhaps fictitious initials to conceal the libeller's identity.

You that be wise listen a while
And mark the tenor of my style,
And weigh the cause in each degree,
The matter is manifest to be.

As for all fools, let them be still,
For wedded they are unto a will
To slander eke both foe and friend,
But gallows tall will be their end.

Some say a battle late there was
Between a lad and a bonny lass,
John Whale's wife that lofty lad,
Old William Shether was her dad.

The other was a Barber born,
Which Edwick's minikin held in scorn,
Called Mary Whale that bonny lass,
But her husband is a very ass.

For if that he were very wise,
He would shore open both his eyes
And see the doings of his wife
And learn her to amend her life.

For if she do not tell him true,
Both head and horns shall be his due.
The barber as I understand
Did take her co in his hand.

But if Clim Poope were now alive
He would not wish himself to thrive
Till he had cuckold his brother Whale,
But tut, this news is very stale.

For Thomas Phillipps swears the same,
The same that he did occupy his dame,
And got of her a goodly boy
Called Robyn, all her only joy.

Some secret thing was in the wind,
I am persuaded in my mind.
Which made the battle to begin,
John Whale by this did six pence win.

Money enough considering all
The barber's beating and his great fall
Among the nettles which did him sting
Because a token he did bring.

Which was devised by her husband John,
No cogging knave, but an honest man,
If Edwick nubs not Mary Whale
And gives her store of Watkin's ale

Hang me at the next tree that grows
And let me have as many blows
As Barker had at that same fray.
I know not but as some do say

Whether he had any yea or no
But by hearsay, but let it go.
But if he had it was no hurt
The discredit longs to such a flirt

As Mary Whale that Flanders mare
That care not who doth touch her gear.
I understand there is a song,
Made by a dishonest throng

Of Mary Whale and Hugh Barker,
And Mistress Almond loves John Parker
And will do so still and so she says
If Beelzebub lighten forth her days.

But whosoever made that song
Let him repair to me John Long,
He shall have me at Goodman Fuller
A dyeing of him in divers colour

Which shortly shall a drying hang,
And nip you all with a lurry come twang.
Vale from my chamber in Duckes Street lane,
If this will not give you your bane

I have another ready made
Which will unfold your knavish trade.
Commend me also to Mary Whale
And if she needs of Watkin's ale

Clim Poope is dead but Phillipps lives
With Watkin's ale to such mates gives,
Yours as you use him John Long the carrier
Dwelling next house to Evans the farrier.

The indictment then proceeds, 'The said libel was endorsed by the said Hugh Barker as follows: "To my approved good friends Mistress Clim Malden, Mistress Anne Sandes and to all the rest of the administering females in Chelmsford and Moulsham with the suburbs thereupon

adjoining, deliver these with all speed possible, W.P.', and further, 'He that finds this song let him make copies and give to his friends.'
It then reads, 'Also in other libels'.

Sometime a mighty huge Leviathan arrived
In brave Albion's eastern parts,
It was a mighty fish and now and then he went abroad
And glanced forth his darts.

Men, women, boys and girls he held as one,
And all men know a whale is big of bone.
What though his entrails like the Caron's flood do
Swallow up the giddy headed crew.

We often see this mighty Cetus' blood
With needles pressed and I'll approve it true.
But what he cannot do his female make
Will undertake to finish for his sake.

Admit the Pope did practise glover's art,
And come to Chelmsford bragging of his skill
In Venus' may games spite of all his heart
She'll meet him at the point and fit his will

And if her husband takes him at the fray
Up goes his hose and fast he runs away.
She knows her wards and in the fencers' game
Hath proper knowledge, let her use it well

Lest soaring high she lose inferior fame
And so her note with Cerberus do dwell.
Well, Whale, look thy wife, I am thy friend
I wish thou what thou hast and
    So farewell.

To the whole generation of vipers health.

The indictment concludes, 'He endorsed this one : "To his very good and loving friends Mistress Anne Wood, the best of the Woods, and to all the rest of the gallant female kind in Chelmsford hundred, deliver these with all speed, Yours humbly to command, Timothy Purkys the joiner dwelling in the same town, Vale, W.P.".'

Chitham had put in an even more lengthy statement entitled, 'The practices of Hugh Barker of Chelmsford barber, written by Thomas Chitham of Boreham schoolmaster.' Whatever his merits as a pedagogue and as a versifier with some classical knowledge, he certainly showed no skill in confining his statement to the essential facts. Written by himself in a fine, small 'secretary' hand, with key phrases in italic, it fills four large pages. Whether the Assize judges allowed its being read out seems doubtful, but it explains the machinations to which the alarmed barber stooped in an attempt to cover up his guilt. It is clear that penury had driven the schoolmaster, much against his better judgement, to be an accessory to the libel. No indictment to that effect, however, is filed, though his appearance as a witness, together with John and Mary Whale and Richard Browne, against Barker is recorded.

In October 1601 (Chitham began) he visited the New Inn in Chelmsford to see a sick friend and at the same time called at Barker's house. On one occasion Barker asked him a favour. 'It is nothing (quoth Barker) but to have you pen a few verses for me upon a pretty jest which I shall tell you.' He twice refused. Going for the third time to be 'trimmed', he was again asked by Barker, while cutting his hair, to write the verses. Still he refused. Drawing his purse to pay, Barker would not take the money, and in the end persuaded Chitham to 'make the poem'. The barber then began to tell the schoolmaster a 'tedious discourse' of one Clement Pope, a glover of Chelmsford, and of one Whale's wife. 'And with such lascivious terms and undecent speeches did he intermingle his discourse as I am ashamed to think on, much less can I with modesty dare (for fear to offend the virtuous and chaste minded) to presume to set them down.' Chitham declared that 'if his intention was to publish it to the disgrace of any, he would not set his hand to paper for a thousand pounds. Then Barker with great oaths swore, it should not come to anybody's sight, save his own.' Chitham questioned the purpose of the 'rhyme'. It was only for his own private use, Barker replied, 'to sing to his citron (cithern) and to laugh at when he was melancholy.' The barber fetched pen and ink and 'in a most villainous sort plotted how he would have it done.' Chitham exclaimed that he would not 'write so beastly, but would cover the filthiness of the fact under as cleanly terms as he could.' Barker asked him to 'grace it with as good an exordium (or, as he termed it, preface) as he could.' Chitham accordingly 'penned four staves of verses (six lines going to every staff).' The barber took them into his house, and on returning said he liked them very well but he could not understand two words in the beginning, Leviathan and Albion. Barker then read the verses to his wife, saying that they were made by the wife of John Whale the tailor and by Clement Pope the glover, now deceased, whose widow Barker had married. When Chitham heard this he asked to have the verses back, but was refused, and he returned to his own house at Boreham.

On his next visit to Chelmsford to see his sick friend at the New Inn, he drank with 'certain honest townsmen of Chelmsford' including Mr. Fitch the apothecary and John Long his landlord. One of the company mentioned 'certain libels' which were then spreading through the town, of which Barker was supposed to be the author. As he was 'noted to be familiar with Barker', Chitham was questioned if he knew of the libels. He denied having any hand in them, adding that, even if he had, 'the alebench was no fit place to reveal such matters,' but he would talk with Whale, if he so wished. Next Friday Whale the tailor, hearing of this, asked Chitham about the verses, and he admitted that he had written some for Barker. Whale then showed him a copy of what he, Chitham, had written, also a copy of 'certain lascivious, villainous and beastly rhymes', which 'I protest before God I never saw before goodman Whale showed them me.' Whale requested Chitham to report the matter to Sir Thomas Mildmay, his nearest J.P., which he did. A fortnight later Sir Thomas summoned him to attend at Moulsham Hall, where 'I did approve the same to Barker's face,' in the presence of 'divers townsmen of Chelmsford.' Doubtless on the justices' advice or order, Chitham preferred an indictment (he stated) against Barker at the Epiphany Quarter Sessions, 'and the bill was found (i.e found a true bill) by the Great Inquest' (grand jury), but was postponed to the next Sessions, as Barker's counsel sought time to traverse the indictment.

In the meantime, on 5 February, Chitham met 'Father Ellys', another Chelmsford barber, who asked Chitham for the right title of the Earl of Sussex in writing. (The earl lived at New Hall, Boreham.) Having no paper or ink, the schoolmaster went to Boxford's house in Moulsham. Boxford (he explained) had married Barker's own sister. He was out, but his wife was sitting by the fire with two young men, musicians, who lived in Moulsham with Crane, 'an honest man', also a musician. Boxford's wife said, 'Mr. Chitham, I marvel what is the cause of my brother Barker and you be such enemies, I would all things were well and all controversies ended.' He replied that he had not wronged Barker. Just as he was leaving she told him that one of the young men 'had occasion to crave my help for penning a love song'. In his statement Chitham declared that this was not true; the fact was that she had secretly sent for Barker, who came and told him that if he prosecuted the suit against him he (Barker) would be 'utterly undone', and entreated Chitham to stay in Chelmsford that night at his expense, adding, 'Because it shall not be apparent that I waged (pledged) you to this, my wife shall from time to time give you money.'

On the same day (5 February) Barker sent his boy to Boxford's house to trim Chitham and would take no money for his labour. Next day the barber 'wished me to forsake my great charge of children and my poor wife, and to shift for myself, alleging that I was fit to live anywhere and wherever I went he would help me.' On Sunday 7 February Barker suggested, as 'policy to cover his practice', that 'I should write a letter to him, wherein I should acknowledge some injury I had offered him,' which he agreed 'very unwisely' to do. Having written it, he was directed by Barker to go to Cawdle's house in Chelmsford (Cawdle had married another of Barker's sisters, Chitham explained) to ask him to carry the letter. He found Cawdle and his wife and one Graves and his wife at the fireside. Cawdle refused to take the letter but his wife 'yielded', and brought back a message that Barker thought it should be delivered by a stranger, not by her. This Graves consented to do, for which Cawdle's wife gave him a pot of beer. He returned with the message that Barker would speak with Chitham at Boxford's house. Then he was taken to Barker's house, where they supped together in an upper chamber 'hung around with painted cloth whereon was described the history of Hammon and his sons.' Barker persuaded (urged) him to write yet another letter, which he did. Barker then said, 'I think it meet to talk with you before some of my friends', to which Chitham replied, 'I think it not amiss', and gave Barker the letter. Sending for three or four of his friends, he told them that Chitham had written to him to desire to speak with him, 'giving me terms at his pleasure (myself being in the house within the hearing of my own doom).' Barker pretended to send his boy to fetch Chitham. 'Barker's wife came up to me into the chamber, and taking me by the hand led me downstairs (for it was dark) and opening the street door softly bid me go forth and knock', which he did and was admitted. 'There Barker repeated certain speeches, and I soothed him up with yea and nay.' Afterwards it was arranged that Chitham should meet Barker at the house of Richard Brewer, a shearman living in Colchester Lane in Chelmsford.

Next day, 8 February, they met, when Barker caused Chitham to write a letter to 'Mr. Towze, Mr. Nightingale and Mr. Wiseman' (justices of the peace) 'to colour' his (Barker's) cause, and also a petition to Sir Thomas Mildmay and the whole Bench to the same effect.' These Chitham gave to Thomas Burles to deliver to Barker. Waiting at Brewer's house, he was brought 10s. by Barker's wife, all in groats; she also gave him 2d. for a drink as he went home.

The schoolmaster then explained in his statement that he was 'living very poor'. But, having an uncle, Mr. Justinian Carey, his mother's own brother, living at 'Evensham' (Eynsham)[1] in Oxfordshire, who was wealthy and childless, he went to him for help, meaning to return to Essex before the (Easter) Quarter Sessions 'to bewray (divulge) the whole drift of Barker's deceiptful practices.' He stayed with his uncle until 11 March. Reaching Chelmsford on 13 March, he went to Boxford's house and sent for Barker, who was not at home, but his wife came and 'bid me welcome, saying that she wondered to see me.' She then sent her boy to Boxford to trim me and would let me pay nothing. 'She gave me 6d. to drink and told me that her husband had a doublet for me, and that I should want nothing if I would stick to her husband.' 'I soothed her,' Chitham stated. She also told him of 'divers practices which goodman Whale had practised against me in my absence, which afterwards I proved to be mere fictions, only to make me fly the country and forsake my wife and children.'

When he appeared at the Easter Sessions to testify against Barker, the latter 'sought all means in the world to disgrace me, bringing in my own

---

[1] I have to thank Lady de Villiers (through the kindness of Mr. H. Walton, County Archivist of Oxfordshire) for telling me of the probable connection between the Careys and Eynsham.

letter which I could not deny.' Sir Thomas Mildmay declared that 'it was the pleasure of the Reverend Judge Gawdy to hear the matter at the next Assizes' (18 July), to which Barker and Chitham were bound over. In the meantime Barker had brought a 'bill' (indictment) of perjury against him at the Quarter Sessions on 2 July, charging him to be 'a rogue, a counterfeit soldier, a beggar by the highway, etc.' (But there is no such indictment on the Sessions roll.) He had also 'privily' procured a writ by which Chitham, John Phillips of Chelmsford tailor and John Whale and his wife were to be sued at one of the courts at London next term. Being bound over, Chitham sought the Assize judges' opinion that Barker's action was illegal. Furthermore, a short time ago, Barker met Chitham by chance in Chelmsford in the dark, exclaiming, 'God's wounds, you are Chitham,' and drawing out a dudgeon dagger, without a hilt, struck at Chitham's head; but he avoided the stroke, as also another 'stab at his breast.' Chitham finished by stating that he had himself written the whole truth, 'desiring the Reverend Judges that I (being poor) may be heard with indifferency.' The schoolmaster added his signature, dating his long effusion 17 July, the day before the Assizes opened.

A few facts about the other people in the case can be traced. The marriages of Hugh Barker and Bridget Pledger in 1575, of Clement Pope and Elizabeth Whale in 1589, and of Simon Cawdell and Joan Barker in 1583 are in Chelmsford register. Clement Pope died in July 1598. By his will, dated a month before his death, he left his buff doublet to his brother-in-law John Whale, whom he had cuckolded. He was a trustee for the children of Robert Whale, a maltster, and of Sibyl Whale, widow of Robert, both of Great Baddow and both dead; and Pope assigned these trusteeships to his own widow, 'to have a special care to perform the same with a good conscience towards the said children as ever she bore faith to God and goodwill towards me.' Sibyl was his residuary legatee and sole executrix. The wills, if any, of Barker and Chitham have not been traced. Nothing can be found about the unfortunate schoolmaster. The act books of the Essex archdeacons, which will be used extensively in the next volume of *Elizabethan Life*, contain hundreds of cases of sexual misbehaviour, and it may be that the promiscuous Mary Whale's doings came before the Church court.

A brief note will be attempted regarding the place of the libellous verse in the context of Elizabethan ballads.[1] From about 1550 to the early eighteenth century a ballad meant a popular, scurrilous song against a person, or, less frequently, against an institution. An example of the latter

[1] I am especially indebted to Professor J. Murphy of the University of Colorado for his generous help in this connection while staying in London in 1970. I also wish to thank Dr. Lena M. Goldstein of Cambridge, who is editing the Pepys ballads and Professor P. Edwards of the University of Essex for their comments. Dr. Goldstein states that there is still no comprehensive survey of verse libel, either ballad or non-ballad, although much of the ground is covered by Claude M. Simpson, *The British Broadside Ballad and Its Music* (Rutgers University Press, 1966).

is the anti-Anglican seditious verse which has already been seen (p. 60). Chitham's testimony that Barker wrote the verse 'to sing on his citron' makes it clear that the libel is not only in ballad form and metre but is also itself a ballad. It was not at all uncommon for Elizabethans to compose such ballads. The Star Chamber records yield a number of contemporary libel suits brought by victims of malicious ballads. There is some evidence that less substantial people were often the objective of neighbours' recriminations, righteously offended on moral grounds, or the butt of acquaintances' rough humour; and ballads, more or less obscene, probably circulated at one time or another in many towns.

While the barber-scrivener's ballad has no literary merit, it is strong, vernacular stuff of much interest from the standpoint of linguistic and social history and immeasurably more authentic in its homely phrases than formal records. It also throws a little light on the popular provincial literature, still largely obscure, of the age of Shakespeare and Jonson. 'lurry cum twang' is apparently a phrase not encountered elsewhere, and probably one borrowed from northern or western England.[1] Lurry meant a jingling rhyme. Among punning lines, that about the fuller's dyed cloth hanging on the tainter is a reminder of 'Taynter Crofte', lying behind Duke Street, shown on John Walker's manuscript map of Chelmsford, 1591. Of the various sexual allusions, Watkin's ale was a contemporary euphemism for copulation.[2] Although the schoolmaster's shorter libel abounds in classical monsters it is scarcely less obscene than the barber's, which accounts for the former's cringing statement prepared in the hope of persuading the Court that his part in the defamatory versifying was forced upon him, unwillingly and on account of his poverty. It is the inordinately long statement which distinguishes Barker's case from most Elizabethan libels, though the interest is domestic, rather than literary, with its insight, e.g. into the barber's upper chamber walls hung with stained cloths depicting the story of Amon of Judah (such biblical scenes were common enough). The documents as a whole give us an intimate picture of the sexual delinquencies of the ordinary folk in a town in 'Albion's eastern parts.'

Later documents tell of Barker's decline and fall. In 1615 a Writtle apprentice and his mother put in a petition against him at Quarter Sessions. The lad had been bound for eight years to be instructed by Barker in the trade of 'barber, scrivener, toothdrawing and bloodletting', which shows that he was a barber-surgeon. But the term had run for only two years, by which time the master, 'being now greatly indebted and having no place of habitation put him to his mother to be maintained and alloweth him nothing for his maintenance, by which he loseth his time and

---

[1] Comment from Dr. Goldstein.
[2] The ballad and music of 'Watkin's Ale' are given by Claude M. Simpson, *The British Broadside Ballad and Its Music* (1966).

hindereth his mother'. Barker refused to release him from his indenture unless the mother gave him money for the lad's discharge. But she 'dare not keep him for fear of bringing herself within the danger of the law', so she asked the justices to discharge his apprenticeship. The Court did so, and ordered his 'dame' (Barker's wife) to return his clothes. Having fled after being indicted for 'transgressions and contempts' and failing to appear after the statutory three proclamations, Barker's career ended in 1618 with his being outlawed.

Defamation is a rare occurrence in the Elizabethan records of other counties, and appears only in Middlesex and Worcestershire. 'One Saxton' complained in 1592 that Thomas Maddy, a gentleman of Staple Inn (one of the inns of court), had come to his house 'to have a woman lodged' there. Saxton refused, whereon Maddy shouted in the street that the plague was in his house. There is nothing which would lead us to identify the plaintiff with Christopher Saxton, the cartographer. In 1601 a schoolmaster was in trouble, but, unlike Chitham, not for an obscene libel: Nicholas Foster of Westminster confessed, when 'a scandalous ballad or libel in print between a Papist and a Protestant' was found in his house, that he had received it from a certain Mr. Skinner.[1] A Worcestershire midwife was slandered as 'not fit to bring a dog to bed, much less a woman.'[2]

---

[1] *Middlesex County Records*, i, 211, 272.   [2] *Worcestershire County Records*, 44.

5

Forgery

By the Treason Act of 1351 the forging of the monarch's great or privy seal, the counterfeiting of the royal coin, or the importing of counterfeits, was high treason. Under Mary and Elizabeth there was a spate of legislation dealing with these crimes. The punishment, as for other convictions for high treason, was drawing, beheading and quartering.

Attempting to pass off as genuine a document with a false royal seal was alleged in 1567 against John Segrave of Barking, a mariner. He was charged with counterfeiting the Great Seal of England attached to forged letters patent, but was found not guilty.

Before narrating the coin-counterfeiting cases it must be pointed out that the large range of English and foreign coins, new and old, in current use in Elizabeth's time, and especially their values, cannot be briefly explained, partly because the exact values at some periods are not easy to ascertain. The royal (or ryal) was worth approximately 10s. The value of the sovereign is more difficult to define, all the more so as the word sometimes seems to have been used for half-sovereign, which, like the ryal, had a value of about 10s. (p. 82).[1] Nearly all the coins above the value of a shilling were of gold, whilst the shilling and lesser denominations were of silver.

Two counterfeit coins were referred to in a Quarter Sessions case in Mary's time (p. 1). The editor of the *Acts of the Privy Council* commented that the improvement of the coinage by Cecil in 1560–1 'proved to be an irresistible temptation to many.'[2] More recently a distinguished historian, taking the opposite view, held that the earlier 'monetary chaos gave way to order, and the counterfeiter was held in check.'[3] During 1577–78, at any rate, a minor wave of coining struck Essex, with no less than five convictions.[4]

Michael (or Nicholas) Coxe yeoman and Thomas Swetinge weaver, both of Roxwell, made twelve 'penny-pieces' of counterfeit money there. They were condemned to be drawn and hanged. Two months earlier

---

[1] Cf. *Middlesex County Records*, i, index *s.v.* 'Money'; despite his long introduction the editor, like the present writer, does not grasp the monetary nettle.
[2] *Acts of the Privy Council*, ix, p. xxx.
[3] S. T. Bindoff, *Tudor England* (1950), 199.
[4] For three of these cases, see *Acts of the Privy Council*, vols. ix and x.

the case had come before the Council, who referred it to the Assize judges. The culprits had been committed to Newgate Gaol for high treason, but Swetinge died there before the Assizes.

A more serious charge engaged the Council's attention in 1578. John Browning and Walter Eldred, both of Peldon, and Marcel Goodwin of Newport, all termed yeomen, were indicted for counterfeiting at Peldon three Elizabeth ryals of gold and a sixpenny-piece. The Council enjoined Lord Darcy and Mr. Tey, Essex J.P.s, to arrest the men and make a house search. A week later they sent a letter to Lord Darcy, thanking him for his pains in apprehending Browning and Goodwin. But, as they were vehemently suspected of coining, the Council sent them to the Tower and asked Darcy to make a further search in Browning's house, because he was 'expressly charged to have two false stamps, one of 6d. and the other of a sovereign, which were not amongst the rest of the trumpery sent up by his lordship'. The noble lord was also required to lock up safely 'such refining pots and other bowls not yet sent up,' the Warden of the Royal Mint having been instructed to dispatch to Peldon a skilled man to examine them. As the Warden was 'well acquainted with such instruments, having discovered the like practices before', he was to attend on the Lord Chief Justice, the Lieutenant of the Tower, the Attorney General and the Solicitor General, who were assigned to examine the two men and Eldred. The Council took these steps because they had received new evidence. A man condemned for false coining at the Norfolk Assizes had accused others, including Browning and Goodwin. In the meantime Darcy had also arrested Eldred, 'a cunning smith and maker of instruments found in Browning's house', who denied having any part in the affair.[1] The four magnates were ordered to use every effort in conjunction with the Warden of the Mint to ascertain before his execution whether the Norfolk coiner's accusation was true. The matter was dealt with at four further Council meetings in the next two months, and it was then referred to the Essex Midsummer Assizes. After all these proceedings, the jury brought in a verdict for all three men of – not guilty!

William Lewes of Manningtree weaver was found guilty for coining and clipping twelve penny-pieces and some sixpenny-pieces with shears; and George Choppin of High Roothing labourer confessed his treason in making twelve penny-pieces and four sixpenny-pieces and was sent to the Castle prison; both cases arose in 1578. The escape of Henry Chittam of Great Bardfield, a convicted coiner, was on the Council's agenda for many of its sessions in 1577.

[1] The Norfolk convict's name was Eloye Mensterell. About 1560 an attempt was made to introduce coins made with the French screw press. Mensterell brought over a press, and produced milled coins far superior to hammered coins, but the Royal Mint workmen were hostile, and he ended on the gallows. See *English Gold Coins* (Cleveland Museum of Art, U.S.A., 1968), 46. I have to thank my friend, Meredith Colket, Director of the Western Reserve Hist. Soc., Cleveland, for a copy of this book (see plate 7).

G

Another minor outbreak occurred in 1586–88, with three more cases. Giles Walworthe of Colchester was haled before the Council on suspicion of coining.[1] Edward Bacon of Brightlingsea coined twelve pieces of money called Utrecht nobles which he gave to William Hubberd for good money at Little Clacton. He had not been arrested, or had escaped from custody. Two Aveley labourers who had made a counterfeit twelve-penny-piece and uttered it to an unknown man were found guilty of uttering only.

In 1591 Matthew Levet of Leaden Roothing clerk (rector from 1571) made an angel of gilded tin, but he also was dead when his case came up at the Assizes: the end of a villainous career (p. 143). Ten years later two Saffron Walden persons were caught. James Bardney, a pewterer, made three fake Elizabeth shillings which he uttered to many persons, and Clemence wife of Robert Underwood, a glazier, in the same month uttered five such shillings of mixed metals; but both were acquitted. The prosecuting witnesses were headed by the town's treasurer.

It is difficult to say why, with many convictions for actual coining, there are few only for uttering counterfeit coin, but one of them is a little treasure in itself. The offender was Robert Lodge, a tapster, who had at Michaelmas 1568 moved from the 'Crown' at Brentwood (see plate 19), where he had served for six years, to the 'Boar's Head' at Chelmsford, as a covenant servant to George Burges the innkeeper. At Hallowtide following (first week in November) a Chelmsford tailor gave him a counterfeit gold piece of 10s. called a sovereign, 'willing' him to 'play it away' or dispose of it otherwise as 'partners'. So Lodge 'laid it to gage' (pawned it) for 6s. with the wife of the innkeeper of the 'Greyhound' at Moulsham (in Chelmsford), who still had it. Also about Hallowtide Mr. Burges's under-ostler found in the river on the backside of the inn a counterfeit angel of 10s., which Lodge borrowed, promising to repay him before Christmas. A fortnight later Lodge borrowed another 4s. from a sailor, which he (Lodge) lost the same afternoon at 'tyck tack at tables', but the sailor being importunate to get his 4s. back, Lodge handed him the counterfeit angel, taking 6s. to make up the 10s. As soon as the sailor realised that he had been duped he told the constables, who apprehended Lodge. The story comes from his deposition on the Epiphany 1570 Sessions roll, but nothing more is known. 'Tables' is backgammon, and 'tyck-tack' an earlier variety of it (p. 221).

Passing foreign coin as coin of the realm was another crime. In 1597 four Rochford men 'falsely and traitorously gave a silver Spanish twelve-pence gilt worth 12d. for a gold double pistole worth 12s.' to another man. One was found guilty of uttering, and he was whipped, pilloried and released. One was acquitted; the others had fled.

[1] *Acts of the Privy Council*, xiv, 204.

Forgery of documents, or uttering false documents, was also a fairly common offence. Indictments were laid under the Act of 33 Henry VIII, c.1 (1541), a 'Statute against the use of false tokens' (as such documents were termed).

A solitary indictment for forging deeds in 1575 revealed how a Laindon husbandman 'procured' a lease of a farm called Paradice in Dunton as well as a bond by which a Hempstead man acknowledged that he was bound in the sum of £200 to the accused. The latter was also charged with making a counterfeit licence and passport in the name of Sir Anthony Cooke (the well-known J.P. of Gidea Hall, Romford).

An Epping husbandman was charged in 1586 with obtaining 'by a false token' six steers in the custody of William Neale, an Epping inn-holder, belonging to a Cambridgeshire drover. The defendant was examined before James Morrice, J.P. He confessed how, after overhearing the terms of an agreement between the innkeeper and the drover and by impersonating the latter, using that token, he had got possession of the cattle and sold them next day at Romford market for £17.

An extraordinary case came before the Court at the Midsummer Sessions in 1587. A labourer of Wickham (probably Wickham Bishops), using a false name each time, must have been a plausible fellow to have extracted a total of £26 in cash from four people. Examined by Thomas Mildmay, he confessed to having used 'this counterfeit token'. On the previous 26 October he went to Mr. Bretton's house at East Tilbury with the tale that he was Mr. Wiseman's man of Rivenhall, who had sent him to fetch £14, part of his rent due at the previous Michaelmas, whereupon Bretton gave him £3 and sent a lad with him to Horndon for £5, which he also received. At High Easter on Twelfth Eve he told a woman that he had a message from her husband, 'who rode a black gelding and had four capons behind him', to lend £5 to Mr. Mannock his master. On 'sennight before Shrove Tuesday' he informed a Feering woman that her husband had ridden into Dengie hundred where he had bought two milch beasts of the defendant for £3. Finally, on 6 April, he called on a Laindon Hills man with the story that his landlord, Mr. Mildmay of Springfield Barnes, had sent him, declaring he was Mr. Mildmay's servant, to collect £10, part of his rent due at Lady Day. All his gullible victims had handed over these sums.

The remaining cases all arose under the vagrancy laws, which demanded that every poor traveller should provide himself with a 'passport'. They yield seven stories of uncommon interest, all derived from justices' examinations preserved in the Sessions rolls.

The nefarious practices of a couple of skilled passport forgers came to light when Edward Sympson was arrested for vagrancy and suspected pilfering in 1581. Brought by the constable of Terling to Anthony Maxey, J.P., Sympson was duly examined and gave the following account. His last master was Sir John Cove in Warwickshire about nine months ago. He served him only for four weeks and was then in Bedfordshire three weeks and Hertfordshire a fortnight. Since then, Sympson confessed, he had been in Essex with Bartholomew Newell *alias* John Johnson, whose companion was Mary Anderson, generally called Fine Mary; she had previously consorted with one Banforde. Sympson then told the justice that he knew two 'great counterfeiters of licences in Essex', Davy Benete and Tom Whitinge. The former had made many false passports for Newell, representing him to be a soldier from Berwick or as one travelling to visit his friends. He can counterfeit, Sympson testified, any J.P.'s seal or any other seal. If he can see it in wax, he can carve a perfect copy (matrix) in wood. He carries about with him a little bag full of these counterfeit seals. He can forge any signature because he writes 'sundry hands'. Can be thus recognised: age about 24; face full of pockholes; travels in an old cloak; sometimes in company with Mary Philips who at present has a two-months infant with her; often visits an old man in the parish of Ugley whose name he does not remember but his house has a glass window on the right-hand side of the entrance-door, not far from one Carter's house of Ugley Hall. Whitinge, the other counterfeiter, is an old man and goes about very simply with a white woollen night-cap with two ears commonly tied under his chin. Sympson added that Whitinge usually makes a white chalk mark shaped like a whiting where he stays, 'to the intent if any chance to lodge there that it was not long since he was there, to the end if any would have any counterfeit licences they might seek after him.' When arrested, Sympson said he had on him 'an old black frize cotton apron, a swaddling band, and white woollen linen.' These, he alleged, had been given to him by Newell who had asked him to go with Fine Mary to Widow Sexton's at Halstead, because Newell and another vagrant did not dare to be seen in the town after escaping from the constables to her house. They had intended the next night to meet him and Fine Mary at the widow's house, but Mary had also managed to escape at the time of his own arrest.

Five vagrants were arrested in 1583. One was examined by Edward Rich, the other by Sir Thomas Lodge, to whom he told a story of a false passport, setting out that the bearer, Thomas Wolson, had by great misfortune lost his house and corn and cattle worth £40 in Little Shelford near Cambridge by fire, and was travelling to his sister in Bedfordshire and to his brother in Essex to obtain their help for himself, his wife and children. Dated 25 March 1583, it was sealed and signed 'Frauncis Hine' and 'Jhon Gooldeinge.' The passport being suspected as counterfeit, Sir Thomas asked where he dwelt and who made it. Wolson deposed that he lived at Little Shelford and that it was written and signed by the two Cambridgeshire justices about Easter last. He had been to Bedford where his sister gave him 20s., and had in his purse £5, which sum he lent to Thomas Adcock of Royston who repaid it with 5s. interest at Easter. He did not know how long ago the fire was, nor exactly where his brother lived in Essex. He desired the justice to challenge his statement. Sir Thomas accordingly sent Thomas Smyth of Plaistow (in West Ham), a man of good credit, to Shelford, who reported on his return that the whole story was untrue, and he brought back a letter from John 'Goldwell', the son of the second Cambridge J.P. The writer declared that no such man as Wolson had lived at Shelford, nor had the village suffered any fire in the past twelve years except one five years ago at Mr. Freville's house. He knew the hands and signatures of Sir Francis Hynde as well as his father's, and therefore the passport was a forgery.

A vagrant's examination, taken by Maldon borough officers, is preserved in the county records. The culprit was John Harte, and he was brought to the Moot Hall before Thomas Eve, one of the two bailiffs, and Edward Coker, a borough justice (he was one of the bailiffs who submitted the borough arms at the herald's visitation in 1558).[1] Harte had been taken up within the borough with a forged testimonial. He said that he was born and dwelt at Yarmouth. For ten weeks he had 'rogued about from place to place'. About a 'seven night since' he was at Rye (Sussex), whence he came to Gravesend three days before Christmas, thence to Blackwall on the north bank of the Thames (then a hamlet, centuries before the tunnel). Coming to Brentwood, he met a schoolmaster, whose name he knew not, dwelling near an alehouse with the sign of the 'Rose and Pot'; this man wrote the testimonial for 2d. Further questioned, Harte confessed he was an Irishman and a sailor. While at Rye he was 'fishing in the boat of one Tamesone before the holyday of Christmas for whiting and gurnard.' Later he was begging with his false testimonial on Sunday after Christmas in All Saints' church in Maldon. He asked alms of Vincent Harrys esquire, who refused. He retorted that 'his ear would breed a scab before Easter Day', whereupon he was committed. Harrys who had bought the house of the former Black Friars at Maldon in 1563 and built a mansion on its site, was not a man to abuse with impunity. The despoition is giend by Eve and William Vernon, the other bailiff.

The malpractices and the miseries of the hordes of rogues and vagabonds are very well documented in the Essex Sessions rolls. The seven cases which have been related were selected solely because they concern forged passports. Other aspects of vagrancy, which was a constant source of anxiety to the County Bench as well as to the Council, will be discussed in Volume 3, and this will include an analysis of their wanderings, based on several remarkable sets of petty constables' returns.

Depositions taken in 1590 reveal how pedlars lurking in fairs found vagrant customers willing to pay for forged passports. Arthur More said

[1] *Essex Review*, xxiii, 63.

that he came into Essex last Thursday out of Norfolk, where he had been for a month, that he arrived at Dover on 1 March last accompanied by John Grene whose name is in his licence, which was made by William Roberts, Clerk of the Captain's Band, and Mr. Herington their Captain signed and sealed it at 'the Ramekynes' in the Low Countries. But afterwards he confessed that it was made at Saffron Walden by John Crofts a soldier, and the name of Anthony Herrington and the seal were set thereunto by one called 'Kytte Myller', a pedlar, who is a maker of passports and goes apparelled in a Spanish leather jerkin with long cuts (slits revealing an under-garment) and a pair of venetians (breeches) of canvas cut, and who made another passport for himself and two others at Chelmsford Fair on May Day last. He also confessed that he was in Leicestershire and had wandered in divers shires with his counterfeit passport. Thomas Hastings, who first declared his name is John Grene, as in his passport, affirmed in every respect as in the former part of More's confession, but afterwards confessed his name to be Thomas Hastings. He had long been a companion with More in Leicestershire, Cambridgeshire, Suffolk, Norfolk, Essex, Kent and other shires, using that trade of living, and confessed that their licence was forged by Myller, whom he first met at Chelmsford Fair in an alehouse in Moulsham, where Myller made them a new passport for which More paid 12d. He had also told the constable that Myller used to lend money to many persons of their quality, and when they 'had gotten any cheat' they repaid him with interest; More had thus paid about 8d.

An unmarried couple, who had kept company for three and a half years according to the man but only half a year by the woman's version, were examined by Israel Amyce in 1587. The man confessed that 'one Smyth a walker' counterfeited both his passport and his testimonial. He had served in Flanders under Sir Walter Waller, returned half a year ago with 'Sir Walter's passport', which he left with Smyth, who gave him the lead seal with which his passport was sealed. Three years ago he was in gaol and burnt in the hand (i.e. branded, having claimed benefit of clergy).

Robert Buck, who described himself in 1592 as a sawyer of Dedham, when examined by John Ive about his passport, admitted that, although it bore the names of the minister and constables of Dedham and of 'one John Quarreles his master', it had been counterfeited with false seals by Thomas Elmes of Dedham, a crippled tailor, to whom he gave 2d. for writing it. Elmes, questioned about Buck's licence to leave his master's service, confessed to the forgery and to receiving 2d. The forger was ordered to be imprisoned in the village cage for two days, with an inscription, 'For counterfeiting of passports'.

Later in the same year William Randall, described as the minister of Langdon Hills, had evidently succumbed to the same temptation, if the allegation is true; but the story, told by a West Tilbury labourer, apparently an alehouse keeper, is not supported by any other documents. The labourer said that last Tuesday one Alice Martin of Hartley (Kent) had come to his house and two hours later Randall arrived and drank a pot of beer with her. She showed Randall her travel licence, who after reading it told her that it was 'very well'. Next day Randall turned up again, this time with a sailor. They and Alice and two more women went up to a chamber. There they drank and ate a 'mess of peasen' together, after which Randall taking paper and ink wrote something. About Whitsuntide last, Alice had come to his house, followed shortly afterwards by Randall and three men 'apparelled like sailors', all of whom went up to a chamber where he wrote a counterfeit passport for Alice, who gave him 8d. for it. The examination was taken before Edward Rich in the presence of one of the constables of West Tilbury. John Frith, rector of Langdon Hills, had been removed from his benefice, and Thomas Edmunds his successor was instituted in the month before Randall was involved. The forger may therefore have been a temporary curate.

A stout denial by James Naylor of Weeley that he neither knew nor made a false passport for Elizabeth Sawfer has to be set side by side with depositions of Robert Patrick and Richard Tillar, both of Beaumont. All were taken by Edmund Pirton in 1593. Patrick said that the woman, who belonged to Beaumont and was suspected to be pregnant by him, had been examined through his means by Dr. Taylor at Colchester. There she cleared him on oath, laying the matter to a Suffolk man whose name he did not know. Afterwards, Naylor meeting him by chance at Thorpe, made a counterfeit passport for the woman for a whole year under the hands and seals of the bailiffs of Yarmouth, changing her name to Elizabeth Bowen widow, for which he was paid 2s. by Naylor, handing it to her in a barn of her uncle Tillar at Beaumont. He had not seen her since then, but heard that Tillar's wife carried her to Bromley or Manningtree. Naylor had 'willed' him to keep out of the way, as he only could accuse Naylor. Tillar said that she told him that Naylor had made the false licence, one Briant, late of Thorpe, having supplied the names of certain justices near Yarmouth whose signatures and seals he had counterfeited. Patrick gave it to her so that she could leave the district. At her departure she asked her uncle, if he did not hear from her before next Easter, to have Patrick before some justices, 'because she feared some evil usage to be done to her by him.' She told one of the bailiffs of Colchester that she was with child by Patrick, but denied it before Dr. Taylor because Patrick threatened to get her punished; but returning from the Court she asserted to Tillar that Patrick was the father. Recognizances had been taken for the two men's appearance, Tillar to give evidence against Patrick, the latter to give it against Naylor for counterfeiting and for conveying the woman away.

Forged passports are also mentioned in three cases which are not expanded by depositions. In 1573 a Bristol man was apprehended at Maldon for begging with a false pass bearing a counterfeit seal of the city and was sentenced as a vagabond to a session in the pillory. At the following Assizes two of six vagrants who had been taken up were indicted for having 'counterfeit licences and passports'. The forger of a licence, committed to Colchester Castle gaol in 1594, was whipped and released.

The Marian and Elizabethan Middlesex county records disclose only four cases of coining and three of forgery, all of writings, but none of them were vagrants' passes. Sentences are given in two instances : not guilty of coining but guilty of uttering, to be imprisoned and to forfeit all goods ; and guilty of coining, to be drawn and hanged.[1] Very little evidence about the incidence of these crimes seems to be recorded in the printed calendars of other counties, but they were occasionally brought to the Privy Council's notice.

[1] *Middlesex County Records*, vol. i.

6

Extortion, Bribery, Perjury and Cozening

Counterfeiting and forgery were only two of the devices used by fraudulent persons. The vice of dishonesty manifested itself in many other ways, and the Elizabethan lawyers had almost as many words for the means by which it was practised. In a broad sense, extortion, bribery, cozening, embezzling, procuring, subornation and perjury were all forms of fraud, though of course man's dishonesty has always been most evident in committing larceny, robbery and other thefts.

It was not at all an uncommon thing for ignorant or illiterate country folk to be pestered by petty local officials, or by people impersonating officials, who managed to extract illegal fees or bribes (extortion).

The worst offender was James Chapman, bailiff of Chelmsford hundred, who was presented in 1578 by the hundredal jurors, some of whom had been among his victims. He had clearly decided that his unpaid appointment ought to produce a few perquisites, so he took bribes for exempting certain men from jury service. As a result, the jurors stated, 'poor men are oppressed, and those that are of ability are not seen but overpassed', that is, those able to pay up were not summoned to serve. 'There are some of our jury that will be sworn that he has compounded with them for a yearly rent, and so long as they gave him that composition they were overpassed, but when they refused to give him such bribes then they were called continually.' Four men had thus been mulcted of between 2s. and 4s. a year; a fifth, 2s. and some bacon; a sixth, a bushel of white wheat. Another refused to give a bushel of rye, so he had been often summoned for jury service. 'If he would do as other men doth,' Chapman bullied another, 'he should not need to serve so often as he doth.' A housewife even had to buy cheeses to hand over, because he said hers were too big to give to him. He was careful not to concentrate on one place, so he practised his tricks in half a dozen villages in the hundred. For serving arrest warrants three bailiffs of hundreds were indicted between 1562 and 1580 for extorting illegal fees, in each case from one person only.

Should threats prove ineffective, arrest would clinch the matter. So thought John Keale, shoemaker of Braintree and sheriff's bailiff, who in 1579 not only levied 2s. 4d. on a Stisted man but also assaulted and imprisoned him until he paid a fine for his release. Two hundredal bailiffs in 1568 and 1592 each took similar sums. One arrested three men; the other assaulted two, one being William Strutt, clerk, at Ballingdon: he was the rector of Little Henny (1577–1620) and was himself before Quarter Sessions two years later (p. 173). A solitary deposition by an unfortunate sufferer is extant. In 1582 a White Colne labourer stated that an Earls Colne weaver, 'as a special bailiff' appointed by the Exchequer, had arrested him under the Statute of Usury, but compounded for 30s. by promising him full discharge by the Court. There are also two indictments against petty constables. The high constables of Chelmsford hundred had summoned twenty-four jurors for their petty sessions. A Mountnessing constable levied 6d. to discharge two of them from appearance. A Kelvedon constable took a fee for returning a mare to its owner, for which he was fined 20s.

In 1572 John Collyn, a goldsmith, of St. Margaret Pattens in Rood Lane, London, and John Prentice, a Colne Engaine yeoman, at Cockfield (Suffolk) frightened John Fynche with a writ of *subpoena*, stating that he was indebted to Prentice for 40s. under penalty of £100 to appear in the Court of Chancery, and they extracted 20s. from him. Three weeks later the same pair descended on Fynche's home at Colne Engaine, assaulting him and demanding 40s. This time, however, he was not so easily duped by their alleging he had been declared an outlaw in the Queen's Court for a £6 debt. About the same time, Collyn was annoying others in Alphamstone, where Edward Pam gentleman and Nicholas Grice the rector heard him say to one of his victims, 'Come to London, if thou dare, and I will trounce ye.' The case appears in the records until 1574, when it was Collyn who was outlawed for non-appearance. Richard Goodwyn, a grocer of Harwich, seems to have been another trouble-maker. In 1574 he was indicted as a common barrator and a man of bad name who had often fraudulently taken money from unknown people under pretence of writs. He was remanded for good behaviour.

Edward Huberd, a Chancery official and lord of the manor of Bentfield Bury in Stansted Mountfitchet, was accused in 1589 of detaining £100 'under colour of a privy seal' (forced loan to the Crown). The money 'should be employed towards the erecting of a free school at Stansted'.[1]

In 1590 two men pursued a plan for getting their victims to compound for alleged and unspecified penal offences and obtained sums ranging from 2s. 6d. to 10s. from four Great Dunmow persons, including Richard Vaughan clerk (who was instituted as vicar a year later) and John Bridge miller. The accused were Thomas Shovelard of High Ongar tailor and John Estland of Braintree fletcher. The former was awarded a session in the pillory on Dunmow market day. In 1598 Thomas Austen of Aveley clerk (vicar, 1592–1609) was accused of extortionately taking

---

[1] *Acts of the Privy Council*, xvii, 410; cf. *Essex Review*, xxxix, 124–8.

10s. from one of his flock for a mortuary fee on his father's death. A mortuary was the customary gift received by an incumbent from a deceased parishioner's estate. Presumably the fee demanded was higher than the normal sum. The vicar's offence was also tried in the Archdeacon's court.

There were always bogus officials. Two men, posing as purveyors for the Queen's household, extracted a few sums of money in 1574 and 1587. Similarly, in 1590, Hugh Wylson of East Tilbury was indicted for pretending to be a purveyor for collecting timber and trees to make 'bowstaves'. He felled and squared twelve elms worth £3 in all growing on the lands of John Bawd esquire at Corringham and three other Fobbing men, and sold the lops and tops of four of the elms for 6s. 8d.

Another officer of the royal household was the Knight-Marshal, who had judicial authority within the palace and a radius of twelve miles around it. In 1574 the grand jury presented 'the men of Henry Percivall, one of the Knights Marshal,' for arresting nine persons and illegally taking from each sums ranging from 21s. to 27s. 8d. Described as 'of London, and one of the servants of Robert Hopton, Queen's Marshal', Percivall himself was indicted for assaulting and taking into his custody by violence at Chelmsford and other places the nine men and for extorting money for their release. Three were members of hundredal juries, one being a Woodham Walter constable.

A Tollesbury labourer in 1600 evidently got hold of a certain John Mowse's licence to practise physic, issued by the Archbishop of Canterbury, and brandished it in front of several unnamed people. It would of course have been written in Latin, and they were led to believe that it was a citation to attend at the Court of Arches and that he was the apparitor. He was found guilty of defrauding them by taking discharge fees and was whipped.

'By extorciouns I lyve', confessed Chaucer's friar, and many Tudor churchmen were guilty of the same sin. Among the most hated officers were those of the ecclesiastical courts, who often charged excessive fees. Occasionally, to everyone's delight, they were brought before the secular courts. The Hinckford hundred jury in 1566 presented that 'one Mr. Cole, scribe unto Mr. Donnell, Commissary, receiveth of most men that be warned to Visitation and other spiritual courts for every bill (churchwarden's annual presentment) 4d.' Two J.P.s fined him 2s. A commissary was a deputy authorised to act in certain parts of a diocese or archdeaconry. Donnell may have been Thomas Donnell, the rector of Birdbrook and vicar of Toppesfield; both parishes were subject to the Commissary of the Archdeacon of Middlesex 'in parts of Essex', as his jurisdiction was termed.

In 1581 John Cavell of Great Dunmow husbandman, a summoner of the Bishop of London's Commissary for Essex, was charged with extorting 3s. by grave threats from a Little Saling man cited to appear before the Court of Arches (the Archbishop's appeal court); with taking 10s. for discharging a Dunmow man from appearance at the Commissary's court; and with falsely summoning eleven Stebbing men to its sessions at Braintree and Dunmow on two successive days.

A further triple complaint was presented by the Hinckford jurors in 1582. The 'Official and the scribe' (their names, Dr. Bingham and Mr. Lynne, were interlined) take 4d. for every bill put into their court or else refuse to accept it. Bingham, the Archdeacon of Colchester's Official, was involved in a big dispute with his predecessor as rector of Rettendon (p. 189). Thomas Tiler of Birdbrook, apparitor, cites men who have not been presented by the churchwardens (another charge of extortion, as he would demand his fee for each citation). And the clerk of the market takes for sealing (weights and measures), 2d. for each bushel or peck, 4d. for each clothier's or smith's weight, 4d. from each victualler, and 4d. for each miller's 'dish' even though his dish be sealed. Two years later the grand jury submitted an even more general criticism of the Church court officers at visitations: they 'exact further than right or reason, extorting of the churchwardens and sidesmen, to the great impoverishing of every parish.'

In 1591 a Moze man handed over to Peter Phillips of Manningtree, an apparitor of the Bishop of London, £3 17s. 4d. and a cheese worth 3s. into the bargain, for his fee and a 40s. fine in the Prerogative Court of Canterbury for ploughing on St. Bartholomew's Day. On his admission that there was no such suit or fine, the justices sentenced the apparitor to the pillory in open market. Two years later John James of Stock, the 'late' common apparitor of the suffragan Bishop of Colchester and of the Bishop of London's Commissary, cited a Stifford woman before the Church court and extorted 2s. to excuse her from attendance. In 1595 John Ruddleston, of Bocking, registrar of the Archbishop of Canterbury's Commissary, took extortionate fees, viz. £3 for probate of a will (goods not exceeding £50) and 6s. 8d. for letters of administration and an inventory (goods not exceeding £3 3s. 4d.). This refers to the deanery of Bocking, a 'peculiar' of the Archbishop consisting of Bocking and six Essex and Suffolk parishes, which were exempt from episcopal and archidiaconal control.

The justices received a petition in 1597 from a Great Bromley man. Ralph Kinge clerk, late commissary of Lord Darcy, had granted him administration of a Thorpe intestate's goods. Having paid the fees, he supposed he was quit from further charges. He was however cited before the court at Thorpe by Christopher Cooke, apparitor of Dr. Thomas Corbet (Kinge's successor), on 3 August, when he was very busy carrying his harvest during 'variable weather'. Ecclesiastical proceedings were prohibited in harvest time. Kinge was rector of Little Bromley, and Corbet was rector of Abberton and Stanway. The soke (Thorpe, Walton and Kirby-le-Soken) was a private peculiar of Lord Darcy. The petition was referred to two J.P.s, Edmund Pirton and Edward Grimeston, who found the complaint without any foundation. But although Dr. Corbet was completely exonerated in their view, he was 'deeply moved with just cause of grief to be so openly accused by this complaint', which had also been notified to Darcy. The justices, however, earnestly urged him to forgive the petitioner, 'which in the end he condescended to do only on the complainant's penitent submission and acknowledging his error before us, which in truth he did with knees and tears'.

In 1578 some of the clergy were cheated by a bogus officer. This is learned from a long letter addressed to Lords Rich and Darcy from Tilty by Henry Medeley, who lived at the Abbey House, and James Morice, who apologised for their absence from the Sessions because neither was able to travel. John Founten, arrested at Ongar after hue and cry, was examined by them. He had called on 'divers of the clergy', sometimes naming himself John Walker, cousin of Archdeacon Walker (Archdeacon of Essex), sometimes Mr. Nowell, Dean of St. Paul's, sometimes Mr. Willoughby, Dean of Rochester, and claiming kinship to both deans. Demanding payment of the clerical subsidy, he had 'cozened' money from them on the archdeacon's authority. Under questioning he prevaricated, so the two justices sent him to the County Bench to deal with restitution of the money, and they had bound over Patrick Fearne clerk (rector of Sandon, 1567–87) and a layman as prosecuting witnesses.

A foolish impersonation of the Bishop of London's clerk of the market for Kelvedon led to the prosecution of Thomas Pygrem of Kelvedon, bailiff of the bishop's liberty in Essex, in June 1589. Receiving a false episcopal warrant, Kelvedon tradespeople duly turned up with their weights and measures. They must have been dim-witted, for the bogus clerk of the market, according to the indictment, held no court, had no jury and showed no commission; and he began by halving a 16d. fee because a blacksmith lent a hammer, chisel and other tools! He collected a total of 2s. 6d. in fees for weights and measures: from John Foster blacksmith for 22 1-lb. weights, John Goldwayt (a very appropriate name) for 3 1-lb. weights, Christmas's wife for a pewter quart pot, John Knight butcher for 20 1-lb. weights, William Cooper 'clover' for divers weights, William Laston for a yard, John Lyngwood for a yard and a 1-lb weight. At least the last man should have been suspicious, as he had been a juror for the liberty at the previous Sessions. Eventually the trick was found out, and it resulted in the bishop writing from his manor of Much Hadham (Herts.) to James Morice, who apparently presided at the Midsummer Quarter Sessions. The bishop stated that one Mr. Powell, 'her Majesty's servant, my honest neighbour at Fulham, since my late coming hither, did within my manor of Stortford' act as clerk of the market by the Queen's grant. 'I pray you and the rest of the bench,' he added, 'to sift it out to the utmost and let him (Pygrem) in God's name have according to law as he has deserved.'

Closely related to extortion was bribery. A briber, until late Elizabethan times, meant a person, especially an official or judge, who received a *douceur*, rather than, as now, a person who offers it. Nearly all Tudor statesmen and courtiers (and some lower officers) accepted money or other offerings from suitors. They regarded them as payment for services to be rendered and as a normal increment to their inadequate remuneration from the Crown. But some were highly unprincipled in regard to the amount of their bribes. Sir William Petre, the Custos Rotulorum of Essex and former Principal Secretary to Henry VIII, Edward and Mary, if his unusually full account-books can be relied upon, seems to have been one of the exceptions in this respect, though even he occasionally accepted gifts designed to secure his influential help.[1]

The taking of *douceurs* by judges was a somewhat different matter. If one is to give credence to the testimony of several people in 1587, a significant if not slightly sinister light is shed on the integrity of an Essex judge. The first scene is at one Reynold's house at High Easter about four days before the Lent Assizes in that year. Present there were John Seriche of High Easter, a husbandman, John Peter *alias* Sparke of Woodham Mortimer, a tailor (his son-in-law), and Thomas Robiant (or Robjant) of Good Easter, another husbandman. They were talking about some trouble that had befallen Seriche and his daughter Joan, wife of Giles Ellis, who sojourned at Reynold's house. Goodman Seriche and Mistress Ellis were due to appear at the Assizes upon suspicion of felony, having been bound over by 'Mr. Baron Clarke' (Robert Clarke, Baron of the Exchequer, and an Essex J.P.). Robiant recommended this course of action to Seriche : 'If you will look to have any favour in your matter at Mr. Clarke's hands, you must do as I have done, namely, to carry a fat capon now and then to him and put a red capon closely into his hand.' Seriche borrowed an angel (10s. coin) from his son-in-law and handed it to Robiant to deliver to Mr. Clarke 'for the good word that he spoke.' Meeting Robiant at Chelmsford about a fortnight later, Peter enquired about the angel, and was told that it had been given to Mr. Clarke. But a week later, by which time Peter learned that Robiant had dealt deceitfully, they met by chance at a butcher's shop in Chelmsford where Robiant had taken money out of his purse. Espying an angel amongst the coins, Peter demanded it, and on being refused he snatched it up. Angered, Robiant would have struck Peter, but was stopped by some bystanders.

---

[1] Emmison, *Tudor Secretary*, 274–6.

The next scene reveals the three men being examined by Lord Rich, who was told this story by Peter. Seriche's deposition is almost identical, but adds that Robiant also advised him to dine with Mr. Clarke and said, 'Give me a ryal (10s. coin) for Mr. Clarke and I warrant you shall find friendship. You shall see what I can do.' Robiant in his examination admitted his having failed to give the 'piece of gold of 10s.' to Mr. Baron Clarke 'to show favour' to Seriche and Joan. There is no record of this case of suspected felony in the file for Lent Assizes 1587, at which Clarke indeed was absent. He attended the preceding and the following Assizes, and it was between these dates that he had been appointed an Exchequer judge. He had recently purchased the manor of Newarks in Good Easter – from Rich. His first appearance as an Essex J.P. was at the Easter Sessions 1582.

Assize judges' salaries were paltry, but they were granted generous daily allowances, those on the Essex circuit being the lowest at £5 14s. *per diem*. Their expenses were largely defrayed by hospitality and by 'presents' of venison, fish, wine and the like from corporations, but no other reference to defendants' gifts has been found by the writer.[1]

In medieval and Tudor England judicial corruption, in contrast to the acceptance of bribes by statesmen, was a rare crime, and the celebrated cases of Lord Chancellor Bacon and Lionel Cranfield, Earl of Middlesex, who lived at Copt Hall near Waltham Abbey, belong to the generation after Robert Clarke. Near the end of our period, in 1601, a Member of the Commons made a violent attack on J.P.s, accusing them among other things of corrupt practices. He went so far as to say that some were known as 'basket justices' from their habit of carrying a basket for the reception of the offerings of those who appeared before them, but he later withdrew some of his charges.[2]

There is only one specific indictment for bribery. Giles Claydon of Bury St. Edmunds gentleman, an informer of the Court of Exchequer, was charged by an Earls Colne shoemaker at the Michaelmas Sessions 1600 with 'divers briberies'. Roger Harlakenden, J.P., took sureties for his appearance from William Sweetinge innholder and Reginald Blande clothier, both of Halstead. The case was adjourned to the following Sessions, when he defaulted. At Easter 1601 Harlakenden put in a memorandum that Claydon had taken bribes from many persons instead of informing against them. He had unwisely written a note (produced to the justice) to an Earls Colne victualler undertaking not to prosecute him. For that Claydon received part of a flitch of bacon : an appropriate Essex present. At the same Sessions the Court decided to start process against Richard Punt of Manningtree linendraper, one of the town's constables,

---

[1] Presents to Assize judges are found in the Maldon Borough chamberlains' accounts (Essex Record Office, D/B 3). Cf. *Somerset Assize Orders, 1629–40*, ed. T. G. Barnes (Som. Rec. Soc., lxv, 1959).
[2] B. Osborne, *Justices of the Peace* (1960), 58.

for offering money to a man to bear false evidence against John Tyffyn, a Wakes Colne gentleman. A further case of subornation, which is the offence of procuring another to give such evidence, was brought in 1596. Richard Stanton of West Ham gentleman accused John Thorowgood of the same, a yeoman of the Queen's chamber, of plotting to persuade a woman to testify against him with the aim of taking away 'Stanton's life and lands'. The woman, however, denied that Thorowgood had actually pressed her to prosecute Stanton, but she did state that he had committed the crime, taking from her by force in Duck Lane (parish not given) a waistcoat and a silk apron and cutting or plucking from her a purse containing gold and silver pieces, as a result of which she caused Thomas Powle, J.P., to apprehend him. The justice, she added, bailed Stanton to appear at the next Sessions. But he failed to attend because Mr. Wetheringe, another yeoman of the Guard, 'willed' her to take the stolen articles back and to 'cease her suit', threatening her with prison until the Sessions if she refused. Fear led her to obey and to accept also a bribe of 20s.

Subornation was a much graver offence than simple perjury, for which four indictments are found. In 1584 three Stebbing men were charged at Quarter Sessions with perjuring themselves in their evidence against another villager in a case of assault which had been tried at the Assizes ; and a Little Hallingbury man in 1574 committed perjury in somewhat similar circumstances. The Chelmsford barber-ballader, in a tight corner, tried to exculpate himself by bringing a counter-charge of perjury (p. 77). By far the most interesting charge is that against Thomas Dennis of Mountnessing and John Weste of Moulsham yeomen for falsely declaring on oath that 'all the boards of one side of the long house at Master Johns and of the end next the lane were down, the space between stud and stud is four feet, and a great ox might easily go between the studs, in at one side and out again at the end, for no boards were upon the long house to hinder the ox.' Four feet was an exceptionally wide interval between the upright timbers of a framed building. The case refers to Master John's Farmhouse (since rebuilt) in Mountnessing, which derives its name from a fourteenth-century owner. Unfortunately there are no further details.

Thomas Bonner of Thundersley perjured himself in 1597 before what was evidently a jury summoned by the county escheator at Chelmsford to 'enquire concerning the lands of which Richard White of Runwell died seized from 4 December, 24 Elizabeth' (1581), that is, the 'inquisition post mortem' held on the death of a tenant of Crown property. His false testimony was to the effect that White 'did buy Grysted Hall in Rochford of Mr. Harrys within a quarter of a year then last past.' According to Morant, William Harrys held this manor, now called Gusted Hall, in 1556 from Lord Rich as part of the royal Honour of Rayleigh.[1] In 1542–46 there seems to have been some doubt whether it then belonged

[1] Morant, *History of Essex*, i, 271.

to Harrys or Sir Thomas Darcy,[1] and little is known about the ownership of this small manor.

Cozening, a word now almost obsolete, meant cheating or defrauding and was used when no more specific term such as extortion was appropriate. Cozening was occasionally resorted to by 'promoters' – persons who prosecuted in the names of the Queen and themselves, in order to obtain part of the fines or penalties imposed on the offender if convicted. This unsavoury species included informers. In 1580 a man was charged not only with abusing a constable but also with 'polling' the Queen's subjects 'under colour of his office of promoting' (a rare mention of the word poll, referring to extortion). In the same year the grand jury presented that 'one Richard Golding useth most about Thaxted the art of a counterfeit promoter, and under that pretence doth cozen men of their money.' A 'procurer of promoters' was one of the charges brought by a J.P. who concluded with three Latin adjectives (p. 142).

'Certain cozenages and misdemeanours by them practised and done' was the vague charge against Richard Wilson innholder and Ralph Graves tailor, both of Stock, brought by a Kent man in 1602; and in 1589 a Coggeshall labourer was indicted for 'subtly and astutely deceiving and defrauding' William White of 7s. in money at Tolleshunt Knights.

A letter dated 1598, written by two Kent men, was read out to the county justices at their Midsummer Sessions. They had been credibly informed that William Clibury, 'terming himself to be of Halstead, gentleman', having by sinister practices deceived many Kent men of money, secretly left the county. Although no sums were mentioned, the amounts embezzled could not have been trifling, as the letter was brought by no less than four men, perhaps the injured parties. The Essex court was asked to aid them in their search for the alleged culprit. The cheat, described as in the letter, was bound over to appear by John Clibury of Milcote (Warws.) gentleman and John Harvey of Halstead clothworker to answer three Kent men (not the letter-writers). The recognizance was taken by the Suffragan Bishop of Colchester as J.P. (John Sterne, vicar of Witham 1587–1607), who was evidently not satisfied with the sureties and committed him to gaol for his 'cozenage' until the Assizes. John was the son of William Clibury, vicar of Halstead (p. 193), who had died in 1590,[2] and William, the defendant, was presumably his brother. Cozening charges, without any details, were also laid in 1597 against Robert Ardley, a clothier of Braintree, and in 1572 a Harwich widow, aged eighty, was cruelly cozened of £12 13s. 4d. by three men who threatened her with arrest and imprisonment by falsely pretending that she had no title to her house.

---

[1] *Feet of Fines for Essex*, iv (Essex Archaeological Society, 1964), 252, 287.
[2] *Trans. Essex Archaeological Society*, vi, 306.

H

7
Arson

By the Act of 23 Henry VIII, c.1 (1531), arson was among the grave felonies for which benefit of clergy could not be claimed, so all convicted arsonists were hanged. As in other centuries harvested grain or hay stored in barns was a main objective of Elizabethans who committed the crime of arson.

There was evidently a feud between Richard Rose and Henry Sylles (Silles, or Celles), a Little Clacton husbandman (or labourer), and Cecily his wife. On 31 August 1581 Sylles stole from Rose's barn grain worth 100 marks (£66 13s. 4d.), but was acquitted. On the following day Cecily and a Thorpe spinster burnt Rose's barn and also a field of grain worth 100 marks : a heavy loss. They were found not guilty. On 31 March following she and her son set fire to Rose's barn full of grain, 'which would have been burnt but for the quickness and diligence of the neighbours.' Again, not guilty. These cases were tried at the Lent and Summer Assizes 1582 respectively. At the former Assizes she had also been charged with bewitching John son of Thomas Death on 4 June 1581 'whereby he died on that day.' On that indictment she was found guilty and remanded. If the indictment and the dates are correct two barns were involved, but this seems unlikely. The fact that both arson charges were dismissed suggests that Rose perhaps had a grudge against the Sylleses whom he maliciously prosecuted, rather than the reverse.

Alleged sorcery led to a fire on 10 March 1584. A barn (worth £30), a stable (£10), a cartload of hay (20s.), a waggon with harness (£3), a saddle with harness (10s.), and many unspecified domestic utensils (£5), all belonging to Edward Burgess, were burnt at Wivenhoe. The defendant was Edmund Mansell who is described as 'of Fingringhoe yeoman *alias* of Feering clerk' (he was certainly not the incumbent of either). According to the indictment, the outbreak was caused by Mansell exercising magic and incantation. The calendar of prisoners has 'Edmund Mansell clerk – a witch.' At the same Assizes he was prosecuted for having used the same arts on Burgesse on 10 September 1581, causing him to languish for six months. The victim was the rector of Wivenhoe (1572–89). As already explained (p. 28), witchcraft charges at Quarter Sessions and Assizes will be considered in the next volume in conjunction with those tried at the Archdeacons' Courts.

In 1590 a Copford labourer burnt Edward Mountjoye's barn with grain and hay in it and was found guilty. The two remaining cases relate to attempted or threatened arson. In May 1601 a Springfield spinster 'would have burned down' a malt-house containing eight bushels of wheat, but she was acquitted. Arson was a crime triable only at the Assizes, but Quarter Sessions in 1587 received a Chancery writ reciting that William Folkes of Rochford yeoman, fearing that Joseph Berrie of Eastwood gentleman and his servant would do him bodily injury and would fire his house, had petitioned for aid. The sheriff was ordered to obtain sureties from both men, and if they refused he was to commit them to gaol.

An unusual case came before the Lent Assizes 1599. Mary the wife of Alexander Mascall of Great Leighs clerk (rector 1588–1619) about 2 a.m. on 16 October 1596 went to the barn of Henry Robinson clerk (rector of Fairstead), taking 'a pan of gunpowder', which she fired with a dag (pistol). The barn and its 24 quarters of corn and 24 sheaves of barley were entirely consumed. Was she demented, or did she wreak vengeance because the rector of the adjoining parish had wrongfully taken tithes from land in Great Leighs? She was convicted and committed to Colchester Castle gaol. Nothing would have been learned of the incident as the files for the three Assizes from Summer 1598 to Summer 1599 are lost, were it not for her escape, as a result of which William Ayers, keeper of the gaol, was indicted at the Lent Assizes 1600. He was found guilty of negligence but not of felony. How Mary Mascall was traced after an interval of at least two years cannot be known; had her indictment been preserved the unfortunate rector of Fairstead would probably have been given as her prosecutor. The calendar of prisoners reveals that two men as well as Mary Mascall 'broke prison': the only detail that can be added to this mysterious affair. Escapes were not uncommon. The calendars of prisoners show that the gaol at this period must have been overcrowded, and another escape is recorded in 1601. Alexander had been unlucky; in 1595 four pieces of gold worth £4 were stolen from him.

County records elsewhere yield nothing about arson for the reason given. Those of Middlesex with its Assize jurisdiction contain only a solitary charge against a Charterhouse Lane man for 'threatening to burn divers houses' in 1601.[1] This scanty evidence points to its having been a rare or rarely detected crime in Elizabethan England.

---

[1] *Middlesex County Records*, i, 274.

8

Riot

Lawyers, juries and judges have always striven, often in face of conflicting evidence, to distinguish between murder, attempted or intended murder, homicide, killing through severe provocation or in self-defence, infanticide, suicide, and death by misadventure. Throughout the ages, too, distinctions between the various ways in which assault is committed have posed problems in the criminal courts. Men's hatred, malice, jealousy, anger, hunger, drunkenness and lust have led them to attack their fellow beings, murderously or otherwise. Common and statute law of course provided many categories of such disorder, but the differentiation was often theoretical or superficial. Long before Elizabeth's time the lawyers had struggled with the niceties, and the records of the Elizabethan Quarter Sessions and Assizes reveal that even the formal indictments often failed to make a distinction between the many kinds of riot and assault or combined into a single indictment two or more offences, with or without assault. It is futile, therefore, to attempt anything in the way of definite analysis.

It is well known that no revolt took place in Essex during our period, but, as we have seen in the chapter on Sedition, outbreaks might well have arisen at two periods (p. 62). Although the records frequently refer to riot, only a few supply evidence of riots in our current non-legal sense. A glance at William Lambarde's *Eirenarcha* (1614) exemplifies the contrast between the hot tempers of menacing malcontents and the cold definitions of learned lawyers. An unlawful assembly, Lambarde wrote, is a company of *three or more persons* 'disorderly coming together, forcibly to commit an unlawful act, as to beat a man or to enter upon his possession', that is, his house or land, 'or such like'. A rout (there he quotes Marrow) is such a disordered assembly, for example, in a dispute about rights of common, whether a crowd of townsmen or villagers, or merely three of them, 'moving forward to commit by force an unlawful act', but dispersing without further trouble. A riot is 'thought to be' where the assembly actually committed trouble. But the last term covers anything from a rebellion to a trio of sourminded rustics trampling down another's grass. The punishment under the statutes was a fine, not imprisonment, but the Acts of 1 Mary, c.12, and 1 Eliz., c.17, dealt with three degrees of riotous and seditious assemblies – three or more persons, twelve or more, and forty or more, with punishments accordingly. If Lambarde's thoughts were not clear, malcontents amid the clamour of voices and hurly-burly certainly gave no thought if they proceeded from unlawful assembly to rout and then riot. Although most of the indictments against groups of such folk include the technical term 'riotously', some, even where their number justifies the term, omit it. A few of the indictments were specifically preferred under the Riot Act of 1411 (13 Henry IV, c.7), which obliged neighbouring justices to respond when aid was sought by going to the scene of a riot in person – in 1591, for example, two J.P.s and the sheriff, in a forcible disseisin case, which cites the ancient statute (p. 124).

What seems to be a case of anti-enclosure violence came before the Privy Council early in 1563, but there is no corroborative evidence in the Sessions or Assize records. Sir Henry Tyrell, Thomas Mildmay and William Ayloff, J.P.s, and Edward Bell gentleman, were instructed by the Council to report on 'a certain disorder in Essex in the breaking up of hedges and pales' by unnamed women and boys.[1]

The long story of enclosures and encroachments in the royal Forest of Waltham, which culminated in the epic struggle leading to the saving of Epping Forest in the 1870s, has an Elizabethan instalment. The Act of 35 Henry VIII, c.17 (1544) for 'the preservation of woods' authorised the lord of a manor to enclose for his own use one-fourth part of any wood or waste land held in common with the tenants of the manor, in consultation with the tenants. Accordingly, Bernard Whetstone, lord of the manor of Woodford, initiated such an enclosure, and James Altham and Thomas Frank, J.P.s, on 22 April 1572, summoned before them the lord and twelve commoners 'living near the waste woods'. But they refused to give their consent to the 'severing, dividing and bounding out' of the fourth part of the woodland, 'although they were thereunto persuaded' (i.e. strongly urged). The J.P.s, however, a week later, 'by men of good skill, measured and bounded out the soil, which they found to be in sundry parcels of wood ground, after 21½ feet to the pole – 246 acres' (the pole was then a measure of length which varied according to the region). The men set out the one-quarter in 'Layghton Grove', 61 acres.

The two justices' award was stoutly disobeyed by the commoners, after Whetstone, anxious to enclose his 61 acres, had begun to employ a large gang. A major riot ensued, which we shall describe shortly. Almost exactly a year later, there was a further disturbance. The result was an inquisition held at Woodford Hall (Whetstone's house) on 7 April 1573 by Henry Denny, James Altham and John Stonard, J.P.s, with a jury. The jurors' report was that, on the preceding 27 March sixteen persons, all of Woodford, 'riotously entered Kingston Wood' (a clerical slip for Knighton Wood), belonging to Whetstone, against the Statute of 5 Richard II

---

[1] *Acts of the Privy Council*, vii, 137; cf. several cases of destruction of hedges in Oxfordshire and Hertfordshire in this volume.

(1381). Of these rioters, Henry Johnson, William Hicks and William Palmer are described as yeomen : all the rest were women, mostly yeomen's wives. The J.P.s then proceeded to deal with a further and bigger disturbance which had taken place on 1 April. This time the jury returned that there had been an affray in the wood upon Whetstone and on John Rigby, John Garbett and Rowland Bowdye yeomen by fifteen of the same persons (Johnson being absent), together with William Dymsdale and his wife of Chigwell and sixty others unnamed.

By good fortune, we learn a lot more about the 'affray' from a letter addressed to 'Sir Thomas Mildmay, Mr. Altham and other Justices' by Whetstone and written at Woodford Hall on 1 April. He stated that he was possessed of Knighton Wood, that he had licence from the Earl of Sussex, justice of the forests, to fell it, and that the fourth part of his woods had been laid out under the Act of 1544, 'as is well known to Mr. Altham and Mr. Frank, who have travelled (travailed) therein.' He had sold his quarter to John Rigby, 'against whom have been committed divers outrageous riots'. (Knowing the hostile attitude of the commoners, Whetstone may have been especially anxious to effect the sale, hoping that he would draw violence away from himself.) One of these riots, if we may believe him, involved no less than 300 men, 'who cast down 400 rods of hedge and ditch and burned 8 or 10 loads of bushes and stakes'. And this riot case, he added, 'was found at the Assizes at Brentwood in Lent twelve months past' (but our luck in having the letter does not extend to the Assize record, which is one of the few lost files). He then went on to mention a further riot on 27 March 'by divers women who beat Rigby's workmen and took from them their axes wherewith they wrought, and yet detain them', which we have already related. Whetstone referred to the incident which had just happened that day (1 April), explaining that Rigby had been 'fully determined to have waited upon their worships at this Quarter Sessions' (it was held on 2 April), 'had not the said women with more in number this afternoon assailed himself and Rigby with those workmen that he had there, to beat them out of the woods, in which fray they have hurt Rigby on the face and on the head very sore, to the great hazard of his life, so as he cannot attend upon their worships as his meaning was.' Escaping from the insurgents' fury, Whetstone hastily penned this missive to the Court, 'humbly desiring their wisdom by the consent of the Bench to appoint Mr. Denny, Mr. Altham and Mr. Stonerd or Mr. Frank to take pains to call a Petty Sessions to enquire and punish these rioters out of hand.' (As we have seen, three were duly appointed.) He concluded : 'I fear greatly there will ensue murder, for they boldly affirm to our faces that they will kill Rigby and myself, although half a score of them should be hanged.' The verdict and punishment are not recorded. Knighton Wood (near the Chingford boundary) was, in fact, the scene and subject of many later anti-enclosure disputes. Bernard

Whetstone was the first of a succession of four Bernards, his father Robert having acquired the manor in 1553. The second, Sir Bernard, was sued by the Attorney-General in the next reign for making illegal fences, and in his defence he enlarged upon his severe losses caused by deer from the forest damaging his crops.[1] In 1670 the inhabitants of Woodford again threw down an enclosure of 80 acres in Knighton Wood, when it was ordered to be destroyed and the illegal encloser was fined £6 13s. 4d.[2] The wood seems to have been partly enclosed later, as it contained only 42 acres in 1781, when there was another and very expensive trespass case.[3] Knighton Wood, 'a rather pathetic island of forest, striving to survive in a sea of genteel suburbs'[4] between Woodford and Buckhurst Hill, was not declared open under the Epping Forest Acts, but was added in 1930.

Disputes occurred in 1566–67 at Salisbury Hall in Walthamstow. Sir William Petre, Secretary of State, in 1557 had obtained for his friend Roger Ascham, who had been tutor to Princess Elizabeth, the reversion of a lease of this manor for forty years to begin in 1564.[5] Peter Copland and Lawrence Dixon yeomen and Peter Uvedall gentleman, all of Chingford, broke into the Salisbury Hall lands belonging to Thomas Rampston, wasting his crops, chasing and ill-treating one of his men and assaulting two more of his servants there. Copland inflicted such a blow that 'the nerve and vein' of one of the men's hands became withered so that Rampston lost his help for a whole month.

Next year William Byllinge waxchandler, John Trowghton shoemaker and Nicholas Fludd pinner, all of London, and nine Walthamstow men including John Turner schoolmaster, armed with divers weapons, broke down the gate and walls of William Casse husbandman at Higham Bensted in that parish, ejected his goods, drove away nine cows and two horses, imparking them at Salisbury Hall, and assaulted and imprisoned Casse in his house for six hours, threatening to mutilate his body. (Each fined 12d.) On the same day Trowghton also assaulted Casse's wife and maidservant there. (Fined 2s. 6d.) These were two early incidents in a long and violent feud between the lords of Higham Bensted and Salisbury Hall manors in Walthamstow, in which Rampston took a leading part. In 1589 he even 'locked up the (manorial) jury in a very narrow room and threatened to keep them fasting there until they gave direct verdict as commanded.'[6] The story will be told when Manor Courts are dealt with in the next volume.

At the Lent Assizes 1567 appears an indictment against John Maynerde, one of the two bailiffs of the borough of Colchester, Benjamin Clere, both

---

[1] Fisher, *Forest of Essex* (1887), 59.
[2] *Ibid.*, 328.   [3] *Ibid.*, 331.
[4] J. A. Brimble, *London's Epping Forest* (1965), 148.
[5] Emmison, *Tudor Secretary*, 259.
[6] Essex Record Office, D/DFc 185.

clothiers, Robert Lambert, alderman, and John Best, merchants, Robert Myddelton woollen-draper, William Ramme and William Bramford, gentlemen, three yeomen and seven mariners, with twenty unknown accomplices. At the instigation of Thomas Lucas esquire, the town clerk, they riotously assembled and struck and ill-treated Henry Morrant on the 'common river called Rowhedge Reach' in the parish of East Donyland and carried off five boats belonging to five (named) men. The judges fined each offender 2s. 6d. Behind this unusual charge lay a violent quarrel between certain fishermen of Rowhedge and Donyland (on the Colne estuary) and the Corporation, which is explained in the Privy Council minutes.[1] Lord Darcy, supporting the former, who dwelt on his estate, had written on their behalf to the Council in February. Their ancient rights in the Colne oyster-beds had been forcibly challenged by the bailiffs of Colchester who had forbidden them to 'use their accustomed trade of trailing (trawling) oysters', and to send their fish to the New Hythe at Colchester. These were new arrangements, but were disobeyed, where-upon seven of their boats were confiscated, which the bailiffs justified under one of the borough charters. The Council ordered the Corporation to return their boats and to restore their rights of trawling and trade until the controversy should be settled, if possible, by the judges at the next Assizes. Hence the indictment. In revenge, they threatened not to bring their fish for sale at the New Hythe at Colchester.

There was trouble in the Belchamps and Foxearth in 1567–70. In 1567 six men of Long Melford (Suffolk) and three of Foxearth, armed with pitchforks and pikestaves, broke the bars, locks and chains of a field-gate there. (All fined 12d. by two J.P.s.) Next year six men of Belchamp Walter and Otten assaulted the wife and sons of Henry Wayte, upsetting his cart laden with corn-sheaves and damaging them to the value of 20s. (Each fined 20s.) It flared up again in 1570. On 4 April four men of Long Melford and Sudbury and thirteen men and women of Foxearth broke into part of the land called Snokeshill and Horsemarsh containing 300 acres in Foxearth, owned by the Earl of Oxford, taking away growing trees worth 40s., and assaulting Henry Kent and Ann Kent working there. (Each fined 6d.) Nearly all the Foxearth folk were named Lowe and in-cluded two in the previous case. On 27 April one of the Foxearth labourers assaulted Barbara Kent at Belchamp Walter, wounding her with his dagger. (Fined 12d.) On 23 June eight yeomen and husbandmen of Belchamp Walter, Borley and Foxearth, including Henry Kent, and twelve others unnamed, entered the meadow of John Mayor (one of the Sudbury men) at Belchamp Walter, taking away two cartloads of grass worth 26s. 8d.; two of them with two more assaulted Mayor with a forest bill at Belchamp Otten; and four of them with two Bulmer men broke down 30 perches of hedge in Snokeshill, carrying off certain trees

[1] *Acts of the Privy Council*, vii, 331–5; G. Martin, *Story of Colchester* (1959), 36, 70.

(£3), and assaulting his wife in the field. (Each fined 6d.) On 16 July the same two Bulmer yeomen damaged the wheat (valued at as much as £20) in the field of John Low of Belchamp Otten at Belchamp Walter called Bevingtons; 'rescued' ten horses of theirs from the field, distrained by Low; and one of the Foxearth men rescued forty sheep of his from another of Low's fields called Eison Field, likewise distrained by Low. On 11 August seven Lows of Belchamp and Foxearth, including John, and five Long Melford men, assaulted Charles Kent in his field at Foxearth, trampling down the grass. (No verdict.) For appearance at the Sessions two of the Lows had been bound, with John Worroll of Belchamp Walter gentleman as surety for John, as also for keeping the peace towards John Kent and his servants. Clearly, all these disturbances reflect one or more family feuds such as are disclosed in other pages.

One December evening in 1574 ten Rayleigh men including Henry Bode gentleman with twenty malefactors unknown broke into the inn of Thomas Lorkyn there called the 'Bull' and assaulted two men asleep in their beds. The incident took place between 7 and 9 p.m. and this may be one of those rare records which reveal that Elizabethan travellers retired to bed very early in the winter.

In August 1576 the Privy Council considered trouble caused by 'certain lewd persons to move some rebellion' in Essex 'and in parts thereabouts'. John Newton and Matthew Petloe of Colchester were suspected to be the 'chief doers', and the matter was referred to Sir Thomas Lucas, Sir William Waldegrave, Henry Golding and Rowland Hyegate (his usual name is Reginald, and they were all Essex J.P.s). They were required to 'sift the same to the bottom and to cause all persons touched to be apprehended and examined' very thoroughly. Hyegate had been commended a little earlier for 'his diligence and discretion in meeting with such evil disposed persons'. The men refused to confess and were sent to the Tower, whence they were released in the following June.[1] We seem to be left with the tantalizingly uninformative Council minutes unless a meagre reference to the arrest of four men at Aldham (near Colchester) in 1577 'for suspicion of a rebellion' is linked with it; but Newton and Petloe are not among these four, and nothing else is to be found about them. (See Sedition p. 46.)

A riotous assault, which had taken place at West Donyland (Berechurch, two miles south of Colchester) in April 1576 also seems to be unconnected with the 'rebellion'. The attack was made on Richard Southwell esquire by John Chrystmas gentleman, John Wykes alias Wygges, both of St. Giles, Colchester, Edward Green of St. Runwald and Nicholas Brown of St. Botolph, all yeomen, with thirty unnamed persons. The only extra fact vouchsafed is that Chrystmas held a caliver 'and would have shot him'. The charge against the riotous gang, headed by Chrystmas, came to

[1] Acts of the Privy Council, ix, 182, 187–8, 263, 373.

Quarter Sessions from the sheriff's tourn (his half-yearly circuit in which
he presided at each hundred-court) held for the hundred of Lexden on
29 September 1576. The leader re-appears in another riot some years
later. The case illustrates the rudimentary police system. In June 1583
Robert Stowe of Colchester during an assault in the east ward struck John
Eve on the head with his sword, wounding him in the skull and brains so
that he was paralysed. The assailant fled. A hue and cry was raised at
once and he was captured by the constables. But John Norton, Richard
Alcock, both gentlemen, and John Prestman and Edward Newman
yeomen, riotously assaulted the constables and rescued Stowe, who in
escaping shouted extremely threatening words to them and the 'faithful'
bystanders. (True bill for all except Newman.) On the same day George
Christmas of Stanway, John Christmas and Goldringramford Christmas
gentlemen, Peter Tewke esquire, and James Barwicke weaver, all the
rest of St. James, Colchester, with seven others unnamed, assaulted and
beat Alcock; and Prestman also made an affray in the same ward on
John Christmas. The quarrel was resumed at Dedham in September when
John Christmas and George Darrell of Colchester esquire were accused of
assault and battery on Newman.

Wistan Browne, the sheriff, who lived at Weald Hall in South Weald,
and Henry Graye of Pyrgo in Havering and James Morice of Chipping
Ongar, justices, summoned on 5 August 1577 under the Act of Henry IV
to Brentwood chapel, witnessed an extraordinary commotion. Crowding
into the chapel and the 'steeple' (tower) and around the chapelyard were
thirty 'spinsters' (used in the legal sense of women, married as well as
unmarried), all of whom are named. They had pulled Richard Brooke
schoolmaster (of Brentwood grammar school) out of the chapel and beaten
him; they had obstructed the chapel doors, locking themselves in; and
they resisted arrest by Wistan Browne's servants and others, brandishing
their weapons, to wit, pitchforks, bills, a piked staff, two hot spits and hot
water in two kettles (which must have been prepared in advance and
rushed in from a nearby house!), three bows and nine arrows, a hatchet,
a great hammer, and a great sharp stone. They were eventually all
arrested by the sheriff and the two justices, but it is not surprising that
seventeen of them managed to escape so that they could not be committed
to gaol. John Mynto of Brentwood yeoman, being commanded by
Morice to help in suppressing the riot, refused; and Henry Dalley also
of Brentwood labourer attempted to rescue their leader, Thomasine Tyler,
widow of the owner of the 'Swan' and 'Bell' inns.[1]

This was the third occasion in the annals of Brentwood when its chapel
was the scene of an unusual incident. The extensive parish of South Weald
contained three main manors. One of them, Costed, included within its
bounds the hamlet of Brentwood. This manor belonged to St. Osyth's

[1] Gladys Ward, *History of South Weald and Brentwood* (1961), 19–20.

abbey, which founded a chapel about 1221 for the use of its tenants. In 1232 Hubert de Burgh, Henry III's chief minister, fell out of the royal favour. He fled from the court. One night, passing through Essex, he was warned of imminent arrest and ran naked to the nearby chapel of Brentwood, claiming sanctuary. He was sent to the Tower, but after an outcry about the abuse of sanctuary he was returned, only to surrender, half-starved.[1] A very different arrest took place in the chapel in 1554 : that of young William Hunter, to be examined by Anthony Browne of Weald Hall after a dispute about religious beliefs with the vicar of South Weald. His courage in refusing to recant led to his being burnt at the stake near the school in the following year.

It was Anthony's great-nephew and successor, Wistan, whose action led to riot in 1577. He decided not to pay the chaplain's stipend nor to allow the inhabitants to use the chapel. Three days after his removal of the pews, the cost of which the inhabitants had recently borne, the Brentwood women took the matter into their hands, as related. The affair reached the Privy Council two days later (7 August). Browne was summoned to appear before them on the following Sunday and forbidden to pull down the chapel ; the women were to be released from gaol under bail. Shrewdly the councillors gave their opinion that he was 'the chiefest cause' of the riot, and the justices at the next Quarter Sessions were not to deal with the amazons severely but to lay some small fine on them 'only for form's sake', and then acquit them.[2] The Court at its Michaelmas Sessions fined the women 4d. each, the two men 2s. each. The record is signed by the defeated sheriff, the two J.P.s, and eleven others. Dalley was up at the next Lent Assizes, charged as a butcher with stealing several sheep from a field in Childerditch belonging to William Hollingsworth of Stondon Massey esquire. But that was not the end of the controversy between the inhabitants and Browne about the use of the chapel. It was again before the Council in January 1578, when they appointed learned lawyers to adjudge the dispute.[3]

There were disturbances at Rivenhall in the winter of 1582-3. On Christmas Eve Ralph Wiseman esquire, four yeomen, four husbandmen and two labourers, all of Rivenhall, with others unknown, riotously assaulted Thomas Burnett of Cressing yeoman and four other men there, and took away three cartloads of timber worth 24s. belonging to John Watson gentleman, also of Rivenhall, and Burnett. (The first-named offender is probably the second son of John Wiseman of Wimbish ; he was to buy the manor of Rivenhall in 1590 and to be knighted in 1603.) More violence occurred on 8 March. Four of Wiseman's servants, two being among the earlier assailants, and others, made affray upon Watson's and Burnett's servants, who were ordered by their masters to make

[1] Ward, op. cit. (1961), 10–11.
[2] Acts of the Privy Council, x, 12, 16, 34.   [3] Ibid., x, 141.

formal complaint to two justices, Francis Harvey and Anthony Maxey. The assault took place in Grove Land on a 'chaseway' for carriage of timber. (In Essex this is the usual meaning of 'chase' – a private right of way or access way over another's land : not unnaturally, therefore, a common cause of disputes.) The two justices went at once to the riotous scene, finding eight or more people there. The same four had long piked staves and daggers, and one had a weapon 'not usually to be borne in our country', viz., an eleven-foot staff, piked at both ends. They arrested the four servants and assessed their fines at 12d. each.

The Burnham horns affair must have enlivened the town in the dull mid-Winter days of 1584. To adorn the outer doors with horns was an ancient method of telling the goodman of the house that he had been cuckolded. For the details we are indebted to that active magistrate, Arthur Herrys of Creeksea Place, for his full account. Jeremy Haven, a tailor of Southminster, and William Ward of Bradwell first related their stories. A month before Shrovetide, Haven and 'his fellow, a minstrel', were in bed. In the same chamber lay Robert Gybbyns, a tailor of Bradwell, who told him of his plan to hang a pair of horns at Kempe's door and another at Knyfe's door in Burnham. Apparently Gybbyns and Kempe had been 'brabbling by the ears' (quarrelling hotly) at Bradwell on the previous Sunday. According to Ward Haven told Gybbyns last Candlemas that he was very sorry to hear about the brawls between the two men. Gybbyns' threatening comment was to the effect that he would deal with Kempe or his brother at the first opportunity. Next month the J.P. examined Agnes Moore and Philpott's wife, both of Burnham. The former said that on St. Matthew's Day, the day on which the horns were hanged up, she chanced to meet Philpott's wife of Burnham in the street, who told her that the defendant's brother, Gybbyns, had carried out his threat at her master's door. Agnes added that about a month before Shrovetide Gybbyns had used 'very great railing speeches and evil words' against her 'dame' (mistress) and said that he would shortly set up a pair of horns upon the sign of Kempe's, her master's, house. The other woman told the J.P. that she had gone to Southminster on St. Matthew's Day about an hour before dawn, when she saw five men unknown to her coming from Burnham with long staves on their shoulders. Herrys then prepared his own version. On the night of 23–24 February five or six 'disordered' men raised a pair of horns on Kempe's and Knyfe's doors. The noisy laughter awakened the neighbours, who in the morning saw the 'ensigns'. Herrys, of course, does not mention the townsmen who jeered. This 'lewd and riotous' act, he wrote, caused great offence among them, especially between the cuckolded men and their wives. The J.P. had no doubt that Gybbyns was the chief culprit.

A dispute about some property at Chingford led to angry scenes in May 1585. The land belonged to Sir John Branche, who had leased it to William

Uvedall, but forcible trespass was made by Robert Lee *alias* Lygh gentle-man, Richard Preston yeoman, and three others, all of Chingford, with six more unknown, who proceeded to break up and overturn a boar's pen called 'a boar's-frank'[1] and then wounded Henry Uvedall gentleman with their naked swords. Pursued by the five men, he fled eight rods down the lane towards William's home called Fridays Hill House, getting there just in time to close the doors after him. Frustrated and furious, they beset it on all sides and 'vehemently bounced and knocked' on the doors, trying to break in, to the inmates' terror. The indictment also charged two local labourers with illegally cutting down and removing two maple trees on the same ground. A jury of fourteen men, headed by Thomas Rampston (see p. 103), lord of another Chingford manor, was summoned to enquire into the case before Robert Wrothe, Thomas Colshill, Henry Archer and William Heigham, neighbouring justices, but their findings are not given.

A riotous affair at Finchingfield about New Year's Day 1585, alleged to have involved over fifty people, looks as though it was a village feud of long standing, because it was referred to by Thomas Gent, J.P., of Moyns Park, Steeple Bumpstead, eight months later as 'the old quarrel', in a letter addressed to Quarter Sessions, to be related shortly. John Kempe gentleman, John Warner miller, three yeomen, William Bincks (the seditious tailor, p. 47), two Stebbings, and three husbandmen, all of Finchingfield, together with thirty persons unknown, were indicted for making an assault and affray on William Pasfield of Finchingfield and John Stebbinge of Stambourne yeomen. It took place as they returned to Pasfield's house after morning prayers in Finchingfield church. Nicholas Broade, one of the gang, was also charged with receiving and helping Kempe and the other defendants in his alehouse, knowing that they had intended to attack Pasfield and Stebbinge. Recognizances were taken by John Wentworth, J.P., from Kempe and the three yeomen, Broade, Bincks and two others for keeping the peace towards Pasfield and Stebbinge, the sureties being Kempe, Nicholas Stebbinge and Alexander Baley smith, also of Finchingfield.

Thomas Gent's letter, dated 29 September 1585, explained that the constables of Halstead (and eslewhere) having been enjoined to warn 'such idle and masterless men as might be spared' to attend the first (militia) musters to be viewed and impressed as soldiers, ordered Thomas Keape, who had lived idly and disorderly in the town for seven or eight weeks, to attend before two justices. His reaction was not exactly favourable. He 'very rudely and disorderly railed on the constables with opprobrious words, threatening to beat them.' The constables had complained to the writer. Keape not only maintained his stubborn behaviour towards the constables, but when summoned before the justices 'very proudly and disorderly behaved himself.' Bound over, he 'procured a young gentleman under

1 The earliest mention 'in olden times' in *N.E.D.* is 1880!

whom he protects himself (though in truth no daily attendant) to come down to Halstead to have beaten the constable.' He left the justices, 'proudly vaunting himself to have the favour of this Court, and being in my hall amongst my men uttered that his master did come down purposely to have beaten the constable if he durst have shown himself.' The examination was conducted by Gent jointly with his neighbour from Tilbury-juxta-Clare, Israel Amyce, and they bound the defendant over to the Sessions with John Keape and John Wignall, both of Sible Hedingham yeomen.

That Keape failed to reform is apparent, because in 1587 he was up again at Quarter Sessions, indicted for having been continually for the past two years a common barrator and disturber of the peace and having many time 'stirred up strifes' against the constables and watch of Halstead and put them in terror of their lives. And his recognizance to appear (his father and Thomas Bentall clothier, both of Halstead, being his sureties) discloses that he had broken the peace also against Edward Smythe tailor and Isaac Medcalfe glover of the same town. Apart from the fact that he and his father were both tailors, nothing else can be ascertained about him or his alleged 'protector'.

But Thomas Gent had not finished his letter to the Court. 'There is also one Charles Hopkyn', he added, 'one of Mr. Kempe's men, sent by warrant before you for the peace, being demanded against him by two men that he had abused.' The justice explained that Hopkyn had offered 'very mean sureties, whereof one was neither a landed man nor assessed in subsidy' (the contemporary tax), 'and besides a poor man', and that 'many men so far as they durst found themselves aggrieved' because he was a quarrelsome man, and they sought better sureties. So such insecure bail was refused, whereon Hopkyn very scornfully charged the J.P. with injustice and contemptuously refused to give his name for an arrest warrant, telling the justice to find out, until he had been committed to the constable. 'I found him very stubborn and arrogant'. The affair was too tedious to report in full, he concluded, 'and I perceive the old quarrel by Mr. Kempe's men against Pasfield and Stebbinge is not yet quenched, but this man being a newcome quarreller doth renew the grudge, and so if there be not good care taken there will grow another outrage, and in that his disorder was before me I thought it good to commit to your consideration rather than proceed against him myself.' (Another echo of Stebbinge's misdeeds was apparently heard in 1592, p. 146.)

The county justices must have found their 'considerations' problematical because another squire had also sent them a letter. They had to weigh the matter therefore between Thomas Gent, who was not merely one of their number but also a Baron of the Court of Exchequer, and the other writer, Robert Kempe of Spains Hall, Finchingfield, who, incidentally, had married Elizabeth, daughter of Clement Higham, Chief Baron of the

Exchequer, and was the father of William, renowned in Essex annals for his seven-year vow of silence after unjustly accusing his wife of infidelity. Robert Kempe himself had been a county justice until 1571. Addressing them as 'The Right Worshipful his very friends and good masters, the Queen's Highness' Justices', Kempe asserted that the complaints against Charles Hopkyn his warrener were altogether untrue, 'if it shall please you to give me credit.' He was not aware of the cause that had led 'Mr. Baron Gent' to bind Hopkyn over to the next Sessions. He begged the Court 'to be favourable to the poor man', for he had great need of his service. His warrener had never struck anyone since coming into his employment except those he had taken for killing his conies, which 'are a great part of my living, my wife being departed this world, and if they may not be defended by my warrener it will prove to my great hindrance' : an interesting comment on the pecuniary value of a rabbit warren. Stoutly supporting his servant, he added, 'What my man's demeanour was before Mr. Gent I do not know, but I trust your worships will bear with a man of stomach, albeit he spoke more than needeth when that without cause he is reviled with divers unseemly crimes. I am sorry to say it that Mr. Baron Gent is my heavy master without desert, as I take God to record, but I may without offence to any crave at your hands for my poor servant favourable justice.'

The lord of the manor of Spains Hall added a postscript. 'If I may be so bold under reformation to inform your worships, before this time the parish of Finchingfield never had but two constables until now of late that Mr. Serjeant (William) Bendlowes would have three constables, more of will than for any other just cause, and in truth the parish hath been in more trouble since than before.' Mr. Maxey and Mr. Hubbard (J.P.s) had ordered, he explained, that all the old constables should be removed and others put in, and the two new constables were sworn, but one of the three remained by what warrant he was not aware, and he therefore asked the Court to discharge the old constable, who was present at the Sessions. His name was W. Flackey. 'You shall do the parish' – his parting shot – 'a good turn and the Queen's Highness better service, for he is a troublous man *et id verum est*.' Another document, unconnected with the dispute, records that Hopkyn served as one of the Finchingfield constables in 1585.

Eight more attacks by rowdy groups, all technically classed as riots, but probably no more than violent local quarrels, occurred near the end of our period. John Smith of Belchamp St. Paul's gentleman and six others of the neighbourhood assaulted another John Smith in St. Paul's parish on two harvest days in 1586, carrying off a cartload of barley worth £3. Four weavers, two cutlers, a tailor, a shoemaker and a glazier of Thaxted, two cutlers and a tailor of Henham, and a labourer of Manuden were bound by their own recognizances and those of two more Thaxted cutlers to answer at Michaelmas Sessions 1587 in connection with a riot at Clavering.

No details are vouchsafed apart from the fact that a jury of twenty-four men had been summoned to meet at Stansted Mountfitchet, that it included assault on a Clavering man, and that a true bill was found for four of the gang. A riotous dispute between rival clergy occurred at Burnham in 1589. Peter Lewes and Thomas Stempe, the vicar and curate respectively, a labourer and a mariner, entered the house of Richard Allyson, M.A., clerk, with staves, daggers, pitchforks and bills, and beat him and Mary and Rhoda Allyson. Was Allyson an unbeneficed lecturer? Christopher Chibborne bound them to keep the peace towards Allyson, but Arthur Herris a week earlier had bound Allyson likewise towards the labourer, so there was evidently guilt on both sides. The case against those who assaulted the Allysons was transferred to the Assizes. Lewes was a troublesome fellow, having been indicted for barratry a little earlier (p. 144). In 1590 nine men broke into the barn of Matthew Grey gentleman, all apparently of Little Wenden, and assaulted him (all fined 6s. 8d. or 3s. 4d.). Two years afterwards a nasty skirmish took place at Wix. The assailants were William Veisey gentleman, a weaver, a cooper (probably the weaver's son), a sawyer and a labourer, all of Wix, and a labourer of Bradfield, who beat Michael Rolfe. The cooper cut through the hamstrings of his left thigh with a sword thrust, maiming and crippling him. One of the Wix constables appeared on the scene, and Veisey and the sawyer assaulted him, the former striking him with his dag (pistol). Within the next year the weaver was also charged as a common barrator and Veisey was presented to the Archdeacon's court for abusing the churchyard with his cattle.[1]

The timbers for building a framed house at Pentlow were ready to be used in midsummer 1590, but four men of Cavendish, the adjacent parish in Suffolk, threw them into the Stour. The men were armed and wore the private livery of an unnamed magnate. The frustrated owner was Ralph Cavendish gentleman, doubtless a descendant of the Suffolk family that had possessed Pentlow Hall in the fourteenth century.

In July 1593 fifteen named Coggeshall folk (twelve husbandmen and three spinsters) and twenty unnamed rioters, 'with great malice and fury', assaulted Samuel London and others unnamed, exercising their lawful business there. All confessed and submitted to be fined, but the fines are not given. On the following day a yeoman and three husbandmen of Bishop's Stortford (Herts.), with other rioters, assembled at Thremnall Green in the parish of Hatfield Broad Oak, to the great terror of the people. Neither plea nor verdict is stated.[2]

The yard of the delightful and small early 16th century manor-house of Little Warley, close to which the busy Southend arterial road now runs (see p. 126), was broken into in 1596 by an armed party led by Thomas

---

[1] *Essex Review,* xlviii, 188.

[2] D. Shorrocks, 'Hatfield Forest 1547–1857 : A Story of Conflict' (*Essex Review,* lxiv, 57).

Fines *alias* Clinton of London esquire with seven Westminster watermen and others unknown. The indictment records that Little Warley Hall was then in the occupation of Fabian Philips and Richard Broughton. In 1597 three men were wounded in an armed attack by two men and their wives and eight more wives. The husbands of all these women were Witham labourers. Some pleaded guilty, but no more can be learned of this affair.

The Old Lock near Waltham Abbey was the scene of two separate incidents of a different nature in 1592. Sixteen named bargemen, one of London, all the rest of Ware (Herts.), with thirty others unnamed, riotously broke the bank of the mill-race at Sir Edward Dennye's mill, diverted the stream and severely beat his servants when they came and ordered the gang to desist. The inquisition was conducted before Robert Wrothe, Barnard Whetstone and Robert Leigh, Essex justices, who fined the Londoner £5, one man £3 6s. 8d., three 40s. each, and the rest 10s. each, heavy fines which are a criterion of the grave view taken by the justices. On 18 December ten men of Ware (only one of whom was also among the July rioters) and one of Stratford Bow (Middlesex), with thirty others, were indicted in almost identical language. No fines are recorded. These documents in fact chronicle only a small part of a lengthy controversy about Waltham Lock.[1]

Throughout the centuries parochial and manorial boundaries were the subject of much discord. Our records reveal three riotous affairs. At Rogationtide, the three days before Ascension Day, parish boundaries were perambulated. Beating the bounds was a religious obligation, and, as we shall see in the next volume, churchwardens were not infrequently presented at the Archdeacons' courts for failure to make the annual 'processioning'. Disputes about doubtful stretches between adjacent parishes had to be settled as most land was liable to tithes and rateable to church repairs. Common land on boundaries was of course a fruitful source of inter-parochial quarrels. The county records reveal two incidents of this nature. In 1578 Christopher Pecocke clerk (presumably the curate, as Edmund Bicknoll succeeded in 1579 on the death of Thomas Forster), David Sympson and Thomas Churche gentlemen (perhaps the church-wardens), Richard Clarke constable, together with other Runwell parishioners unnamed, going around the bounds and proceeding from a close called Reden up to part of Rettendon Common hitherto accepted as within Runwell, were riotously assaulted there by eleven named and fourteen unknown parishioners of Rettendon, wishing to hinder the pro-cession, who 'beat them so that they despaired of their lives' (doubtless exaggerated legal language).

¹ Cf. *Acts of the Privy Council*, xxii, 537, 553; Dr K. N. Bascombe of Waltham Abbey kindly drew my attention to other records, too long to quote.

I

A clash, apparently over rights of common, took place in 1580 at Stock Common and at 'Pressons Common', presumably near Great and Little Prestons, in South Hanningfield. Whether the quarrel was between the lords of the manors supported by their tenants or between the rival villagers is not clear. John Pascall, who described himself as of the Middle Temple (but lived at Great Baddow and was also lord of the manor of South Hanningfield), was indicted with Benedict Strutt of the latter parish, yeoman, and nine husbandmen and labourers of Stock, Ramsden Bellhouse and Buttsbury, with others unnamed, for an armed assembly on part of Stock Common in the parish of South Hanningfield. They riotously assaulted a male servant of Edward Atslowe, doctor of physic, and 'divers other tenants' of Edward Earl of Oxford, the common being in his manor of Downham Hall. (Incidentally, Pascall and Atslowe were both to be often indicted in the years to come as Catholic recusants.) Likewise the servant and twenty-one yeomen, husbandmen and labourers of Downham and three others of Ramsden Bellhouse and Wickford, with thirty others unknown, were charged with armed assembly at Prestons Common in Hanningfield and for assaulting Paschall and most of those in the first indictment, the common being that of Francis Burie in right of his wife Ann. The Court treated the whole affair lightly, fining all except two in each group 6d. each.

A third inter-parish dispute had come before the Privy Council in 1564, but has no counterpart in the Sessions or Assize records. The quarrel had arisen about Ongar Park in the previous Rogation Week, as a result of which three men of Greenstead and Stanford Rivers had been accused by Thomas Cole, Archdeacon of Essex, in his capacity as rector of High Ongar (1559–71). No details are vouchsafed, but the matter could not have been a trifling one, as the Council requested the Bishop to convene a meeting with the Attorney-General and other lay members of the Court of High Commission for Ecclesiastical Causes in order to examine the defendants and to report their findings urgently. Ongar Park was a detached part of High Ongar parish and not unnaturally therefore a focal point of parochial rivalries.[1]

Such were some of the acts of riotous disorder in Elizabethan Essex. Other riots are described in the sections on Sedition, Burglary, Assaults on Officers, Disseisin, Trespass and Church Assaults.

The law regarded as a riot any assembly of three or more persons who committed assault or the like, so there still remain a few more cases which fall in this category. The indictment of 1575 of Edward Grevell gentleman (he lived at Harold's Park), Thomas Badger and John Postans *alias* Little John yeomen, all of Waltham Abbey, was for 'riotous assembly' at Stapleford Abbots in which they beat William Cooke esquire and Thomas Maddoxe his servant, as a result of which Cooke lost the services

---

[1] *Acts of the Privy Council*, i, 145.

of his man during a month's convalescence. To call this riot seems a legal nicety, and one would be inclined to dismiss it as a minor quarrel. But the record happens to give the punishment, which shows that the evidence before the Court must have revealed an aggravated assault, for Grevell was fined £20 and the others £5 each.

It is curious how the justices seem to have alternated between trifling and heavy sums in riot charges. William Clibury of Halstead, woollen-draper or gentleman was fined £5 for a riot in 1602 in company with six others and sentenced to prison in default of finding sureties for appearance before the Queen's Bench. Three armed men in 1602 broke into the close of George Skingle, a Witham yeoman, at Faulkbourne between 9 and 10 p.m. and assaulted his servant and three other men. Two were fined £5 each, a third £3 6s. 8d.

In complete contrast was the fine of 2s. each imposed on several men who broke down a wall to the damage of £20 ; on this occasion it was evidently deemed only one of trespass (p. 136). Fines of 2s. 6d. had also been awarded in 1563 to Peter Wentworth esquire, Paul Wentworth gentleman, and two yeomen, all of Lillingstone Lovell (Oxfordshire), a North Shoebury mariner and an Epping yeoman, who with others unknown had 'riotously made silent affray' on Henry Baker of Canewdon and two boys in the coastal marshlands called Grapnelles, Garden and Aye Marshes in Paglesham and Little Wakering. They were also ordered to pay 27s. legal costs. The Wentworths were brothers, both of whom were afterwards to become the well-known parliamentary leaders in opposition to the Queen, who put Peter in the Tower in 1576 for his offensive conduct in the Commons. Henry Wentworth of Codham Hall in Wethersfield, who died in 1482, had acquired the manor of North Shoebury through his second wife, and their son, Sir Nicholas, was the founder of the Oxfordshire branch of the Wentworth family.[1]

Parallel evidence from other counties regarding the incidence of riots cannot readily be assessed because the editors of the printed calendars, like the present writer, have been foiled in their attempts to differentiate between riot, sedition, forcible entry, disseisin, assault, trespass, and even unlawful games. The lawyers' use of 'riotously' where three or more persons were involved adds to the confusion. Only by using the indices and reading every entry under these headings can serious riots be weeded out from the chaff of petty assaults. Even so, the surviving (mostly late Elizabethan) records of other counties seem to disclose few cases of a grave nature, and virtually nothing similar to the charges of seditious speech tending to insurrection (p. 62) ; nor are there any depositions, in which the Essex records are so rich. The county records of the Catholic North all begin too late to add to our knowledge of the revolt of 1569.

[1] *Trans. Essex Archaeological Society*, iii, 209.

These aspects of Elizabethan Disorder are illustrated in the *Acts of the Privy Council*, and many of the more violent riots are recorded only in the archives of the Court of Star Chamber, which, however, are unpublished and are not catalogued in detail.[1] But published calendars of Sessions records reveal some sidelights, for example, a reference to the unruly Shrove Tuesday assemblies associated with riotous games of football.[2] A more serious riot took place in 1576. The pale of Sir Thomas Gresham's deer-park at Osterley (Middlesex) was thrown down and burnt about 2 a.m. on 7 May, when the Queen and the court were in residence in the mansion. The editor of the calendar (1886) was not able to consult the printed volume of the Council's minutes (1894), which reveal their apparently genuine concern about the inhabitants' complaint against Gresham for having enclosed certain common land into his park, but the outcome is not recorded.[3]

[1] For Star Chamber Proceedings, 1485–1558, see *Lists and Indexes*, vol. xiii (List and Index Society, 1968).
[2] *Middlesex County Records*, i, 278.
[3] *Ibid.*, 99; *Acts of the Privy Council*, ix, 160, 167.

9

Disseisin

Most of England enjoyed the relative quiet brought by the early Tudor kings after the lawlessness of the Wars of the Roses. Few manor-houses were then built with defensive walls or turrets. The mid-sixteenth century Gosfield Hall must be one of the last Essex houses intended to put up a defence if need be, as one long windowless outer wall clearly indicates. Ingatestone Hall, built by Dr. William Petre about 1540–45, is partly crenellated, but its parapet battlements were probably ornamental rather than defensive.

The firm governments of Henry VII and Henry VIII were however succeeded under the boy king by an insurrection in the south-west because of religious and economic discontent and by bitter rivalry between the court parties. These in turn were followed under Mary by bitter religious strife and another revolt in Kent and London, which led Sir William Petre alone to muster at least 142 footmen from his Essex estate.[1]

'The Englishman's home is his castle' is said to have originated with 'My house is to me like my castle,' in Sir William Stanford's legal textbook *Les Plees del Coron* (1567). It is interesting to find that Michael Dalton, in his text-book, *The Country Justice* (1618), has two long sections on Forcible Entry and Disseisin in which he writes 'Everyman's house was his Castle.' To what extent was the tenure of his home weakened by the middle of the sixteenth century after the unrest and unruliness of Edward's and Mary's reigns? As Essex possesses numerous and almost complete Quarter Sessions indictments, there is valuable evidence, and the reader may judge for himself how safe and secure Essex homes were. The Sessions rolls are extant from 1555, the year after Wyatt's Rebellion. We are now able therefore to draw upon a rich corpus of material. At least two of the manor houses involved in the incidents to be described are still surviving.

Disseisin, or the unlawful dispossessing of a man's house or lands, was regarded as a serious offence at least as far back as Magna Carta, but in Tudor times the operative statutes were 15 Richard II, c.2 (1391) and 8 Henry VI, c.9 (1429), especially the latter. One or both are cited in some of the indictments. The law provided the victim with the right, on complaint to a neighbouring justice of the peace, to require him without delay to go to the property forcibly held. On arrival, sometimes accompanied by the parish constables, the justice was to restore possession to the

[1] Emmison, *Tudor Secretary*, 170–1.

plaintiff. If this was withheld, it was the justice's duty to arrest the disseisor, to arrange for his removal to gaol, and to take away any weapons used in the forcible detainer, valuing them as property forfeited to the Crown. If however resistance was offered, the justice could not restore possession, but a jury of twenty-four men was to be summoned to enquire into the circumstances. His final duty was to send a record of personal view of the disseisin to the clerk of the peace. The fine was sometimes fixed by Quarter Sessions, but was more often assessed by the justice apprehending the disseisor, and on payment or on his finding sureties by recognizance to appear at Court he was to be released to await trial. Occasionally two, and in one case three, justices went to the scene.

A less common offence was forcible entry without actual expulsion, often termed entry 'by strong hand'. If either offence was committed by three or more persons, it became technically a riot (pp. 100–114). Weapons used by the culprits were often stated; in some cases they were general 'omnibus' phrases, in others clearly specific.

The Marian indictments (in the Sessions rolls) include no less than eighteen cases of unlawful dispossession. The earliest roll records, behind the screen of legal phrases, a violent dispute about the ownership of the manors of Great Stambridge (Hall) and Colemans in Prittlewell (the latter is not mentioned by Morant in his *History of Essex*). On 9 December 1555 William Poley of Great Stambridge, variously described as esquire or gentleman, with two Eastwood yeomen, forcibly entered and expelled Thomas Shaa of Terling gentleman from the manor of Colemans. The affair warmed up six months later. On 3 July 1556, Shaa, with Thomas Gymlet *alias* Barbar gentleman and Clement Gymlet yeoman, both Terling men, John Coke of Rayleigh gentleman, three yeomen, three labourers, a bricklayer and a painter, all of Prittlewell, and a Rayleigh labourer, turned out Poolye and Alice his wife from Colemans. (The Court gave him an order for restitution.) Not to be defeated, Poley ten days afterwards, with seven yeomen and labourers of Eastwood, Prittlewell and Stambridge, expelled Shaa. In the previous month, on 20 June, Poley with a yeoman and a spinster of his parish had evicted Shaa from Great Stambridge Hall (restitution given); but on the same 3 July, accompanied by the Gymlets and Coke, also four labourers, two weavers and a spinster, all of Rayleigh, Shaa turned the tables on Poley, regaining possession. The clue to this dispute is that Alice Poley was the four-year-old daughter and heir of Edmund Shaa when he died in 1532. Thomas Shaa sold the manor in 1579.[1]

The manor house of 'Cabornes' in Stanford-le-Hope[2] witnessed on 14 December 1555 the forcible expulsion of John Odingsales gentleman by

---

[1] Morant, *History of Essex*, i, 319.
[2] G. M. Benton, 'Manor Farm, formerly called Cabborns' (*Trans. Essex Archaeological Society*, xxiv, pp. 1–5), with illustrations.

Thomas Mathew gentleman and a tailor and a labourer, all of Stanford. A writ of restitution was granted.[1] Mathew had been one of the defendants in an earlier case of disseisin of the manor of Cabborns (plate 13). The house was demolished in 1940. The other disseisin cases in the Marian records relate to smaller properties. The eighteen indictments found in the three extant Sessions rolls of 1556–7 are equalled in number by those of 1558–70 : clear evidence of the insecurity of holding property in Mary's time. But it is noteworthy that the sixty cases under Elizabeth are spread fairly evenly through the reign ; in other words, security of land tenure, judged merely by disseisin charges, was not any higher towards the end of her reign.

While the records of the disputed possession of Great Stambridge Hall and the neighbouring manor in Prittlewell might leave some doubt whether physical violence was actually employed, there are plenty of Elizabethan cases which definitely refer to strong-armed disseisin. The tiny village of Sutton, a few miles away, was the scene of serious disorder in the 1560s. The trouble was apparently initiated by George Monoux, described as a merchant of London. He was the grandson of Sir George Monoux, Lord Mayor of London, the founder of the grammar school at Walthamstow that still bears his name. Five men, mostly labourers, of Prittlewell, Great and Little Wakering and Foulness island, who were jointly accused with Monoux and John Bond another London merchant and Richard Hammond of Prittlewell servingman, had probably been hired for the job. On 11 May 1562 they descended on a thirty-acre farm called Smythes stated in the indictment to belong to Edward Hedge of Hockley yeoman, broke the farmhouse window and assaulted him. The affray lasted an hour and he was 'so maltreated that his life despaired of' (a phrase which as already seen was not uncommonly used). They 'drove away his cattle to places unknown' and carried off twelve cartloads of wood. Next day Hedge and three Hockley and Sutton yeomen forcibly expelled Monoux from Smythes. Four days later the same Monoux party of eight with ten others unnamed again assaulted Hedge ; in this second attack they 'destroyed the dwelling house, kitchen, etc.' Few indictments could be more specific. But on the same day, 16 May, Hedge, the ejected farmer, retaliated in force with seven yeomen and husbandmen of Hockley, Eastwood and Sutton between 10 p.m. and midnight, and assaulted Monoux at Smythes, 'putting him in fear of his life'. Among Monoux's supporters each time was a somewhat mysterious figure. Called a servingman of Prittlewell in May, he was indicted again as Richard Hammond of London gentleman for assaulting Edward Hedge junior at Sutton on 6 August, but ten days later secured a writ of *supersedeas* to stop

[1] This writ is given in full in *Quarter Sessions Records for Cheshire* (1940), 39.

proceedings against him and if in prison to release him. Finally, Monoux and Hammond, now both termed gentlemen, of London and Saltash (Cornwall) respectively, were indicted for entering Smythes and forcibly disseising Hedge on 1 June 1563. In the course of these charges and counter charges, at least three of the cases were removed by Queen's Bench writ of *certiorari* from Quarter Sessions to Assizes, the files of which are missing for 1562. It is impossible, without search in the public records, to deduce from the confused litigation whether Monoux or Hedge was the legal owner of the farm.[1]

In 1562 Reginald Hollingsworth gentleman, Lawrence Hollingsworth and William Hollingsworth yeomen, all of Stondon Massey, evicted William Bradburne esquire from his manor of Myles in Kelvedon Hatch. He had acquired it in the previous year by marriage.[2]

One night in August 1574 a 'capital messuage' (substantial house) called 'Fannes in the Lane' or 'Fannes House' in Kents Lane with its 110 acres of farmland in Thaxted was forcibly entered and five men, then in the house, were assaulted. The house had three owners, who were dispossessed, but only for 14 hours. The raiding party consisted of John Broke, his three sons, and two others, all of Thaxted, a Little Bardfield man and a Swavesey (Cambridgeshire) man. They were fined 40s. each. In 1586 a glazier and his wife and four spinsters, everyone named Starlying, and two other men, all of Thaxted, together with the same Cambridgeshire man, 'armed with staves, swords and daggers', broke into the unnamed house of Richard Brooke (apparently one of the assailants of 1574) and disseised him.

During the Elizabethan period forcible disseisin cases before Quarter Sessions included at least twenty involving manor houses and other sizeable properties. The defendants in these instances were mostly gentlemen, with or without bodyguards, and it may be assumed that such cases concerned legal disputes rather than attacks by ruffians.

Four assaults (one a riot, another in church) and, a decade later, disseisin – all apparently associated – exemplify the minor feuds which were not uncommon in Elizabethan disorder and reminiscent of the lawlessness of the previous century. In 1572 Edward Jobson of West Donyland and Edward Yorke of Colchester, gentlemen, with five other named men and 'ten malefactors unknown', broke down a stone wall at Hatfield (Peverel) Priory, belonging to John Sawyne gentleman, 'preventing him and his servants from coming out or going in.' How long the siege lasted is not related. They also assaulted another Hatfield man.

In 1573 three Londoners stabbed one of Sawyne's servants on the head with a dagger, 'so that Sawyne was deprived of his services for a long

---

[1] Cf. *Calendar of Ancient Deeds* (P.R.O.), vi, 502. Hedge's nuncupative will and inventory reveals him at that time (1599) as a relatively poor yeoman (E.R.O., D/ABW 19/344).

[2] *V.C.H., Essex*, iv, 67, 145.

time'. Apparently on the same day John Jobson of Colchester esquire, William Purle of Boreham miller, two Hatfield men, Nicholas Minstrell *alias* Fiddler, Denis the Frenchman, two of the same Londoners, and ten other malefactors broke into Hatfield church, 'to the great terror of all the people congregated there to hear divine service'. They entered the choir, seized Sawyn's wife sitting there, threw her out, and beat two of his servants trying to protect their mistress. Nine years later, in 1582, the same John Jobson, this time described as of East Donyland, with Robert Prowe, also a gentleman, and four other men of the same place, were indicted for an armed assembly at night, breaking into the manor house of East Donyland belonging to Edward Jobson esquire, ejecting Clement Nuse gentleman, his tenant, and dispossessing him.

A mass attack on Layer-de-la-Haye Hall, stated to be owned by William Tey esquire, took place one evening in 1587. The party consisted of Thomas Warren esquire, his wife, George Kempe gentleman, John Blouden cleric, and five other men, all of Layer-de-la-Haye, the wife of Roger Gwyn of London grocer, Richard Lambe of Brightlingsea gentleman, and sixteen unidentified malefactors. They made an affray upon William Bullman gentleman and his wife and four others in the house, all of whom were forcibly expelled. The benefice of Layer-de-la-Haye was only a curacy, and this record gives an otherwise unrecorded curate; but his recognizance to keep the peace towards Bullman he is described as John Blundell of Hemley (Suffolk), with Simon Cooke of Great Birch clerk (rector from 1585) as his surety.

The beautiful Elizabethan manor house of Edwins Hall, Woodham Ferrers (formerly Edwards Hall) was built by Edwin Sandys, Archbishop of York (1577–88). The manor had belonged to the Sandys (or Sandes) family from the beginning of the century. His widow Cecily was the victim of forcible expulsion from a messuage and 200 acres of land in Woodham in May 1594, which clearly refers to Edwins Hall. The defendants were Roger Gittins gentleman and four Woodham men, and six others of Maldon, Witham and Purleigh; the last was a sawyer. This case was presented by the hundred jury. The Court ordered a writ of restitution, which however was stayed (postponed) 'upon the opening of the matter on both sides' until 1 September following. For the first time the record relates what lay behind the usual terse statement. 'Meanwhile', it adds, 'Mr. Gittins has promised to attend Mistress Sandes and take some reasonable end with her and she shall quietly have all the rooms excepted in the lease according to covenants made between them as also such other sufficient and necessary rooms and lodgings for herself and her household'. Failing agreement, the dispute is referred to Mr. Towse and Mr. Chibborne; and if they also fail, then the writ of restitution is to be executed. And the Court ordered that no waste be committed meanwhile on the property. What transpired comes as a shock, and the violent sequel is recorded at the following Michaelmas Sessions, which incidentally states that Mistress Sandes was life tenant of the manor. (Gittins was apparently lessee of part of the Hall.) On 9 September she was in the house with Miles her son, John Gawber gentleman and her servants, when it was raided at midnight by fourteen men (four of Woodham, six from Brentwood and four from Ongar), 'with many others'. They were armed with cudgels, swords, corselets and 'guns charged with shot and powder'. They broke the doors and windows with axes, assaulted those in the house, and wounded Gawber and three of the servants. The record could not be more specific : all this was done 'by the procuration of Roger Gittins, who had incited them to do it with the intention of killing Cecily Sandes.' The laconic note added to the indictment unfortunately says no more than that four of the men (those of Woodham) were arrested and imprisoned. We do not need to waste much sympathy on the widow : the archbishop, like most of the higher clergy of the time, had plundered the property of the Church for the benefit of himself, his wife and family.[1] In fact, another of her seven sons may have started the trouble. An indictment dated the same day in May 1594 charged Henry Sandes and six named villagers and sixteen more unnamed with breaking into Gittins's barn, driving out forty ewe sheep being milked, and assaulting his servant.[2] Cecily died in 1611. Her magnificent monument is in the chancel of Woodham Ferrers church.[3]

The Edwins Hall affair is paralleled, though not closely, by a case in 1602 of violent ejection at Gaynes Park Hall in Theydon Garnon. On 14 June William Fitzwilliam junior with four or six parishioners made a forcible entry into the house, owned by his younger brother John, and on the following day, with others unknown, they repeated the operation. Quarter Sessions ordered a writ of restitution, but 'many circumstances moved the Court to delay its execution, among them the undersheriff's statement that 'the goods remaining in Gaynes Park Hall were by him lawfully seized to the Queen's use.' The Court ordered all the parties to be bound by recognizance for their good behaviour and to appear at the next General Gaol Delivery, 'now here at hand', there to be censured for their offence 'as by the Justices of the Assizes should be advised to the justices of the peace'. Meantime, unlike the Edwins Hall affair, the party actually in possession, William, with one servant to wait upon him, was allowed to remain in the house until the judges' opinion was declared, but in company with two nominees of the undersheriff. This decision John clearly had no intention of obeying and he counter-attacked. On 9 July a

---

[1] Christopher Hill, *Economic Problems of the Church* (1963), 19.

[2] Camden, writing in the previous decade, had commented with amazement on the 'cheeses of extraordinary bigness' made from ewes' milk in the marsh pastures of south-east Essex. Ten milch sheep were reckoned as equal to one cow (F. G. Emmison, *Tudor Food and Pastimes* (1964), 38–9).

[3] See R. C. Fowler, 'Edwins Hall and the Sandys Family' (*Trans. Essex Archaeological Society*, xviii, 216–21).

preliminary reconnaissance was made by Robert Browne and Henry Fitzwilliam gentlemen and four labourers, all of Theydon Garnon; armed with knives and pitchforks, they 'riotously assembled' in the park grounds 'to the great terror of the populace'. On 14 July John Fitzwilliam, Browne and Gilbert Beck gentlemen and three others, all of Theydon Garnon, armed with swords, hammers and pitchforks, broke the locks of the entrance gates, a door and mud wall, and entered the park grounds in a horse-drawn coach, assaulted and carried away two of William's servants including his warrener, and 'beset' the house for two hours. The siege apparently failed, so the assailants then tried to break into the warrener's house. On 12 July William availed himself of the Act of Henry VI and complained to Sir Robert Wrothe, J.P. (of Loughton Hall), who went to the park to find three of the four labourers armed with pitchforks and long ironforks, holding the land. The justice caused them to be arrested and committed them to gaol. A further raid took place on 16 July. A stronger contingent made up of John and Henry Fitzwilliam, Browne, Beck and seven different Theydon labourers entered the park and assaulted the village constable. More about this incident is learned from a warrant written by another justice, Robert Legh, from his home at Epping, to the Keeper of Colchester Castle gaol, dated 16 July, stating that he also had been involved as a result of a further complaint from William and had gone to the park to find the seven labourers, 'forcibly and with strong hands and armed power and weapon drawn' holding the park. They, too, were packed off into the gaoler's custody.

The public records give the cause of the trouble. The contestants were sons of Sir William Fitzwilliam, who as Treasurer of the Wars in Ireland from 1559 to 1573 had incurred heavy debts to the Queen, some still outstanding at the time of his death in 1599 and his wife's in 1602, when John secured the Essex estates under his father's settlement. Saddled with this burden, William disputed John's title and mortgaged the manor to the Queen. The case finally went to the Court of Exchequer, but, although John regained possession, details are apparently not recorded.[1]

At least ten other forcible disseisin cases are preserved in which a neighbouring justice went to the scene, as was his statutory duty in case of forcible entry. The earliest belongs to 1584. By formal sealed certificate addressed to the Court of Exchequer dated at the Easter Sessions, William Ayloffe relates how a month earlier Francis Helmer of Dagenham husbandman called at his house at Hornchurch, 'pleading' that James Leach painter-stainer and Thomas Fowley merchant, both of London, with other unknown malefactors, had just broken into his house and forcibly expelled him, and 'requiring' the justice to go to the scene of the 'riotous assembly' and execute the law. On arrival he found the two Londoners in possession, with sword and rapier drawn. He committed them

---

[1] This paragraph is entirely from *V.C.H. Essex,* iv, 267.

to gaol (by what means the record is silent), there to remain until they redeemed themselves by paying the fine to the Exchequer under the statute. Their arms were valued by four Dagenham men. The culprits were released from gaol on 16 April by the bond of two other London painters by payment of 6s. 8d.

In the following year another case of eviction and counter-eviction is found. Five Newport men including a mercer and a butcher on 29 September riotously disseised George Wheatley of a 40-acre farm. In the Epiphany 1586 Quarter Sessions roll are three certificates put in by justices. Edward Huberd went on 2 October to a messuage of Thomas Cole and his co-feoffees in Newport, held by Wheatley with a bow and twelve shafts, pitchfork, pease-hook (a sort of sickle), and a piece of an old sword. He was sent to gaol to remain there until he paid his fine. The second and third certificates, one signed by Huberd and George Nicolls, the other by Nicolls only, and both dated 13 December, relate to their visiting Cole's house and finding Wheatley again in possession, holding it with a pitchfork and 'hot water cast out of the house', almost emulating the besieged in a medieval machicolated castle casting down molten lead! Arrest and gaol followed. The Court fined Wheatley 2s.

At the succeeding Easter Sessions Walter Mildmay certified his having gone to the house and park of Edward Turnor at Great Parndon, who had handed a Chancery writ to him under the two statutes. There he found two men in illegal possession, holding out with a harquebus charged with hailshot, a bow and twelve arrows, a piked staff, a long sword, and a pitchfork with iron tines (teeth). He sent them to Colchester gaol, re-seized the property and put Turnor in possession again. Valuing the weapons at 7s. 9d. in all he delivered them to the village constables.

Another Essex park figured in a case of some interest which came before the Council in December 1581, but does not appear in the county records. William White, keeper of the Old Lodge in the Great Park of Pleshey, complained that Lord Rich, who owned it, had 'besieged' him for a whole week, despite the keepership having been granted to White by the first Lord Rich and confirmed by the second baron. The plaintiff alleged that the whole of his family was famished. The Council enjoined the Sheriff to go in person to the Lodge, 'and finding any such force maintained, to call unto him other justices thereabout, with a sufficient number of the power of the county, immediately to remove the said force'.[1] Here we have the only Elizabethan Essex reference to the *posse comitatus* (the power of the county), that is, in theory, all males above fifteen, which the Sheriff could raise under the ancient Statute of Westminster. The young and impetuous third Lord Rich, who also received a stern missive from the Council, had succeeded on the premature death of his father earlier in the year. The Lodge lay on the south side of the Castle.

[1] *Acts of the Privy Council*, xiii, 297.

On 17 June 1585 Anthony Maxey wrote a very long letter without a day's delay to the Court from his house at Little Dunmow. He and Francis Harvey had been called by one Mr. Pilburrow, a servant of the Earl of Sussex, to a house called Teyes in Little Dunmow owned by the Earl and leased to George Digby. There they found John Bust, who refused to open up after due proclamation. They broke a door, to be confronted by him 'weaponed with one dagger and the house furnished with sundry weapons.' He confessed that he and three Halstead men with a fowling piece, sword and so forth on 10 June had violently put out Digby's manservant, a lad and two maidservants. Bust was dispatched to gaol. The Court fined him 6s. 8d.

Another justice, Edward Eliot, in 1590 also used his own language instead of a formal certificate. Called to view the forcible dispossession by Henry Streetes and James Streetes of William Eve's house called Hottofts at Chignal St. James, he wrote : 'I found the said Henry and James there and the doors shut, who also against me (using her Majesty's authority) contemptuously denying to open the doors and violently withstanding my entry, until with a more strong hand I brake in, at which time also they resisted me and my people with pikestaves and suchlike weapons of force ; whereupon, and after their submission hardly yielded unto, I committed them to gaol, who now (at the sessions) are to appear upon their bail hereunto annexed.' But the fines imposed by the Court were only 2s. each.

In the following year Eliot was again summoned in company with Thomas Mildmay, the Chelmsford justice, and Ralph Wiseman, the sheriff, by Ursula Grave, a widow of Great Baddow, who had been expelled from her house by William Peckever gentleman and three labourers. They were 'threatening many evils' against her and 'harming certain of the Queen's subjects with weapons called spits'. They were each fined 5s.

In 1595 Edward Grimeston certified that he went immediately after receiving complaint to a house at Little Clacton owned by a Suffolk man. He found two other Suffolk men forcibly holding it with bolted doors and armed with two long staves, a javelin and a hatchet, who refused to open up. On the way to Colchester Castle gaol in charge of the village constable, they assaulted him and one of them escaped. Similarly, in 1601, John Sames arrested Henry Baker, John Baker and Peter Shakerley, all of Shoebury gentlemen, for holding with swords and daggers the house of James Valentine yeoman at Ulting. He committed them to gaol until their fines were paid. The last Elizabethan act of disseisin, found in the first roll of James I, records Thomas Kighley's proceeding to a labourer's cottage in East Tilbury from which he had been evicted by Isaac Goslinge gentleman and a fisherman, both of the same parish, whom he committed to gaol until their fines were paid, which in this instance were £3 6s. 8d., in marked contrast to those in some of the earlier charges.

In 1568 four Little Warley yeomen, with unknown malefactors, armed

with swords, sticks, shields, arrows and knives, forcibly expelled John
Tyrell esquire of 'Little Warley Hall otherwise Castle Warley' from his
house and 300-acre manor. Restitution was effected. There are two
points of interest here. Castle Warley as an alternative to Little Warley
was not found by Dr. Reaney in compiling his *Place-Names of Essex* (1935)
nor does it seem to be otherwise known; and the indictment is most
unusual in its implicit statement that the act of disseisin was carried out by
the order of Lewis Gryvell of Little Warley esquire. Ludovick Greville, as
he was generally known, had married Thomasine, the seventeen-year-
old daughter of Sir William Petre of Ingatestone Hall, and their eight
children were born there.[1] Petre's second wife Anne had first married a
Tyrell of Heron Hall, a few miles from Little Warley. Three years later
Thomas Veere was dispossessed by ten local men and women of the
neighbouring manor house of Childerditch Hall and its 270-acre estate
leased to him by the widowed Lady Anne Maltravers. They were all fined
4d. No less than thirty others, unidentified, also took part.

The most vivid account of a disseisin case concerns a house called
Paternosters in Canewdon which was attacked with determined fury in
1597. Climbing down the chimney and other incidents are related in
detailed examinations, which have already been fully described.[2] In the
course of the first of the two assaults, the besieged flung leads of cheese
(a lead weighed 56lb.) and heavy pins out of the cheese press. Taking one
of the female attackers 'furiously by the neck' the rightful occupier swore,
'By God, if you do not leave meddling and be still I will have your blood.'
The weapons used comprised a sheaf of seventeen arrows, a pikestaff, a
long pitchfork, a sword, a bill, and a halberd.

There are two other cases, where the disseisors, not satisfied with one
raid, descended a second time. In 1583 Roger Parkins (or Parkinson), a
blacksmith of Fryerning, and two others expelled Richard Drynker and
his wife and household from his home at Writtle belonging to John Bond.[3]
Ten months later the blacksmith was apparently the leader of a mob,
twenty-three strong, mostly labourers with some women, all of Writtle,
'together with other malefactors unknown to the number of sixty persons'
who forcibly disseised Bond, now described as an innholder of Ingatestone,
from a messuage called Taylors in Writtle, presumably the same one. The
Court gave possession again to Bond. Unfortunately we learn no more
about this record number of accomplices. Next year Bond's wife complained about disseisin in Writtle to Eustace Cloville, J.P., who found 'a
widow woman and three children having in the house two pitchforks'.
She confessed that she found the longer of the two in the house, but the
other she had brought for her own defence if besieged.

---

[1] Emmison, *Tudor Secretary*, 287.
[2] J. Holmes, 'The Affair at Paternosters' (*Essex Review*, lxiv, 259–66).
[3] There is no evidence to connect him with his namesake on p. 119 above.

Two members of the Rochester family of Terling disputed ownership of an acre of the demesne of the manor of Loys in that parish in 1571. Led by William Rochester yeoman, five men and women forcibly disseised John Rochester esquire and were fined 12d. each. A quarter of a century later, Richard Rochester husbandman with five local men expelled William's tenant from a house there called Bettes. What lay behind the incident in this case is explained. On the preceding Michaelmas day 1595 (when most rents were due) Richard had distrained twenty sheep and lambs for arrears of rent from Bettes. Not to be outwitted William and three other yeomen and a widow violently attacked Richard and 'rescued' the beasts. Next day Richard with three Great Leighs men retaliated by assaulting one of William's party and two others at Terling; and on the same day William and his party, armed with pitchforks, expelled Richard from Bettes. All the people concerned were indicted for the affrays. At the Lent Assizes 1596 Justice Owen deputed John Ive and Henry Appleton, J.P.s, to try to settle the whole dispute, but if they failed it was to be referred back to an 'open hearing' at the next Quarter Sessions for the county justices' determination. This is one of the rare instances when an Assize order, other than a verdict or sentence, is recorded. As likely as not, the judges were baffled by the Rochesters' charges and countercharges; the final outcome is not recorded.

In February 1594 Thomas Carowe gentleman and three labourers of Navestock forcibly expelled Richard Lovelace gentleman from 'Lafte Hall' and 300 acres in that parish, and he still remained dispossessed at the time when the case came up at the Epiphany Sessions in 1595. The manor of Loft Hall was owned by the Sedley family from 1507 to 1654, so that Lovelace must have been the tenant.[1]

John Thurston's house called Walton Hall barn was the scene of assault and disseisin by twelve Walton and Kirby men in 1571. On the same day three of them, with Richard Badcocke merchant and two mariners, all of Moze, burgled John Tendring's house at Walton, stealing ten 'wayes' of cheese worth £17. This was a massive quantity, a weigh of cheese being either 224 or 256 lb.[2] Six years afterwards John Thurston of Frinton Hall gentleman, with two men of Canewdon and Paglesham, expelled Philip Mitche from his house and 20-acre farm called Ames in Canewdon (restitution granted). The Thurstons of Colchester in the next century were woollen-drapers,[3] but little seems to be known of the family in Elizabeth's time apart from Robert and John of Great Holland, whose wills were proved in 1571 and 1588.[4]

Other cases involving manor houses or large estates may be briefly related. The manor-house of Deanes in Debden with 100 acres of land had

[1] V.C.H., Essex, iv, 145.
[2] W. Harrison, Description of England, 457.
[3] Essex Review, lx, 216.
[4] F. G. Emmison (ed.), Wills at Chelmsford, 1400–1720, 425.

been acquired in 1566 by Richard Barnard. Four years later he was disseised by two Debden yeomen, who were ordered to restore possession. In 1577 Henry Wentford gentleman, with four men and women, all of Tendring, expelled Frances Price widow from her manor of Tendring. Two clothiers and seven labourers, all of Nayland, just over the Suffolk boundary, with many others unknown, in 1573 riotously expelled Edward Reynouldes gentleman from his estate called Nayland Park or Horkesley Park, destroying the grass valued at £20. Two J.P.s fined everyone 2s. 6d. Dovecotes could only be owned by lords of manors, and there is a single indictment in 1580 against two local men for disseising the dove-cote of John Brett of Broomfield gentleman. Edward Hodiern gentleman, Martha his wife and six men and women, all of Frating, were charged in 1597 with armed entry into the house of Edmund Wythepoll esquire, in the occupation of Peter Wythepoll, D.D., and assault and ejection of two men.

In 1577 the Privy Council asked Sir Thomas Mildmay, Sir John Petre and George White to call before them and to settle the controversy between John Cliffe, Clerk of the Signet, and William Maddison 'servant' (probably steward) of William Plater esquire of Suffolk. Cliffe had been the law steward to Sir William Petre, Secretary of State, and was one of his executors, and Plater was evidently William Playters of Sotterley (Suffolk), who had married one of the four daughters and co-heirs of Edmund Tyrell of Beeches in Rawreth, a relation of Sir William's first wife. By the marriage Playters acquired the manors of Barrington in Ramsden Bellhouse and Canewdon. Cliffe had complained that Maddison had 'detained' a mansion house in Essex. Perhaps Barrington was leased to Cliffe. White, at any rate, lived nearby at Hutton Hall.[1]

A few of the remaining cases involving small properties have minor points of interest. The owner and the tenant of a house called Pratts in Black Notley were riotously ejected in 1589 by Elias Frend, described as a minstrel of Braintree, his wife and four others. The island of Foulness had one disseisin case affecting the house of Nicholas Reynolds in 1593, when three local men expelled him. A butcher was charged in 1571 with disseising the owner of the 'George' at Moulsham in Chelmsford. A disseisin indictment involved a house at West Hanningfield and abduction of the owner's infant daughter (p. 196). In 1569 James Raymonde of Dagenham husbandman and Edmund Cheveley alias Lacie yeoman (who appeared before the Court on other occasions), with others unknown, expelled John Legatt gentleman from his house called Eastbrook End alias Field End with sixty acres of land in Dagenham, on which a true bill was found. The Legatt family also owned two manors in the parish. An unorthodox indictment of 1602 charged a Sandon yeoman with ejecting a widow from a house there 'in which she had lived for a long time without

[1] *Acts of the Privy Council*, x, 52.

11 ANOTHER NEW MANSION

Edwins Hall, Woodham Ferrers, *circa* 1575
Said to have been built by Edwin Sandys, Archbishop of York.

12 CECILY SANDYS, THE ARCHBISHOP'S WIDOW

13   MANOR OF CABBORNS, STANFORD-LE-HOPE

South-East front, showing 15th century windows discovered in the hall during demolition of the building in 1940 (p. 118).

disturbance'. The act was perpetrated 'by the malicious instigation of his uncharitable mind.' Among the few indictments for 'entry with the strong hand' under the Act of Richard II, without actual dispossession, is one which seems to have occasioned a special 'Sessions of the Peace' held at Stratford Langthorne (in West Ham) on 22 May 1567 before John Southcott, justice of the Queen's Bench (of Witham), and Clement Sysley, J.P. (of Barking). The jury of seventeen men dealt with the breaking into a capital messuage called New Barns in West Ham, the property of Robert Staunton gentleman, by eleven men, mostly Londoners. They were also charged separately with riot. In 1566 the county justices received a writ stating that the Queen was willing that the indictments concerning forcible entry against Clement Tusser and John Tusser, gentlemen of Rivenhall, be quashed. No details are given. Clement Tusser was one of the two county coroners. He and John were the eldest and third sons of William Tusser of Rivenhall and brothers of Thomas, the author of the *Five Hundreth Good Pointes of Good Husbandrie* (1573). Between 'entry with (or by) the strong hand', forcible entry, and close-breaking there is sometimes no clear distinction. Close-breaking with theft is dealt with under Larceny; without theft, under Trespass.

There are other cases in which the justices' record states that he sent the offender to gaol until the fine was paid. Amounts varied, but were usually about 6s. 8d. Most of the incidents narrated have involved manor houses, farmhouses and the like, but there are in addition forty-six indictments for disseisin of little interest except to the parish or family historian. Some relate to farms, but the majority concern smaller properties. The number given includes the fifteen cases in Mary's time. Quite often the disseising party included a dozen or more people: the Writtle riot, as we have seen, embraced sixty, as well as the twenty-three named assailants. In some of the disputes relating to manors which have been described one cannot tell whether the parties were owners or lessees until the *Victoria History of Essex*, based on detailed research, has been completed.

Essex is a large county, and Elizabeth's reign was a long one, but there are too many indictments to warrant their being dismissed as in any way exceptional. There have always been disputes between neighbouring landowners and between landlord and tenant. There always had been aggrieved parties who took the law into their own hands rather than await the result of protracted litigation, for the law was slow. But even allowing for the usual tendency to exaggeration in plaintiff's language, two pictures emerge. One is of the lord of the manor or the yeoman farmer enlisting the help of his neighbours, servants and a few strong-arm yokels to evict someone who is deemed to be in unlawful possession. The other portrays, in more colourful and striking tones, the riotous attack of a determined group of trouble-makers, with a mostly inactive mob of village hangers-on who had joined in for the fun or perhaps because the

K

victim was generally disliked. Yet, as one editor observed[1] it is curious and perplexing that throughout many generations people persisted in so turblent and futile a way of asserting their claim to real estate. Nearly all disseisin acts terminated in the same way – by fine, with or without imprisonment, and the restoration of the 'status quo'. Despite the deforciants' discomforture one after another went on with their characteristic Tudor element of disorder, possibly in some cases from an inherent urge or delight in rioting.

A number of clergy and lay rectors, that is, the owners of the rectorial tithes or lay parsonages, figure in disseisin cases, some brought under an Act of Henry VIII. William Pullen, a tailor, with others unknown, forcibly disseised his priest, John Holmes (1567–69), of High Easter vicarage house and glebe soon after he had been instituted. Three J.P.s fined him 12d., and a writ of restitution was granted at the Assizes. And Matthew Levett had scarcely arrived as rector of Leading Roothing before he was expelled from his parsonage by four men of the Roothings.

Disseisin and counter-disseisin took place at Pentlow. In 1571 Nicholas Bushe, the rector, with six men and women of the neighbourhood, unlawfully entered Pentlow Parsonage (a secular house) belonging to Thomas Strachie of Saffron Walden draper. Nineteen months later George Smythe of Pentlow gentleman expelled Nicholas Walles the rector and Thomas Strachie, then described as of Pentlow, his 'farmer' (lessee), from several of the glebe fields.

The lay Parsonage House of Chigwell was tenanted by Robert Spackman yeoman under a forty-year lease from James Calshill, a prebendary of St. Paul's, to Nicholas Fulham dated 1567 and assigned by Thomas Fulham to Spackman. In 1570 the house was forcibly broken in to by Benedict Barfot of Lambourne gentleman, two London watermen and three Chigwell men including a useful blacksmith. Restitution was given by the Court.

In 1566 Shellow Bowells parsonage and 14 acres of glebe belonging to John Wright the rector (1564–73) was forcibly entered by Ralph Madyson, a yeoman of the parish, who was also charged as a common barrator and fomenter of contention among his neighbours. But it was the incumbent who was the defendant in 1563 when Robert Lewykin *alias* Luckyn, vicar of Takeley (1561–98), and Prudence his wife forcibly disseised William Collyn from his house and land, for which each was fined 2s. But these were all mild disputes in comparison with the acrimonious affair at Rettendon. In July 1588 William Bingham, LL.D., rector of Rettendon (1588–1611), was evicted from his rectory by an armed party of ten men and women, mostly from Chelmsford and Writtle, who held it until the following day. The case was transmitted to the Assizes. On the following December 1589 Robert Buckberd of Writtle clerk (rector of

[1] *Middlesex County Records*, ii, p. xlii.

Rettendon 1562–88) and Helen his wife and nine men of various parishes 'with many other unknown malefactors', armed with swords, pikes, daggers, staves and pitchforks, assaulted Dr. Bingham and Katherine his wife, and disseised him from his kitchen (a separate building) and barn, and were still in possession when the case came before the county justices.

The evidence from other counties which have preserved their Elizabethan Quarter Sessions records is sketchy. The indices to their printed calendars mostly fail to differentiate between forcible entry and actual disseisin. West Riding (1598–1603) had only five cases,[1] but Lancashire (1588–1603) had many. 'The great frequency of forcible entry upon lands in dispute', wrote the editor, 'shows that the lawlessness for which Lancashire had been notorious in the Middle Ages was not yet extinct. In 1592 no less than forty-two cases were presented.'[2] In Staffordshire too (1582–1603), forcible entry was a fairly common offence. The editor gives his view that they were probably in the majority of cases associated with resistance to enclosure or some form of agrarian development which affected the interests of the peasantry.[3] The Middlesex court had relatively few cases of disseisin: four in Edward's and Mary's reigns and eight in Elizabeth's; a few were riotous, but none serious, and none took place after 1583.

---

[1] *West Riding Sessions Rolls* (Yorks. Archl. Soc., Record Series, iii, 1888).
[2] *Lancashire Quarter Sessions Records* (Chetham Soc., 1917).
[3] *Staffordshire Quarter Sessions Rolls* (William Salt Archl. Soc.), vol. i, p. xxxviii.

10

Trespass

Trespass is any actionable wrong committed against a person or his goods or lands, but for our purpose it is the last only. In this restricted sense, 'it signifies', wrote Blackstone, 'no more than entry on another man's ground without a lawful authority, and doing some damage, however inconsiderable'.[1] The trespass was done by 'breaking X's close', and the offences to be related are therefore either simple close-breaking, with or without assault, but without theft. All cases of stealing cattle or sheep from a field and clothes or cloth from a garden or a tainter-field are considered in special sections of Larceny (pp. 280–299), but we have no section on Close-breaking (p. 257).

At the Lent Assizes 1563 the judges determined that all indictments for trespass should be dealt with in future by the county justices and their clerk of the peace and not by the clerk of assize.[2] Trespasses therefore figure only in the records of Quarter Sessions except where the case was removed by writ of *certiorari* to Queen's Bench for trial at Assizes.

Trespass was committed in many ways, and for this reason the indictments exhibit a much greater variety of form and detail than for any other offence. Except in fact for the initial close-breaking clause, there is no regular form. The lawyer's textbooks in this respect sometimes failed him, and the indictments tend to be refreshingly free from set phrases. There is a wide range of trespasses, such as digging or filling in a ditch or trench, cutting down mark (boundary) stakes, breaking or throwing down hedges or pales, uprooting a new quickset hedge, uprooting trees, unlawfully ploughing land, turning a horse or cow into another's field and damaging his grass or crops, or driving a laden cart through a pasture field.

Sometimes the damage is assessed, at sums between as little as 1s. and as much as £20. Where punishment is recorded it is always a small fine, even as low as 4d., an indication that the justices probably regarded such cases as trifling or as petty squabbles. There are many more, where such trespass was combined with removal. Taking away hay or crops, or cutting down and carrying away trees or timber or paling were common offences. Again, fines seem low, even allowing for the contemporary value of money.

---

[1] Blackstone, *Commentaries on the Laws of England* (1768).
[2] E.R.O., Q/CP 2, page 5.

For example, only 12d. levied on John Porter, a fishmonger of West Ham, who in 1567 broke into a close in the New Marsh there, cutting and carrying away in his cart John Shipman's crops to the value of 40s. ; only 8d. each on two Hockley husbandmen in the same year who dug a trench ten perches long in the ground of Edmund Tyrrell esquire at Rawreth (the lord of the manor of Beeches) and cut down with axes and carried away two oaks worth 20s. ; or only 2s. each on five Ashdon husbandmen in 1561 who cut down and carried off sixteen cartloads of firewood from John Cornell's close there called Grygges. Produce thus removed is often specified by the number of cartloads, e.g. five cartloads of wood (3s.), three of logs (20s.), one of turves (60s.). It is not always easy to see the lawyer's distinction between larceny and such acts of trespass involving the actual removal of valuable corn and timber, for which the punishment was a small fine, in contrast to hanging for theft of goods over 1s.

In 1576 two men of Layer Breton and Feering broke into the close of a Goldhanger husbandman, assaulted his wife and threatened her, destroyed the 'bartlings' of his house and despoiled 'victuals and other domestic things' there worth five marks (£3 3s. 4d.) : close-breaking, not house-breaking, because they apparently did not enter the house.

The commonest and mildest form of trespass was trifling damage to herbage or crops, which was the lawyer's way of dealing with unlawful entry into anyone's field. Such was therefore little more than 'treading by feet', mostly human but sometimes animal. But it often involved assault. For example, in 1562, when two Hatfield Broad Oak men broke into the close of Francis Frank gentleman there, trampling his growing crops under foot, and assaulting him. Each was fined 2s. Or trampling on the grass in the 'Castle Land' (next to Colchester Castle) belonging to Henry Mackwilliam esquire; or in 1576, when Richard Ferrers of the Middle Temple gentleman and a servant of Henry Ferrers of Baddesley (Warws.) yeoman broke into the close of Sir Thomas Smythe, one of the Queen's Chief Secretaries, at Theydon Mount, destroying the grass to the value of 10s. This is an incidental reference to the author of *De Republica Anglorum* (1583), who built the remarkable mansion of Hill Hall there, which suffered a disastrous fire in 1969. In 1563 Henry Snelloke of Toppesfield gentleman, three Finchingfield labourers, and many others unknown entered Henry Brokhole's three-acre pasture there called Mardeley Green or Brokholes Green, being his 'several ground' (private land), assaulting him and destroying his herbage worth 26s. 8d. ; probably the dispute settled whether the green was a common waste or not. Fined 20d. each. Brokhole had been assaulted and wounded by another parishioner in the previous month.

In 1562 Nicholas Fuljambe, a merchant-tailor of St. Stephen's, Colman Street, London, his apprentice, and two Theydon men, broke into Thomas Wilbrand's field in Theydon Mount and destroyed his oats through being trampled down by their cattle. Fuljambe was evidently a quarrelsome person, as he was also indicted for barratry. John Harrison of Wheatley in Rayleigh must have nursed a grievance against Humphrey Hasteler. He could not keep out of Hasteler's twelve-acre pasture field called Lamp Land in that parish. Three times, in 1562, 1564 and 1568, he went into it, first assaulting the owner's servant and destroying the crops with his own cattle to the value of 40s. (fined 20d.) ; then, with ten others unknown, again destroying his crops and digging a pit (result not given) ; finally, with another local labourer, assaulting Hasteler with a 'grained staff', wasting his crops and carrying off a load of stakes (each fined only 6d. by two J.P.s). Four Orsett men, with many others unknown, in 1567 wasted the crops in a field called Fulgars at Horndon-on-the-Hill, digging up the soil with 'lees' (defined only as a North Country word for scythes), mattocks, shovels and spades. In 1570 Robert Cooke husbandman and two labourers, all of Feering, trampled down the grass of William Marshall gentleman called Bullocks Oavers *alias* Howchyns Oavers. (Each fined 2s.). This appears to relate to a paddock adjoining the three-storeyed, double-jettied house known as Houchins, a substantial building lying to the north of the Coggeshall–Colchester road (plate 14). By chance the first of the alternative names is explained by an indictment of 1567, but filed on the 1570 roll, against Cooke, James Bromeley and John Sponer of Coggeshall fullers, for digging up the soil in John Bullock's close similarly named. (Each fined 2s.). Another simple trespass indictment in which the grass-trampling formula was used is of interest because it is the sole Elizabethan case tried by the Essex justices arising out of an offence which strictly should have come before the Kent Sessions. Two East Ham labourers in 1589 unlawfully entered land in 'Wolledge' called Gallyons Ground. From time immemorial about 500 acres of marshland lying next to Gallions Reach and known as North Woolwich belonged to the parish of Woolwich and was regarded as part of Kent.

Inquisitions taken before Thomas Meade serjeant-at-law and Kenelm Throckmorton, J.P.s, in August 1577 at Finchingfield disclose six separate indictments for trespass there, all nominally close-breaking in the first place. The facts, as expressed in their cold language, were that certain parishioners on 4 July mowed and took away the grass in John Glascock's field ; on 10 August ploughed the land of Henry Harrington and William Bett ; on 13 August ploughed the land of Robert Parre clerk (vicar, 1562–85), assaulted two of his servants and led away four cows and bullocks depastured there ; on 13 August led away John Wakelyn's cows from his field ; and on 17 August, arriving with staves and knives, took Harrington's corn worth £10. In every trespass Robert Vere esquire and Barbara his wife and William Barners gentleman took part, together with Robert Edwards in four, Thomas Poole *alias* Welchman in three, Robert Reed's wife in two, Robert Reed in the first, and William Celey, six wives and one spinster in the last. No ready explanation offers itself; but here and elsewhere it seems probable that the actual offence was carried out by the servants on their employer's orders. Trespass with assault occurred in 1579, when John St. John of Hatfield Peverel gentleman with several other villagers broke a gate and destroyed the grass in two of William Bastwick's fields there and wounded him as well as assaulting William Studhanger gentleman.

In 1578 three cases were tried: John Watson gentleman and seven labourers, all of Rivenhall and Cressing, for taking ten cartloads of hay from the land of Francis Harvye esquire at Rivenhall, also for obstructing the highway there from Cressing to Blackwater (hamlet on the Braintree–Colchester road) by digging 'a great ditch called a moat'; and a labourer for digging a ditch to enclose some land, by the order of Thomas Kightley of Grays Thurrock gentleman. In 1564–5 three close-breaking expeditions on the lands of Edward Cousin and Thomas Blackwell gentlemen at Dagenham and Barking involved thirteen culprits of these two parishes, who broke down a gate, dug ditches, damaged crops, cut down three elms, and bound a farm-worker, 'detaining him as a prisoner for eighteen days'. For the last act three of them were each fined 12d. Two other cases of assault with temporary imprisonment each occurred after breaking into a garden. In 1571 William Pawne of High Ongar (lord of the manor of Chivers Hall) and William Marsey of Great Easton gentlemen, with two labourers, assaulted the owner's wife, shutting her up in the garden barn for three hours. (Fined 6d. each.) And in 1594 three husbandmen, two of Horseheath (Cambs.) and the other of Hockley, with five unknown men, broke into the garden of John Barnardiston of Hawkwell gentleman and assaulted his maidservant, imprisoning her for two hours.

Some of the trespasses on land arose out of deliberate malice but many were probably minor acts of careless damage which some owners would have overlooked but others decided to prosecute. To have broken down 45 perches of hedge, unless newly quickset, must have been a wilful act of the three accused Little Hallingbury husbandmen; and the same remark applies to damage assessed at £10, caused by three West Ham yeomen charged with destroying grass with their feet, and to 'great damage' which the house called Wynnes in Walthamstow owned by Thomas Browne gentleman sustained in 1581, when the pales also were twice pulled down. A field called Pragelles in Dagenham was entered in 1567 by three men armed with quarter-staves and ten-foot pikes, who damaged the crops and took four cows which were so badly beaten that they prematurely calved. All were fined 3s. (12d. for each offence) by two J.P.s. In 1573 three Belchamp St. Paul's men pulled down and carried off the palings of William Golding's park there. He was the brother of Arthur Golding, the translator of Ovid's *Metamorphoses*, and brother-in-law of the Earl of Oxford. A dispute about the taking away of part of the frame of a house of Lord Morley on Hallingbury Green in 1587, as revealed in a deposition, evidently involved horses being used to pull the house down. George Withers of Danbury clerk (who was Archdeacon of Colchester as well as rector) was accused in 1585 with four labourers of riotously throwing down a brick wall there belonging to Thomas Emerye of Little Baddow yeoman. The incident took place at 5 a.m. on a September day, and the damage was assessed at £20. But as Sir Thomas Mildmay and Eustace Clovile fined them only 2s. each it seems clear that this was regarded only as a trifling trespass and 'riotously' was used because more than three persons took part. The recognizance bound over only 'Dr. Withers' men'.

Unlawful entry into a meadow resulted in an indictment laid in 1567 under the Act of 5 Richard II (1381) against Henry Ravens of Dedham, Richard Serly (or Saly) of Langham, shearmen, and two men from just over the Suffolk border for breaking down a perch of fencing on three acres in Nether Hall Meadow in Dedham belonging to Edmund Robinson, a weaver there. Ravens and two Ipswich and three Dedham men had themselves been bound with Edward Babington of the Old Hythe, Colchester, gentleman, and Thomas Waslington of Colchester merchant, as their sureties, to appear at Sessions two years earlier and to keep the peace towards Robinson, but had produced a writ of *supersedeas* liberating them 'if in prison'. For the appearance of Henry Ravens and one of the others William Cole, a clothier of Dedham, acted as surety, and they duly appeared. All four men were bound to appear at the following Sessions, when the case was apparently removed to the Assizes, at which their indictment was preferred under the Act of 5 Henry IV 'against entry with the strong hand' and adds that possession of the bit of meadow was taken at 1 a.m.

Four Braintree and Bocking men at 11 p.m. on Sunday 6 July 1568 carried off a cartload of hay of Richard Manne, 'farmer' (lessee) of Lord Rich, from two acres in Ludham Mead at Ford Bridge in Braintree. Although formally termed a close, the boundaries and abuttals are given, and it was clearly a strip in a common meadow. While haymaking in Panfield Mead at East Hanningfield on land belonging to Thomas Pyke in 1571, his wife and three of his men were unable to withstand the assault of a crowd of thirty-four labourers, half of them unnamed, the rest of East and West Hanningfield and Runwell, who took away eight cartloads of hay worth £6. Pyke's men then apparently entered the field or meadow of John Skelton, first-named of the crowd, and got their own back on him and three of his party. The case against Skelton and his sixteen men was transferred to the Assizes (but does not seem to be in its records), while Pyke and his servants were fined 2s. 6d. each. Disputes about strips or doles in the common meadows (and in the open fields), where boundaries were often uncertain, are on the vague borderline between trespass and larceny.

Richard Grene's vicarage garden at Great Maplestead was raided in 1571 by three male and six female parishioners, who carried away hops worth 20s. and assaulted his wife. Each was fined 2s. The vicar, John Wilbore, died two months later, so Grene was either curate or lessee. Harrison's reference to hop-growing in the Hedinghams area, which included the Maplesteads, is now taken back a few years.[1]

What do these heterogeneous trespass cases really amount to? Apart from the probable tithe disputes, it seems that they fall mainly into three categories – trespass with deliberate intent to make off with crops or wood, secretly, especially after dark, and, if caught, often leading to a skirmish; contested ownership of land or crops; and village feuds or quarrels. In actual fact, how 'riotously' involved were these close-breakers, especially where no assault was alleged and the adverb was included because the number of people exceeded two? Before dismissing them as mere squabbles or petty trespasses, we should bear in mind that at least seven of the early cases were removed to the Assizes, yet the language of the Sessions indictments is quite mild. A reminder that most of the trespasses related were technically riots is given by the grand jury in 1583 finding a true bill for trespass, but no true bill for riot, three Burnham men with the usual 'other malefactors unknown' having been charged with damaging the grass in an eight-acre pasture called Easterns there and turning up the soil by cartwheels. In another incident three years later the grand jury found a true bill for four, but *ignoramus* for the remaining eight, men and women, mostly of Roydon, but including George Ward the miller of Hunsdon (Herts.). They were indicted for an armed breaking into 'Ten Acres' field owned by William Cole gentleman at Great Parndon, throwing down the hedges and fences, and assaulting three of his servants. The attack was made at the instigation of goodwife Helen Buckberd and her two servants. But there is a countercharge by Robert Buckberd on account of 'Ten Acres' being broken into and by Helen his wife and the same servants for being beaten, although all in peaceful possession (the usual phrase), by Cole and his three servants, John Tadly gentleman, and six other Parndon people on the same day, 8 August 1586. To whom did the field belong? Ten months previously Robert Buckberd, then termed 'clerk', the two servants and others had so forcibly disseised Edward Turnour esquire of a house and land in his park at Great Parndon (he owned the manor of Canons) that he ordered his keepers, if possession was not surrendered, to arrest them and cause them

---

[1] Hop garden at Ingatestone Hall, 1548 (Emmison, *Tudor Secretary*, 148); Harrison, *op. cit.*, 217. An action for trespass at Bocking was brought at the Assizes in 1599 (for which the two files are lost) by John Wentworth, lord of the manor of Bocking, against William Pawfflyn, lessee of the manor of Fennes in Bocking, the lord being William Bendlowes (copy in E.R.O., T/A 153/4).

to be put in the nearest gaol. Buckberd must be the rector of Rettendon (1572–88), but in what capacity he was creating these disturbances at Parndon is not clear.

One remarkable aspect is that these offences are very numerous in the first decade of the reign. After 1570 they become relatively infrequent. As no other counties have preserved such complete Quarter Sessions records for the early period comparison is impossible. Does the mass of evidence quoted justify our drawing the conclusion – one which would be of some importance – that the Essex records reveal the very last stage of insecurity of tenure through strong-arm action, so prevalent in medieval England? The reader must judge for himself, and in doing so should not overlook some conflicting evidence in the section on Disseissin, which deals with the more aggravated disputes (p. 119).

There remain one or two little puzzles. Many trespass indictments include gentlemen among the defendants, often in company with labourers. Were these more substantial persons not indicted, we might have regarded most of the offences as those committed by gangs of village ruffians. Doubtless in some instances the labourers were hired or were in the employment of the gentlemen, though if the latter they were generally termed their 'servants'. In other cases it seems probable that the victims of the trespass and assault were unpopular, even hated, by their fellow parishioners.

11

Barratry

Michael Dalton found that barrators were of three sorts : '(1) disturbers of the peace, viz. such as are either common quarrellers or fighters in their own cause, or common movers or maintainers of quarrels and affrays between others; (2) common takers or detainers (by force or subtlety) of the possessions of houses, lands or goods which have been in question or controversy; (3) inventors and sowers of false reports, whereby discord ariseth or may arise between neighbours'. The delinquencies of some of the Elizabethan barrators, or troublemakers, were therefore akin to assault or to slander. Barratry was a sort of omnibus name for the numerous nuisances which such men and women inflicted on their neighbours : a convenient term for the Elizabethan lawyer, which his present day counterpart lacks.

On two occasions barrators' activities in Essex were reported from high constables' sessions. One wife was 'a common scold and disturber of the neighbours'; another was 'a common disturber of the peace by quarrelling, railing and living unquietly with her neighbours'. Barratry, in fact, being a somewhat unspecific offence, was often informally expressed, as the charge against William Holleyday of Ramsden Crays and his wife for being 'unquiet persons who trouble and disturb their neighbours continually'; or, more forcibly, against Hugh Barker, the Chelmsford barber, 'a very troublesome and dangerous fellow and a raiser of great sedition amongst his neighbours' (for the racy story of the scandalous libel, see p. 71) ; or against Thomas Keyes of Goldhanger, for 'causing out of his own diabolical and perverse mind divers false clamours and quarrels without any reasonable or just cause against many of his neighbours, and for being a common brawler'.

Such unruly folk were mostly indicted for being 'a common barrator', or 'a common disturber of the peace', or both : the distinction, if any, is negligible. The catalogue may be much longer. Thomas Kelton of Earls Colne gentleman was charged in 1587 as 'a common barrator, disturber of the peace and oppressor of his neighbours, and a common malefactor, calumniator and spreader of strifes and discords between his neighbours'. But his behaviour was perhaps no worse than if only the first two words had been used, the rest having probably been added by the deputy Clerk of the Peace, though he may have been influenced after drawing a further indictment against Kelton for violence. Some indictments may be more to the point, as for instance that against two of the rowdy Sampford family at Willingale (p. 187), the man a whoremonger and common barrator, his wife a common brawler.

But of course brawling was not the prerogative of the poor. In fact, the middle and upper classes indulged both in common brawling and in the more refined forms of calumny; and many of them were intensely litigious.

Simple indictments for being a common barrator were laid in 1597 against Richard Stanton of West Ham gentleman and against John Chambers of Dunwich (Suffolk) and Benjamin Clere of Boxted, also against Thomas Vincent of Waltham Holy Cross armourer (1564), Richard Fawell of Writtle miller (1576) and George Beale of Bocking shoemaker (1584). The last was fined as much as £5, but the penalty for barrators is rarely recorded, nor indeed the verdict.

Perhaps the liveliest character sketch of one of these many turbulent fellows is found in a petition to Lord Mordaunt 'and the other justices at Brentwood' (Mordaunt, who lived at Thorndon Hall, evidently presided at this Easter Sessions 1564 and the following one). It came from the inhabitants of Ingrave and referred to John Pattryke, one of their number, whom they termed a yeoman. 'He is a very troublous and disordered person of evil name, fame and conversation, a common quarreller among us and other our neighbours, a railer against such as be the honest of the parish, in calling them thieves, villains and other odible names of reproach and infamy, daily seeking and procuring by false lies and devices of his busy brain to set variance and strifes between the parishioners.' Even allowing for contemporary usage in such petitions, there is little doubt about John Pattryke's behaviour. He had been indicted in the previous year for cony-catching and belonged to an Ingrave family which evidently had poaching in their blood (p. 244). The villagers sought the justices' 'warrant for good abearing for the better stay of him in good and civil order.' With Mordaunt, who was lord of the manor of Ingrave among other manors, on the Bench, the petitioners might have hoped for reform following punishment; but he was before the noble lord again at the following Sessions, charged for the second time with the same kind of poaching offence.

The events leading to the indictment in 1583 of John Walford senior of Wethersfield, yeoman or husbandman, merely for being a common barrator and disturber of the peace are of much interest because of the second witness's allusion to the 'godly preachers then assembled there' – one of the early meetings of the Dedham 'Classis', the important puritan conference which had begun to meet at Dedham and in the neighbourhood in the previous year. On 11 March nine Wethersfield men attested against the farmer before Lord Rich. Robert, who had succeeded his father as the third Baron two years earlier, was already a deeply-committed puritan, and clearly instigated Walford's prosecution for derogatory comments about those who had attended the religious exercise at Wethersfield. The witnesses were Lancelot Warde, John Parker, John Clarke, John Smith, John Livermore, Josias Sansom, Thomas Whitehand, Edward Pasfield and Bartholomew Waighte.

Warde deposed that Walford, on a Sabbath evening about a year and a half ago, meeting one of the ushers of the school at Wethersfield, beat him with his cudgel and 'bruised him very sore', frightening the other usher. This incident was confirmed by all of the witnesses. Parker referred to a day shortly before Michaelmas last, when Dr. Chapman, preached at Wethersfield, and 'sundry other godly preachers and other persons were there assembled to hear him.' On that day Walford railed against them in Roulston's victualling-house there: 'What make all these knaves here today? What, will they make a god of Rogers? There were forty of the knaves like rebels indicted at the last assize, and more had been if they had not made friends.' And when Lord Rich was at Mr. Wentworth's house at Gosfield about the end of last summer, he sent for Walford, who refused to go without a warrant. Whitehand and Pasfield declared that Walford exclaimed, when he was told that Lord Rich's warrant had been sent to the constables and headboroughs, 'If any headborough comes to serve his warrant, I shall try what my dagger can do.' Sansom said that, on another occasion when he was one of the constables and had Lord Rich's warrant for arrest, Walford was about to go hunting and declared that he had appointed his business for that day and if the constable came again on the morrow he would then go. Next morning Walford came to Sansom's house, demanded to see the warrant, and then swore with bitter oaths that he would not obey it, and Lord Rich must send another. Waighte deposed how, when he met Walford hunting, he asked where he was going. 'I take my pleasure today', he answered, 'for I should be hanged tomorrow, because then I must go before my Lord Rich.' And on another day, at his brother's house at Finchingfield, Walford railed as usual against the preachers. His brother rebuked him, speaking in their defence, whereon Walford cast a pot at his head and spilt drink in his face. At Easter last Walford was in the company of a wicked fellow and others in a Wethersfield alehouse. Some were already drunk, 'yet for all that he caused fortypennyworth of drink more to be presently filled in.' Finally, all the witnesses said that he was a common ringleader and practiser of evil rule and great disorder, both in the village, especially on Sabbath days in time of prayer, and elsewhere, and encouraged many others through his misdemeanours and evil example to oppose good order. The long document recording these depositions bears Rich's signature.

Richard Rogers, host at this Wethersfield 'assembly', was the lecturer at Wethersfield church and was to become a very well-known puritan divine, presbyterian leader and religious writer. Dr. Edmund Chapman, who was the preacher, had earlier been town preacher of Bedford, was expelled by the bishop, and had been lecturer at Dedham since 1578. He was a moderate puritan. A recent author in a brief reference to Walford's indictment, expressed the opinion that the Assize mentioned was probably that at Bury St. Edmunds of the previous July, when many puritan preachers and laymen were prosecuted.[1] On the previous February William Rust, the vicar of Felsted, had spoken his mind too bluntly about Rich and was prosecuted for slander (p. 67).

The document following the depositions against Walford is a testimonial given by John Wilkinson, 'minister' of Stansted Mountfitchet (vicar, 1573–91), two parishioners and a midwife on behalf of a woman whose bastard child had been fathered by John Walford of Wethersfield, who was £4 in debt for its maintenance. He was presumably the son of the barrator, described as 'the elder'.

In 1593 Robert Legh wrote to the County Bench from 'Chingford Pauls' (Chingford Hall, of which he was lord of the manor) about a Walthamstow man whom he had bound to appear at the Sessions, but would himself be unable to attend. 'He is by profession a fencer and sometimes he taketh upon him the trade of a butcher. He is continually in variance with some one or other of his neighbours, a common threatener and braver of poor men, and a procurer of promoters to vex his neighbours.' 'In a word', Legh added, exhibiting his classical learning in three words, 'he is *jurgosus, rixosus et pugnax*.'

Three years later the Assize judges received a letter, signed by John Pragell, the high constable, Thomas Shawe and John Thorowgood churchwardens, and five parishioners of West Ham at the request of 'their neighbours, being the bakers of Stratford Bow' (over the Middlesex boundary) 'and one baker of their parish', testifying to the behaviour of a parishioner who had maliciously prosecuted the bakers because one of their number, as a headborough, had served a warrant on his sister. They declared him to be 'a man of very riotous behaviour, a common frequenter of alehouses, a quarreller and disquieter of his honest neighbours, one that keepeth continual carding and dicing in his house and daily companioneth with men of lewd and licentious life, and hath not only cloaked but also publicly defended the wicked life of his sister, which lived in adultery with a married man by whom of late she hath had two children, and doth daily in this time of Lent without licence kill and sell flesh to the great offence of his neighbours.' The writers craved punishment for this 'troublesome person.'

A much briefer note from five Danbury men in 1599, after a quarrel between two beer brewers of the parish, declared that the assailant was 'a

[1] P. Collinson, *The Elizabethan Puritan Movement* (1967), 220.

very lewd person and very often misbehaving himself.' The first signatory was Dr. George Withers, the rector (and Archdeacon of Colchester).

That barrators' activities might lead even to violent death is postulated in five further cases, all of which were tried at the Assizes. Silvester Walden of Little Dunmow gentleman was indicted in 1567 as a common barrator 'so that murders, homicides, quarrels and disorders are likely to arise among the inhabitants unless some remedy be speedily provided'; and almost the same language is used against William Metham of Manningtree blacksmith in 1571. Four years later Henry Puplett, a yeoman of Great Horkesley, was indicted as a barrator and procurer of divers murders, 'etc.'; found guilty, he was fined 6s. 8d. These are of course phrases taken out of justices' textbooks, but may well have been reserved for the more determined barrators. And the turbulent temperament of Walden, for one, was not exaggerated, for within a year he gave the parish constable three wounds when he tried to arrest him (p. 174).

A remarkable feature of Elizabethan disorder is the part played by some of the clergy. Patrick Ferne, rector of Sandon (1567–87),[1] was a common barrator, also a common quarreller in his church and elsewhere (fined 20d. on the first charge and 3s. 4d. on the second). An order made at the Midsummer Sessions 1575 concerned Matthew Levett, rector of Leaden Roothing, one of the most notorious of the Essex clergy (p. 82). It was for a minor offence – refusing to pay his share, 10d. a month, of the poor rate. The parish was 'very poor and small', and had to keep a newly-born bastard as well as three other 'aged and impotent persons.' The Court had learned that his benefice was worth £40 a year and he had 'of his own temporal living' another £16 a year. He was enjoined to pay 10d. monthly 'so long as the parish shall be charged with so great a charge as now it is.' An extra payment of 5s. to the collector of the poor for arrears was deleted from the order, first made probably because the bastard had been born in his rectory, the mother having died within a week and the named reputed father having absconded. He next appears in 1587 and was bound over by Francis Barrington, J.P., for good behaviour and appearance at the Midsummer Sessions 1588. He had been in the custody of the the Provost Marshal (in a London gaol) immediately before. At the Sessions he was charged with being a common barrator and disturber of the peace there, and a common malefactor, calumniator and spreader of strifes and discords among his parishioners and neighbours. In the well-known report of the Privy Council to the Archbishop of Canterbury in 1584 on the 'lamentable state of the Church in Essex' appears another catalogue of Levett's delinquencies: 'a notorious swearer, a dicer, a

---

[1] The periods during which the clergy held their benefices are taken from Newcourt, *Repertorium* (1710), vol. ii.

carder, a hawker and hunter'; he quarrelled and fought with the parson of Stoke (Stock) in a common inn in Chelmsford.[1] The other party was William Pinder, rector of Stock for half a century (1580–1625), and there is no doubt that there was little to choose between these fighting parsons. 'A common disturber of the peace, and caused discord among his neighbours' were the words used in his indictment at the Assizes in 1585: commonplace, but especially true in regard to Pinder. Evidence from the manorial and the archidiaconal records shows Pinder to have been both quarrelsome and litigious.[2]

John Goldringe, rector of Laindon Hills (died 1590),[3] was reported by the hundred as a drunkard and a quarreller in 1585. Nicholas Wallis, rector of Pentlow (who succeeded Nicholas Bushe in 1571, p. 200), was brought by the constables before Quarter Sessions in 1586, bound in the meantime, with two of his parishioners as sureties, to keep the peace towards a Cavendish (Suffolk) labourer. The court records say no more, but the Church report gives 'now in trouble for incontinency.'[4] Three years later Peter Williams, rector of Latchingdon (1584–1608), was presented by the grand jury as a quarreller amongst his parishioners, a fighter, a brabbler, a common player and gamester.

An indictment for barratry against Peter Lewes, vicar of Burnham, in 1587 charged him as 'a common barrator and disturber of the peace, and procurer of many insults, strifes and discords between his neighbours there and in divers other places, and has put them in terror of their lives, the mutilation of their limbs and the firing of their houses, and is very likely to commit murders, homicides, rebellions and disturbances and other damage in the county.' His sureties were George Cowell of Staple Inn, London, and Thomas Moore of Dagenham gentlemen. But his appearance was by proxy: Edward Makyn his attorney (it was very rare to find an attorney engaged) pleaded that the indictment was insufficient in law. The prosecutor for the Crown was John Popham, the Attorney-General, a criterion of the gravity of his offence. The jury of 24 (their names are given in a special list) found him guilty. Soon afterwards he was involved with others in a serious fracas with Richard Allyson, M.A., also of Burnham, whose clerical status in the parish is not at all clear (p. 112). One of his sureties for good behaviour was John Chandler, who was presented within a year or so for immorality and abetting intended murder (p. 199). The vicar, however, kept his benefice until his death thirty years later.

Five other clerics were accused of various forms of barratry. Richard Halywell, rector of Twinstead (1555–67), and Anne his wife, 'are common barrators, disturbers of the peace and sowers of quarrels among their neighbours, and keep a bawdy house there at which divers men and

---

[1] T. W. Davids, *Annals of Evangelical Nonconformity in Essex* (1863), 91.
[2] F. W. Austen, *Rectors of Two Essex Parishes* (1943), 81, 89.
[3] *Transactions Essex Archaeological Society*, vi, 323.   [4] Davids, *op. cit.*, 89.

14 HOUCHINS, FEERING

A fine example of a double-jettied, late 16th-century house (p. 134).

15 HARLOW BUSH FAIR, LATTON, 1616

women of ill condition and conversation frequent, and keep divers whores there' (1566). Lawrence Lyde of Ardleigh clerk (vicar, 1569–1602) 'is a common barrator and incites his neighbours to murder, homicides and contentions' (1574). At his trial he pleaded not guilty by his attorney and was found not guilty. William Drywood of Downham clerk (rector, 1574–1608) 'is a common barrator and disturber of the peace' (1579). The case was adjourned because a further charge was to be made. This appears at the following Assizes, when he was indicted for illegal gaming (p. 219) as well as for calling his parishioners 'boors, steers, notorious liars, drunken knaves.' The same Church report of 1584 awarded him the title of 'gamester.'[1] Challenging two vagrants in 1576, he had been attacked by both of them. John Whyte, vicar of Ramsey (1575–92) was a common barrator and disturber of the peace (1584). George Darlowe, vicar of Ugley (1591–96), was also a common disturber of the peace (1590). He was in Court again three years afterwards, in company with other parishioners, for assault (p. 167). The general account of 1584 had commented, 'a common swearer, a proud careless man, a riotous man ; absent from his benefice and preacheth not.'[2] The Essex clergy also figure in the sections on Church Assaults, Riot, Games, Larceny, and even Rape. The evidence now available in the Essex Sessions and Assize records bears out many of the charges made against some of the Essex clergy in the sweeping report of 1584, biased and exaggerated though it obviously is.

In 1575 it was a schoolmaster of Billericay whose conduct was unsatisfactory. Lord Rich, writing from Leighs Priory, informed the justices at their Easter Sessions 1576 that Marmaduke Middleton, who 'greatly misliked his trade and occupation', had been brought to him by the constable. Because of his behaviour at Billericay and 'in other places in Kent where he beforetime dwelt', Rich thought good to put him under house arrest till the Sessions, at which he was formally indicted as a common brawler and disturber. The schoolmaster appealed to the Privy Council in July. As a result, a letter was sent to the Assize judges. 'Whereas Marmaduke Middleton', they wrote, 'hath exhibited a complaint of certain griefs against the Lord Rich and certain of his tenants, which by reason of his poverty he is not able to pursue by order of law, they are required when they shall be in the county to take information of the matter by the poor man's own report and to confer with the Lord Rich and such others as shall be touched in the case, and to use all good means they can to bring the matter to an end or quietness.' The file for the Midsummer Assize is missing, but in any case it would probably have contained no record, as orders of this nature have rarely been preserved. After failing to appear, Middleton was eventually outlawed ; in the last two writs before outlawry, 1580–81, he is given as a schoolmaster of Colchester.

[1] T. W. Davids, *Annals of Evangelical Nonconformity in Essex* (1863), 99.
[2] Davids, *op. cit.*, 100.

Into Michael Dalton's second category of barrators – takers by force or subtlety of lands in controversy – seems to fall a complicated case about which Thomas Gent, a Baron of the Exchequer and J.P. of Moyns in Steeple Bumpstead, wrote to the county justices in 1592. It concerned 'the strife and the obstinate demeanour' of one Allen and 'the bad counsel given by one Stebbinge' (presumably the John Stebbinge who had figured in the Finchingfield feud of 1585–87, p. 109). Lady Cheke, widow of the learned Sir John Cheke, had married Henry Mackwilliam, lord of the manor of Stambourne, who himself had died in 1586.[1] She owned some land in Finchingfield which had been acquired on condition that the 'old tenants' should not be turned out. Allen thought he had managed to obtain a house and ground in the ancient tenure of one Flacke, the bearer of the letter, and violently evicted 'a poor woman who was there charitably kept and now lies on the charge of Finchingfield.' Gent reminded Lady Cheke of the proviso, so money was charitably offered by her to Allen to remove himself and his family, and Gent would have asked the parish of Stambourne to grant him 'a void place of the highway to have builded him a house with this money.' But Allen refused the offer 'with very evil words and unreverent demeanour', and gave 'worse words' when examined by Mr. Bendishe, J.P., of Finchingfield. All the chief parishioners had complained to Gent about the 'outrageous dealings' of Flack, who 'railing most impudently refuses and so he will in the end live most miserably without relief.' Gent left the matter for the Court's consideration.

The third category – false reports – is closely related to the less violent but merciless offence of Slander (p. 66).

All over England, in the sixteenth century and later, those accused of various crimes and offences were bound by the recognizances of themselves and usually two other sureties to appear at the Court to answer the charges against them; and the recognizance generally bound the offender also to keep the peace towards the plaintiff. In some cases a single or double justice (the term used by lawyers for a J.P. acting alone or a pair) satisfied himself with binding to good behaviour or to keep the peace without committing to the gaol or the Court. This often applied in the less serious charges of assault or barratry, but what proportion were thus dealt with we have no means of ascertaining.

There is however a single document which suggests that sending recognizances for the peace to the Clerk of the Peace merely for filing on record against any future breach was the only action taken in the majority of these misdemeanours. Edward Bury, writing to Mr. Ramme, the clerk of the peace, from his house 'in the Little Park of Rayleigh' on the morning of the Easter Sessions, sent him 'divers recognizances in paper for lack of parchment, praying you to bear with me for this time.' He explained that he was old and lame, and it was a great trouble and pain either to ride or

---

[1] Morant, *History of Essex*, ii, 357, 365.

go. He added a long postscript. 'Whereas I have made mention of divers recognizances, the parties hath desired to be quiet and are agreed'; but, he emphasised, 'except this one man, and who I assure you is naught and very troublesome among his neighbours, and in especial to this simple poor man John Marshall, and hath kept his wife and hath used him otherwise in suit in the spiritual court, for that the wife hath the parsonage of Little Wakering in ferm (lease), where the said Marshall did dwell, and hath so troubled him that he hath been driven to suffer him to avoid further trouble, much to his harm and undoing. Many others doth complain of him, as my Lord Rich can partly declare, if his honour do call to memory how he did use a poor widow, that my said Lord did grant the good abearing against him (i.e. took a recognizance for good behaviour) for his lewd behaviour. Therefore I assure you it is meet that such men should be bridled, otherwise it will be a discouraging to quiet and honest persons.' Thus the aged J.P. informed Ramme so that 'order may be taken as shall be meet.' The recognizance given by the delinquent, William Wiggon or Wygon of Little Wakering husbandman, with Henry Hasyll of South Shoebury husbandman and John Deane of Eastwood surgeon (probably barber-surgeon) as his sureties, is attached to the letter. But it is be noted that the others have not been preserved. And even Wiggon's could have been destroyed, as the Court 'released' (discharged) it when he duly appeared.

Thus, in Elizabeth's time, as well as generations before and after, this universal form of human disorder was challenged in the two higher civil courts for the county after presentment by the hundredal juries or complaints by neighbours. In these august courts the ubiquitous nuisance-makers were charged as 'common barrators and disturbers of the peace'. They were presumably among the worst or most persistent offenders, and many more were reported to the archdeacons' courts and the manor courts. There they were usually presented as 'common scolds', and some highly abusive epithets issued from their barbed tongues, as will be recounted in the next volume.

Barratry crops up in county records elsewhere, but the evidence is patchy. It was a fairly common offence in Lancashire and Wiltshire. In 1580 the Wiltshire Quarter Sessions ordered that no indictments for barratry should be received 'unless open evidence given in Court' : a wise safeguard against malicious prosecution.[1] As a specific offence it seems never to have been before the Middlesex justices. The only Worcestershire indictment, 'for being a common barrator, calumniator, curser and stirrer up of strife', was preferred against the parson or curate of Inkberrow in 1602.

[1] *Wiltshire County Records*, 59.

12
Murder and Homicide

Unlike other crimes, the records of which are largely in the form of indictments, the murder cases are drawn from both indictments and coroners' 'inquisitions' preserved in the Assize and Queen's Bench records. The great majority come from the inquests, which are set out as in the following case. Inquisition taken at Little Bromley, 10 April 1571, before William Vernon, gentleman, the coroner, on the view of the body of John Elder of the same, aged 74, on the oaths of (fourteen named) jurors, who say that John Robbins *alias* Roberts and Richard Wilson, his servant, of Great Bromley sawyers, on 5 March about 10 o'clock at night, assaulted John Elder in his house. Wilson held him on his bed while Robbins struck him a mortal blow with a dagger on the right cheek and then strangled him. Both plead not guilty; verdict, guilty.

Murder indictments are briefer, as in the next case. William Robiant of Orsett yeoman, at Margaretting, strangled Thomas Waight, and then, apparently to make certain, threw him into the river where he was drowned. Eight cases of murder or homicide in 1559–61 were described in the chapter on the earliest records (pp. 7, 11), including the only burglary in which an alleged murder was perpetrated. In this chapter, and indeed in some of the later chapters, we shall not give the years in which the crime was committed, when the date is of no significance, as in the next seven murders: all violent cases, but typical, we may assume, of what was happening all over the country in every decade of Elizabeth's reign.

A Debden labourer broke a woman's neck and hanged her while still alive. He was found guilty. The name of his alleged accomplice is struck through. An Inworth carpenter attacked a bricklayer, striking him on the head with a cudgel and felling him. Throwing himself on the victim, the carpenter with his knees and hands squeezed and struck him again. He died two weeks later. Not satisfied with flagellation, a Hadleigh man broke his wife's neck with the cord with which he had thrashed her. He was hanged. The inventory of his forfeited goods is on p. 165. A foul murder was committed by a London painter-stainer. 'Wickedly devising to despoil' a Barking widow, he persuaded a maidservant to steal £8 12s. belonging to her mistress. Presumably to silence her from giving evidence against him, he twisted her neck. She died instantly; guilty. An Althorne labourer one Christmas Day at 6 p.m. strangled a widow in her own house, then 'with an iron instrument called a bodkin' (either a dagger or small instrument for piercing holes) struck her a mortal blow on the head. The victim died instantly and the defendant was found guilty. A particularly brutal murder of a pregnant girl took place at Maldon. A local tailor had got the wench into trouble. He struck her on the belly and 'did spurn and crush her to make the child to be untimely born.' A Paglesham tailor was attacked by a widow and a labourer. The amazon gripped his throat, violently twisted it and broke his neck, causing instant death; the man 'was present and helped' her; and another tailor 'advised and helped her'. She only was found guilty, and she was pregnant when the case came before the judges. The imagination boggles at what lay behind her fury, and, equally, that of the cordwainer (p. 8).

Only twice do the records show that a murderer claimed more than one victim. On a February evening in 1589 a labourer broke into the house of John Catterall at Black Notley and murdered him and his sister. The assailant struck the man with an axe on the right and left of his head and then plunged his knife into the man's brain and throat. The woman received four head wounds with the axe. The gory details are extended, as in many other cases, to the depths in inches of each wound. Both died instantly. Another labourer, apparently his brother, helped the murderer to bury his victims. The labourer was found guilty, the accessory not guilty. One morning in 1597 a Mile End (Colchester) labourer, at Great Horkesley, struck both his wife and his two-year-old son on the head with a staff, giving each a mortal 'bruise'. While still alive he drowned them in a water-filled sawpit. The Assize judges learned that he had died in gaol.

There are only a few fairly definite cases of premeditated murder. Thomas Marshe senior, a Stebbing butcher, took his axe with him 'of malice aforethought' to the house of Walter Algor at Great Bardfield, where he killed Alice Wakelyn, a spinster, with a single expert blow. Not satisfied, he gave her a second head gash, 'of which she would have died if she had not been killed by the first wound'; guilty. A Little Clacton labourer, also 'of malice aforethought', murdered his wife by wringing her neck. Guilty. (Stands mute: judgement that he be pressed, etc.) The words in parentheses are struck through. They refer to one of the rare occasions when the accused refused to plead, in order to save his property from forfeiture. This terrible death, being pressed by heavy weights, was resorted to by a few courageous men, usually possessing an estate which was thus preserved intact for the heir; it is most unusual to find a labourer associated with the *peine forte et dure*, as lawyers termed it.[1]

The records provide five instances of fatal poisoning. A Great Wakering woman murdered her husband with poison mixed in a drink, so that he instantly died; not guilty. A Wakes Colne servant put mercury into a mess of porridge for her mistress, who died after languishing for a fortnight.

1 For the *peine forte et dure*, see *Middlesex County Records*, i, pp. xxxii–iii.

A man had abetted her. Despite the evidence of five witnesses (not given), both were acquitted. A Thundersley man gave his wife ratsbane in her broth. An Ipswich (Suffolk) woman mixed 'poison with rosasolis (aqua rosarum)', which she gave to her husband, who died next day. Nicholas Tooley, yeoman, also of Ipswich, had abetted her and afterwards received her at Ilford. The examinations of five witnesses were taken. Both were acquitted. (Rosasolis by itself is not poisonous.) It has not been possible to ascertain whether Nicholas was a relation of Henry Tooley, the richest merchant of Ipswich, who on his death in 1551 left most of his fortune to the poor of his town.[1] A Great Wakering labourer's wife murdered him with 'poison in a drink, so that he instantly died'; not guilty.

Among the murder charges are those resulting from three sailors' brawls, all of which took place at Harwich. A St. Osyth sailor attacked a Ramsey mariner with his sword, killing him there in 1596. He escaped away in the ship Foresight, whose master and owner was a Harwich man, John Cobham, termed an 'esquire'. Two mariners, 'aliens born in the parts under the obedience of King Philip', were involved, one knifing the other on 'the Common'. The last case records how a Harwich sailor knifed another.

John Collins of Braintree went to Bocking about his father's business, when along came John Noke of Stisted, aged 23, and they quarrelled. Said Noke, 'Thou, boy, use the weapon if thou be a man as thou boasted thyself; for I will fight with thee and be revenged of me. Pray thee content thyself, and a-touching the malice thou bearest me from last playing together at backsword play I pray thee forget, for I tell thee for my part from henceforth I will have nothing to do with thee. But if thou be a good fellow and go drink I will give it thee'. Nevertheless, the record (1565) laconically adds, they fought. The coroner's inquest was adjourned for three months, when the verdict was that Collins murdered Noke. A blacksmith, a tailor and a husbandman of Faulkbourne with others unknown attacked four named men, whose abode is not stated. The husbandman, with the aid of the other two, knifed one of the men in the throat (1602). All three were apparently convicted and were presumably hanged at Colchester; none was buried at Faulkbourne.[2]

These may all have been drunken fights. Only twice is there a record of tempers fatally flaring up in an alehouse (the other is related later under homicide). Three men were drinking together 'in a friendly way' (one is surprised to find this phrase used as far back as Elizabeth's day). The scene is the house of Thomas Cooke at Witham. He brought a pot of beer, asking payment from Stamford, who promptly knocked him down. Field joined in the affray, and with Cooke attacked Stamford, crushing him to the ground. He died instantly. Field escaped but was captured by the constable and other townsmen. Neither was found guilty. Like Ben Johnson,

[1] J. Webb (ed.), *Poor Relief in Elizabethan Ipswich* (Suffolk Rec. Soc., ix, 1966).
[2] Transcript of parish register (E.R.O., T/R 20).

who was killed in a drunken brawl at Deptford in 1593 (p. 164), more of these recorded victims must have met their death in similar circumstances. Little imagination is required to visualise some of the scenes. Occasionally a four-centuries-old echo of their taunting words reaches us. Two servants of Edmund Sherbrooke, 'Master of Theology', of Ashdon (rector, 1565–84), quarrelled because one made two 'taypinnes' (tie-pins, doubtless to fix together the members of the timber-frame of a building). For some reason the other disapproved and with a cart whip lashed his fellow servant, who 'being moved by wrath' threw his knife, causing instant death. He was convicted.

Despite Harrison's remarks, there is not much evidence of murders by vagrants,[1] though perhaps a little more about non-fatal attacks. There are many contemporary allusions (Harrison is only one of the writers) to the hordes of unruly vagabonds and discharged soldiers and sailors wandering about the country. In a few cases we may perhaps equate untraced murderers with vagrants, but this would be mere supposition. The savage incident at Leytonstone has already been related (p. 8). In 1568 one 'wayfaringman' assaulted a labourer in Springfield parsonage barn yard at night with a 'forage knife'. He died six days later in the barn. His assailant fled. A violent attack with sword and caliver was made at Vange in 1590 by a Hatfield Peverel labourer with others unknown on a man who died next day (the labourer fled) ; and another in 1598 on the Great Essex Road to Colchester, but just within the city of London boundary, where a Londoner assaulted Walter Overed of Great Warley gentleman with a penknife, as a result of which he died seven months afterwards.

There are several fatal quarrels which took place on the highway. Two Writtle husbandmen 'happened to pass in the highway from High Ongar to Chelmsford and opprobrious words arose between then'. A mortal blow with a hedging bill led to death three days later. The coroner had the assailant's goods valued at £6 13s. 4d. ; but he was not in custody. A spinster aged 26 of Sudbury (Suffolk), walking home, was attacked at Belchamp St. Paul by a Bures cook, who cut her throat; guilty. Two Dagenham labourers were walking on the Dagenham church path when they 'quarrelled and wrangled', one dying two hours later from a cudgel blow. The attacker had no goods; guilty, read as a clerk.

Two Maldon shoemakers were fighting with their fists in Friars Mead, when a third man separated them. Determined to have it out, they met again next morning (9 January 1582) between 7 and 8 in a field belonging to Heybridge rectory, both equipped with pikestaves and daggers. A chest stab caused instant death. The survivor 'escaped to some place unknown', and the verdict was murder. A dawn rendezvous, each with the same weapon, strongly suggests a duel, in which a fatal wound was accounted in law as murder. Although no pre-arranged duel is specifically referred

[1] William Harrison, *Description of England*, 185.

to in the Elizabethan Assize records it may perhaps be deduced when one (or, more probably, both) of the parties was a gentleman and the weapon was a sword or rapier.

At 8 a.m. on 26 September 1597 at Braintree Edward Larkyn of Finchingfield gentleman, with his dagger stabbed William Parkington, giving him a deep belly wound, of which he died next day; the verdict is illegible. Three more fatal deaths by sword and rapier in the same decade, which would otherwise call for no comment, occurred at 8 a.m.; of the survivors, possibly duellists, one was found guilty, another was at large, and the third confessed. The most intriguing case concerns a gentleman of the family chiefly remembered because of the Stock almshouses, the building of which Richard Twedy provided for in his will of 1575, and of his well-known brass in the church where he was buried, though he describes himself in his will as of Boreham.[1] At Lent Assizes 1579 Robert Twydy *alias* Twyttye of Stock (Richard's brother) gave Thomas Tabor yeoman there on the previous 16 September a dagger wound causing death three days later. But the jurors' statement in the coroner's inquisition, taken at Stock on 20 September, clearly says that about 4 p.m. Tabor kicked Twedy to the ground, whereon he retaliated (as narrated in the indictment). An inventory of Twedy's goods made on 20 September and valued at £9 12s. 8d. unfortunately gives few details.

Two fatal quarrels, possibly duels, occurred in 1603. Edward Wylbore gentleman gave Robert Potter yeoman, both of Colchester, a rapier wound; and John Davenant of Poslingford (Suffolk) gentleman gave William Toftes of Danbury a sword wound. Both men died instantly. Wylbore 'gave himself up' (the sole instance in the whole period). On 29 June 1598 a coroner's jury, after viewing the body of Percival Clovell of West Hanningfield esquire, said that he had been instantly killed by Robert Fryer of Chelmsford yeoman with a three-inch deep sword thrust. Fryer fled and was still at large. It is interesting to find that the victim was the son and heir of Francis Clovile of Clovile Hall in West Hanningfield. The Cloviles had owned the manor since the time of Henry II, and Percival had inherited it in 1589 when he was 16. The Herald's visitation of 1612 records him as 'slayn, without issue', a sinister line on which local historians have previously sought some illumination.

In 1592 there was an encounter between George Haven of Coggeshall surgeon and Thomas Warner yeoman there. With one knife Haven gave Warner a 'thrust' in the throat five inches deep and with another knife three more stabs in the belly, one five inches and the others half an inch deep respectively. Not surprisingly the victim died at once; guilty. Another surgeon, John Fyssher of Brentwood, in 1583 at West Ham, violently flung a bricklayer twice to the ground so that his body was crushed, and he died later that day. The verdict was 'Not guilty, but that a

[1] Austen, *Rectors of Two Essex Parishes*, 66–68.

certain John Style killed him'. Both were probably barber-surgeons, and it is doubtful if they were duelling. This verdict introduces the contemporary nomenclature for the present-day 'person unknown', corresponding to John Doe and Richard Roe, the ubiquitous men of straw in the ficititious property suits known as 'common recoveries'.

Four men found a woman aged 21 dead with a broken neck in a hay barn. Verdict: John atte Style with both his hands murdered her. We find a number of these imaginary gentlemen. A fight between two men with fisticuffs at Barking was broken up by the onlookers, but the first assailant followed the other and re-started fighting. Retaliation led to retribution and death six days later. Not guilty, but John at Nok was. At an inquest on an unknown man found by a wood near Lepers Lane in Dagenham the jury declared that John A Style had clubbed him and then cut his throat. 'The said A Style fled, by default of the vill', that is, the folk neglected their ancient communal duty of raising a hue and cry. After viewing the dead body of a Basildon woman, the coroner's jury found that she had been clubbed on the head by John Atnoke of Basildon and died instantly. They added that he also gave her another head wound of which she would have died if she had not already succumbed. He fled, by default of the inhabitants.

A very human quarrel suddenly arose on the edge of the great royal Waltham Forest one early autumn day in 1571. Two Waltham men, one of them John Garbett being of the household of John Ryggesby gentleman, a forest keeper, were passing through a close of William Alee husbandman in which does were grazing. They spotted two dogs after them and chased the dogs to their home. Alee's wife was standing at the door, having doubtless heard the hubbub. The keeper demanded to know who sent the dogs on the hunt. The woman declared that she had done it. Garbett threatened to kill them if found chasing the Queen's deer again. The wife, a little nettled (*paululum commota*) by these words, called Garbett a fool (*nebulonem*), adding that if she had been present when he killed a neighbour's dogs she would not have borne it, and putting down the infant she was holding she threw a brickbat at Garbett's head, hurting him, on which he struck her on the back with his nine-foot pikestaff. She died on New Year's Eve. Not guilty, but John atte Noke was.

Two boys found the decaying body of an unknown girl aged 12 in a ditch by the lane in White Colne leading to 'Lowne Hall' (probably Little Loveney Hall in Wakes Colne). The jurors said that Richard Nemo murdered her. But another jury eschewed such appellations and found that an unknown man had murdered a spinster servant in Waysingwell Field in Great Braxted by choking her, and had fled.

It mattered little whether the jurors placed the guilt on an unknown murderer, or on Richard Nemo, or John a Style, or John atte Noke. But the last three cases in their turn lead to the inevitable question whether their victims had first been raped. There are nine further cases, together with the murder in a wood at Leytonstone (p. 8) ; but in all rape is only hypothetical, and some or all may have been the victims of the man's anger, or theft, or, in one case, burglary. One February evening in 1600 Thomas Winckfield of Brentwood gentleman killed a London spinster by a dagger wound in her buttock; that night he fled and remained at large. A Rayleigh tailor killed a woman at Basildon by a headwound with a hatchet; not guilty. A Stebbing butcher, of malice aforethought, killed a spinster in another man's house at Bardfield Saling by a head wound with an axe, of which she instantly died ; after which he gave her further slashes. A Hornchurch labourer struck a woman on the head, so that she fell into a pit of water, and a second blow killed her ; he confessed to the charge and was hanged. Maurice 'le Roge of Ingatestone labourer' (evidently a vagabond) broke the neck of an unknown girl aged about 19 and fled the same night.

A curious case arose in 1581, when a coroner's jury, after viewing a South Weald widow's body, 'knew nothing'. The coroner adjudged this as recalcitrance. They were each fined the stunning sum of £5, which loosened their tongues. Then they stated that John in le Winde of South Weald labourer had cut her throat at night in her house with her own scissors and then fled. Another unusual incident, originating under James I in Quarter Sessions, was first dealt with as the aged Queen lay on her deathbed. Gamaliel Capell, J.P. had examined Nicholas Clarke of Beauchamp Roothing painter, charged with the paternity of his servant's bastard, when the news came that the infant had been murdered. The justice's clerk, reporting this event, asked the Court to bind Clarke over to the Assizes. In the meantime Mr. Long the coroner was to take sufficient security for his appearance.

A cuckolded husband came before the Assizes in 1602. He was Richard Cofield, the miller of Sible Hedingham. The woman was at a Finchingfield man's house at 6 a.m., when the incensed spouse turned up, stabbing her in the heart with his knife. Provocation did not avail in his defence and he was hanged.

A right-of-way dispute at Ashdon proved fatal in 1572. A yeoman's servant stopped four villagers from crossing his master's land with a cartload of wood. Next day they re-appeared, and the same servant with two other men armed with bows, arrows and pitchforks prevented their passage. A member of the defending party was mortally wounded in the struggle. One of the villagers was found guilty ; two not guilty ; the fourth was tried only for felony.

The case of a murderer of Bures St. Mary (Suffolk) has two unusual features. One night in March 1588, on the bank of the Stour (the boundary between Suffolk and Essex), he gave a mortal head wound with his quarter-staff to a man of Bures Mount (Essex), killing him instantly. His widow was indicted for procuring the murder and receiving the Suffolk man. She was found not guilty. In the file for the following Assizes is a letter from John Wolmer, the clerk of assize in Suffolk, to the justices of gaol delivery, which states that the murderer had been hanged.

In seventeen further cases both murderer and victim were men, the offensive weapon being a cudgel (three times), sword, rapier, dagger, knife, hedging bill, axe, hatchet, spade, stake, 'loakestake', stick or pike-staff. Where verdicts and sentences are given, they show that seven murderers read and were branded, three had fled and were still at large, and one had died in gaol. The others, of course, were hanged. Only in two cases was the verdict not guilty – an attack with an axe, and an assault with 'a wand or stick' in which the victim was struck four times and died three days later.

An aspect of Tudor social history of which little is known concerns the conditions under which domestic servants and servants in husbandry lived. The Essex petty sessions presentments have exceptionally good statistics about their wages and other items in their hiring contracts (these will be given in a later volume, and depositions in the Quarter Sessions rolls also contain some details of their lives. The criminal records give some lurid stories about the ways in which a few met violent deaths. At least ten died at the hands of their master or mistress : a significant proportion of the total number of murders. Equally significant is the fact that nearly all the pleas of not guilty were accepted, but there are too few cases to allow the conclusion that employers were exonerated by juries ; furthermore, one charge – that against a member of an armigerous and substantial Harlow family – was reduced from murder to homicide by the jury (p. 8).

A twelve-year-old servant of William Thedam of Little Waltham, who was his wife's stepdaughter, was working in the 'entry' of his house, when the woman gave her a mortal wound with a hatchet, and hid the body first under a plum tree, then in an oat field, and finally in a pond near Palmer's Way in the parish. The jury had met on 21 July but sought an adjournment. The coroner ordered them to meet at North End (in Great Waltham) at dawn on 17 August. They then found her not guilty and said that John at Love killed her. A Stanford-le-Hope husbandman, angry with his servant-girl at 6 a.m. because she had been too long in feeding the pigs, struck her violently and her nose bled too freely. She survived for six weeks. Not guilty ; John at Style killed her. Richard Gollyns of Rainham yeoman threw down his maidservant aged 14, and struck her. She died four days later. Not guilty ; killed by John (?)Watts (the writing is faint and it might be another of the 'atte' species). A servant girl of 15 was many times 'unreasonably abused and corrected with wands of hull and hazel by her mistress', and she died of such ill-treatment ; not guilty. Corporal punishment was often inflicted by a labourer on his servant aged 11. It was alleged that he had chastised her on the legs and thighs with his buckled belt and the bruises putrified. Not guilty; John Staff (yet another fictitious name) killed her. One evening in 1597 John Grant of Abbess Hall in Great Wigborough (evidently the tenant of the Duke of Norfolk's manor) inflicted a deep dagger wound in the head of his maid-servant aged 24 in Wheat Field there. His plea was that John Love murdered her, but Grant was found guilty. A Navestock sawyer killed a maidservant by a head wound with his axe. He fled, but later confessed. An Aveley spinster struck her maidservant several times with a 'broom-stalk'.[1] Not guilty; William Nobody killed her. A Great Clacton husbandman's wife beat her manservant with a 'slivery stick' (a piece of wood split off) so that he died three days later; guilty, remanded for pregnancy.

Murder of young servants leads to murder of children and then to infanticide. Four cases of child murders have already been related (p. 7), verdicts of not guilty being returned in two of them. A ten-year-old boy was stuck on the head by his guardian's wife, wielding a 'hazel stick with a snag growing thereon' (a knot left after cutting off a small branch), which penetrated the skull. The wound became putrified and death occurred within four months, by which time the woman had also died. A girl of the same age was struck by her stepmother on the hips and back with a rod and died three days later; not guilty, John Anoke killed her. A nine-year-old girl was violently struck by a man with a 'walking staff' and died within two weeks; not guilty. A solitary charge of starvation was brought in 1571. A Twinstead man received a boy aged five into his house to bring him up, but his wife, intending to kill the child, deprived him of food and drink over a period of seven months; not guilty, John a Style killed him.

Verdicts of guilty were given in the remaining cases. The most revolting murder is that of the pregnant woman who put her young son into an oven (p. 7). A girl of eight was beaten by her father with a 'broomstalk' and died six days later. A girl of six was found dead. She had been ill, and the coroner's jury said that her stepfather threw her out of bed against the boards and next day struck her violently while in bed. She died within a week. An unmarried mother drowned her two-year-old son in a pond. Alice wife of Benjamin Kyngsman of Springfield gentleman murdered their daughter aged two by breaking her neck. A widow, of malice aforethought, murdered her son, age not stated, by wounding his head with an unknown instrument. One coroner's inquest led to no charge: a widow murdered her daughter aged five and then drowned herself.

Infanticide was woefully common, and there were probably many other violent deaths by smothering or bruising which were concealed from the coroner. The Essex records disclose at least thirty unwanted babies whose brief lives were cut short by their mothers. Except for three, they were all

---

[1] Not a misreading of broomstick but an earlier form (unrecorded in this sense in *N.E.D.*) of broomstaff; another fatal assault with a broomstalk is given below.

apparently unmarried. One spinster, on 21 October 1570 between 12 and 1 a.m. at the house of William Fytche gentleman, her master, at Little Canfield (Hall), gave birth to a dead infant in the backhouse and threw it into his horse pond; no verdict given. Another, in the house of John Perrye yeoman, her master, at Stanford-le-Hope, secretly gave birth at night, after which she cut the baby's throat and threw him into the nearby stream, weighted with stones; guilty. A baby was born in Cludens Close in Copt Hall Park, Epping, and thrown into the 'mud or slud' of the ditch; not guilty, but John Stile did it. Another, born in a field on a December night, was drowned. Another was left to die in the cold of January. A servant of Richard Harte of St. Mary's, Maldon, yeoman, bore a daughter without a midwife's aid and put her naked into a chest in the bedroom. Next day she took the infant, then dead, and by advice of her master, the putative father, buried it in a heap of horse dung in the garden; 'not in prison' (refers presumably to the mother). Another infant, born 'without the help of any woman', was strangled. Only in one other case is the father or putative father specifically named. The mother of a stillborn infant took him to a pond full of water, and tying a weight to his neck threw him in. William Draper, the father, knew nothing of this. A coroner's jury returned that a Little Bardfield widow 'gave birth by abortion to a female infant born dead' at Lindsell. Before absconding she carried it to her home parish and hid it in a haymow of William Chapman, who was the finder: a man of good name and fame, the jurors added. The year is 1589 and until much later the meaning of abortion was as given by Andrew Boorde in his *Brevyarye* (1547), 'Abhorsion is when a woman is delyvered of her chylde before her tyme.'

A widow strangled her newly-born infant; another widow was present and abetted her. The mother was hanged, and the abettor acquitted. A woman buried her offspring close to the house of William Grey gentleman at Danbury; and a servant of Humphrey Mopted of Frinton yeoman secretly delivered herself and then 'defaced' the baby among her pigs; in the jurors' view it was born dead through her negligence in not seeking a midwife's help.

Analysis of the causes of death in the thirty infanticide cases, including those already referred to, gives: strangled, five; smothered, two; suffocated —by pillow, one, in oven, one, in ditch, three; in haystack, one; drowned —in pond, four (one stillborn), in well, one; buried in a hole, one; broken or twisted neck, three; put in chest and then in dung heap, one; cut throat, two (one then drowned); struck against bedpost, one; struck by a man, one; cause not stated, three. The verdicts, etc., were: guilty, seventeen (three women were remanded because they were pregnant again); not guilty, five; John a Style guilty, one; guilty of homicide but not of murder, one; not proved that child was alive, one; killed by a man, one; inquests without verdict, three; 'abortion', one.

The three forms of justifiable homicide, according to the lawyers, were manslaughter, misadventure, and necessity. Manslaughter properly covered all homicides, but was popularly used for unpremeditated (and therefore not malicious) attacks, usually arising from sudden quarrels; its quaint legal synonym was chance-medley, a term found in the Middlesex records but not in Essex. Necessity was pleaded, for example, where an officer killed a man resisting arrest in a hue-and-cry or in a journey to gaol, but it applied mainly to self-defence. Misadventure implied an accident.

In a plea of self-defence, the accused had to prove that he had been unable to flee beyond a wall, hedge, ditch or other obstacle; mere counter-attack without running away and being cornered was not by itself justifiable manslaughter. Hence, as we shall see, the precise particulars of such obstructions. But in some cases a plea of self-defence without being cornered was accepted.

Homicide or manslaughter, other than by chance-medley, misadventure or necessity, differed from murder only in that it was committed without malicious intent; it was a felony, the punishment for which was hanging, as with murder. If, however, the verdict of the coroner's jury included the words 'by misfortune', 'in self-defence', or the like, then a royal pardon was granted 'of course', that is, as a matter of right. But all persons convicted of manslaughter, as well as murder (and other felonies) forfeited their goods and chattels. Two inventories of felons' belongings have been preserved (p. 165).

Michael Dalton, in his *Country Justice*, devotes as much space to the various ways in which homicide could be pleaded as he does to murder. Statute law, as already seen, had defined some means; case law had provided other loopholes but does not always seem to have been consistent. Self-defence, of course, was the plea whenever there was a chance of its being accepted; and, if so, the verdict ran, 'guilty of homicide but not of murder', 'homicide in self-defence', or 'manslaughter but not of malice aforethought'. Such a plea was certainly justified in the eyes of a coroner's jury which met at Wivenhoe on 14 and 23 December 1566 to consider a violent incident there between two Wivenhoe men. One was 'quietly going about his business' near his house in the road, called the 'entry', from the quay leading to Colchester. The other, intent on murder, ran up, shouting 'Whoremaster' and attacking. The victim, in self-defence, used his bill, killing the assailant instantly.

An enraged labourer, assaulted by John Fowell, a miller of Shenfield, drew his knife and mortally wounded the miller, who died on the same day. Richard Oseley, termed a gentleman of Chelmsford but possibly a traveller, was assaulted one afternoon in 1601 in the 'Boar's Head' there by a Boreham man, but struck out with his sword; the man died sixteen days later. Two upper servants of Sir Henry Tyrrel of Downham were arguing and fighting. A labourer was trying to separate them, when Henry Rainebird, a fellow servant, came up and suddenly attacked one of the brawlers, who turned on him, giving a dagger thrust on the cheek, from which he died three days afterwards. Four men were drinking together at Coggeshall. About to depart to Colchester on his horse and holding a stone pot, one was challenged to pay for a 'drinking glass' that he had broken. Throwing the pot against a wall, 'by misfortune' it hit the man demanding the cash, who died a few days later. The plea, strangely enough, was self-defence.

Among cases not involving self-defence, there is another mortal attack on a servant. Joan wife of William Ive of Horndon-on-the-Hill fletcher (arrowmaker) struck her 18-year-old servant with a bedstaff under her short ribs. Presumably the plea was one of unpremeditated anger. Two Waltham Holy Cross men were quarrelling. The brother of one of them, 'not willing to break the peace, quietly left them in order to stop the affray', upon which the other violently struck him on the eye with a boar spear; the culprit fled. One February day at dawn a carpenter killed a weaver's wife with his staff and knife in Windmill Croft in Coggeshall, to which they both belonged.

One of the four fatal highway assaults which reached the courts took place in 1566 at Ilford (probably on the Great Essex Road). The victim was attacked with a hedging bill by a man described as 'of Ilford labourer' (but this may be a fictitious appellation); the case was heard at a special Quarter Sessions at Barking. An inquest of 1590 reveals an unusual incident. Two men had sued Thomas Foster gentleman in the Queen's Bench. Under a writ of *non omittas*, four sheriff's bailiffs had arrested him at Bedfords near Romford, but two men and others unknown had rescued him in the highway at South Weald (evidently the same main road). Equipped with gauntlets (some of which at this period had metal plates), dogs, privy coats (coats of mail worn under ordinary dress), swords and daggers, they attacked the bailiffs, one of whom was killed instantly by a rapier thrust. Perhaps the sight of the gallows, the memory of which is preserved in Gallows Corner, emboldened him to force an escape. Both Foster and the assailant were found guilty of homicide. Had the bailiffs known the law, they could have killed the ruffian with impunity. Under an Act of Henry VII Foster was treated as an accessory. Killing an officer was a serious crime, and the jury's verdict of 'guilty of homicide and not of murder' for both seems too lenient for Foster's rescuer.

Orsett villagers witnessed a strange scene on 1 June 1597. It was the 'festival of Whitsun Wednesday' and John Adams the curate was celebrating evening prayers. Thomas Griffin, a parishioner, created some sort of 'disturbance', so the constable and churchwarden with the help of others arrested him. As they took him through the street he put up a resistance, so the officers struck him with their staves. He received internal injuries and died next day. No verdict is given, but it was probably not guilty, or the charge was homicide. Another violent encounter took place at Stanford-le-Hope, also in 1590 (p. 82).

Three Great Dunmow labourers in 1603 broke into the park of Robert Kynwelmershe gentleman (he was lord of the manor of Newton Hall in Dunmow), intending to take coneys. But two of his men were watching, and in the skirmish one of them sustained a four-inch head wound with a pikestaff. It became infected and he died a week later. The poacher was convicted; the abettors were guilty of felony but not of murder. This was the only fatal poaching encounter except for the borderline incident in Waltham Forest.

There was also a wildfowling fatality which came before the coroner in 1600, but the verdict is illegible. Two Manningtree sailors, rowing at 12.30 a.m. in Brantham Creek on the Suffolk side of the Stour, espied what they thought was the plumage of a heron feeding on another water-fowl. One discharged his fowling-piece but it proved to be the head of a solitary wildfowler moving stealthily among the rushes in the salt-marsh. He was mortally wounded.

Accessories were indicted in five more homicide cases, but all were acquitted. Two of these involved procurers, but Essex records yield none of hired assassins. Strong feelings about ownership of some land at Wethersfield in dispute between William Cranford and Alexander Walford of Shalford yeomen lay behind an attack which took place at Thaxted in 1580. The latter and his son, also Alexander, 'procured' William Baker, a baker of Thaxted, as their strongarm man, giving him a good meal beforehand. William 'Barnish' (Berners) of Finchingfield gentleman was also implicated, having sent a lad of his with a black horse to the land 'in variance', who delivered to Baker over his hedge a pikestaff, ten foot long, with the message, 'Take this staff, it is better than thine own'. And with this useful weapon Baker struck Cranford on the head. He died within three hours. After the murder Walford senior sent Baker 5s., bidding him to be of good cheer. Cranford had apparently been warned in advance by Berners. 'There are come,' he told him, 'those now that will keep possession, and I can tell it will cost knocks'. The verdict against Baker was homicide; the Walfords were not charged; and Berners was acquitted. He was the grandson of John Berners, whose fine altar tomb is in the south chapel of Finchingfield church, and his house, Petches, still exists.

Three years later Robert Stowe gave John Eve a sword thrust on the back of his head, of which he died within four days. Richard Alcocke abetted him. The jurors stated that John Norton, gentleman and brewer, procured the two men to commit the felony. All three defendants belonged to Colchester. In 1588 two bookbinders named Pratt were indicted. William hit Gabriel Thurgood on the head with a cudgel, of which he died instantly, and Roger and his wife abetted William. All were of Saffron Walden. *Ignoramus* for the wife; not guilty for her husband. Robert Coxe of Canewdon blacksmith and Thomas Coxe of Rayleigh husbandman assaulted a man at Woodham Ferrers, Robert striking him with his dagger on the 'cannon bone'[1] on the left side of the chest (died two weeks later), Thomas abbetting. Instead of a normal sentence, Robert was remanded for the Queen's service (the date is 1602, England continuing at war with Spain until her death). Two charges of infanticide also produced verdicts of homicide.

A plea of self-defence was submitted to nine assault charges, in seven of which the fleeing man was held up by a hedge, stile or other obstruction. A labourer attacked another; the victim fled but could not get beyond a hedge, so to save his life he struck out, instantly killing his assailant. Two fighting clothworkers, both apparently of Great Dunmow, were 'parted'. The man assaulted then went to his master's house, found an axe, counter-attacked, forcing the other to a pile of tree trunks whence the first could not escape, and in self-defence he wielded a rod with fatal effect. The fourth highway assault, with a three-foot cudgel and a rapier, occurred at Abbess Roothing. Running to a hedge which he could not get through and being followed 'furiously', the man attacked drew his sword in self-defence, giving a mortal wound. Edmund Fortescue of Barking esquire reproved his servant for drunkenness. In a rage he drew his rapier and attacked his master, who fled to a ditch, drawing his own rapier and inflicting a seven-inch belly wound, of which the servant died two days later. At 'Ketton' (Kedington, a hamlet on the Suffolk border) John Chote saw one of Peter Jobson's pigs doing damage in his field. He ordered his man to chase it out, but Jobson made for him with a six-foot fork. In fear of his life he fled and failing to get through the nearest hedge he pulled out an 'eyther' (edder, a hazel-rod) from the hedge and struck Jobson in self-defence, giving him a wound two inches long and a 'grain of barley' in depth and across, of which he died five days afterwards. 'Herd, turn thee, for I will strike thee', the words followed by action, caused flight on another occasion to the nearest stile, where the attacker was resisted and killed. Thomas Nicholson shoemaker was one evening at the house of Richard Joye. They were both of Moulsham in Chelmsford (Joye was a tailor who committed burglary seven years later). Nicholson assaulted John Neuberye of Chelmsford butcher with a cudgel. The butcher ran outside, falling into a roadside ditch. 'Angrily' scrambling out, he drew his knife and thrust it into the body of the shoemaker, who died nine days later. The jury, sitting under two coroners, found the butcher guilty: exceptionally in this case, the jurors presumably rejecting a plea of chance-medley or self-defence. The inventory of the butcher's goods is at the end of the chapter. John Pamplyn of Great Waltham shoemaker was digging

---

[1] Not in *N.E.D.* except as bones in a horse's leg (earliest ref., 1834).

M

at Broad Green, where he 'beat the brains out of the head' of a boy aged nine. A spinster threw out her six-weeks 'natural child' into the 'entry' of Nicholas Bonnye's inn at Witham; seeing the infant, he told Peter Archbone to take it to its grandmother's home. On his way William Farthinge of Witham yeoman assaulted Archbone and struck the infant with a staff, of which she died three weeks later. Was he the father? Gilbert Hyndes of Brentwood yeoman, at Tiptree in Tolleshunt D'Arcy, furiously assaulted Ralph Elzynge of Little Horkesley yeoman on the face with his sword. 'After some time', to save his life he defended himself, killing his attacker. The scene was probably Tiptree Heath, a wild open expanse. John Mettleman, a bellfounder of London, had long been retained by Philip Browne as 'caretaker' of the rectory of Manuden. Thomas Harrys entered the rectory on behalf of Thomas Punford, who claimed title to it, and fell upon Mettleman, who escaped with Harrys hot in pursuit. In self-defence the former killed his adversary.

There are twelve cases of attempted, intended or suspected murder, the earliest having already been noted (p. 11). In 1562 John Fludd of Brentwood, John Waker of Dunmow and William 'with the wry (i.e. twisted) mouth' of Sheering, all shearmen, burgled the house of Thomas Smythe and his wife at Sheering with murderous intent. Walter died before the case was tried; the others were found not guilty. A letter sent in 1574 from two Barnston men to Lord Rich and Lord Darcy complained that the wife of one of them, 'forgetting her duty and obedience as a wife, had sundry times maliciously attempted to bereave her husband of his life, so that he stand in great fear', not only of her but also of two Dunmow men, her 'adherents', who haunted his house in her company at night. He sought warrants for their arrest. In 1579 a London silkweaver and four others broke into the house of Lewis Benner of Kelvedon clerk (rector of Kelvedon, died 1605[1]) at night, 'intending to murder and plunder' him and his wife. When Edward Pynchon gentleman (of Writtle) late one evening in 1602 marched with a constable into Thomas Tabor's inn at Brentwood to arrest a man, bearing a warrant from John Butler, J.P., he was attacked by unruly customers and nearly strangled by the innkeeper's brother.

A few suspected murderers lurk in the shadows. Henry Barbor, vicar of Grays Thurrock (1598–1605), was 'bound in bail' in 1602 by John Wyld of Barking and William Page of Thurrock gentlemen to appear at the Assizes to 'charge Mr. Kyghtly for keeping in his house persons vehemently suspected for felony and murder, knowing them to be suspected'. This curious charge refers to Thomas Kighley (or Keightley), J.P., lord of the manor of Grays, who had presented Barbor to the benefice.[2] The records are silent about any proceedings. In the same year a case of

---

[1] *Transactions Essex Archaeological Society*, vi, 322.
[2] H. E. Brooks, 'The Kighley Family of Grays Thurrock' (*Essex Review*, xxxviii, 130–42).

'most palpable suspicions of murther' worried Sir Edward Denny (of Waltham Abbey). He could not attend Quarter Sessions, so he wrote to the Court about a Londoner suspected of 'destroying and burning privately in a dunghill' a bastard child of which he was the putative father. But no indictment is found against the man, nor against another whose name occurs in a gaol calendar of 1565, imprisoned on suspicion of murder.

From the deposition of a Kelvedon man 'touching the conspiracy against Mr Sames' in 1585 the examining justice, Anthony Maxey, learned how Henry Miles boasted that he had a 'dag' (a heavy pistol or handgun) in a long chest in Henry Turner's chamber with which he intended to kill his father-in-law and mother, viz. Mr. (Richard) Sames and his wife of Feering, saying to his father-in-law, 'Now you have me in prison you think yourself without danger, but Turner hath another dag as well as I and doth intend therewith to procure your destruction with my mother's.'

A Fairstead man 'had conspired to murder' a Terling butcher in 1580, 'as by his own confession before the whole assembly of the justices did appear'. They therefore bound him to be at the next Quarter Sessions. 'The whole assembly' consisted of Lord Morley, Lord Rich, Sir Thomas Barrington and Sir John Petre, meeting at Chelmsford on 26 May, a date which coincides with neither the ordinary Quarter Sessions nor the Assizes and seems to refer to one of the rare special sessions of the county justices. In 1596 one of the constables of Belchamp Walter struck Edward Coo gentleman there, 'intending to murder him'. Later that year Henry Snellock junior of Toppesfield gentleman broke into the house of Thomas Harrold blacksmith there with intent to murder him. Seeing her husband in danger of being killed with a long piked staff, she came to his help, at which Snellock broke her right arm. (He was charged at the Assizes two years later for killing a deer in Little Sampford park.) The story of the alleged murderous attack on Cecily Sandes, the Archbishop of York's widow, of Edwins Hall in Woodham Ferrers is told in the section on Disseisin (p. 121), and that of the plot to murder a cuckolded man of Burnham under Immorality (p. 199).

Finally, there are several cases of barratry, in which 'it is likely that murders and homicides will arise among neighbours unless a remedy soon be found', which is largely formal language (p. 143).

Killing in self-defence; homicide; murderous attempt or intent; suspicion of murder: in these various ways, a substitute for the capital charge of murder has often been found. There remains death by accident or misfortune caused by another: twenty cases, all recorded in coroners' inquests. Had they all been found to be pure accidents, we should have deferred them, with many other incidental deaths such as falling into a well, for a later volume of *Elizabethan Life* (and death); but three encounters were not free from malice and are therefore described here.

In 1586 two servants of John Wood of Greenstead (juxta-Ongar)[1] gentleman exchanged abusive words. One struck the other on the ear. The latter retaliated with his dagger, and the wound proved fatal. The accused was found not guilty of homicide, the death being by misfortune, and he was reprieved by procuring a pardon. Two Great Braxted men in 1574 came into the house of a Kelvedon saddler, aged 60. One of them asked for 'trappings for his saddle', which had been brought by an unknown woman to sell. He refused, and they quarrelled. The other man sought to appease them, but the saddler, cursing, turned on him. The go-between struck the saddler, who rushed out of his shop, but he was a sick man, collapsed and died on the one-mile journey to fetch Francis Harvey, J.P. Verdict: visitation of God. Early one morning in 1576 a man obtained leave from Richard Gowers, master of a 15-year-old apprentice tailor, to take the lad to a house at Studley Green in Danbury to fetch a skein of black thread for Gowers. Having 'a secret malice in his heart' towards the boy, he hit him with a cudgel. The boy fled to a hedge to pull a stake to defend himself, whereon the man desisted. They found nobody at the house. Getting through the window, he asked the lad to help him, when he again attacked the boy. In the struggle the man fell on his back and the boy with all his weight fell on him, but because of a long sickness the man died two hours later. Verdict: death by misadventure.

A unique death came before a coroner's jury in June 1587. A maid was on her way at 4 a.m. to milk her master's cows, when she was attacked by two mastiffs belonging to Barnaby Barker, a Prittlewell tanner. They had broken their chains and escaped from his yard, tore the milkmaid's throat, killing her instantly. Their owner averred that they had never before bitten anyone. The verdict was misfortune.

Elizabethan society, to whose violence and cruelty the Assize files are a monument, was haunted by the fear of witches, and death by witchcraft was an even more common charge than murder. We shall touch on witchcraft, which was also a Church offence, in the next volume.

Murder, being a crime not cognizable at Quarter Sessions, is virtually absent from the Sessions records of other counties, but five cases of manslaughter were heard by the Lancashire justices.

The Middlesex justices, with their unique Assize jurisdiction, received forty-six true bills for murder between 1551 and 1603, including a few for manslaughter, infanticide and highway assault, one of which took place in the notorious Mile End road, close to the Essex boundary. When the Middlesex records were calendared eighty years ago, the indictment of Ben Johnson in 1598 for mortally wounding Gabriel Spencer in a duel was first discovered. The poet pleaded guilty, was convicted of manslaughter, pleaded his clergy, read his neck-verse, was branded by a hot iron with

[1] *Registers of Greenstead* (ed. F. A. Crisp, 1892), 3, 4.

the letter, known to the populace as the 'Tyburn T', and then released.[1] The editor of the Middlesex calendar equates in his index all fatal assaults by one person on another as duels, but this seems to be contrary to the contemporary (and modern) meaning of duel. Among the Middlesex murders were four cases of poisoning including two in which 'mercury *alias* ratsbane' was administered. One of the unlucky victims was the wife of Edward Crumwell (later Lord Crumwell).

Inventories

Inventories of the goods of two murderers were found in the Assize files. An inventory should have been made in all cases where a felon possessed any goods worth valuing, but many indictments are noted, 'No goods'.

John Neuberye of Chelmsford butcher, 1581.

In the hall: a joined table with a frame, price 6s. 8d., a firepan and a pair of tongs, 6d.; in a chamber, a joined bedstead, 10s.; in another chamber, a little bedstead, 2s. 6d.; in another room, two chests and a table, 2s. 6d. Total 22s. 2d.

John Kyttar of Hadleigh husbandman, 1597.

Oats 3 bushels, 3s.; barley, ½ bushel, 14d. An old flock bed, 3s. 4d., old iron 18d., an old kettle and a posnet and a pewter platter, 18d., a lock and 2 earthen pans, 8d., a pair of quern stones, 18d., wood and old boards, 5s., a posnet, a gridiron and a candlestick, 12d., a pail, 4d. The cattle – 3 mares and 2 nags and the furniture (i.e. harness, etc.), £8. A cart, 26s. 8d. 2 young bullocks, £3, 2 kine and a bullock, £5. A debt of 30s. owing to him by Joan Landys of Hadleigh, 30s. Total (according to the record) £19 14s. 2d.

---

[1] *Middlesex County Records* (ed. J. C. Jeaffreson), xxxviii, xlii; this indictment is also in F. G. Emmison and I. Gray, *County Records* (Hist. Ass., 1967), 18–19.

13

Common Assault

In 1562 Robert Offyn of Great Baddow yeoman broke into John Lydgeard's house in Witham and assaulted Alice his wife with a pole, for which he was fined 2s.; and John Parker of Arkesden husbandman assaulted John Sarle at Elmdon. In 1602 Elizabeth wife of Henry Cannoudon of Rochford blacksmith beat Margery wife of Walter Samon there, so that she despaired of her life. In the forty-year interval between these incidents scores of similar assaults were brought before the county justices at Quarter Sessions. Petty assault, however, did not figure as often as petty larceny. The former accounts for hundreds of entries in the rolls of manor courts, which disposed of the great majority of minor quarrels, though the steward usually included the ancient phrase 'and drew blood'. The customary fine in the manor court was 3s. 4d., and it remained stable throughout the reign. Owing to the depreciation in the value of money, assaults were therefore cheaper in the later years! In Sessions indictments many of the victims' 'lives were despaired of'; but that is little more than common form. Only a few yield any details about the weapons used (fists often sufficed), and very few give any hint whether the assault was the result of sudden, hot temper, or long-standing enmity. It matters little, as this aspect of Elizabethan disorder needs no extra illumination, for violent quarrels or merely neighbours' scuffles differ little between medieval, Elizabethan and modern times. We shall draw therefore only on exceptional documents.

In most of the indictments the key-verb is 'beat' – hence 'assault and battery' – by anything that was at hand : knife, pitchfork, and so on. At first sight, a Spanish weapon was wielded by a High Easter man, who beat another on the head with a 'bastinado', drawing blood. The date is 1583, only six years after the lexicographer's earliest mention of the word (in Holinshed's *Chronicle*) ; then, and later, it refers usually to the act of cudgelling rather than the cudgel itself, though the Essex records once used the word to mean the weapon (p. 195). In 1565 John Graves of East Ham yeoman assaulted a male servant of John Lacye gentleman in his house there, shooting him in the face with an arrow (fined 2s.). The pregnant wife of a Hatfield Peverel man was beaten with a stick by William Bastwick who himself had been wounded in the previous year in a local dispute (p. 135). Two Finchingfield men were are variance in

1574. Thomas Crackeneale husbandman, 'being servant' (perhaps bailiff) of William Thurgood yeoman, wounded his master; on confession he was imprisoned and whipped.

'Assault and battery' was the charge in 1591 against four husbandmen and two sailors of Thorpe and Kirby for attacking William Gosling, a glover of the former parish; against two of them and a Great Holland husbandman and 'Sander' (Alexander) Wynde, a mason of Kirby, for a second assault on him next day; also against John Crescye, constable of Kirby, for a similar assault on the first day.

One document of 1584 used phraseology much fuller than that of the normal indictments, and, even more exceptional, was written in English: not necessarily evidence that the scribe knew no Latin, for he put his verbs at the end of each clause, and his construction is identical with the orthodox Latin form. Henry Andrew, a Chelmsford butcher, threatened a neighbour, John Tatem, in his 'backside' (rear garden)[1] 'and by whorling his dagger, him the said John upon his head did hit, grievously wound, beat and evil intreat, and in great peril of his life did put, and in the common highway of him belonging to the freehold messuage of one John Eve gent. did deny, interrupt and let (impede).'

As is noticed elsewhere (p. 143), some of the clergy were prone to violence. George Darlow, vicar of Ugley, who had been charged with disturbing the peace three years earlier, was in graver trouble in 1593 for having abused and wounded, in company with four labourers of his parish, a man and his wife.

Some variations from the usual assaults are found. A labourer cut off another's thumb; a man was 'assaulted' by a drover's wife 'inciting a mastiff to bite and chase him' (fined 12d. by three J.P.s), but as so often there was a counter charge that he had first assaulted her; William Norrys, a Billericay butcher, in the open market there, struck another violently on the head with a quart pot, drawing blood (and he was also indicted for being a common drunkard); two men violently assaulted a woman in Thomas Frank's field at Hatfield Broad Oak and also wounded four of Frank's carthorses (each fined 4d.); and a Belchamp St. Paul's yeoman attacked a farm labourer, breaking up his plough and cutting up the horse-traces. Many assaults were combined with trespass (pp. 133, 137).

Very occasionally a hundredal jury felt constrained to report assault. Even so, nothing very serious appears. Two men had a bloody fight as they returned home from ploughing; and a Tilbury (juxta-Clare) man 'violently thrust' a bundle of straw from a parishioner's shoulders, battered and maimed him. So we turn to the more animated stories in the justices' examinations. An Aveley woman accused her husband, Henry Grigges, of pulling off her headkerchief, pulling her hair, and beating her. Two

---

[1] All the long, narrow closes behind the houses in the High Street are termed 'backsydes' in John Walker's well-known map of Chelmsford, 1591.

neighbouring wives testified; one had come to weed, found her looking ill, and was told that she was 'very evil at ease' after being knocked about. Edward Barrett, J.P., of Belhus in the same parish, who took these depositions on 19 April 1583, had two weeks previously with a fellow J.P. bound Grigges to appear before the Bishop of London and the Court of High Commission because of 'his incontinency and his wicked life', when he was committed to the Fleet prison. Jerome Garrard, a Witham husbandman, was met with 'very stubborn words' from his servant on being ordered to do a job; and when finished it was done so negligently that the master rebuked him 'by speeches'. Thereupon he struck Garrard with 'a great bullock's set' (probably a goad) a yard or more in length, and continued to strike as he fled. From this dangerous situation another, more loyal, servant came to the rescue; and he and another servant confirmed their master's story. The accused was sentenced to be whipped.

In the next case, the boot seems to have been on the other leg. It has always been the lot of justices to try to adjudicate on conflicting versions of assault. Whose story is to be believed in the depositions taken down in 1582 before Sir Edmund Huddleston and Anthony Maxey – the allegations of the master, Martin Skinner, a Braintree haberdasher, and his wife, or that of Thomas Yeldham, his apprentice, supported by an onlooker's statement? Thomas deposed first. Returning from his 'errands' after being sent to warn a labourer to report for work next day, he was suddenly struck by his master who chased him as he fled. Pulled hard by the ears, he struggled free and in so doing his master fell backwards, dragging him on top, so that he accidentally broke his master's leg. A Braintree man said that he and others were sitting on a bench by the smith's shop when he saw Yeldham running from his master's shop down the lane towards Coggeshall but was overtaken, and when grabbed by the shoulder they both fell down. The apprentice got up, 'without showing any token of violence towards his master', and went down towards Bocking Street leaving him lying there. Rachel Skynner alleged that, about six months past, she reproved Thomas for his 'lewdness' (rudeness). Tom answered back that 'hereafter he would be worse than ever and do worse than ever he did'. Next morning, meeting his dame in her shop, she being pregnant, he gave her such a thrust against the shop chest that the child was still-born. To this charge the apprentice stated that 'there was never such a falling out between his dame and him', nor had she ever complained before that 'the child she went then withal was decayed by any such hurt.'

Martin Skynner's counter-statement ran thus. About to ride out of town, he ordered Tom to 'rape brassel.' Returning to find that Tom had done no work, he gave him a few words of reproof 'for his slothful negligence' and ordered him again to get on with the task. Grumbling, he began but was so careless that Skynner sent him on the errand already related. 'Having tarried somewhat longer than cause required', the master demanded an explanation. 'Standing very near to his master and facing him boldly with his hat on his head', Tom said, 'Whither did you send me? I have been there'. The master, 'seeing this malapert boldness of his over-saucy servant, did with the back of his hand give him a blow on the ear'. He was just about to retaliate with the 'waster' (cudgel) in his hand, so Skynner snatched it away, when 'the boy closed with him, and casting his leg between his master's, and they striving together he overthrew his master and broke his leg in sunder.' To 'rape brassell' (the literal and legible spelling, occurring twice) confounded a lexicographical specialist,[1] and equally puzzled the writer, because 'rape' was assumed to mean reap, which made little sense. To 'rape' is in fact an obsolete dialect word for 'rasp', to scrape with a rasp, file or rough instrument, and the lad was therefore ordered to rasp brazil, an extremely hard wood, formerly spelt 'brassell' and having no etymological link with Brazil. Rasped brazil wood was infused to produce a brick-red dye. It suggests that Martin Skynner was a haberdasher of hats rather than of small wares and dyed some of his goods or sold his dye to the local clothiers. Evelyn, in his *Diary* (1641), refers to a Dutch rasphouse, a house of correction in which the prisoners were employed in rasping wood: 'very hard labour', he adds. It is no wonder, then, that the apprentice was 'slothful'.

Martin and Rachel Skynner signed their depositions in the presence of John Goodday the elder, Joseph Man, John Lyngwood, Jeffery Lyngwood, and William Skynner. The master had also secured Edward Venyall, another apprentice, to testify on his behalf, but the lad, doubtless feigning dumbness, could 'say nothing that was material.' Thomas Yeldham, of Finchingfield husbandman, probably the father, had stood surety for Tom's appearance in Court, which ordered him 'to be punished with the rod by the bailiff of Braintree' (doubtless the manorial bailiff). The mildness of the sentence suggests that the justices only half-believed the haberdasher's statement.

A very long deposition made by John Crushe of Laindon in 1576 disclosed not only assault but also a series of threats, which forced him to surrender a deed. At Michaelmas 1573 Matthew Bell of Ramsden Bell-house had hired six of his milch cows for three years at an annual rent of 20s. Their re-delivery at the end of the term or 33s. 4d. for any cow not returned had been guaranteed by a bond given by Bell and John Knightbridge of Laindon. Edmund Croxon of Billericay, Bell's son-in-law, had many times, however, tried to get Crushe to give the bond to him, promising to deliver the stock, explaining that he had to sue Bell for unpaid legacies and would make him unable to make any recompense for the cows; and further that Knightbridge was worth nothing. Croxon had also told this twice to Crushe's wife; all to no effect. One day 'at

[1] *Essex Review*, lxiii, 45, 102.

the sun's going down' Crushe went to Croxon's house to fetch some hay of his. Croxon's wife called, 'Come hither'. Going into the parlour, he was struck down with a short crabtree staff by Croxon who swore by God's blood that he would thrust his dagger into him. But that evening John Nevell of Laindon came to his house, 'at the instrument of Croxon, as it seemeth', asserting that he had injured Croxon, who demanded money as damages. Drawing Crushe into a field by pre-arrangement with Croxon, the latter exclaimed, 'Crushe, thou has lost £5 by coming into my house,' Nevill adding, 'Ye must give him some recompense'. Crushe, denied long having injured him, but terrified at last offered him an oak, on which Croxon replied, 'By God's blood, I will not take all the trees thou hast for amends.' So Crushe asked, 'What would you have?' Croxon then demanded the bond, 'which,' he said, 'is not worth 2d., and thou shalt in the morning deliver it to my brother Nevell,' which through great fear he did.

Not long afterwards, when Crushe was riding to market, Croxon accosted him in the highway with a hedging bill and vehemently swore that he and Nevell would misuse him. Accompanying him to the town, Croxon brought along one Drier of Billericay, who said that Croxon complained he had bought some cattle from Crushe, who must give him a letter of attorney for the cattle. Through fear, Crushe went to one Freeman's house (presumably a lawyer), who there wrote the letter of attorney, which was handed to Croxon. Crushe submitted his complaint, to the Court, seeking redress for his safety of life, 'whereof I walk in no small peril' In this case the result is not known.

For centuries the clergy, when collecting their tithes, were involved in disputes (pp. 3, 113). Occasionally, taking tithes was forcibly resisted, and even more violently in 1595, when it was the parson's wife who was assaulted. On 16 August Roger Harlackinden, who had purchased the manor of Earls Colne from the notorious Edward Earl of Oxford in 1583, examined Grace wife of (blank) Garrett of Great Tey clerk (Robert Garrett had been instituted vicar two years previously). On 4 July she had gone into a field to 'stay' (prevent) George Sache from carrying off some tithe hay that was 'in controversy' between him and her husband. He threw her into a ditch, then against his cart, often striking her with a pitchfork, though she entreated him to leave the hay alone until her husband came home. He refused, and then attacked her maidservant and her two sons with the pitchfork. The justice also took statements from two women, who confirmed that Sache had abused Mistress Garrett. Taking her home, they said that she twice swooned.

Unusual circumstances were briefly related in a letter of 1596 written to Quarter Sessions by Arthur Herrys, J.P., from Woodham Mortimer. He had bound over Mr. Hugh Cole, who was separated from Elizabeth his late wife *a mensa et thoro* and had leased his house there for her maintenance. Cole, however, had many times entered it and 'intolerably vexed the poor gentlewoman', and, more recently had 'committed foul battery' upon her, her manservant and maidservant, and upon his children. His appearance at Court, the J.P. added, was all the more necessary because he was generally disobedient in response to any public services, as the high constable would confirm.

It was usual, and indeed obligatory, for a J.P. who had examined a person accused of any form of assault or disorderly behaviour to bind the party, with one or two sureties, to keep the peace or to be of good behaviour, until the next Quarter Sessions. There are several hundreds of such recognizances or bail bonds. A few state that the person who sought the bond 'stands in fear of some bodily harm'. A fair number of recognizances are not followed by indictments and may therefore be the sole evidence of quarrels or the like ; but the nature of the offence is rarely stated.

Anyone who wishes to find out more about the extent and ways in which common assault was committed may consult the well-indexed printed calendars of Quarter Sessions records of Caernarvonshire, 1541–1558, and Worcestershire, 1591–1643.

14

Assaults on Officers

There is plenty of evidence that the lower ranks of those who were obliged to keep the Queen's peace, especially the sheriff's and hundredal court bailiffs and the petty constables and watchmen, were liable to be assaulted in the execution of their duty or to have prisoners forcibly 'rescued' (the legal term).

Only once was a chief constable attacked. In 1568 John Abell gentleman and two others of West Bergholt assaulted William Lyn senior, one of the two chief constables of Lexden hundred, William Lyn junior of Colchester, and another man. Abell struck all three men, as the chief constable in his official capacity took them into custody. Each was fined 12d. by four J.P.s.

Each hundred had its own bailiff. Like the itinerant bailiffs who were nominally employed by the sheriff they were lowly but strong-armed officers, always unpopular. In 1569 Francis Warner of Great Warley clerk (not the rector) and a parishioner assaulted the bailiff of the hundred and rescued two horses belonging to another villager which had been distrained by the bailiff on the sheriff's warrant. In 1585 William Hollingworth of Stondon Massey gentleman and three other villagers beat a sheriff's bailiff, took away his dagger, and let Roger Parkyns, a Fryerning black-smith, go at large. Self-rescue from the sheriff's or hundredal bailiffs was another form of assault, as when a sheriff's bailiff in 1587, having made an arrest in Rayleigh market place, was violently assaulted and beaten by his prisoner, who 'went at large'.

Half the adult population of Newport apparently turned out one day in March 1575 to take part in a determined attack on the sheriff's bailiff and the hundredal bailiff, who had been called upon to assist the former in apprehending Nicholas Harvey of Newport, described as a gentleman, to answer in the royal courts a few days afterwards in a case of £25 damages brought against him by Thomas Swallowe. The bailiffs went inside Harvey's house. Then the hubbub started. Nineteen persons, including Robert Harvey tailor and glover, Agnes his wife, and Ann Harvey, violently assaulted the bailiffs and rescued Nicholas. All belonged to Newport except for one Widdington man. It was largely a women's scuffle – sixteen of them, mostly wives. Probably their menfolk were busy in the fields. But, if the bailiffs were not stout liars, the amazons had in the background as moral support 'an hundred and more other malefactors unknown'. With such a crowd milling round his door, no wonder Nicholas boldly spoke his mind. 'I care not for the high Sheriff nor the undersheriff,' he shouted contemptuously, 'nor for any knave of you both,' when they called on the folk in the Queen's name for aid. He was annoyed that they had found him unarmed. 'If I had my dagger,' he exclaimed, 'I would make you both sure that you would not go out of the house.' With such determined opposition, the bailiffs probably beat a hasty retreat, deciding that it would be useless to summon the constables. The grand jury found a true bill for all except Robert and the Widdington man. 'Each fined', the indictment reads, and then disappoints us with a blank. Nothing is known of Harvey, but Swallowe seems to be Great Chesterford man.

A serious case of obstructing the officers of the law came before Easter Quarter Sessions in 1576. A general precept to the bailiffs of no less than ten hundreds and to the sheriff's itinerant bailiff had been issued for the arrest of Richard Young, a gentleman of East Hanningfield, who had been outlawed at the suit of John Warren for debt. The Sheriff's bailiffs found him in the house of William Young gentleman at High Roothing. Although one of the parish constables and other villagers came to the bailiff's help, two labourers, also of High Roothing, and two unknown persons effectively prevented the arrest and assaulted the bailiff and the constable into the bargain. On 8 July John Petre, the Sheriff, received a sharp letter from the Privy Council, referring to Richard Young having 'very disorderly disobeyed not only the process served upon him, but also the said Sheriff being with him in person', when summoned to appear before the Court of High Commission.[1] 'Such disorders are not to be suffered in any man of what degree so ever', the letter emphasised, and Petre was enjoined to produce Young before the High Commissioners without delay. At the end of the month Young, now described as 'of High Roothing gentleman', was charged at the Assizes for disturbing the peace.

A distraining bailiff of the royal honour of Clare aroused the ire of a Halstead woman in 1587. The goods (a flock bed, a pair of blankets and a spit) belonging apparently to her father or brother were ordered to be distrained to answer John Mott in a case of trespass to be heard at the court of the honour in the Moothall at Halstead. She assaulted the bailiff and rescued the goods. In 1594 William Strutt clerk (rector of Little Henny, 1577–1620) was taken into custody at Great Henny to appear at Westminster in a case of trespass brought against him by Thomas Fuller, when his wife, Thomas Strutt of Henny and his wife, and the wife of a Twinstead man rescued him. Two years earlier Henry Calton of Saffron Walden gentleman was arrested, to answer William Clerke in a plea of trespass by Thomas Greene gentleman, deputy of the sheriff; but John Triplove of Ickleton (Cambs.), John Ballard of Ashdon clerk (not the

[1] *Acts of the Privy Council*, ix, 155.

rector), and Roger Bybye of Walden innholder, with many others un-named, assaulted Greene in a riotous affray and rescued Calton. Triplowe was fined 3s. 4d.; the others apparently were acquitted. Bybye however was charged on a separate indictment because he, being one of the town headboroughs (constables), and enjoined by Greene to assist, 'speedily withdrew', but the verdict is not given.

Four further rescues from sheriff's bailiffs (later called riding bailiffs) afford no details of interest apart from the fact that on two occasions the wives stoutly defended their menfolk. There are two cases of rescue of distrained goods – an ox worth 30s. and a settle worth 5s. from one man, and a horse from another to pay for 14s. 1d. damages which William Taylor, the Tendring blacksmith, had recovered in the Hundred Court of Tendring. The lot of officers responsible for arresting and taking culprits to prison was sometimes dangerous, as the killing of a sheriff's bailiff demonstrated (p. 159).

The parish constables often suffered the same treatment. A Grays Thurrock constable was assaulted by a quarrelsome labourer; and Richard Potter, a smith of Kelvedon, assaulted a constable in his own garden (both 1562). A London fishmonger's servant, evidently about to be arrested, struck one of the constables of Walthamstow on the face and was rescued by his 'fellows' (1565); and Peter Jerome, a gentleman of Woodham Mortimer, attacked a petty constable of the parish for which he was fined 6s. 8d. (1572); in both cases the assailant drew blood with his dagger. In 1567 two millers, Robert Marshall of Shimpling and John Marshall of Boxsted (both in Suffolk), with Nicholas Bushe of Pentlow clerk (rector, 1560–71), assaulted both constables of Pentlow when they were arresting the two Suffolk men by the warrant of Sir William Cordell (Master of the Rolls) and with Bushe's help they escaped. But one of the constables was charged with negligence on that account. When trying to apprehend Silvester Walden of Little Dunmow gentleman on a warrant to take him to the Assizes, the constable was struck by his staff which inflicted three wounds on his head and elsewhere (1568); and a Castle Hedingham man not only resisted the constable about to take him into custody but also tore up the warrant, escaped and remained at large (1573).

Another self-rescue was effected in 1583 by Nicholas Eve and Christopher Eve, both yeomen of High Easter. After being taken up by the constables on a warrant from Sir Thomas Mildmay, the Eves assaulted them and escaped. Nicholas was fined 40s., Christopher 20s. Two days later they were bound over by Lord Rich, with Christopher Scott of Felsted yeoman and John Doughty of Barnston gentleman as their sureties, to keep the peace towards a Pleshey housewife; and Doughty and the woman were concurrently bailed to keep the peace towards Christopher: presumably the result of an affray. The Eves were evidently quarrelsome people. Both

had been bound over a year earlier, but forfeiture of Nicholas's recognizance was sued soon afterwards by John Wilkinson, a Pleshey mercer, who
also kept an alehouse. A girl had taken six beehives out of Nicholas's
garden on his mother-in-law's instructions. Trouble ensued, of which no
details are given, and the girl obtained surety of the peace from a J.P.
against Nicholas, which she renewed at the Assizes. And while in Wilkinson's alehouse there was further trouble when he challenged a customer
with having stolen his 'brach' (keen-scented hound), who vehemently
denied it, whereupon Wilkinson 'made as though he would jostle or
thrust' against Nicholas, saying 'Thou dost misuse my guests.' Nicholas,
accused of striking mine host, claimed that he was merely defending
himself. Curiously enough, however, Nicholas was one of Wilkinson's
sureties for the renewal of his licence later in the year.

Bush Fair, one of the important Essex fairs, at which the chief trade was
horses and cattle, was held on part of the great Harlow Bush Common
two miles south of the town at Potter Street on the London–Cambridge
road. In 1577 a Netteswell man, ordered by the constable to stop fighting,
soon went at it again, and 'railed' on him after the fighters had been
parted. The affray occurred on 'Bush Fair eve, commonly called St.
John's day in latteren', the jury foreman's way of trying to name the feast
of St. John the Evangelist *ante portam latinam*. (See plate 15.)

Evidently a Bocking shoemaker had assaulted or insulted the headboroughs in 1584, as he was bound, with another Bocking shoemaker, to
keep the peace towards them. The actual charge, of being a common
barrator, was made a week later (fined £5). He seems to have incurred a
further fine of £2, and was committed to prison, apparently because he
failed to find surety for payment. In the same year an alehousekeeper's wife
of Birdbrook was indicted for striking the constable with a billet of wood
and speaking opprobrious words to him when he came upon a hue and cry
to their house to search for certain persons suspected to be there. Next year
a Dunmow constable was beaten, trying to stop football (p. 226). In 1589
a deputy constable of Blackmore took up a man for suspicion of felony, but
Charles Smyth gentleman (probably the son of Thomas Smyth, the lord
of the manor) and two yeomen, all of Blackmore, assaulted him and rescued the prisoner. Smyth was 'not in prison' (evidently he fled) ; one of
the others guilty but read ; the third not guilty. A Chelmsford constable
complained in 1590 that he had risked attack, probably at the fair. A
London upholsterer was standing at his booth, when a Chelmsford
servingman cut three holes in it and threatened to burn the booth. He
violently resisted arrest by the constable, threatening to stab him. Thomas
May grocer and Christopher Tatam innholder, both townsmen, stood
bail for the defendant.

A violently resisted arrest is narrated in a warrant dated 1593 from
Francis Barrington, J.P., written at Barrington Hall, his home in Hatfield

Broad Oak, to the keeper of the County gaol at Colchester. His earlier warrant to the constables of Great Bardfield to bring Thomas Snelloge before him had led Snelloge not only to disobey but to attack them with his dagger, 'and had not the company there present stayed (stopped) him he had slain them.' Snelloge could not produce sureties for his good behaviour, so he was sent to gaol. An obstreperous man, in similar circumstances in 1587, was able to produce a surety, probably his brother, and it is the recognizance which relates how, on being warned by one of the constables of Wethersfield to appear before Israel Amyce, J.P., he 'not only very evilly' ill-treated the constable but also 'very contemptuously' refused to obey the justice's warrant and threatened to shoot the constable. Many neighbours testified against an Easthorpe man for stoutly resisting the arrest of his wife and servant by the constable on a J.P.'s warrant for felony. His contempt sent him to the Castle gaol for ten days to cool off, after which he was to be brought to the same J.P., Christopher Chibborne, fined 40s., and to produce sureties for appearance at Quarter Sessions. It seems to have had little effect, as he was up again a year later for burgling an Easthorpe house and beating an occupant.

The night watchmen, not unnaturally, also come into the picture of violence and disorder against petty officers of the peace. A breach of the peace was committed one night in 1585 against the constables and watchmen at Newport by three townsmen and two from Widdington. Two men, duly elected and sworn by the constables of Harlow in 1584, were keeping their watch, when two Harlow poulterers, having gathered to themselves other persons unknown, were wandering in the town at midnight and brutally attacked the watchmen, one of whom was wounded with a pikestaff. Each was fined the large sum of 20s. Two years later the Aldham watchmen were wounded by two villagers with a pitchfork and a bill, who threatened them and other folk with malicious words during the watch. This is what Martin Chapman told Christopher Chibborne on 19 September. He, with three others, had been appointed to watch for the parishes of Fordham and Aldham on Thursday was 'sevenight'. Seeing lights in William Hyls' alehouse about midnight, but 'hearing no stir', he went back to the place of their watch. Returning to walk along the street, Hyls came out and challenged John Waylande, another watchman, 'to have eavesdropped his house', who declared it was a lie. They walked on, but Hyls and one Joshua Newton soon appeared with a pitchfork and a bill, intent on picking a quarrel. 'Ye have been skulking about the backsides of the houses to steal poultry'. Hyls told the watchmen 'to get them out of their parishes'. They naturally refused. Newton bade Hyls to lay hold of Waylande and put him in the stocks. Waylande fended him off with his weapon, whereupon Newton began shouting, waking up the villagers. Getting out of bed, the constables' deputy told Chapman and Waylande to depart for fear of further mischief, so they were fain to forsake their watch, Newton threatening that if Waylande ever came again to watch there he would lay him by the heels. The three others confirmed Chapman's statement.

There was probably little distinction in the justices' minds between actual assaults on officers and threatened assaults or oral insults (both words of course have a common origin) or obstruction. Among petty constables' duties was 'privy search' for suspects. Their right of entry into houses for this purpose was sometimes firmly resisted as an intrusion against the Englishman's liberty. One of the two earliest cases (for the first, see p. 33) was when a Langford constable searched a house in 1575. The occupier refused to open up and shouted contemptuous words, which cost him a 5s. fine. Other constables received the same sort of abuse. They were reviled with 'quarrelsome talk and unseemly words' at Ingatestone, and with 'opprobrious and threatening words' at Blackmore when putting a vagrant in the stocks. In 1588 William Bayley and John Porter, two Brentwood blacksmiths, were charged with refusing to shoe a mare brought by the constable and for giving him 'evil words'; they were bound to better behaviour by Sir John Petre and Edward Rich. And of course the watch got even worse treatment. Late one August evening in 1580 Edmund Hunt of Maldon hatter and haberdasher and Randall Redgeway glover and John Saffold hatmaker, both of Heybridge, called the two Heybridge watchmen varlets and knaves; and next month William Longborough of Heybridge was indicted for abusing the watch as well as for extortion. In 1598 Freshwell hundredal jury presented a Hempstead victualler not only for disorder in his house on two nights but also for calling the watchmen knaves for snooping too near it.

The Essex records go a long way towards explaining why the unpaid offices of constable and watchman were so unpopular with their holders. Those of Halstead suffered from the activities of a very refractory fellow, Hercules Turner. His was a case of 'like father, like son'. The three constables of Halstead in 1592 had put him in the stocks for disturbing the watch. William Turner, a weaver, had come to his son's aid, and between them Hercules got loose. The father was in disfavour with the constables for abetting the son in other disorders, and was bound over to answer for his contempt; William Hudson clothier and Isaac Medcalfe glover, townsmen of Halstead, stood surety. Perhaps they had second thoughts, as William's appearance at Sessions was later secured by two Earls Colne men, who in the meantime were to see that he produced his son before Sir Edmund Huddleston, J.P. On 1 October 1595 Huddleston wrote to the justices from his home at Pattiswick. He referred to the constables' complaint to him 'about two years sithence' and to his having ordered Hercules to be stocked, because he thought that this punishment would repress his insolence. He added more details of the incident. On being 'rescued', the culprit behaved outrageously, threatening the officers

N

and others to such an extent that 'the whole town was (he was later informed) in tumult and disquiet'. To get his own back, Hercules 'molested' the constables by suing them in the Court of Exchequer for false imprisonment (a session in the stocks counted as such), and only desisted when he knew the action would be unsuccessful. 'But now of late', Sir Edmund wrote, Hercules, now described as of Roydon (Norfolk) and Hitchin (Herts.), had renewed his suit 'to the great hindrance of the poor men' and had threatened and misused them. They had of course complained to the justice, who had bound him over to answer for his 'lewd misdemeanour', and at the earnest entreaty of some of the townsmen he had sent this letter to Quarter Sessions. The County Bench was clearly determined to have done with the dispute by making a most unusual order. The 'controversy' was referred to Thomas French and William Sewell of Halstead, 'arbitrators indifferently chosen' by the parties' consent, for settlement before Hollantide (1 November) ; if unsuccessful, then Arthur Breame esquire was to act as 'umpire' ; if he also failed, then Hercules Turner was to appear at the next Sessions. Breame was Halstead's chief magnate and lord of two of its manors, but whether his services were called upon is not recorded. French was apparently lord of Stansted Hall manor. Another constable of Halstead, in 1602, was assaulted and abused.

A second case, 1599, also tells of opposition to both constables and watchmen, by Thomas Aylett, a Dunmow weaver. The constables were carting through the town two persons who had committed fornication. Meeting the cart, Aylett attempted to 'rescue' the offending couple by taking away a boy in relief of parish alms who was leading the cart, resulting in a 'great concourse of people' and general disturbance. On another occasion the watchmen came across two men fetching beer from an alehouse about 11 p.m. Charging them in the Queen's name to say whither they were carrying it, the men 'brangled' (squabbled) with the watchmen. Calling on neighbours for help, Aylett very obstinately refused but 'animated' the beer-carriers against the officers, urging the former to find pins to prick the watch. This time the parish officers were stoutly supported by Ralph Wiseman, the examining J.P., who sent him to prison till he paid up and bound himself to good behaviour and to appear at Quarter Sessions. Bating the despised watchmen seems to have been a popular pastime.

John Swetinge, a surveyor of highways, as well as Edward Swetinge, a constable, perhaps brothers, were both insulted in 1578 when they served these parish offices in Margaretting. The former had made 'a sufficient causeway in the highway' according to his statutory duties towards the house of Edward Hoye yeoman, who destroyed the causeway, abusing the surveyor with contemptuous words and calling the constable 'coxcomb'.

There is a single case of an attack on one of the hated royal purveyors.

When they came to collect provisions, which are not specified, the wife of a Kelvedon alehousekeeper drew her knife and thrust it through the cloak of one of the officers in three places.

Most of the assaults afford laconic reading, but they are so numerous as to supply a fairly reliable idea of the ineffectiveness of the Elizabethan police system. Many constables were of course ignorant fellows. Some, like Dogberry, were doubtless both foolish and consequential. The majority probably loathed their term of office, fearing to bring on themselves their neighbours' curses or on occasion their physical attacks. So little were the constables and watchmen respected in some towns and villages that men who were easily provoked did not bother to think twice before handling these petty officers roughly, guessing that they would not dare to complain to the nearest justice. Assaults on them and on the bailiffs, or merely a half-hearted respect towards them, form a vital element in Elizabethan disorder.

It is curious that cases of assaulting and abusing officers are so rare in the records of other counties. In Middlesex, into which the city of London had already spread, one would have expected to find many sorry stories of constables and watchmen being manhandled. But perhaps their paucity is made up by the solitary incident in 1576 when a constable of St. Martin's-in-the-Fields, questioning a scrivener, was bade to kiss his own tail.[1]

[1] *Middlesex County Records*, i, 100.

15

Highway Assault

As already explained, it is not easy to assign many of the documents about Elizabethan Disorder to a definite crime or offence, and there is therefore much overlapping between the contents of our chapters. Although we are able to differentiate between Highway Assault (that is, without robbery) and Highway Robbery, there is often little difference between cases of Common and Highway Assault or between the latter and Riot.

Two or three cases of death following attack on the Queen's highway have been referred to under Murder, and a third will be mentioned shortly. But none of these encounteres could be regarded as involving highwaymen. Other incidents arose through various circumstances and will be related in order of date. The reader in search of highwaymen may skip this and turn to a later chapter (p. 272).

An assault by Evan ap Rice of Tendring gentleman (p. 196) on a Great Bentley man took place at Elmstead in 1566. In the next year Richard Pease of Ulting husbandman was fined 12d. by two justices for assaulting William Bastick with a bearing bill in the highway there. He, with three local men, each had to pay another shilling for reaping and carrying off five 'shocks' of rye in Broom Field in Hatfield Peverel, belonging to Bastick, who was similarly treated in 1579 (p. 135). A scuffle with swords occurred in 1569 at Easterford (i.e. Kelvedon, on the London–Colchester highway) in which Robert Cole and Richard Cole, both clothiers of East Bergholt (Suffolk), wounded Robert Tompson of Layham (Suffolk) gentleman and Eleanor his wife and Welthiana Answorth, a spinster of Colchester.

One long story comes from a petition dated 1569 by Robert Cokerell of Great Maplestead husbandman. It is preserved in the Sessions roll although addressed to Sir Nicholas Bacon, Lord Keeper of the Great Seal. Cokerell was travelling with his cart, when Edward Glascock of Castle Hedingham gentleman, passing him, suddenly turned and struck him over the shoulder with a short 'waster' (single-stick or perhaps cudgel), saying, 'Take thee that.' Dismounting, he defended himself with his whip. As he returned homewards Glascock, lying in wait for him in a house, attacked him with a long piked staff and would have killed or maimed him had he not 'shifted himself under his horse.' Glascock refused Cokerell's offer to 'come to some reasonable talk and order with him.' So he went to Robert Kempe, the justice (of Finchingfield), who granted him a warrant, whereupon Glascock promptly got a writ of *supersedeas* from Sir Thomas Golding, another justice, and 'still lies in wait for him.' On St. James's Day at Hedingham Fair Glascock fell upon him with sword and buckler as Cokerell passed by his house in the village street. There would have been manslaughter, had not people 'sundered them', so that he is constrained to seek further justice. He gives the names of two or three witnesses of each assault. At the last attack one of them, George Strond, seeing Glascock with drawn sword, bade him keep the peace, pulling them apart three times, when he too was set upon, but struck down both their weapons. Glascock called for another weapon. Suddenly the constable appeared and arrested Strond and put him in the stocks, 'which was contrary to equity and justice.' Like most petitions, this was evidently penned by a scrivener, but, strangely, ends with no specific request. If it reached Bacon, he must have passed it to the Essex Bench.

An assault occurring within the liberties of the borough of Colchester led to an examination by John Hunwicke, one of the bailiffs, and two aldermen, in 1578. Robert Ellys explained how he, aged 26, and his master, Henry Johnson, were returning from Berechurch, where they had been with Mr. Wentworth (probably John Wentworth, who was later to inherit the Gosfield estate). Beyond Monkwick (a large farm which lay a mile nearer Colchester), one Barnaby Smythe suddenly stepped out of the hedge and gave Johnson many blows with a crabtree cudgel, and at length felled him to the ground, breaking his leg and hurting his arm. Before striking him, Ellys said, Smythe had thrown Johnson's cloak around his head, Johnson having no weapon. While he lay on the road, a man came riding by, whereon Smythe went off, Ellys in pursuit. But the assailant, turning his own cloak the wrong side outwards, threatened to give Ellys the same treatment if he followed him, 'and so he escaped to Sir Thomas Lucas his house at Saint John's, so that he could not be then taken'. It is not apparent at first sight why his house should be considered as sanctuary, but St. John's Abbey was one of the religious houses which enjoyed the privilege of sanctuary by royal charter,[1] and presumably Smythe, in his plight, thought that the right extended to the precincts, on the site of which Sir Thomas Lucas's mansion was built. It suggests that this privilege was a matter of common belief with the townsmen, although in fact Colchester was not one of the towns allowed sanctuary rights by Henry VIII's Act of 1540. All three parties were tailors of Colchester, and the indictment adds that Johnson was also Smythe's master. The assault had taken place in August, and Lucas, who not surprisingly was the

[1] Morant, *History of Colchester* (1768), 144; cf. *Trans. Ess. Archl. Soc.*, ix, 352.

examining magistrate, had committed Smythe to Colchester Castle gaol (the county, not the town prison) for one month without bail, to be released only if he found sureties for appearance at the Michaelmas Sessions. What the verdict was is not given.

In 1584 Robert Wynche, a grocer of Woodford, wounded William Stackforde in the latter's 'little close' there with a 'sharp instrument called a scavell (small spade) of iron and steel', and ordered his apprentice to beat Stackforde. They both dug and removed his turves some months later. Between these dates Wynche made three separate assaults on him in 'Seise Elm Lane' in Woodford, shouting abuse at him. On one occasion Wynche snatched away and broke his 'instrument called an angle rood'; on another, the victim also sustained a murderous dagger thrust from Wynche's companion, but was rescued by others. A man was riding along the Colchester highway at West Ham in 1585, when John Ardes of Chelmsford drew his sword and put him in fear of his life. The accused was fined 2s. by Sir John Petre, Sir Thomas Mildmay and Lord Rich.

A hundred jury in 1590 presented Thomas Pinner, son-in-law of Mr. George Dorrell of Stanford-le-Hope, who had assaulted Mr. Willett in the highway, drawing blood. In danger of being slain, the constables and other villagers came to his aid, but Pinner's mob numbering eight counter-attacked, driving them to John Rattell's house. There one of the constables charged them to keep the peace. They retorted that the constable would have not been spared had he also not taken refuge in the building. A much longer document, headed 'Instructions for the indictments', shows that this was only one of four violent assaults on Willett by Dorrell, Pinner and his gang. About Shrovetide they attacked him in 'Hassingbrooke barn' (which he occupied), and pulled off the hay being loaded on to his cart. One day in Lent they 'did beat, punch, thump and kneel' on one of his servants, who died five weeks later, his right side being very black and bruised. 'Woe worth Mr. Champion', the victim had declared of his attacker (Richard Champion) in his dying hours, 'that ever he knew him.' On 4 April, Dorrell by fair words allured Willett into the highway and there suddenly struck him with a crabtree staff with two iron 'grains' in it. Three days later occurred the melée with the constables. Finally, on 11 April, when Willett was travelling to London, Edward Glemen gentleman and four others unnamed assaulted him on the highway near Ilford town. A few miles nearer London, the Great Essex Road at West Ham was the scene of another attack in 1600 by two blacksmiths, Richard Cover of Navestock and Owen Williams of Kelvedon (Hatch), the victims being the pregnant wife of a local man and his servant.

In the same year three yeomen of Layer Marney with others unknown assaulted one Golding Raynesforth Crismas gentleman in the highway at Messing. The first-named struck him with his sword, giving him a two-inch wound in his left hand whereby he lost the use of his hand for a long time; the others aided and abetted. True bill for the first, no true bill for the others. 'Goldringamford' Christmas and two other Christmases were themselves the mob-leaders in 1576 and 1583 (p. 106).

In 1602 Edward Goldingham of Wormingford gentleman on the highway at Lexden assaulted William Pasfield clerk, 'so that his life was despaired of.' The indictment is endorsed: 'At large. Let a *venire facias* be made.' Pasfield is evidently the vicar of Tolleshunt D'Arcy, whom a parishioner had called a dunce three years before (p. 193).

16
Church Assaults

In many places in Elizabethan Essex the House of God was the scene of violent disorders. Laymen were involved in the majority of these incidents, which probably had little connection with their religious views. In a period when church attendance was compulsory nearly all parishioners met together for divine service, and their petty rivalries and smouldering jealousies occasionally broke out in the places where they all assembled – in the church or churchyard. The same were also convenient spots for arrests.

The Act of 5 Edward VI, c.4 (1551), forbade the drawing of weapons in churches and churchyards. The alleged murderous assault in Takeley church, which is the only indictment under this statute in Mary's short reign (p. 4), is followed by many under Elizabeth. But the two earliest church disturbances do not actually mention personal assaults. Within a few months after her accession the Privy Council referred to Lord Rich a 'supplication by the parson of Shoebury wherein he complaineth of some disorder done in the church by one Thomas Pyke', requesting Rich to examine him and if found guilty to punish him.[1] Both Sessions and Assize records are deficient at this date, and nothing else can be found about the allegation. Nor are there any details beyond the terse charge against a man for breaking a window stanchion during service in Walthamstow church in 1564.

At 9 o'clock one Sunday in 1565 Thomas Freborne yeoman was sitting and praying in his parish church of North Benfleet before public worship, when Robert Dreywood yeoman, a parishioner, hit him in the face. Defending himself, he struck his assailant on the head with his dagger. Both were charged under the Act, but their indictments were quashed by royal writ. In 1577 Hinckford hundred presented that John Akershed broke the peace in Newport church at the feast of Pentecost by fighting with one Thurston, another parishioner. Akershed had also confessed to having recently stolen a pair of 'sweet gloves'. Samuel Fylpott, a husbandman of High Easter, struck Elizabeth Pyckett with his fist in the church there on 'Sunday fortnight before Christmas' 1584. Thomas Hollowell, described as a yeoman of Sandon, on a Sunday in 1594, seized John Slaughterford in Horndon-on-the-Hill church while Robert Willmott

[1] *Acts of the Privy Council*, vii, 17.

the vicar was reading divine service. Slaughterford had been bound over ten years earlier to keep the peace towards a Horndon housewife standing in fear of him. The nature of the disturbance in Orsett church in Whitsun week 1597 is not disclosed, but it had a fatal end (see p. 159).

The case involving the very early use of the word 'puritan' in 1574 was described under Sedition (p. 45). The incident followed a sermon preached by Michael Mayshort (or Mayshott), vicar of Writtle, on 18 April, when he was arrested. An even more remarkable affair had occurred on Wednesday 31 March, which doubtless led to the vicar being apprehended on 18 April. According to the indictment, which unfortunately is not supported by any depositions, serious destruction in his own church had been led by the vicar. Charged with him were five of his parishioners (two yeomen, a tanner, a minstrel, and a labourer) and three Moulsham men (Bartholomew Dutchman a joiner, another joiner and a carpenter), which suggests that the 'riotous assembly' of these nine persons 'with many other malefactors' in the churchyard was a premeditated plan to remove certain internal structures, the existence of which was contrary to the vicar's liturgical views. The actual charge is that the defendants broke into the church and destroyed the Jesus Chapel, Cope's *alias* Pynchon's Chapel and a pulpit, against the two churchwardens' will and without the parishioners' consent, the damage being assessed at the extremely high sum of £100.

The serious disturbance in St. Thomas's chapel at Brentwood in 1577 was a purely secular affair, and is narrated in the section on Riot (p. 106). Hundredal juries reported a Lindsell woman in somewhat naïve language, because she 'did uncharitably strike' a Great Easton man in his church, calling him murderer and declaring that he had 'killed' her (1599) ; also a Stanford Rivers man who with some strangers struck blows and drew blood in the church there (1602). In this medley of disorderly delinquencies of little-known villagers it is refreshing to come across one whose affairs extended far beyond parochial bounds. In 1602 Chelmsford hundred jurors presented Mr. John Troughton of Rawreth for fighting in the church on the last sabbath, striking the collector for the poor and others with a 'walking stick.' He was also presented in the Archdeacon's court in the same year for not receiving communion.[1] As Captain John Troughton he had been appointed commander of the *Lioness* on a voyage into the Mediterranean to suppress unwarranted English privateering. His instructions, signed by Nottingham, Lord High Admiral, in 1600, were discovered in the present Lord Petre's archives : the sea-dog later became a member of the first Lord Petre's household.[2] The marble mural memorial (he died in 1621 aged 66) in Ingatestone church reveals a bold, spirited face (plate 17).

[1] Essex Record Office, D/AEA 22, f. 204.
[2] A. C. Edwards, *English History from Essex Sources, 1550–1700* (1952), 15, 22.

Ill feelings occasionally arose when a parishioner, resenting the church-wardens having allotted him a family pew or seat which he deemed inferior to his social position, appropriated another place. Such may account for one or more of the following incidents. Richard Pilsedon yeoman and Robert Noke and Edmund Noke gentlemen violently ex-pelled Francis Franke gentleman from his pew in Hatfield Broad Oak church in 1564. Two years earlier he had been assaulted by two other parishioners, but there may be no link between the two encounters. In 1570 there was a similar scuffle in Thaxted church, when George Pygott and John Taylor *alias* Moore yeomen violently removed Jane wife of John Brooke, but that was her 'usual' seat, and they were both fined 12d. by Robert Kempe, J.P. The casting out of Mistress Sawyn from her choir seat and the thrashing of two servants who came to her aid in Hatfield Peverel church in 1573 was apparently only one of three skirmishes between the Jobson and Sawyne families (p. 120).

The last pew case (1598) is of interest because the victim had been the heroine of an elopement episode in which the lovers' steed swam a noted Essex ferry against a strong tide. Her youthful courage is related in a story told by 'Mr. Malden of Rayne, servant to the Earl of Warwick,' about 130 years later to Morant, whose own note is now copied.[1] 'The Earl of Warwick going from Leighs to Rochford Hall was attended by Capt. Cammock, who courted his daughter. He carried her off upon a horse, and came to Fambridge Ferry, where the boat was on the other side, and the tide violent. They found themselves pursued, and had no shift but to swim over. The Captain advised her not to venture; but she said she would live and die with him, and took the water. When they were half over, the Earl's servant came to the water-side, and his horse neighed; upon which the horse that carried the lovers turned round, and with much difficulty was brought to keep his course. They rode to Maldon; were wedded and bedded; and the Earl said, seeing she had ventured her life for him, "God blesse 'em".'

There is one discrepancy in this romantic tale, which is understandable as the events took place long before. Robert, third Lord Rich, was not created Earl of Warwick until 1618. As the second Lord Rich, father of Frances, died in 1581, the captain may have been in the suite of the third baron. He was a widower when he carried off his intended bride. By Ursula his first wife he had had nine children; by Frances he was to have thirteen more of whom only one is named in the incident about to be related. The twenty-five Cammocks are all portrayed in the alabaster and marble monument erected after his death in 1602 on the east wall of the north aisle of All Saints church, Maldon.[2] Ironically, the ferry

[1] Morant, *History of Essex*, i, 323. Perhaps Hames Malden of Rayne, grocer (will proved 1770).
[2] Chancellor, *Sepulchral Monuments of Essex* (1890), plate xciii.

belonged to William Harrys of Creeksea Hall who held it from Lord Rich, lord of the honour of Rayleigh.

Apparently there was disharmony between the two chief families in Layer Marney, the Tukes and the Cammocks. The facts are set out in the indictment, which is not accompanied by other evidence. On Sunday 23 July 1598, Frances, wife of Thomas Cammock gentleman (she being further described as daughter of Robert Lord Rich deceased), went to church with her children and servants, only to find that Elizabeth wife of Peter Tuke esquire and a carpenter had fixed a lock on her pew. They were 'threatened' while trying to enter the locked pew, by Mistress Tuke, her manservant and others unnamed, and she and the servant beat and ill-treated Mistress Cammock, Martha her ten-year-old daughter and her man-servant. The lawn apron which Frances wore was torn, and she had to be vio-lently 'withheld' from her pew. 'So,' the indictment ends in somewhat fulsome language, 'they were not able to hear Divine Service quietly and peaceably without peril of death.' Frances' spirit had showed itself again in the scuffle.

Peter Tuke, J.P., was the third son and heir of George (died 1573), who was also third son and heir of Sir Brian Tuke, chief secretary of Cardinal Wolsey. Sir Brian, High Sheriff of Essex in 1533, had purchased Layer Marney Hall and estate from the two daughters and co-heirs of John, second and last Lord Marney. It was his father who built the spectacular four-turreted gatehouse, but the main house was never begun so it became known as Layer Marney Tower. The Cammocks were an old-established family in the parish. Thomas was the son of Robert Cammock (died 1586). The west cross-wing of the house built by the father or the son still exists : then known as Cammocks, it has been called Duke's Farm for two centuries. Two years after this disturbance Mistress Tuke's manservant was charged with highway assault (p. 182), and a year after James's accession Cammock and three yeomen, perhaps his tenants, all of Layer Marney, were indicted for assaulting the constable of a neighbouring village.

No less than ten attacks in churchyards came before the secular courts. A fight took place in Willingale Doe churchyard on 30 May 1565 between several villagers. Richard Sampford struck Richard Bright with his dagger and Thomas Sampford and Agnes his wife with his staff. Helen (or Ellen) wife of Richard Sampford assaulted Thomas, pulling out a bit of his beard and striking him on the head with a leg of mutton, for which the Court fined her 12d. Richard pleaded not guilty by Thomas Wallinger his attorney, but he was also indicted at the same Sessions as a common whoremonger and barrator and his wife as a common brawler. Both were fined 12d. by Richard Rich and Thomas Frank, J.P.s. A slightly earlier indictment discloses what lay behind the quarrel (p. 66). One of the first deeds enrolled with the clerk of the peace shows that one branch owned Duke's Farm in Willingale Doe in and before 1538.[1]

[1] Essex Record Office, Q/RDb 1, no. 37.

In 1578 'an ignorant simple fellow' of Nazeing, aged 18, drew his
dagger in the churchyard 'among a company of maidens, striking one
but hurting none'; the jurors, mercifully inclined, 'craved that he may
have his correction'. It was no half-wit but a gentleman, Francis Smith of
Blackmore (lord of the Priory manor), whom the hundredal jury presented
in 1588 for striking the constable at the church-gate with drawn sword
and for fetching John Reve out of the church, in which the constable had
locked him. Reve was a mercer and alehouse-keeper in the parish. A
few months afterwards another violent rescue occurred in the neighbouring church of Writtle. John Wylde, a parishioner, had been outlawed
after conviction for debt. The hundred bailiff arrested Wylde, but he was
released by no less than twenty men, all named, in the congregation,
after they had wounded the bailiff and his man, 'so that their blood was
drawn and murder was like to have been committed.' Wylde then escaped.
One may wonder what took Thomas Sherlock of Chelmsford to Bradwell-
juxta-mare in 1598. He apparently went berserk with his 'longstaff',
crashing it down on three heads in the churchyard. In the same year,
William Markant gentleman and John Playse yeoman, both of Great
Bentley, stoutly resisted arrest in the churchyard, striking with sword and
cudgel both the village constables who were executing a justice's warrant.

Other incidents in which hot tempers flared up in God's Acre were
attacks by dagger at West Ham (1566) and Terling (1574) and assaults
by staff at Alphamstone (New Year's Day 1578), Great Parndon (1588),
and Great Waltham (1602).

A very different if not unique affair at Upminster was presented by
the hundredal jury in June 1586. James Robotham gentleman had been
buried in the parish church about six weeks earlier. His corpse was afterwards taken out of the grave in the night-time, and re-buried the following night in the churchyard. The incident was affirmed by Thomas
Latham and three others including the sexton. (William Latham, lord
of the manor of Gaines in Upminster, was presented by the jury at the
same Sessions as a recusant.) But they had been unable to find out who
carried out the exhumation, so no indictment could be preferred.

Such were the physical assaults and disturbances of a secular nature
in Essex churches and churchyards which reached the Courts. Some of
the clergy were subject to disturbances of a very different character to
those in which laymen were involved. Apart from the rector of Mashbury
being called a crying rascal in his church in 1556 (p. 4), no further
anti-clerical commotions are recorded, despite the Religious Settlement
of 1559, until 1578 when Richard Archer of North Fambridge clerk (not
the rector) was not only threatened but assaulted before the congregation
by Thomas Pryce gentleman, one of his parishioners. No details are
given. They are not lacking, however, in an indictment against Edward
Rothman of Pleshey yeoman, who on a Sunday in 1586, when James

Essex was not directly involved in rebellion against the government. But there is found some evidence in our records (and apparently un-recorded elsewhere) of an abortive attempt at insurrection in the cloth-manufacturing towns in the north-east of the county in 1566; and subversive comments, which could also have led to a rising, were over-heard during famine years in the last decade of the reign (pp. 61–65). Apart from the usual crop of seditious talk at every sovereign's accession, the Assize files regularly echo the cries of discontented subjects, sober or drunken, and ears were strained in later years to listen for any whisper which seemed to come from the twin menaces of Spanish power and Catholic treason. Specific indictments of high treason are relatively few, but they include the notoriously false charge against John Payne of Ingatestone Hall, Catholic martyr, who was hanged (p. 52). Rarely is the sentence given – a common defect of criminal court records of the period – but where the verdict was guilty it may be assumed that the law took its course.

At the Winter Assizes, 1576, Mary Cleere of Ingatestone was charged with having traitorously declared there a few months earlier that the Queen was 'baseborn and not born to the Crown,' but that another Lady was the right inheritor.' She added, somewhat irrelevantly, that it did not become a woman to make knights, which she would justify. Found guilty, she was sentenced to be drawn and burnt (*trahatur et comburatur*). Burning was rightly deemed to be a more severe punishment than hanging : a criterion of the gravity of her crime and the sole instance actually recorded in our Elizabethan records.

A Catholic impostor impersonating the dead Queen Mary would have been less surprising to a Protestant government than one alleging that he was Edward. (Two Essex men had been arrested in the middle of Mary's reign for reporting that Edward was still alive.[1]) This late Tudor pretender, emulating Perkin Warbeck's attempt against Henry VII, first appeared in May 1578, when the Council ordered that 'one Blosse *alias* Mantell' be removed from the Tower to the Marshalsea prison, also in London, to await his trial by the Assize judges in Essex.[2] The indictment at the following Midsummer Assizes states that Robert Mantell *alias* Bloys of London, at Maldon and many other places,' gave out and said that King Edward was alive, that he (meaning the said Robert) was said that King Edward the Sixth, and that if he would find one that was trusty he could disclose that which should rejoice them all; howbeit he could never find such an one.' He was found guilty, but he escaped from the Castle gaol a year later. So Lord Darcy and Sir Thomas Lucas were enjoined by the Council to visit the gaol and interrogate the prisoners. Lucas reported that widow Symonds, a prisoner, had probably helped

[1] *Acts of the Privy Council*, v, 126.   [2] *Ibid.*, x, 223; also xii, 29, 353–4.

to escape. At the Midsummer Assizes 1579 Richard King, the
r (deputy of Henry Mackwilliam esquire, Keeper of the Castle
was charged. The impostor had been sent thither by the Council
June 1578, 'on suspicion of high treason', had been re-committed
conviction by the Assize judges for further trial, but on the Assize
King 'treacherously allowed him to escape'. King pleaded not
of treason but guilty of negligence, and he exchanged his gaoler's
for a cell in his own prison, where he remained until released by
il order in January 1580. Re-captured and thrown into Newgate
, Mantell was sent under secure guard to Brentwood, where he
efore the judges again at the Lent Assizes 1581, this time pleading
Judgement: 'To be drawn from prison to the gallows and there
d and afterwards whilst still living cut down, etc.'

ard, no longer young, was still living in 1587, according to another
r. For spreading it, Walter Mildmay had committed William
s, a smith of Hatfield Peverel, who, being asked what news was at
n, had said, 'There is one in the Tower which saith he is King
d'; then a bystander remarked, 'I dare say that King Edward is
which Francis denied, 'I dare not say so', adding 'I know the man
rried King Edward in a red mantle into Germany in a ship called
rry'. When it was pointed out that he was buried where they used
kings, Francis declared that 'there was a piece of lead buried that
low but there was nothing in it and that it was but a monument',
ch he was told, 'These are naughty words which ought not to be
' He was found guilty of treason.

ours of a highly treasonable and scandalous nature were being
in Essex and Hertfordshire in the summer of 1560. Thomas
, who had become rector of Little Burstead on the death of his
ssor in the same month as Mary's death, was charged by the
ouncil, after their receiving a letter from the Earl of Oxford
at Hedingham Castle), with 'uttering malicious words against
een.' Holland confessed that he heard the vicar of Stortford
say that one had been sent to the Tower for reporting that the
vas with child.[1] He resigned his benefice very soon afterwards.
he same time Lord Rich and Thomas Mildmay, J.P.s, wrote to
closing depositions of certain Essex folk about similar reports,
hat they had committed Anne Dowe of Brentwood, the chief
to gaol. Mother Dowe was alleged to have openly asserted that
n was pregnant by Dudley.[2]
0 fertile rumour in Essex had credited such a liaison with two
a story not matched in reports to the Council from elsewhere.

e Papers Domestic, 1547–80, 154.
7. She was not of 'Brentford' (J. Neale, *Queen Elizabeth*, 86), who cites both
s the only known gossip that the Queen had borne a bastard by Dudley.

Forester (perhaps the lecturer, the vicar's name at this date is not known) was ministering in the church, shouted, 'You should have a purgation to digest your choler, and I do not doubt you shall have it. I know not whether you have authority to preach and read in this place. I hope to have you tamed when the bishop cometh again. You are but a lousy boy, and so you will show yourself always.' The churchwarden bade him to be quiet, 'for the place and time served not for such misdemeanour'.

Rival claims to hold benefices or to preach led to several stormy scenes. The clergy list for Rettendon has these entries: Robert Buckberd clerk, instituted 1572; William Bingham, L.D., 1588. At the Epiphany Quarter Sessions 1591 Robert Buckberd, termed 'of Rettendon clerk', was indicted for an assault one Sunday in November 1590 on William Bingham, doctor of laws, in Rettendon church. Buckberd was alleged to have struck Bingham violently with a little staff or cudgel, giving him a wound in the cheek. A true bill was found, but the verdict is not given. The following Easter Sessions received a deposition taken by Edward Hubberd, J.P., from Thomas Dowcet, a tailor of Harlow, an impressed soldier who was just about to go abroad, which purports to make out that Buckberd had been the victim of a 'slanderous and untrue indictment procured by Dr. Bingham'. Buckberd and the deponent were in the church before morning prayer, when the doctor entered and sat down in the place where Bingham normally read divine service, exclaiming that he had come to perform his duty. Buckberd denied his claim to the benefice and tried to push him out of the seat. In the scuffle, Bingham's cheek hit the edge of the seat. Dowcet on oath had declared his testimony that Buckberd did not assault Bingham to be true and he would be ready to confirm his statement later, 'if God send him well home again into England.' Other members of both clerical families were also bound by recognizances to keep the peace – Bingham on Christmas Eve 1589 for his wife and two sons (£40 each taken before Edward Sulyard), and Buckberd on 4 January 1590 for Elizabeth, probably his daughter[1] (taken before Humphrey Mildmay and Thomas Mildmay); and in the following April Lawrence Bingham of High Ongar gentleman had been bound as surety for three Fyfield and one Willingale Doe men to keep the peace towards Robert Buckberd, 'late of Rettendon clerk.' Dr. Bingham, it should be added, was Official to the Archdeacon of Colchester, and had been reported in 1582 to Quarter Sessions for refusing to accept church-wardens' presentments unless they paid a 4d. fee for each (p. 92). Helen Buckberd had also been the ringleader in a riotous closebreaking and assault at Great Parndon in 1586 (p. 137).

Before describing some exceptionally lively encounters in Stanford-le-Hope church in August 1591, certain preliminary skirmishes must be related. Martin Clipsam the rector evidently evinced popish leanings.

[1] *Trans. Essex Archaeological Society*, vii, 156.

Admitted rector in 1584, he had been previously rector of St. Vedast, London. William Partridge, the leading opponent among his parishioners, had probably involved himself in a dispute with the rector over a legacy for the repair of the church which had passed through his hands as one of the churchwardens.[1] He had at any rate been excommunicated in the Archdeacon's Court for failing to render his warden's account for the year 1587.[2] The first recorded open conflict seems to have taken place on Friday 24 May 1591, when Tristram Blaby, using his newly issued licence, was 'preaching the word of God'. On that day the rector 'did very maliciously disturb and interrupt' him in the pulpit, 'using many lewd and contemptuous gestures to disgrace and discountenance the said preacher'. On several subsequent occasions the rector left the church 'to the great dislike of the congregation.' The story so far is told from indictments and depositions which give the impression of being *ex parte* Blaby. The events of August are taken from depositions made *ex parte* Clipsam, and restore the balance.

It is in the 1580s that the puritan phenomenon, the lecturer, first appears in our records. The word 'lecturer' in fact originates with this new clerical species, usually appointed and paid by the parishioners' voluntary contributions for the purpose of delivering afternoon or evening lectures or sermons. An extraordinary account of the internecine struggle between rector and preacher at Stanford-le-Hope has been preserved in the following decade. At the Summer Assizes 1591 Clipsam was prosecuted on three counts: interrupting Blaby and quitting the church when he preached (as already stated); also 'for administering the sacrament in only one kind, viz. in bread, not in wine, after the Popish manner', on Sunday 1 August 1590.

By the Michaelmas Sessions it was Blaby the preacher who was indicted. The opposition party had struck, and with effect. Serious trouble arose in the church on two successive Sundays. The scenes are described in a statement, unsigned but clearly put in by one or more members of the rector's party against 'the preacher' and his 'faction'. On 8 August, as rector Clipsam had almost ended divine service, 'saving the Collects at the end of the Communion', preacher Blaby went unreverently and rudely into the pulpit, giving no warning to the 'parson' nor to the sexton about preaching, and commanded the people, as the rector was reading, to sing a psalm. 'I pray you', the rector exclaimed, 'give me leave to say forth my service, it is almost done.' Partridge, the excommunicate, and Philip Pery, one of the churchwardens, rebuked the parson, telling him that he did contrary to the order of the Communion book. But other parishioners said, 'Why do ye trouble the parson?' Then they 'multiplied words, one against another', and some said, 'If he would have preached, he might have given warning to the parson that the bell might have been

[1] Essex Record Office, D/AEA 15, f. 73.   2 *Ibid.*, f. 54.

tolled'. As they were contending together, the rector went home. Left in undisputed possession, Blaby preached, and in his sermon he railed on the parson, calling him, 'Dumb dog, idle pastor, unlearned and unable minister, a murderer of their souls', with divers other unseemly words, comparing him to Corah, Dathan and Abiram. He said that all that took part with the parson were like those that murmured against Moses and Aaron, and that 'if some of them die the common death of all men, then say you that I am not sent.' (The characteristically apt reference by a generation steeped in the Bible is to *Numbers*, xvi, 1–35. Dathan and Abiram rebelled against the civil authority of Moses, and Korah tried to intrude himself into the priestly office.)[1]

At evening prayer on the same day, Blaby walked in the churchyard all the service time. Then he came in great haste into the pulpit to preach, and he 'railed most shamefully against the parson and against all other states of people and authority' (the seditious sermon already referred to, p. 57).

Next Sunday the disorder grew much worse. When Clipsam the rector was in his seat at morning prayer, with his surplice on and ready to begin, Blaby came and commanded him to 'come forth of his seat', saying that the Bishop of London had appointed him to say service. Being 'amazed', the rector retorted, 'If my Lord of London have appointed you so to do, show me his authority and I will give you place, otherwise I will not.' Blaby then charged the congregation to witness that the parson would not obey the episcopal mandate, adding that his bond in £40 to the Bishop to say service in the church would be forfeited if he gave way.

At evening prayer, Blaby, Partridge and 'divers other parishioners and some of other parishes of their faction' came into the church, at which the rector said, 'I marvel greatly, Goodman Partridge, seeing you are excommunicated, why you do trouble me and the parish thus every day'. He answered, 'You lie, I am not excommunicated'. Clipsam said, 'If you are absolved, show me your discharge from the Court under the seal and I am satisfied or else get you forth of the church, for so long as you are in it I will say no service.' Blaby countered, 'If you will not say service, I will go preach'. The rector asserted, 'We are commanded at the Bishop's visitation by his injunctions that service should not be said as long as any excommunicate person is in the church.' Partridge then urged Blaby, 'Take your place', at which Clipsam charged the churchwardens, 'as they would answer it', not to suffer Blaby to preach. As the people were reasoning together, standing in the middle alley (aisle), Blaby hastily climbed the pulpit, reading three or four words above the hubbub which doubtless filled the church. (It seems likely that it was at this juncture that the rector delivered himself of a resounding piece of Elizabethan abuse, which we quote at the end from a separate indictment.) Then

[1] I owe this note to my friend, Samuel Marriage of the Essex Record Office.

descending, he said to his faction, 'Come, let us go hence and let the parson do now what he will.' The rest tarried until the end of the service. Meantime, Blaby, Partridge and company consulted in the churchyard. Now came the violence. When the rector was quietly talking to one Christopher Daie, Blaby and his party ran through the churchyard on the south side of the west end to the north side where Clipsam was. Partridge held him by the left arm, 'haling, pulling and gripping him very sore, and Blaby haling, pulling and holding him by the bosom on the other side, hurting him grievously and saying, 'Come and go with us, we charge you in the Queen's name, to the justice.' Clipsam asked if they had any authority from the justice; if so, he would go. But they continued to pull, enjoining those that stood by to lay hold on him and carry him to the justice. Some asked what the parson had done, and Robert Bayly said that he was a rebel and would give 6d. for a halter to hang him with. Clipsam prayed them not to hurt him. Grievously pained, he got out his 'little meat knife', saying, 'If you will not let me go and leave your gripping, I will make you let me go', not hurting them but fearing that they would pull his arm out of joint. They let him go. The final outcome of the dispute is unknown. Certainly the rector was forbidden to exercise his duties, since he appeared in the Archdeacon's Court on 2 October next alleging that 'the matter whereof he was suspended, viz. for brawling and using violent speeches, is now depending before the Judges of Assize', and praying the suspension be lifted.[1] In another document Clipsam was charged with having spoken these 'false, scandalous and opprobrious words' in the church on 15 August against Blaby, 'Come down, thou prating Jack, thou foamest out thine own poison'; later in the churchyard, for addressing Partridge, 'Jack', with other words (not given). This indictment was preferred at the same Michaelmas Sessions, and the justices also received the written statement against Blaby for his remarks on the previous Sunday against higher authority, already quoted under Sedition (p. 57).[2] In his will, which was proved in 1597, Clipsam does not refer to himself as rector.[3]

The Stanford dispute is noteworthy because it illustrates the conditions with which some of the puritan preachers had to contend where the parson and his followers resented their appointment; but the lecturers' supporters were sometimes stronger and often had the influential backing of local justices of the peace. In Essex, Colchester appears to have been the first town to have employed a preacher, who was paid by the 'free and voluntary contribution' of the bailiffs and aldermen and of about forty townsmen. George Gifford's early activities in this capacity at Maldon in

[1] Essex Record Office, D/AEA 15, f. 187v.

[2] An account from the lengthy documents of the Stanford affair was drafted ten years ago by my former colleague, John Holmes, M.A., which I have used.

[3] *Trans. Essex Archaeological Society*, vii, 168, quoting Vicar General's book (Bishop of London).

1582 have already been mentioned (p. 52). The lecturers filled a big gap in the spiritual life especially in parishes where the parson was ill-educated or was a frequent absentee.[1]

While no actual disturbance resulted from the presentment by the grand jury at the Michaelmas Sessions 1583, the language is too cryptic to pass over. On Sunday 22 September William Clyburye, vicar of Halstead (1561–90), preached 'fables and tales and then and many times before uttered vain and foolish invectives against his brethren preachers: "My fine fellows and my jolly fellows can suck out their doctrine out of their finger ends, but I preach my doctrine out of ancient doctors and writers of three hundred years old. I can shake a knave at all times out of my sleeve".' Also, according to the jurors, many other vile, bawdy and uncomely words came from his pulpit, to the great offence of the congregation and to the peril of an uproar against the Queen's Majesty's peace. More flashes of Essex sardonic humour are mirrored in the last two Elizabethan cases, in both of which laymen took the offensive. 'Parson Taylor', exclaimed William Massie gentleman in 1598 to his rector William Taylor in Springfield church, 'we should have had some good or goodly sermon of you this day, but belike you are not well provided (prepared) for the same.' Both assaulted and derided was William Pasfield, vicar of Tolleshunt D'Arcy (1590–1604). On Sunday 4 November 1599 Stephen Beckingham gentleman, one of his parishioners, struck him during service time, exclaiming, 'Thou art a dunce and a bold dunce. I will make thee neither parson nor vicar here, but I will not call thee knave.' Four witnesses confirmed. The grand jury found a true bill, but the verdict is not given. Pasfield had sought security against Beckingham 'on account of divers discords between them before this time'. The accused had been bailed by Francis Harvey of Cressing Temple, J.P., and Robert Veysye gentleman, also of Cressing, but he obtained a writ of *supersedeas* a fortnight after the Sessions. He was the younger brother of Sir Thomas of Beckingham Hall in Tolleshunt Major, the contemporary turreted gatehouse of which has survived. Pasfield was subsequently rector of Chelmsford (1604–13) and vicar of Wethersfield (1613–36). What lay behind their differences is unknown, but Pasfield's benefice was not in Beckingham's gift and the vicar had been at Tolleshunt for a long time. In 1602 he was violently attacked on the highway (p. 183).

But it was not always a case of trouble-making parishioners or contending clergy. In 1571 Patrick Ferne, rector of Sandon (1567–87), was fined 3s. 4d. for quarrelling both in and out of church and 20d. for barratry generally.

Despite the number of church disturbances dealt with by the secular courts, chiefly as assaults, a far greater number and variety was chronicled

---

[1] The best account of these preachers is by P. Collinson, *The Elizabethan Puritan Movement* (1967). He does not mention the Stanford-le-Hope affair.

O

in the Archdeacons' Courts. The combined evidence forms one of the most important aspects of Elizabethan life, with its many facets of violence, slander and unconscious humour. Apart from a little complementary information about the Stanford-le-Hope and Blackmore incidents, the cases are entirely different. They will appear in the next volume.

There is little specific information about church assaults and disturbances in county records elsewhere in England. One afternoon in 1573 a man insulted another in St. Paul's cathedral, waited for him in the churchyard, and then attacked with sword in one hand and dagger in the other. In self-defence, the victim drew his own sword and killed his assailant.[1] Two assaults in churchyards are recorded in Lancashire.[2] A single Hertfordshire indictment, for a fight in the chancel of Hitchin church, recites that the punishment under the statute for attacks in church or churchyard was either cutting off an ear or branding a cheek, but does not give the sentence, and the Essex records are equally unhelpful in this respect.[3]

[1] *Middlesex County Records*, i, 82–3.
[2] *Lancashire Quarter Sessions Records*, i.
[3] *Herts County Records*, i, 4.

17

Abduction, Rape and Immorality

In English law abduction was the forcible or fraudulent taking away of any person, especially a child under sixteen. In Elizabethan times abduction generally implied motives of lucre, the felon's intention being marriage rather than rape or sexual intercourse; but the latter was not excluded. An indictment had to be laid under the Act of 4 & 5 Philip and Mary, c.8 (1558). This statute is quoted in the only prosecution found in the Middlesex records of our period, a girl aged 13 whose father had bequeathed her a £30 marriage portion having been 'withdrawn' from her guardian's custody.[1]

Six cases occur in the Essex archives, 'seized and carried off' being the phrase commonly used: abduction, as such, is a word that does not appear till much later. ('Kidnapping' originated near the end of the seventeenth century and then applied to stealing or carrying off children or others to the American plantations.) An indictment of 1597 corresponds with the Middlesex case. Margery daughter and heir of John Ardleigh of East Hanningfield deceased was under 14. She was in the guardianship of Jeremy Fennynge, who had married her widowed mother also deceased, and she possessed lands of the annual value of £14. The girl was taken away against her will by Matthew Hedge and Richard Segrave, yeomen of Goldhanger. Hedge was acquitted, but Segrave was at large. Margery is not mentioned in the will (1586) of her father, John Ardley, a husbandman of East Hanningfield.

In 1585 a Colchester yeoman broke into the house of Henry Lame, incited his daughter Anne to leave home with him, and two days afterwards abducted her. He was remanded to be of good behaviour. The will of Henry Lambe, a butcher (1588), who lived in a big house, no longer surviving, at the corner of East Stockwell Street and St. Helen's Lane in Colchester, includes a legacy of £20 to Anne at the age of 21.

It seems doubtful whether mercenary intentions entered into the other cases which, as they involved more than two defendants, were riots in the eyes of the law. In 1572 John Pylborowe gentleman and three yeomen, all of Hatfield Peverel, assaulted with 'bastinadoes or cudgels' John Cooke of Rochford gentleman, his wife Frances and his ward Susan daughter of John Biglond of Prittlewell. The incident occurred at Great Leighs as they were riding with their servants from the house of John Rochester

1 *Middlesex County Records*, i, 199.

esquire at Terling to that of Sir Giles Allington, Frances' grandfather, at Horseheath (Cambs.). Susan was seized and carried off. The accused appeared at the Assizes and declared that the indictment was insufficient in law, but in any case they pleaded not guilty and prayed to be allowed to 'make fine.' Their fines were assessed at 6s. 8d. each. Pilborough's will (1603), in which he also called himself a gentleman, is apparently unique among Essex wills in stipulating that 'none suspected or detected (presented) for the devilish art of sorcery and witchcraft' should share in his bequests to the poor.

A prosecution of 1591 would have been treated as one of disseisin, were it not for the additional count that a servant and an infant were abducted. Five West Hanningfield men and women had expelled Edward Tunbridge from possession of a house there. Three days later, with eighteen unnamed persons, they broke into Tunbridge's house (not necessarily the same one), beat his maidservant, and carried her off with Zeafora, his daughter, aged one year. The grand jury found a true bill for three of the four named defendants but no true bill for the rest.

In 1600 a Ling (Norfolk) weaver assaulted Henry Ringe, miller of Fyfield, and took away the daughter of a 'spinster' (female spinner); he was acquitted. In another indictment, the first-named defendant was Thomas Newman of Canewdon clerk (the vicar). With four labourers of his parish he made an armed assault at 8 p.m. one March day in 1602 on Robert Kindlemarsh's house and carried away Augustine Dawney from his keeping. One of the labourers was at large; the others were acquitted and bound in £10 each, presumably against any further breach of the peace.

Three early cases of rape (p. 8) were alleged to have been committed by masters on their servants, but all the defendants are acquitted. Twenty-six indictments for rape are found in the three series of records. Of these the verdict was not guilty in sixteen cases, three of which were preferred against a Hatfield Peverel baker for raping different girls, and four against masters for assaulting their servants. Among those convicted one died of fever in Colchester Castle prison. A Brentwood beerbrewer committed the crime at a house called the 'Katherine Wheel' in Shenfield in 1579. A single document of 1574 combined indictments of two servants of Evan ap Rice of Tendring gentleman (p. 180) for barratry with that of one of the servants for breaking into William Allington's house and raping his wife; and the next document charged ap Rice with inciting many persons to break the peace. A most surprising indictment is that of George Burley, rector of Chelmsford, who was charged in 1588 with breaking into the house of John Elliot, 'who was there with Joan, his wife, whom he violently assaulted and raped.' He was acquitted. 'George Burghley' had been instituted two years earlier, but at what date his successor Ralph Rowley became rector does not seem to be known, though he is described as preacher in the parish register between 1594 and 1601. A Mary Burley was buried in 1593 and Mistress Burghlie in 1594. A similar verdict had been found in the case of another clerical defendant four years earlier, when Thomas Sayer of Wrabness clerk (rector, 1566–1608) was indicted for raping a woman aged 26. A rapist who fled is mentioned incidentally in a deposition about cattle-stealing (p. 285) ; and there may be a few hypothetical cases of rape among the murders (p. 154).

The incomplete Middlesex records yield fifteen indictments for rape. There are also several indictments, in briefest form, for buggery and bestiality in the Essex and Middlesex series, but only negligible number of references in the few surviving Elizabethan records of other counties.

Apart from the crimes just dealt with, Quarter Sessions was little concerned, and Assizes even less, with sexual offences, which came within the purview of the spiritual courts. Hundreds of pages of the act books of the Archdeacons of Essex and Colchester are filled with charges of every sort of immoral behaviour. While the Elizabethans differed in this respect in no way from preceding or succeeding generations, the publication in the next volume of *Elizabethan Life* of extracts from the immense corpus of factual evidence in the Church court records will undoubtedly provide some valuable new material for the social historian. This is no idle statement : out of the 20,000 Essex cases during 1558–1603, at least one-tenth relate to sexual delinquency.

The county justices were indirectly involved with such behaviour in so far as their control of poor relief and victuallers brought to Quarter Sessions many cases of bastardy and a few charges of keeping brothels (p. 26).

'William Tynge of Stanford Rivers is ordered that he shall not further frequent the society of Joan Palmer widow of Chipping Ongar, because they are suspected persons and of dishonest conversation, under a penalty of forfeit as often as they are found associating, to wit, William 13s. 4d., Joan 6s. 8d.' This is an entry in an Ongar hundred presentment of 1562, and a year later an item in a Chafford hundred presentment reads, 'William Aucocke received William Clerk and the wife of Casse, being both known to be ill together in their living.' These are the sole reports of suspected incontinence in the scores of early hundredal presentments. Twenty years afterwards the Becontree hundred jurors stated bluntly, 'Audrey Cooke dwelling at Walthamstow is a common whore and for the space of two years has lived an evil life there.' Another hundred produced one of those curious 'mixed' charges, against Edmund Beare, a gentleman of Doddinghurst who kept a 'defamed woman' in his house, and neither went to church : an echo of a similar double presentment in 1556 (p. 30).

It may be assumed either that these four juries included a foreman or a member of stern attitude or that the persons accused were especially offensive to their fellows. Of the four presentments, the Court apparently dealt only with Audrey Cooke. Tynge was well known to the jurors who presented him and must have been a man of some substance, as he is found twice among grand juries.

The conduct of a notorious lecher led to determined action by Wethersfield – a parish which was to figure prominently in the annals of the Essex evangelical movement a little later. That such a definite step was taken in 1575 by the villagers is of more than usual interest. The series of offences, alleged by them, embraced both barratry and incontinence, and are set out in a petition from the two churchwardens, the four questmen (sidesmen) and six parishioners of Wethersfield to the justices complaining against John Lamberte, 'a very troublesome and disordered person'. Suspected for 16 or 17 years of 'whoredom and incontinency' and 'detected' (i.e. presented to the Archdeacon's Court) many times for such 'crimes' (rumours), he had been ordered to purge himself. (The archaic procedure of purgation in Church courts will be described in the next volume.) For many years he had lived disorderly with his wife, and for a time abandoned her, living very dissolutely in other places, where he 'became the common crime of all the country thereabouts by reason of his unbridled lust'. With no fear of God before his eyes, the petition runs, he 'continually vexes and molests his neighbours and especially those whom he perceives to hate most of all his evil demeanour and to seek redress of his infamous doings, and on the contrary labours to maintain and defend his own unclear and abominable life, to the great slander of God's holy gospel, the great grief and offence of all good men, and to the intolerable burden of the whole township (being otherwise sore charged with a great number of poor and impotent people) with bastards and misbegotten children. Further, he has of late procured many processes and writs against some of the honest inhabitants, for they never quarrelled with him otherwise than travailed in the town's behalf (as all good townsmen ought to do) to be discharged of a base child of his. The parishioners therefore desired the county justices to have his licentious boldness repressed and his wicked and abominable manners amended.' And, as if all this was not enough, they end with an equally sanctimonious peroration. Thus, it is interesting to note, puritan feelings were very pronounced at Wethersfield at an early date. Had Richard Rogers (see p. 141), soon to become well known as the puritan lecturer at this village, already arrived (the date is usually given as *circa* 1577)? If so, he probably wrote this document. John Ludham, the vicar, certainly was not the scribe, and was a frequent absentee, though he is found living in Wethersfield in 1590, when mutual recognizances to keep the peace were extracted from him and a parishioner.

The perennial problem of getting rid of the husband of another's mistress crops up once in the Court records. 'We present', the hundredal jury said in 1590, 'John Chaundler of Burnham for that he liveth very wickedly in keeping another man's wife and gave his consent unto murdering of her husband' : a stark allegation, which is supported by a letter from the ever-active Arthur Herrys of Woodham Mortimer to Robert Machyn, deputy clerk of the peace, a few weeks later. At the last Sessions, it appears, the intended victim, one Philpott of Burnham, had 'exhibited a supplication' against Chaundler, resulting in his being bound over with Philpott's wife for appearance at the Sessions. The officer had received the recognizances, also a deposition of Rowland Gryffyth, who had evidently been bribed to play the part of 'executioner' but decided to turn Queen's evidence against Chaundler about the intended murder. Neither the plotter, who had therefore forfeited his bond, nor the wife, because 'she was then ready to lay her belly', came to the Sessions, and she was still too weak to appear at the Assizes. However, the J.P. added, Gryffyth still remained in gaol and would probably have been released, he thought, at last Sessions, but 'the fellow hath lain all this winter and is very weak (as I hear), the murder intended not executed but disclosed' by him. Herrys therefore asked Machyn to 'move Mr. Baron Clerke' (one of the Assize judges) to deliver Gryffyth out of prison, 'for he only hath been punished and the others hitherto free, saving the recognizance forfeited by Chaundler, who I doubt will no more be found.' The woman, he concluded, would be at the next Quarter Sessions. We find no more about Chaundler later on, but he was one of the sureties for the notorious vicar, Peter Lewes, in the previous autumn (p. 144).

An Elizabethan seduction story refers to a man whose immoral relations were not confined to one wench. A fortnight before Easter Sessions 1582 Dorothy Clarke of Burnham spinster had been examined by Sir Edmund Huddleston. She had lived there for four years, and about a year ago on her way to Maldon market she 'by chance fell into acquaintance' with John Fletcher of Coggeshall, who told her he was a bachelor. Unsuccessful in his approaches, he eventually promised to provide a chamber for her in London and to allow her 20 marks a year, and on Lady Day last at Maldon fair she consented in the house of one Woodhouse at the sign of the 'Saracen's Head'. After dinner Fletcher called for a chamber and a fire and a servant brought in beer. They were to meet next Tuesday afternoon at the sign of the 'Cock' at Boreham, when he would carry her to London. Not knowing the way to Boreham, she was to hire someone, and he would pay the charge. But she could not keep the rendezvous, so thought good to visit Coggeshall, and between Kelvedon and Coggeshall she met Fletcher in company, who scarcely spoke to her, apart from saying he must go on. She therefore went to an alehouse in Coggeshall, and paid a boy 3d. to go to Fletcher's house in order to speak to him, but he was not at home. Four days after she had been examined, a midwife and another woman, both of Coggeshall, were telling of the misdeeds of a strumpet of the town to Edward Derawgh. The J.P. learned that Susan Babye, in the extremity of her travail, had confessed that the father was her only half-brother. But she also admitted intercourse with Fletcher at Witham fair a year ago, and with two other Coggeshall men.

Nicholas Wallis, rector of Pentlow, 'now in trouble for incontinency' according to the 'survey of unpreaching ministers in Essex' of 1584 (p. 143), was prosecuted by the county justices in 1586, but his offence is not stated. One of the few occasions on which a J.P. took action in relation to immorality is learned because he attached a memorandum to a recognizance when forwarding it to the County Bench. Two East Ham men stood sureties for a Little Ilford bricklayer's keeping the peace towards his wife. 'He wholly withdrew himself from his wife', William Heigham explained, 'and refused either to give her house-room or any maintenance, and hath of long time haunted the house and company of one Agnes Turner of Little Ilford widow, his next neighbour, being a woman suspected of lewd life; and for which cause they have been convented formerly in the spiritual court, and there enjoined not to keep any more company together, which notwithstanding they have still done, to the great mislike of divers of their neighbours.' In another case, William Sympson of Lambeth (Surrey), a minstrel, was bound over to be of good behaviour for a whole year and then to appear at Quarter Sessions; in the meantime he must not resort to the company of a Barking man's wife nor even appear in Barking for half a year, but should abide with his own wife. John Sewell, the recalcitrant footballer of Dunmow (p. 226), also lusted after Faith wife of Thomas Virgyn. The 'incontinent life' of a Mount Bures wife with a married man of Wakes Colne led to no less than four men being bound to give evidence against her. The accusation of his pregnant servant resulted in Nicholas Baker of Woodford gentleman being bound with two sureties, to receive the order of the Court; most unusually, the J.P. (Miles Sandys) enforcing the bond added a note, 'He hath an evil name that way, by the report of the most of his parish.' A woman who could not produce a surety was gaoled 'for lewdness of life.' The case of a justice's binding a man accused of incontinency to appear before the Church court and the abortive attempt of a man to release a fornicating couple from their humiliating punishment have already been related (p. 178). A solitary charge of keeping two wives is referred to in a calendar of prisoners in the gaol, but there is no indictment. In 1567 the Attorney General brought a case against the bailiffs and commonalty of Colchester for unlawfully exercising several functions, including the imprisoning without bail of adulterers. This short miscellany includes all the relevant documents.

Although the secular courts had no specific statutory authority to deal with charges of immorality, they also came before the justices of other counties very occasionally. The Middlesex records, for example, show a few indictments for adultery (one offender was sentenced to be carted) and one for incest on which a true bill was returned, but no sentence is given.[1] The Middlesex justices were more concerned with brothel-keepers, several of whom were also ordered to be punished by being publicly carted around (in one case, 'basons to be rung all the way before her') and then imprisoned until fines of as much as £20 or £40 were paid. In a solitary Lancashire case, a Bolton wench was to receive five strokes on her bare back on market-day and to be set in the stocks with a paper on her head, 'This person punished for fornication':[2] the latter was a sentence frequently imposed by the Church courts for such offenders.

[1] *Middlesex County Records*, i, 152, 189, 234–5, 287.
[2] *Lancashire Quarter Sessions Records*, 83.

18

Inns and Alehouses

Much has been written about the many ancient Essex inns which still exist. Some, timber-framed, jettied and gabled, when viewed from the outside, are a delight to the eye. Inside, wall-studs or panelling, ceiling-beams or great fireplaces give equal pleasure. But little has been told about mine host and his customers, and the way they behaved. What follows is drawn wholly from the Quarter Sessions and Assize records. Apart from their names in the annual licences, the publicans (to use a modern term), the travellers seeking refreshment and lodging at the inn, and the local folk resorting to the alehouse are rarely mentioned if they were law-abiding. But several hundreds of those who committed offences appear in the records. Some disorderly alehouses have already been noted in Chapter 2. More will be seen in the next chapter on Games and Sports. Indeed, disreputable alehouses and forbidden games were virtually concomitant, as was aptly expressed but painfully spelt when a West Ham victualler was presented in 1576 for 'kepynge of fytlynge and for kepynge of grete ilruyle of gret gamynge.' Many alehouse-keepers were termed lewd, or disorderly, fellows. In Tudor language the words meant much the same: 'lewd' normally had no sexual implication. This, of course, does not imply that there were no brothels in Elizabethan England. Two were reported in Chelmsford in 1567 (p. 26), and a few later.

'The true and principal use of Inns, Alehouses and Victualling-houses is two-fold, viz. either for the relief and lodging of wayfaring people travelling from place to place about their necessary business, or for the necessary supply of the wants of such poor persons as are not able by greater quantities to make their provision of victuals: and is not meant for entertainment and harbouring of lewd or idle people to spend or consume their money or time there.' Thus Michael Dalton in his *Country Justice* introduces a long section on Alehouses, paraphrasing the preamble to the Act of 1 James I, c.9 (1603), which deplored the fact that neither the Act of 11 Henry VII empowering J.P.s to reduce the number of alehouses nor that of 5 & 6 Edward VI, c.25 for more general reformation of abuses had brought about the desired effect.

By the Edwardian Act any two J.P.s, acting out of Sessions, could 'allow' an alehouse, provided that the applicant produced two sureties prepared to enter into a pecuniary recognizance, or bond, with him for his good behaviour. A very early example has survived in the Marian Sessions rolls (p. 5), in which the licensee undertook not to allow vagrants and other rogues or unlawful games in his house. The operative words in another form of recognizance, taken in 1586, run: 'do keep good order and wholesome drink for man's body, using the true measures and weights of ale and bread according to the Statute, and do not suffer no unlawful games nor no company to be kept in his house in time of Divine Service'. (Had he broken his bond, perhaps a pedagogue could have shown him how to disclaim it because of the effect of the double negative.) There are several other variants. The fullest version made the alehouse-keeper liable to be charged for allowing, or merely encouraging, unlawful games; harbouring rogues, vagabonds and others without passports; lodging women about to give birth to bastards or other paupers who might be a charge on the parish rates; engaging in brothel-keeping or temporarily housing women of ill fame; flouting the law against dressing or eating flesh in Lent or other fastdays or fishdays, or serving customers with victuals or ale in time of service or on holidays. Of these victuallers', innkeepers' and alehouse-keepers' recognizances were brought to Quarter Sessions and were duly filed. The justices held frequent local and probably informal 'binding sessions' for this purpose. This more orderly aspect will be considered in more detail later, with an estimate of the total number of inns and alehouses in the county.

No wonder that some licensees were presented for more than one offence at the same time. A Broomfield alehouse-keeper, for instance, received vagabonds and allowed men's servants and artificers to play at cards and other unlawful games at unlawful hours in the night, and his wife was a common disturber of the peace, quarrelling, railing and living unquietly with her neighbours. An innholder in Chatley hamlet (in Great Leighs) received persons into his house on Sunday afternoons, drinking and misbehaving themselves, and he had not come to church twice in the past quarter but goes abroad to kill and chase poultry and generally perturbs the inhabitants. A Chigwell man was an unlicensed vendor of ale, a common player of cards, a common disturber of the peace of his neighbours, and a keeper of a bawdy house. But before drawing further on the more unusual reports of unruly houses, something should be said about their utility. The licensed victualler sold ale and bread, providing them chiefly for the indigent. The more substantial house-holders brewed their own beer and baked their own bread. Ale was virtually the only drink of the poor. 'Water', wrote Andrew Boorde earlier in the century, 'is not wholesome sole by itself for an Englishman', and he sang the praises of good ale brewed from malt and water alone. (Before hops were introduced ale and beer were synonymous terms.) The innkeeper, too, pursued his trade for the benefit of the traveller. It was only when drunkenness led to disorder, or when the alehouse or inn was open in church time, became the resort of vagabonds, scoundrels or gamesters, or was unlicensed, that it was reported. All criminal records tend to give a distorted picture in this respect. The presentment at the Witham hundredal sessions in 1572 has as fair a statement as any. The number of 'innkeepers' (meaning clearly in this document both inn-keepers and alehouse-keepers) in each parish is given. In the town of Witham there were six licensed and three unlicensed. Indictments for lack of licences in Marian Essex have already been referred to (p. 4).

Only once is there a hint of favouritism. In 1569 a hundredal jury declared that a Stapleford Tawney man kept an alehouse (unlicensed as far as they gathered), 'by the friendship of Sir Thomas Smith and Thomas Luter, the high constable.' Sir Thomas, the future author of *De Republica Anglorum*, had been ambassador to France, although not yet re-appointed as a privy councillor and Secretary of State, and was an influential J.P.

More than one contemporary writer condemned the multitude of ale-houses. In 1583 two of the hundreds took the same line. Because a Hatfield Peverel victualler allowed illicit games 'we think the place may be very well spared from victualling for there be four besides'; and in Halstead they presented 'divers needless and noisome alehouses and beerhouses, receivers and maintainers of idle and roisterous persons', and they named no less than thirteen men. 'Too many alehouses in our town' was, in fact, a frequent complaint. The presentment for the hundred of Rochford and the duchy of Lancaster in 1592 is quite definite. 'We have nine alehouses in Prittlewell, which fewer would serve as we think; four alehouses in Rochford besides an inn; two alehouses in Pebmarsh, which we think one would serve.' These were all referred to the local justices. In 1596 the Rochford hundred jurors dealt with the other market town. 'We find that there is in Rayleigh ten victuallers and alehouse-keepers, whereof we think that five of them would serve'; and they revert to Rochford town by presenting Robert Brooke who 'victuals and keeps very ill rule in his house, and we have three more victuallers besides.' At the same Sessions another presentment runs, 'We think that there are two ale-houses maintained in Birchanger, which are more than is needed, and thereby many inconveniences arise; we think it very necessary that one or both may be suppressed and especially Philip Steward's alehouse for many causes and disorders.' It was suppressed, and 'none to be licensed there but by special order of this Court.'

In 1598 Chelmsford hundred inveighed against the multitude of houses: six in Danbury Street, 'which we think too many and we suppose that three would be enough for that street' (the long hill); likewise five in Great Waltham, where three would suffice; and four in Rettendon, two of which had been forbidden by the justices. Next year the same hundred reported, 'There be more victualling houses in Danbury than is necessary, to the great trouble of the officers and disquiet of the town' (the Court suppressed three of them for disorder) ; and yet again in 1601, five in Springfield, 'which we think be too many.' The legion of alehouses, in no wise reduced, was brought to the notice of the Assize judges in Midsummer 1600, when the grand jury 'humbly desired your Lordships that the great number of alehouses, being the cause of great misdemeanours and outrages daily committed, may be suppressed.' What such iniquities were is lucidly stated, for example, in a hundredal presentment of 1598 : a Stebbing alehouse-keeper, for drunkenness, quarrelling and fighting; or, more mildly, in the same document, a Hatfield Broad Oak innkeeper, for disorder and maintaining men when they ought to have been in their beds.

Between that year and the end of our period several very disreputable houses were suppressed after complaints had been made to the justices. Many of the 'principal and chiefest' inhabitants of East Tilbury reported John Nicolson victualler in 1602 as 'a man of lewd and evil behaviour, who of his own authority doth obstinately take upon himself to keep a common alehouse not being licensed and hath of his own evil mind procured and by force compelled divers to commit that horrible vice of drunkenness, whereby his good neighbours are greatly grieved, the Sabbath day profaned, God dishonoured and the Kingdom of Satan erected, and the wicked vice of drunkenness increased.' Accordingly, Sir John Petre and Thomas Kighley signed a warrant for his committal to Colchester Castle gaol for at least three days without bail, not to be released until he found good sureties for appearance at the Sessions, and they debarred him from further alehouse-keeping. In the same year the inhabitants of the hamlet of Runsell in Danbury petitioned that Thomas Ingram's alehouse there called the 'Blue Lion' be suppressed because it was disorderly and a harbourage of idle and disordered persons. The petition is endorsed 'True bill'. Two months later William Towse issued his warrant at Dunmow ordering Ingram to cease further trading as he had failed to reform after being admonished. But four months afterwards a Runsell man, apparently the constable, on behalf of his neighbours wrote to Justice Towse, recalling his suppression warrant which had been issued when the Coroner's inquest was held at Dunmow on the death of one slain in Ingram's house, and declaring that he had 'denied' to obey the order read to him by the writer. The justice added, 'He maketh poverty his colour to continue his course ; I think it is not so ; if it be, we were better and will rather contribute to his charge, being a deed of charity, than that he should maintain himself by this, which is evident unto us to be displeasing to God and very hurtful and offensive to all the neighbours.'

In 1600 the inhabitants of Little (Bardfield) Saling petitioned the magistrates to suppress Edward Pratt husbandman, because he keeps a 'lewd and disordered house', unlicensed and having been 'prohibited'.

But he 'continues of malice and set purpose, and being a man having no charge and sufficiently able to live' they hinted that he would not be impoverished by being suppressed. Unfortunately there is nothing to amplify the brief entry about the suppression of two Wethersfield ale-house-keepers, also in 1600, 'at the request of Mr. Rogers, clerk', who was the puritan lecturer there. One of them had been licensed only a short time previously. But it was the hundredal jury, not a puritan preacher, who reported in 1602 an unlicensed West Donyland man for 'such disorder in the nights that there is like to be manslaughter in their company.'

In contrast, the justices were twice asked for an extra licensed house. From Finchingfield folk in 1600 came a petition, headed by the signature of William Bendlowes, who lived at Brent Hall and was a well-established London lawyer. They had considered the 'complaint' of the poor, who, having only one licensed victualler, were greatly distressed because he was unable to provide for the 'four score poor households and upwards.' An additional licence was sought for Richard Cowlete and Cecily his wife, who dwelt in a house of their own which had been a victualling house for more than forty years. The married couple were known 'to have always used the trade of victualling and are greatly desired of the poor because they have been there very well used and relieved by way of lending.' The house stood conveniently both for 'passengers' (travellers) and others, and two of the signatories, being subsidy men, would be bound for their good order.

The other application for a second house came from Thomas Farrar, the rector, and six 'chief inhabitants' of Langham, who told the Court in 1601 that they had had for a long time only one victualling house, built and continued by a 'very meet man', John Rand, near the church. But of late many new cottages had been built in places remote from the church, and 'the poor folks thereabouts are greatly hindered in their work in going far for their bread and beer and other necessaries.' So of their own accord they recommended a second very meet man, Thomas Warner, a clothier; and they tactfully added, 'but not above, for above two we think not necessary.' The justices accordingly licensed 'no more but only the two.'

But there had been some counter-canvassing, and another certificate had since been signed. So the County Bench learned at the next Sessions through a strong letter from Robert Vigerous, J.P. of Langham, whose home was at Valley House.[1] It had been 'gotten of some of the meaner sort' by one William Profytt 'for lucre sake and envy to Warner against the good liking of the chief and better minded neighbours'. The real trouble was that Profytt had also importuned Henry Appleton, J.P., who

---

[1] Not, as popularly believed, the Valley Farm of Constable. See 'Valley House, Langham' (*Essex Review*, xxii, 196–205), with three photographs of the house, probably built by the J.P.'s father.

joined with Vigerous as a signatory for Warner. And, Vigerous added, he 'is not very well acquainted with the state of our town'. He then proceeded to list four objections : the justices have made up their minds not to license alehouses for gain but only for the benefit of the poor ; Profytt's house adjoins Warner's ; it is near no thoroughfare ; and 'it is thought there will be ill rule kept, to the offence of the neighbours, for Profytt's wife hath lately taken into the house her son and his wife being a young woman – Profytt will object that I and the town at the first did move his wife to keep an alehouse, I answer that was before her son and his wife came thither, but since that time our minds altered.' He emphasised that the alehouses are 'only for the poor to buy bread and beer' and added that 'my Lord Suffragan' has been written to by the rector ; and asked for action to 'cross it'. What action was taken is not recorded.

Henry Appleton had been criticised a few months earlier, so it appears, not for complaisance but for severity. He and Thomas Rawlins had forwarded in 1600 a note of their having sent to gaol Henry Forde of Rayleigh for victualling without licence. His case had been remitted to Quarter Sessions, after he had received corporal punishment, for his fine to be assessed. His name crops up again a year later, when it is learned that an unlicensed victualler was not necessarily debarred from further trading. He was in fact granted a licence by two Essex magnates, the Earl of Sussex and Lord Rich, because of a very favourable petition from the townsmen of Rayleigh testifying that he had been a victualler there for a long time and had dealt honestly with his customers. 'Nevertheless', the earl indignantly wrote from his seat at New Hall, Boreham, on behalf of Rich and himself to their brother justices, 'Mr. Appleton goeth about to contradict us, which we cannot but much marvel at', for when he victualled contrary to law Mr. Appleton committed him to prison and he was fined, but 'because the poor man has satisfied the law they desire that their proceedings may not be contradicted'. He added, sententiously, 'if they have done more than by law they might, they are willing to subject themselves when they may be present themselves at any Quarter Sessions hereafter.' Rival landowners occasionally continued their neighbourly disputes in the higher sphere of the County Bench, which was regaled with the spice of local power politics. But, in this matter, it was doubtless futile for Appleton to pit his opinions against two such leaders as Sussex and Rich.

An unusual petition was received at the Easter Sessions 1602 on behalf of Anthony Blande, a baymaker of Halstead, a man with a just grievance. He alleged that he had been requested by the overseers to use the trade of brewing, there being only one other brewer, in order to relieve the poor, 'being very many and none or very few brew their own drink.' He had also provided brewing vessels at his own heavy expense. But nearly all the victuallers bought their supplies from the other brewers, so he sold his own beer to the poor out of doors by the 1d. and ½d. as they needed, which led to his being indicted at the last Quarter Sessions for victualling without licence. 'It is requested therefore that he be licensed to sell to the poor as stated, and that such innholders and victuallers as brew in their own houses be suppressed.' The two constables, an overseer, a churchwarden and ten others signed the petition.

Applicants for licences had to obtain a recommendation or certificate of good conduct from their fellow parishioners, in addition to producing two sureties, and in some cases they had to solicit support. In 1572 five Woodford men signed a letter to the clerk of the peace desiring him to show favour to the bearer, John Lynnet of Woodford Bridge, so that he might be licensed to sell ale, 'for', they averred, 'we know him to be an honest neighbour and one meet for the same.' The inhabitants of Messing in 1589 'certify' that an old-established 'house of victualling called the Vine', which has 'never before been put down' for more than fifty years and was for the benefit of horse and man in the neighbourhood, had recently been suppressed to their misliking without any reasonable cause. The present victualler and his parents had been born and bred in the parish. So the constables and nine villagers signed the petition for the licensing of 'the house of such antiquity'. The justices allowed it. In 1590 a certificate was put in by the 'inhabitants' of Mountnessing at the request of John Abell. 'The place where he dwelleth is meet for that purpose and the man of honest behaviour.' Eight signed, two of whom were his sureties. A similar testimonial from six men of Feering to the (Suffragan) Bishop of Colchester (in his capacity as a county J.P.) and Ralph Wiseman in 1601, reciting that 'no man may keep any victualling or tippling house without a commendation from the place of his abode', declared that Richard Scotte was a very honest man.

In the roll for Michaelmas Sessions 1573 are two letters from Kenelm Throckmorton of Little Easton, J.P. One is addressed to John Pynchon, J.P. A poor man of Dunmow, one Hugh Tomson, he wrote, had been presented for keeping an alehouse. What he had done in the past the writer could not tell, but for a good while he had not kept one. Throckmorton asked Pynchon, if the matter came before the Court, to speak on his behalf. A month later he wrote to Mr. Clarke, steward of the manor of Great Dunmow, and 'the rest of the corporation there', praying them to forbear setting any penalty at their leet upon Tomson, the bearer, for being unlicensed, because Mr. Frank and he had promised Tomson at their recent (petty) sessions at Dunmow to grant him a licence, which they could not do as Mr. Frank had been obliged to ride the next day to Ingatestone on other business. Exceptionally, in Midsummer 1577, the Assize judges granted three licences, two of which were 'at the special request of the inhabitants' of Feering and Salcott.

Another part of the general picture discloses the inn as being essential to weary travellers, such as those arriving in Essex by the Thames ferry

16 *(above)*

**SIR JOHN PETRE'S
EXPENSES AT
ASSIZES AND
QUARTER
SESSIONS, 1594**

Gratuities to musicians and
'Skottishe pipers at Mr.
Sheriffes lodging' and to
Sir Thomas Mildmay's
servants at Moulsham Hall.

17 *(left)*

**CAPTAIN JOHN
TROUGHTON,
INGATESTONE
CHURCH**

Sir John Petre's page; later
a sea-dog (p. 185).

18 BOW BRIDGE, WEST HAM

Over the Lea on the Essex-Middlesex boundary. Said to have been built by Queen Matilda and to derive its name from its bow-shaped arches.

19 CROWN INN, BRENTWOOD

Rear view, from a watercolour dated 1892

from Kent. In 1603 the minister, constables and five parishioners of West Tilbury certified that the house of Benjamin Stannerd (or Stonard), a cooper, was 'necessary and his lodging meet, and that it had been from time to time a common alehouse for the relief and sustentation of such passengers as pass the town, better than all the rest of the other alehouses.' A licence was granted by Mr. Kighley.

But not all travellers were honest. On the not uncommon charge that alehouses were the haunt of vagabonds the evidence of the Essex Sessions rolls is abundantly clear. Too many alehouse-keepers were presented for harbouring vagabonds to allow any presumption that they were reported chiefly because of neighbours' malice. 'He doth keep a tippling house and keepeth a great resort of rogues' is typical. Sometimes it is a bare statement of fact, with no hint of ill-will, such as that against an alehouse-keeper of Chipping Hill, Witham in 1571 for 'lodging rogues and vagrants, with other simple and poor people,' or against one of Goldhanger in 1582 for 'much resort of rogues and beggars, above twenty at a time'. More to the point is the presentment in 1586 of a Heybridge victualler who disturbed his neighbours by admitting a dozen rogues, 'who being drunken fell together by the ears and brake the peace,' or that of an unlicensed Brentwood man who 'harboureth all manner of lewd and wandering persons.'

In 1592 three Widford victuallers were reported for continually harbouring rogues and vagabonds, some of whom stole hay. In the same year not only was a Faulkbourne widow presented as a common lodger of rogues, 'not respecting whether they have licences (passports) or not', but the constable also, having many times been warned to apprehend them, had failed to do so ; and a Dunmow victualler likewise for keeping disorder in his house, for 'hoystering of lewd persons' ('hostering', or 'howstering', of vagabonds and suspected folk was presented elsewhere on two occasions). The presentment in 1566 of a Kelvedon alehouse-keeper for 'lodging guests' without the constables' consent reveals another aspect of the same matter.

The converse is observed in a hundredal presentment in 1579 of three Aveley alehouse-keepers who had frequently denied lodging to passengers from the ferry, brought by the constables and headboroughs after 1 a.m. at night. Doubtless they had been held up by an adverse tide or bad weather in crossing over from Kent. Only one other instance of this offence is found, in 1597, when a Great Ilford man, presumably a victualler on the Great Essex Road, refused to lodge travellers brought by the constables, when he had lodging available. His name, ironically enough, was Taverner.

In Elizabethan times wandering musicians were always liable to be treated as vagabonds. In 1571 a Springfield tailor kept a tippling house, maintaining ill rule 'by common resorting of minstrels to his house

P

where the youth of the parish do resort together on Sundays and holydays, rioting and revelling to the great decay of the use and exercise of artillery (archery practice), which by that means is little used; and upon privy watch and search' two Chelmsford servants, a singleman, a woman, 'and others' were found in his house at midnight one Sunday. But drinking in the alehouse during church service time rarely figures in the Sessions records, though many recognizances prohibited it, expressed in one bond as 'drinking or banqueting', the latter meaning revelling as well as feasting. In fact, the only Sunday offence worth citing is that of a Woodford man who in 1573 served two named local labourers and twenty unnamed men with victuals during the time of divine service.

Parochial obsession with vagrancy led a constable and another inhabitant of Willingale Doe in 1572 to report two villagers, one of whom kept a tippling-house, for receiving vagrants, 'they meanwhile exercising their arts at Turrels Hall around the building there of Henry Josselyn gentleman and elsewhere': an incidental reference to Torrells Hall in that parish which presumably supplies the year when this manor house, still surviving, was built.

'Alehouses to be allowed', Dalton wrote, 'are meetest to be about the midst of the town, but not to be in any blind or by-corner (much less in woods or places remote)', because such a house tended to be the resort of vagabonds and thieves. Four such 'blind alehouses' were reported between 1590 and 1602 at Hempstead, Thundersley, Coggeshall and Eastwood. A victualling house, which 'standeth in a wood far distant from any neighbour very suspiciously', was presented in 1583. It lay in the parish of Gosfield, and Edward Bettes had set up the sign of the Saracen's Head, where he lodged the sort of rogues referred to by Dalton. One Helen Harvie, a widowed pedlar who travelled about selling small wares, slept there one Sunday night. On the same night Bettes also lodged Roger Bensted late of Sudbury (Suffolk), a tailor, and Thomas Lawrence late of Bocking. But the village constables arrived, well supported by many honest parishioners, and searched the alehouse, finding the three lodgers, whom the constables' suspected to be evil persons. The victualler was ordered to turn them out, which he promised to do, but they all lodged there again the following night, being Christmas Eve. And at 1 a.m. that night the two men arose from bed and carried off 'as much of her small wages as did cost her £5', as well as a piece of fine linen and some of her clothes worth £3. In 1602 an unlicensed house 'in an unconvenient place' was presented from Great Burstead.

As already seen (and on p. 205) justices' orders for suppressing alehouses were sometimes blatantly ignored. In 1594, for example, Robert Ardley of Braintree was charged with victualling without licence, although 'he was put down by Sir Edmund Hurlestone and Mr. (Thomas) Bendishe the last time of binding of victuallers.' Next year Roger Milborne of Great

Dunmow was similarly presented, having been 'forbode by the justices twice and yet he doth uphold it, by what licence we know not.'

A presentment from the 'view of frankpledge with the court baron of George Sayer esquire' for his manor of Bourchiers Hall in Fordham is preserved in the Sessions roll for Easter 1598. It states that William Borodale 'was discharged from victualling at the last sitting for binding of victuallers, since which time he has continued victualling one month;' and the county justices ordered process to be made. In the same year James Whats of Childerditch was presented for selling ale and bread without licence, despite an order made by Sir Henry Grey and Sir John Petre; and John Joce and Henry Hickson of Billericay were charged in like fashion in 1600, having been forbidden by Petre and Mr. (John) Butler. The parishioners of East Donyland complained in 1603 that Nicholas Grigges had promised the justices, when charged with 'great disorders and resort of company at unlawful times', not to victual any more. He had not only persisted but 'had very lately taken in more beer to continue his former bad courses.' Evil example to the local youths is emphasised.

The part played by the constables on their own initiative, or more probably on that of the justices, is illustrated several times. In 1576 'one William of Halstead, a carrier' was presented for keeping an unlicensed victualling house, although forbidden by the constable; and in 1597 Henry Haye, a victualler of Great Leighs, for keeping a tippling-house after similar action by the constable and other inhabitants, by virtue of a warrant from Sir Thomas Mildmay, so he was gaoled, his fine being assessed at 10s. by the Court, 'because he was a pauper'. Two Great Dunmow men were before Quarter Sessions in 1593. One for 'keeping rogues and disordered persons three days and nights,' also for playing on holidays in service time and quarrelling at midnight, to the great disquiet of the town. His answer to the constable admonishing him was that 'he does nothing but that he will answer it.' The other, 'old Randall', for continual drunkenness and other disorder in his unlicensed house. Warned to give up, he stoutly declared that he 'will keep a cup of good ale in his house and if any man hath anything to say to it he will answer it.' Both were suppressed. Covering the whole county (except Colchester and Maldon) and the whole reign, these records of disobedience do not indicate serious derision of authority.

There are many more cases of unlicensed houses and a few more of disorderly ones, not of sufficient interest to justify quoting. On the whole, encouraging the local drunkards and gamesters seems to have been a less flagrant offence than 'entertaining' wandering rogues and other undesirable characters. And this conclusion, tentative as it is, coincides with the general view expressed, for example, in a letter to Cecil from a Buckinghamshire J.P. in 1561 : 'I do think (them) to be the very stake and stay of all false thieves and vagabonds; if one or two justices be ready to put them down that be too bad, by and by other justices be ready to set them up again, so that there is little hope of any amendment to be had.'[1]

Leniency was shown, as we have noticed, to the very poor, especially when obedience was finally observed. John Bowles, an unlicensed victualler, was presented by Finchingfield at the petty sessions in 1600. But 'sithence we finished this our certificate', the high constables added, 'we are very credibly informed that he hath pulled down his sign and wholly given over victualling.' He had been ordered to do so, and was presented only because he victualled three or four days after the order, to sell his remaining supplies. They begged the Court to pardon him, 'so as the poor man may not be urged to the extremity, which if he be he is utterly undone.'

In one respect the records differ a great deal from those of three or four centuries later. The magistrates were far more concerned with the economic aspects of running alehouses than with the number of those who got drunk. Hence many more alehouse-keepers were in trouble than their customers, unless they were vagrants. The 'habitual drunkard' was a term of the distant future.

Idle time spent in the alehouse impoverished men: by drinking they might become a charge on the poor rate, and also deprive their masters of worktime. The former theme was a frequent one in presentments of unlawful gamesters in alehouses (p. 29). 'We present,' one hundredal jury declared typically in 1600, 'Thomas Carr of Billericay for living idly, following no trade to live by, being a lusty young man that goeth from alehouse to alehouse spending his time.' Or 'John Harris *alias* Black John of Blackmore liveth out of service and lieth at an alehouse very suspiciously, for that he hath nothing to live on and hath there remained a year or thereabouts'; so he was carried to the 'next justices' to be bound over to Quarter Sessions.

Drunkenness was regarded by the civil courts as an offence chiefly because it led to breaches of the peace. Accordingly, Arthur Harrys, J.P., bound Isaac Sexten of Canewdon husbandman for his good behaviour, being 'an usual haunter of alehouses in the town of Burnham and a common exciter and provoker of others to drunkenness, himself also being often drunken, hath sundry times broken the peace and committed affrays and bloodshed and provoked others to the like offence.' In another document he is termed a common fraymaker. A Stebbing victualler's disorder was expressed as 'extraordinary drinking, provoking divers quarrels.' Naturally, quarrelsome folk were more likely to lose their tempers when drunk. And tempers gave rise to fighting. Yet, strangely enough, alehouse fights seldom figure in the Sessions records. A Billericay victualler was held

[1] *Tudor Economic Documents*, ed. Tawney and Power, i, 330–1.

responsible for various disorders including drunkards fighting and 'one lately like to be slain'; and a Pleshey man for allowing many customers, fighting together, to draw their swords. Occasionally the lower ranks of the clergy got involved in drunken brawls, such as John Goldringe 'parson' of Laindon Hills who was presented in 1585 as a drunkard and quarreller. Some, indeed, were persistent offenders in more than one respect. But as for ordinary laymen, perhaps alehouse scuffles were too common and minor an occurrence to report to the County Bench. Hundreds were presented to manor courts. Three bibulous quarrels ending in death must not be overlooked. One led to a murder charge (p. 150); the others, including an incident at the 'Boar's Head' in Chelmsford, to that of homicide (p. 158). In one of his most pungent passages, Harrison has left a description of some of the more unsavoury drunkards of his time. 'Certes', he wrote, 'I know some aleknights so much addicted thereunto that they will not cease from morrow until even to visit the same, cleansing house after house, till they defile themselves and either fall quite under the board, or else, not daring to stir from their stools, sit pinking (blinking) with their narrow eyes as half-sleeping till the fume of their adversary be digested, that he may go to it afresh.'[1] Does this portray an occasional scene in a Radwinter alehouse? And in a better-known passage referring to the enormous consumption of ale by his countrymen he regarded them as 'maltbugs.'

Indictments for dressing or eating meat on fishdays occur rarely. But among other aspects of alehouse life, one has only been mentioned incidentally. A game tended to take the continuous quaffer's mind off his tankard. But almost every indoor game was prohibited for ordinary folk. Despite this, the Sessions rolls conjure up scores of scenes of unlawful play in the alehouse – some mildly convivial, but one revealing an Elizabethan gambling and night club, furtively sited in remote marshes. (See next chapter.) A more mundane aspect shows the victualler breaking trade regulations, chiefly by defective weights and measures for his bread and beer, but this will not be seen until we study Elizabethan Work in the third volume.

Relatively few of the presentments and indictments name the sign of the inn or alehouse. One jury, however, in 1576 informed the Court that three victualling houses in Woodham Ferrers, the 'Cock', the 'Grey-hound' and the 'Chequer', were all unlicensed. But a number of signs occur incidentally in the records relating to other subjects. All have been brought together in the index under 'Inns and Alehouses: Signs'. Although the paucity of names may appear to be disappointing, it must be remembered that there were frequent changes in the names of some houses. In few cases, in fact only in those of the more important inns, may continuity of name between the times of Elizabeth I and Elizabeth II

[1] Harrison, *Description of England*, 139.

be assumed and even then the assumption may not be justified. With the smaller houses considerable research is usually required to establish that a single sign was used over a long period. In 1564 William Aukyn of the 'White Hart', Brentwood, was presented for allowing unlawful gaming in his house undoubtedly the sixteenth-century inn still surviving, though then two-storeyed. To prevent gaming at the 'White Hart' and the 'Crown' by some of the throng attending Assizes could not have been easy.

Excluding the sentence of gaol and fine for the recalcitrant Great Leighs man, what was the normal punishment for those who plied their trade without authority or without good order? This is rarely stated, but it was always a fine – 1s., 8d., or only 6d. Yet, in 1568, when two Finchingfield labourers were indicted for unlicensed alehouses, they were fined 1s. 'because they are very poor.' Exceptionally, in 1567 a Hatfield Peverel defendant pleaded that his indictment for keeping an unlicensed 'tippling-house' was void because his house was a 'common inn'. He was shrewd enough to spot the lawyer's slip. Exceptionally, too, in 1598, a Chelmsford tailor was charged at the Assizes, with selling from his cellar claret and white wine in retail by the quart, pint and bottle without licence.

Even so we are still some way from completing our reconstruction of the wider picture of Essex inns and alehouses. Although the manor court rolls supply only a few extra details, many more will be recovered from the Archdeacons' court books, which cover most of the reign and nearly all the county and will be one of the chief sources for the second volume of *Elizabethan Life*. In the eyes of the Church the two relevant offences were drunkenness on the one hand, and on the other, being absent from the parish church on Sundays, church festivals or other days during divine service and being in an alehouse at the time. Both were very common delinquencies, and of course those who served customers and should have been with the law-abiding parishioners were equally guilty. For example, 'On New Year's Day', Lawford reported to the Archdeacon of one villager, 'he was so drunken that he was not able to go of his legs, and so was led home'. The punishment? 'To sit on his knees in the church porch with three empty (ale) pots before him till the Second Lesson with a white wand in his hand and then to come into church to the minister and there to speak such words of penitence after the minister as shall be declared to him in writing.' Which does not necessarily mean that he did his penance, and, if he refused to obey, he would after several proclamations have been excommunicated. But the secular court, with its fine of a shilling or less, nearly always got the offender to appear and pay up.

We must not forget the much larger number of houses that were never presented because those in charge committed no flagrant breaches of the law, or, if they did, because the constables and their fellow parishioners failed to detect them or turned a blind eye. This leads to the question of how many licensed houses were there in the county in our period? It seems possible to make a rough estimate of their number from the extant recognizances or lists of licences. Preservation of these bonds or lists is largely fortuitous, and although about 1,000 bonds exist for the latter half of our period they represent only a fraction of the total number taken. There are many for some years, very few for others. But it seems reasonable to assume that there were between 600 and 800 licensed houses in Essex, for the average works out steadily at 1½ to 2 houses per parish, and Essex had just over 400 parishes. A few tiny villages had no alehouse, while the market-towns, especially those on the main thoroughfares, boasted of several inns and many alehouses. Brentwood, on the London–Colchester road, according to a schedule of licences granted in 1578, possessed eleven.

Inns and alehouses are rarely distinguished. But there is a single return to the Privy Council, dated at Colchester on 12 October 1577 and signed by John Davey, Thomas Tey, Edmund Pirton and Thomas Lucas, Essex justices, of the number of licensed houses in their division. This is preserved in the State Papers.[1]

	Taverners	Inn-holders	Alehouse-keepers	
Tendring hundred	3	11	36	
Lexden hundred	1	8	34	
Winstree hundred	0	0	4	
Thurstable hundred	0	0	8	
Witham hundred	0	7	15	
Colchester town	5	5	38	
	9	31	135	Total 175

The principal differences between taverns and inns seem to be that taverns also sold wines but did not take in lodgers. Winstree and Thurstable hundreds possessed no inns chiefly because they included no market towns whereas the other hundreds comprised a number of towns on main thoroughfares. In 1580 the same division excluding Colchester received 112 victuallers' and alehouse-keepers' recognizances. This north-east Essex division, together with Colchester, had approximately one-fourth of the total population of the county, and the figure of 175 licensed houses therefore tallies closely with the estimate based on the county records.

To what extent did an alehouse-keeper engage at the same time in another trade or craft? It is not easy to answer the question. We find smiths, carriers, glovers, tailors, and so on named in their bonds; more naturally, butchers, bakers, fishmongers, and a cook; once a 'sailor victualler' at Manningtree. One may assume that the last plied his boat when he was not drawing his beer. Three women, all widows, are found

---

[1] P.R.O., S.P. 12/116/12; see also 12/116/13 for a return of the recorded number of licences granted annually by Quarter Sessions 1568–77 (copies of both in Essex Record Office, T/A 407/38, 39).

as alehouse-keepers. One is called an alewife. Another, at Navestock, 'is put down', wrote Sir Henry Grey, 'and if she do desire to be admitted at the Quarter Sessions, I pray you that licence may not be granted.'

We will conclude with a few words about the justices' administrative control. In granting the eleven licences at Brentwood, together with two more at South Weald and Brook Street (all nominally in the parish of South Weald), the justices accepted sureties as follows : one man stood for five licensees, one for four, one for three, one for two; and of the fourteen sureties, three were themselves licensees. In another case, not exceptional, two licensees were mutually bound without additional security. Sureties usually stood for the sum of £10 each, principals for double that figure. Occasionally a man was one of the sureties for a number of licensees, doubtless for a financial consideration. The recognizances nearly always give the parties' occupations. They emphasize that, for most of the licensees, the alehouse was a secondary occupation to their normal craft or trade. (See plates 19 and 22.)

Very occasionally a recognizance was forfeited – once by the licensee only, once by both sureties as well. Is it to be assumed from these rare references that the bond was always forfeited when a house was suppressed? In 1592 three Braintree men, presumably all suppressed, stood sureties for themselves not to keep victualling or tippling in their houses ; and in 1576 John Hammond of Great Baddow surgeon (probably barber-surgeon) was surety for a parishioner ceasing to sell beer, ale or other victuals and to lodge anyone in his house. The licence had to be renewed annually, when a fee of 12d. was payable : normally, to the justices or to their clerk, if they had one. The Act of 5 & 6 Edward VI, c.25 (1552) obliged the licensing justices to send or 'certify' the recognizances to Quarter Sessions, when an additional fee was probably collected by the clerk of the peace. 'I pray you', wrote one justice to this officer, when sending him a 'note of licences to victual granted by Sir John Petre and myself' in 1603, 'let all these licences be made and I will cause my man to pay you your fees.' Although the Act required only a pair of J.P.s for giving a licence it is clear that they were granted, at any rate, towards the end of the century, in divisional meetings of the justices – forerunners of the later and regular petty sessions.[1] At the last Quarter Sessions before the Queen's death, the Court stiffened the existing regulations with a general order that all petty constables should hand in monthly certificates at the high constables' sessions of their inns and alehouses.

The reader will be surprised to learn, after reading this long account of the disorders in Essex inns and alehouses, that they figure very seldom in the printed calendars for other counties. In the Worcestershire records,

[1] See multiple recognizance, 1591 (*Guide to Essex Record Office* (1946) 67).

which exist only for the last decade of Elizabeth, there are a few recognizances and indictments, and in 1600 the grand jury presented nine unlicensed houses in one parish. The mass of records for Middlesex strangely enough throw hardly any light on alehouses, though there is a solitary but imperfect roll of 312 victuallers' recognizances, all for 1552.[1]

[1] *Middlesex County Records*, i, 10–11.

19

Games and Sports

If playing games is the best antidote to boredom, life in Elizabethan England must have been appallingly dull, because nearly all Englishmen were prohibited from playing nearly all games. So one would conclude, if one assumed that the folk of Elizabeth's time were all law-abiding. The list of unlawful games comprises tables (backgammon), cards, dice, football, bowls, tennis, coits (quoits), cales (nine pins), logats (the same, using bones), shovegroat, and casting the stone. These are all set out in the Act of 33 Henry VIII, c.9 (1541). Many of them first appeared in the Act of 12 Richard II, c.6 (1388). The ban involved artificers, husbandmen, labourers in husbandry, mariners, fishermen and watermen, and all apprentices and servants, that is, the great majority of the adult males. It applied in all places and at all times (except Christmastide at home or in their masters' houses and then only with their masters' leave).

This almost total prohibition by statute was based on military, economic, and, to a lesser extent, moral grounds. The excepted game was archery – 'shooting in the long bow, that being a great defence of the realm, and a meet exercise for all manner of persons to use, and a means to prevent or divert men from other unlawful, crafty and deceitful games and from the inordinate and common haunting of alehouses and tippling.' The Tudor government looked with especial severity on those of the lower classes who further impoverished themselves by gambling. Both the positive and the negative attitudes were seen in the articles of enquiry at the Essex hundredal petty sessions: Enquire for butts; enquire for unlawful games (p. 29).

The penalties under the Henrician Act were severe: playing an unlawful game, 40s.; keeping 'a common house, alley or place' for unlawful games, 40s. a day; resorting to such place and playing there, 6s. 8d. To enforce its provisions, justices of the peace were enjoined to publish the Act in Quarter Sessions, and mayors and officers to proclaim it four times a year in market places. Justices were empowered to search any suspected ale-houses and to imprison the keepers until they produced sureties for giving up their malpractices; and mayors and constables were ordered to make a monthly search. In face of such minatory legislation, publicly re-iterated, how did Englishmen in the later Tudor age react? The Essex Marian sessions rolls yield nothing about unlawful games, but the early presentments, 1562–68, contain (pp. 27, 33) some fairly representative entries : football three times, cards, dice, tables, and bowls each once, the solitary mention in the Essex records of mumming, and a presentment of the keeper of a house for alleys (bowls), cards and slidethrift. While the kind of game is nearly always specified, a present-ment leaves us in the dark as to what 'unlawful games' brought nine men from neighbouring villages, including 'Martin the miller of Hornchurch', to the house of John Fryth of Upminster to play day and night at Candle-mas 1574.

Cards, Dice, Tables and Quoits

The commonest offenders were those who played at cards or dice, or both, usually in an alehouse. Sometimes tables were indulged in as well as cards and dice. Tables was the name for backgammon until well into the next century. A game for two people, it was played with draughts-men on a hinged board divided into four 'tables' furnished with fifteen white and fifteen black men and two dice-boxes. William Drywood of Downham clerk (rector, 1574–1608) was indicted for playing at dice, cards and tables on New Year's Day 1580 and on divers other days – and also calling his parishioners notorious liars and drunken thieves, with other epithets. Peter Williams 'parson' of Latchingdon (rector, 1584–1608) was presented by the grand jury in 1589 as 'a quarreller, a fighter, a brabbler (brawler), a common player and gamester, not only on working days but also on holidays, and on Midsummer Day he played at cards the most part of the day and said no Divine Service'. In 1565 the grand jury's presentment included Richard Warner of Brentwood, 'a common dicer and carder, and will not obey the Queen's officers'.

Two pedagogues were among the delinquents. In 1590 John Hobson of Terling schoolmaster 'useth commonly to spend the great part of his time from his charge in playing unlawful games as dice and tables in alehouses', in company with a butcher and a husbandman ; and five years later Thomas Gates 'clerk of Walthamstow church' (parish clerk), 'keepeth unlawful games in his school, as dice and tables'. A fair number of alehouse-keepers who allowed illicit games were caught. Ten 'tipplers', all of Moulsham in Chelmsford, were presented in 1572 for 'keeping playing at cards and other unlawful games' in their houses. A Goldhanger 'alehouse-holder' was indicted in 1583 for playing himself, and two of his customers from Great Totham for card-playing in his house. The latter were duly fined 6s. 8d. each, but the record does not say whether the ale-house-keeper paid the statutory 40s. which was inflicted in some of the other cases. Richard Jackson of Mashbury clerk in 1562 played cards and other games in a common alehouse at Good Easter. He was vicar from 1550 to 1554 when he was deprived.

In 1565 a Great Bardfield labourer and his wife not only kept an unlicensed alehouse, 'selling bread, meat and beer to all who came there', but also 'kept common games, as painted cards, alleys and tables', and they received two men's servants who played at cards 'and other ancient and unlawful games'. Somewhat surprisingly, the Freshwell hundred petty sessions presentment, on which his indictment was based, is endorsed to the effect that he desired to be licensed, and he produced sureties. Two years later it was found that a Shenfield butcher, apparently unlicensed, 'doth daily hospitate and succour vagabonds and idle persons and suffer them to play at cards in his house'.

The stern attitude towards gambling was seldom more forcibly expressed than by the Chelmsford high constables' sessions in 1572, when two Little Baddow men were reported for keeping ill rule in their tippling houses and playing at cards and unlawful games, 'poor men resorting thither and often times spend and waste their money when they had more need to do at their daily labour'. The same hundred in the following year presented that Richard Sawyn of Little Waltham innkeeper allowed his neighbours' servants and others to play cards, dice, 'etc.' In 1602 John Sell was indicted for keeping a 'common house of dicing' as well as 'maintaining drunkenness' in Audley End (the hamlet, not the mansion said to have been begun in the following year).

> *Moth.* You are a gentleman and a gamester, sir.
> *Armado.* I confess both : they are both the variants of a complete man.
> *Moth.* Then, I am sure you know how much the gross sum of deuce-ace amounts to.
> *Armado.* It doth amount to one more than two.
> *Moth.* Which the base vulgar do call three.

Shakespeare shows two sides of the dice : the privileged and the prohibited players; and indeed deuce-ace stood for the unlucky, the 'base vulgar' folk.[1]

From a series of documents of 1580 relating to Writtle, it appears that a husbandman and a labourer had a spite against Richard Asser, one of the constables. Their indictment is dated 18 August. On 31 July Sir Thomas Mildmay of Moulsham Hall, Chelmsford, had summoned Asser, with others unnamed, to be at his house on the following Sunday to answer for his misdemeanours as a constable. From prison Asser submitted a petition to the justices. It is a garbled statement couched in obsequious language. He begged to be released, for he fully intended to do his duty and was heartily sorry for having disobeyed a warrant from Mildmay. Trying to get his own back on his 'enemies and persecutors', he prayed that all who had played games on the sabbath and at nights might be punished, and he was 'moved in conscience more than by malice' to complain of those who were being indicted for such offences. He also begged forgiveness for not executing a warrant from the Bench against

[1] *Love's Labour's Lost*, i, ii, 45–52.

another man for disobeying Lord Rich's warrant. The result was that Nicholas Cawarden was charged with allowing card-playing in his house, the offenders being John Newton senior, a tailor, and John Chawke, a husbandman, both constables of Writtle, John Newton junior, also a tailor, and two others.

Only once, in 1595, is there a record of a J.P. acting under the 1541 statute in arresting offenders, apparently after his own search: 'John Adele, John Hoginges, John Trigg and Nicholas Wante I took at play at cards – all these were found playing at cards in the alehouse at Newport.' The justice's name is not given. A Rayne alehouse-keeper in 1571 allowed dice and cards and gave abusive words to the 'officer' (probably the constable). Witham hundred jury in 1585 reported Thomas Leveriche at the sign of the Angel and Robert Shoyle at the sign of the Bull, both in Kelvedon, for keeping 'great disorder of playing in their houses at cards, dice, tables and other unlawful games', also for selling underweight bread.

Allowing play at tables, but no other games, brought a number of cases before Quarter Sessions. A Little Canfield butcher and victualler, having offended in 1583 by keeping table-play 'for bread and beer', had been charged by John Wiseman, J.P., to leave it, and a constable on the presenting hundred jury promised to see that the victualler obeyed. In two cases a customer was indicted with the landlord: (Robert) Rowland, rector of Greenstead (1561–93), in an Ongar alehouse in 1574; and Thomas Maddockes (or Madoxe) of Aveley yeoman, in Francis Quicke's inn there, where he lost 20s. in gambling. A Pleshey alehouse-keeper allowed tables in service time in 1590. A Chelmsford tapster lost 4s. 'at tyck tack at tables' in 1569 (p. 82). Tick-tack was 'an old variety of backgammon played on a board with holes along the edge, in which pegs were placed for scoring'.[1]

Quoits were prohibited as far back as the Act of Richard II. This game was apparently little indulged in by Essex folk, if the two references are any criterion, but perhaps it was regarded as too innocent a game to be presented. In 1585, a Birdbrook alehouse-keeper was charged with permitting three men and others of evil conversation and idle life to play at cards, tables and quoits for the past six months. He and ten labourers of several neighbouring villages were also indicted as common players of unlawful games there. A Great Burstead victualler was presented in 1580 for allowing 'shovegroat and quoits and suchlike games which bred evil demeanour.'

Bowls

Essex records make it clear that a bowling alley was generally an adjunct to an alehouse. Such apparently was not the case at Harlow. In 1580 Harlow petty sessions presented John Bugge gentleman, two

---

1 *New English Dictionary* (earliest reference 1558).

butchers, a shoemaker and a yeoman, all of Harlow, for playing bowls in
Pepper Alley there; and at the same Quarter Sessions the hundredal
jury presented the same men except Bugge and the yeoman for going to
bowl in the adjacent village of Latton. In 1573 Richard Cocke of Great
Dunmow tawyer and William Durdel curate of Barnston both bowled
on Dunmow Down. Other offenders were two men of Stansted Mountfitchet in 1566 and five of unstated abode in 1583. The Becontree petty
sessions in 1577 presented a West Ham tailor for procuring many servants
of the townsmen to play alleys, cards and dice with him in many secret
places and fields in Barking. Bowls were also irresistible to some of the
constables: John Smythe of Lamarsh played on Sunday in 1582, and
John Anderkyn of West Hanningfield in 1583, who was among many of
the parish who were accused in 1583. Five alley-keepers were in trouble
at various times between 1572 and 1590: a Moulsham (Chelmsford)
innkeeper; an Inworth alehouse-keeper; a Barking butcher kept an
alley which was often resorted to by three local men; a Springfield
victualler, at whose house 'there is bowling used very much'; a Great
Dunmow victualler; and a Stanford-le-Hope victualler with three of his
customers, who 'usually play at bowls on the sabbath day and other days
continually'.

Dicing and bowling are among the games censured in the presentment
of the 'great inquest' (grand jury) at the Summer Assizes 1569, which is
preserved in the Sessions roll. Unfortunately a few words have been lost
at the frayed edge of this remarkable paper document and the presumed
words are placed in parentheses. 'We certify that whereas upon Sunday
being the 3rd day of the same month at High (Laver) within the hundred
of Dunmow (there) were silver games before proclaimed (and) in the
several parishes before mentioned practised and played, among which
were (some) new invented and unlawful games (much) used and abused,
whereupon did follow great inconveniences, loss of money and hindrance
(to many) persons, namely youth and men's servants, (which) games were
called riffling and bowling and (nine) holes, which were so abused at
High (Laver) by the space of 2 days that sundry persons (there) lost as it
seemed more than their year's (wages, to) the pernicious example of
others'. An initial 'L' still remains at its second mention, which identifies
it with Laver and not Ongar. The two rendezvous were both at places
with a very small population. A book published in the same year (1569)
gives the earliest known reference in print: 'Theare was none used but
one onlie game, called rifflinge, by which diverse persons weare spoyled
and utterlie undon'.[1] More light on this game is afforded by a slightly
later book, which defines it as 'a kind of game wherein he that in casting
doth throw most on the dyce takes up all the monye that is layd downe'.[2]

[1] *New English Dictionary*, 'riffling', quoting Ellis, *Original letters* (1569).
[2] Halliwell, *Dictionary of Archaic and Provincial Terms* (1889), quoting *Nomenclator* (1585).

That riffling was a novel form of dicing is confirmed by the grand jury presentment at the Michaelmas Sessions 1574. 'There is and has of late been practised and used in sundry and divers places within this shire certain new invented games, as well with dice as with bowls and such like, called riffling and bowling at nine holes, whereby has ensued much inconvenience to many persons as well servants as others, so as they have wasted and lost all the money in their purses. Wherein they pray that the said unlawful devices may be reformed.' (See the Wiltshire record, p. 231.)

In presenting alehouse-keepers juries occasionally linked drunkenness with games: a Goldhanger man suffered 'playing at dice and drinking excessively', and a Great Waltham man for unlawful play and drunkenness. Another jury in 1596 'think good' that a Little Canfield man, presented for keeping ill rule and maintaining men's servants and poor labouring men at play, 'which is an undoing unto the poor men', should be suppressed. These last three cases sum up the antagonistic attitude of the ruling class to all these otherwise trivial amusements.

Shovegroat

Shovegroat, slidegroat, slidethrift, and shovelaboard, according to the lexicographers, were all one and the same pastime and predecessors of our modern shoveha'penny, which is first recorded (as shovehalfpenny) in 1841. Shovegroat dates from at least 1488, and the rest appear in the next century, all somewhat before our period. The players gave a smart push to a groat or other coin, scoring by the position of the lines marked on the table. Such incised marks can be seen on a table at Beeleigh Abbey near Maldon. An 'old shovelaboard' table, $4\frac{3}{4}$ yards long, which is mentioned in an inventory of Ingatestone Hall, 1600, as being in the long gallery, had presumably been engraved at one end.[1]

Our earliest reference is in a Lexden petty sessions presentment of 1568, when a Wivenhoe victualler maintained 'unlawful games, to wit, alleys, cards and slidethrift'. Then, four years later, Chelmsford petty sessions found that a Moulsham (Chelmsford) beerbrewer had likewise broken the Act with 'unlawful games called shovelboard and slidegroat', which suggests that they were slightly different forms of the pastime, though it may be that they were synonymous alternatives. The grand jury in 1574 presented a constable of Boreham for playing at cards, bowls and 'slidegroat' ten times between Michaelmas and Christmas. In 1578 Barstable sessions reported a Vange tippler for allowing 'shovegroat' in his house. Four years afterwards the grand jury presented two Heybridge alehouse-keepers for 'suffering much evil rule in playing at cards and shovelaboard,' chiefly by men's servants. The grand jury in 1590 again presented an offender, an Inworth victualler, for permitting 'shovegroat in divine

[1] F. G. Emmison, *Tudor Food and Pastimes* (1964), 81.

service time'. Finally, in 1592, a Little Burstead victualler suffered play at 'shovel board' in his house on sabbath days by children and servants.

Dancing

The Henrician Act did not condemn dancing, but Puritan preachers and pamphleteers raged against 'the horrible vice of pestiferous dancing', and it is not surprising therefore to find its being attacked, according to our records, towards the end of the Elizabethan period. Harrison, no Puritan, referred harshly to the excessive drinking at bride-ales, where the fun included dancing – until midnight, as some poachers related (p. 245). In 1591 a Stebbing carpenter was presented for keeping 'evil rule in his house and receiving other men's servants in the night-time and at other unlawful times to cards and dancing and other unlawful games'; and a few years later a Woodham Walter victualler and a Springfield alehouse-keeper were each reported for 'disorder and dancing in his house' on the Lord's Day in time of divine service. The Woodham house may have been 'The Bell', which is of Elizabethan date.

The most illuminating description of Essex entertainment is found in a petition submitted to the Midsummer Sessions 1598 and signed by John Ellerton the vicar and six parishioners of Barling. They accused John Collyn of keeping a disorderly victualling house and unlawful games, to wit, 'dice-playing, cards, tables, shovegroat, scales, dancings, hobby-horses and such unreasonable dealing as well on the sabbath days as other holydays, both by night and day, in service time and otherwise; and with his evil and unruly company hath had his daughter gotten with child once at the least; and doth suffer his eldest son to play at dice, cards and tables, and that for greater sums of money, to the evil example of many'. Also, the disgusted villagers add, 'for other causes, as harbouring men's servants and other evil and idle persons, which maketh a common proverb to go of our town almost through the whole hundreth of Rochford, "Whither shall we go to dance, to play at dice, at tables or such like but at Barling?", and this the town has got by this bad house, which stands at an outside of the town far from neighbours, and most fit for such ill rule. And now very lately the said Collyn did say to the constable that he did hear that he and Wiseman and Bunting with others went about to put him down from selling. But, saith he (with reverence be it spoken), "Turd in all their teeth, I will victual and sell in despite of them all".' The petitioners sought from the Bench 'some order and redress'. What the county justices thought of this alleged sink of iniquity is not revealed (and the Assize files are missing for 1598–99). But, judging by the reaction to similar petitions, this isolated alehouse was certainly suppressed. This remarkable document contains the sole references to scales (probably for cales or ninepins) and morris-dancing. 'The hobby-horse is forgot'

(*Hamlet*, iii, ii, 146) is believed to be a quotation from a ballad satirizing the Puritans' opposition to morris-dancing,[1] in which the man who danced the hobby-horse takes a leading part. It was in the following year that Will Kemp danced his famous jig from London to Norwich, along certain stretches of Essex road, the state of which he maligned for all time.[2]

Unfortunately Essex has only one mention, incidental and mirthless, of maypoles. A coroner's record discloses how a Great Wakering man was driving a cart with two horses which was carrying a maypole. The cart overturned, killing a young boy. Cart and horses, worth 53s. 4d., therefore became deodands and were forfeited to the Queen.

Football

After all these physically harmless games, the scene changes to football, which in Tudor times had few restrictions and fewer rules. Essex football in the 1560s has already been referred to – at Brentwood, at Good Easter, and the match between Stondon and Kelvedon Hatch – merely as unlawful games (p. 36). Sir Thomas Elyot in his *Boke called the Governour* (1531) wrote of 'Foote balle, wherein is nothinge but beastly furie and exstreme violence', and Henry Stubbes, after our period, of 'the bloody and murthering game, a devilish pastime'; incidentally, he was clerk to an assize circuit. The Essex Assize records yield some concrete facts.

Football led to four cases in the Essex coroners' courts. At an inquest held on 10 March 1567, which had been adjourned from 4 March, the jury stated that Henry Ingolde of White Roothing husbandman aged 24 and Thomas Paviott of Hatfield Broad Oak yeoman, with many others unnamed, between 4 and 5 p.m., were playing at 'the foot ball' in Branton Mead at Hatfield. Henry and Thomas collided while running after the ball. Henry knocked him down, and being exhausted by over-exertion and not wishing to run any farther at the time fell upon him and held him by his stockings. As they tried to rise together Thomas, without any malice, lightly pushed Henry off and ran after the ball, leaving him on the ground. Henry died at midnight at William Josselyn's house there, from over-exhaustion and not through any injury caused by Thomas. Thus, at any rate, they decided to describe a tough tackle. There is the indictment of Thomas for unlawfully playing football and for assaulting Henry without due cause in the course of the game, throwing him to the ground, so that he died. The jury, it will be noticed, preferred to say 'without any malice' rather than 'without due cause'. But the other players were not overlooked. The game was illegal, and so there is a second indictment, against three yeomen of Hatfield and four husbandmen and four labourers of White Roothing, for playing in the same meadow between 2 and 4 p.m.

[1] *Shakespeare's England*, ii, 438.
[2] *Will Kemp's Nine Daies' Wonder* (1599).

R

on that day. All confessed, except one of the yeomen who 'is not in prison' (at large) ; the two other yeomen were fined 10s. ; the rest 3s. 4d. each.

A field fittingly called Stony Field in Gosfield was the scene of a fatal fall, which occurred in February 1582, during a match apparently between husbandmen of Gosfield and Bocking. John Pye was guarding the goal, when Richard Elye of Bocking, attacking with the ball, violently collided with Pye, who being a weak man collapsed after he fell and died at 9 o'clock that evening. The jurors stated that his death was caused by the fall and not otherwise. On 16 April of the same year, John Warde an East Ham labourer and Thomas Turner yeoman, whose abode is not given, were playing football on opposite sides at West Ham. Thomas assaulted John, dashing him to the ground, and he died instantly. Thomas was found not guilty, but John Astyle was.[1] Almost exactly a year later three weavers including Charles Addesley, a fuller, a tailor, all of Bocking, with others unnamed, were playing 'the football' in John Hodge's field. Isaac Fuller, another Bocking weaver, 'with ill intent', came between Charles and the others and began to play, saying 'We are making work for the surgeon', after which he violently pushed Charles, who fell and being feeble and weak was 'shattered' and died nine days afterwards. The jurors' verdict is illegible, but perhaps on this occasion it anticipated Shakespeare's 'You base football player' (*King Lear*, I, iv, 95). About the same time a game at Writtle led to a quarrel (p. 52).

A game called the foot ball in which Thomas Whistock of White Notley with nine of his fellows unnamed were playing there on Sunday 25 February 1599 did not result in an inquest but was perhaps equally rough, as there 'grew bloodshed'. Indulging in football was only one of the offences for which John Sewell, a yeoman of Great Dunmow, was in trouble in 1585. By three separate indictments he was charged with beating a manservant of Thomas Virgin, a mason of the same town ; for being a common barrator and disturber of his neighbours, stirring up quarrels among them and publishing seditious libels about them ; and for assaulting Robert Melford, a mercer, one of the constables, when he ordered Sewell in the Queen's name to cease from playing 'the football'. Sir John Petre, Sir Thomas Mildmay and Lord Rich fined him 6s. 8d. on the first charge and 12d. on the third ; he pleaded not guilty to the second.

Other Unlawful Sports

Football was not the only sporting combat which ended in fatalities. In 1572 William Egham gentleman and Thomas Hewys yeoman aged 30, both of Moulsham in Chelmsford, were 'playing and wrestling' in Coneyburrow Field there 'for the sport of it and without any malice'.

[1] For John Astyle and other men of straw, see Murders (p. 153).

Hewys put both arms around Egham's waist, lifted him up, and tried to throw him down. They both fell with great force, with Hewys' head underneath Egham's, as a result of which Hewys died next day. The jury's verdict was one of accident. Egham was pardoned ten months later. A plea of not guilty was recorded in another inquest in 1592. Richard Ingolle of Epping, aged 14, liked to play with his companions, at 'wasters' (fencing with single-stick). Having a couple of sticks, he asked Henry Campe yeoman, his friend, to take a stick and play with him. So he took one without any evil intention, and during play Campe struck Ingolle under the right ear, giving him a mortal wound of which he died instantly. Yet another coroner's inquest yields an early and interesting reference to swimming with the aid of bladders. In 1576 many lads were bathing in a millpond at St. Osyth. One tied two bladders round his body, but he began to sink, crying, 'I am drowning, I am drowning, for the love of God help me!' Two of the boys pulled him to land, but their feet slipped and they were all drowned. 'The bladders worth 1d. are a deodand.' Did the Sheriff account for the penny to the Crown? Shakespeare may have witnessed such a tragedy (*Henry VIII*, III, iii, 359) :

> Little wanton boyes that swim on bladders.

While the binding of alehouse-keepers to good behaviour was the normal practice, there is only a solitary instance of recognizances being taken against playing unlawful games – by Thomas Kighley, the active J.P. of Grays Thurrock, in 1601. A butcher of Orsett and a bricklayer and a husbandman of Aveley each produced two sureties for their lifelong abstention from all the games set out in the Act of 33 Henry VIII.

Archery

'To him that compared gaming with shooting I will answer' was a vital line in Roger Ascham's *Toxophilus* (1545), a treatise in defence of the long-bow, but William Harrison, an even stouter patriot, had to admit thirty years later that the long-bow, which had won so many victories against the French, was doomed. Yet archery practice at the town or village butts was still compulsory.

The primary duties of the county justices were to keep the peace themselves and to see that others kept the peace. But an ironical feature of their records is that the details of how some people broke the peace are matched with virtually no details of how most kept it. It is true that *Omnia bene*, 'All is well in our parish', or the like are common enough in the hundred court presentments, but, to take games as an example, we learn only of fatal accidents and not of many incidents which occurred in the one lawful sport in which the men engaged, willingly or unwillingly.

The first scene is at Stisted. The villagers were at archery practice at the butts one June evening in 1566. A labourer was 'shooting with his bow from one butt to another' when suddenly a two-year-old child passed through the butts. His arrow struck one of her eyes, and she died a week later. He was pardoned by the general pardon of that year; in any case, the inquest produced a verdict that he killed her without any malice. The second is at Little Oakley in 1579. A labourer, practising with the young men of the parish, shot another labourer aged 16 in the left eye; he died next day. In the third, a young man standing near the town butts of Barking was fatally wounded in 1581.

There occurs this mysterious entry in the Privy Council minute book, under 1576: 'A licence granted to John Saterley of Stock yeoman to set forth and cause to be practised, tried and played in open places, either by himself, his deputy or deputies, certain games contained in the minute of the said licence remaining in the Council Chest'.[1] One can only guess that the new games were some form of salutary exercise, otherwise the Council would not have authorised them.

Drama

What do other Essex records disclose about games which could be lawfully played by the middle and upper ranks of Elizabethan society and of the sports enjoyed by those with the substantial property qualifications? Unfortunately, very little, with the exception of the one family whose descendants have preserved the remarkably full personal account-books of Sir William Petre and his son Sir John Petre of Ingatestone Hall and Thorndon Hall.[2] We can observe the Petres enjoying their pastimes, free from the prying eyes of petty constables or sneaking neighbours. But Sir William, a privy councillor, saw that those who disobeyed the laws locally were punished. The court rolls of his manor of Ingatestone show how the inhabitants were dealt with for card-playing, dicing and shove-groating. In 1564–65 fourteen men were fined for playing dice and bowls.[3] As already explained, games were even prohibited at Christmas in public places. At that time Sir William always entertained great numbers of his servants and tenants. At Twelfthtide 1556, for instance, they watched visiting mummers, without being prosecuted as several men were who 'went a-mumming' not far away at Christmas 1561–2 (p. 27).

This brings us to plays and other dramatic entertainments. Not being games in the sense of the statute they were allowed and indeed produced by some towns and villages. In Maldon, somewhat exceptionally, the

[1] *Acts of the Privy Council*, ix, 226.
[2] See Emmison, *Tudor Food and Pastimes*, for William, and A. C. Edwards 'Sir John Petre and his household, 1576–77' (*Essex Review*, lxiii, 189–202).
[3] Emmison, *Tudor Food and Pastimes*, 80.

municipal authorities had managed religious plays of local origin until
shortly after Elizabeth's accession, and thereafter they controlled plays
given by travelling companies. In a number of Essex parishes, especially
Chelmsford, native drama flourished, and handsome profits accrued,
even contributing towards the building or repairing of a bridge at Sandon
(p. 22). Sixteenth-century churchwardens' accounts exist for ten Essex
parishes, and from various entries we can take a glimpse at some of the
Whitsun church ales, May days, children's Christmas plays, morris
dancing, Corpus Christi and Plough Feasts, and the like.[1] But visits by
professional players were often discouraged, especially in towns and
villages where there was strong puritan influence. Even earlier, the
Council was antagonistic, as plays, like fairs, tended to breaches of the
peace and vagabondage. In 1551 the Council licensed the players of the
Marquis of Dorset to perform only in his presence – at Tilty Abbey. Five
years later Lord Rich was enjoined by the Council to stop a stage play to
be given at Shrovetide at Hatfield Broad Oak.[2] The subsequent control of
strolling players and the protection of certain groups by noblemen is
well known. We hope to quote from some of the borough and parochial
archives in the next volume.

We have related some of the prosecutions under the Unlawful Games
Act of 1541 which were brought before the two civil courts for the county.
Many more were reported to the borough and manor courts, and the more
unusual cases will appear in the next volume. The Maldon Borough
records reveal several little-known games as well as an intriguing reference
to the game of clicket : clearly an onomatopoeic word, possibly for cricket,
and if so the earliest known reference, but probably an otherwise unrecorded name for a game in which the striking of the object produced a
clicking sound.

The Essex manor court rolls so far searched show that the jurors,
occasionally presented those playing illegal games and more frequently
alehouse-keepers for allowing play. Even where a village had its traditional
'playstall' or playground, those enjoying a game of bowls there were
disobeying her Majesty's laws ; and a Purleigh court roll of 1591 suggests
that so many villagers played bowls that no attempt could be made to
name individuals. But if most village constables turned a blind eye to
man's insistent need for relaxation after the long hours of labour, reporting only those causing disorder, the keen eyes and ears of the churchwardens and questmen (sidesmen) searched out a much greater number,
chiefly those who absented themselves from church to snatch their play.
They were duly presented at the archdeacons' courts, and few were

[1] See the articles by Dr. W. A. Mepham on Drama in Essex in the 16th century in
Essex Review, lv–lvii (1946–48).
[2] *Acts of the Privy Council*, v, 234, 237–8.

spared, least of all any erring clergy, such as the rector of Thundersley, who 'playeth at cards and dice all the week long', or the schoolmaster of Manuden, who 'runneth to the football and dancing upon the sabbath days and holy days.' The diversity of games found in the archdeacons' records is even wider than those in the Sessions and Assize records : more 'shovelgroat', 'wasters', 'scales', more football (with a lot about 'camping', another name for it), and plenty of logats and stoolball.

The Act of 1541 did not refer to one kind of sport, the zest for which has always been in many an Englishman's blood. We now therefore turn to Poaching.

Before doing so, however, we shall take a quick look at a few scenes of play which led to prosecutions in other counties. The first is at Newton in Cheshire, where in 1574 an unlicensed alehouse-keeper suffered bowling on Skeyre Heath, 'by means whereof menservants and children are provoked to unthriftiness', which caused Sir Thomas Venables to write a letter of complaint to the County Bench. The second is at Eaton in the same county in 1591. The village constable saw three men 'playing at dice for money' one Sunday, and on the next evening he went to the same house, peered through a slit, and heard one dice-player say '4 mine' and the other answer '7 mine.'[1]

Next we have three scenes from Middlesex. In 1556 a gentleman was enticed into a game of dice by a fishmonger, who had 'in his left hand false dice that at every fall of the dice came forth at his pleasure', and his legerdemain led to the other player losing 4s. 4d. At Ruislip in Middlesex in 1576 there 'arose a great affray, likely to result in homicides and serious accidents'. This is hardly surprising, as over a hundred footballers were involved. But only five Ruislip and seven Uxbridge men were identified. We can even hear the shouts of abuse between two of the footballers at South Mimms in the same county in 1573, 'Cast him over the hedge', yelled one. 'Come thou and do it', was the retort. A mortal blow and concussion resulted in a coroner's inquest.[2]

The Lancashire Sessions records include two documents which throw a dim but sinister light on the more brutal sports. The conditions in an alehouse licence banned 'unlawful games or disorders in house, backside, garden or alley', and those visiting 'wakes, bullbaitings, bearbaitings, May games, and cockfightings' (1592) ;[3] 'riotous assemblies called wakes' in Cheshire had troubled the Council in 1578.[4] In 1601 a man was indicted for baiting an ape on Sunday.[5]

---

[1] *Quarter Sessions Records of the County Palatine of Chester 1559–1760* (1940), i, 41, 44.
[2] *Middlesex County Records*, i, 26, 97, 138.
[3] *Lancs. Quarter Sessions Records*, i, 51.
[4] *Acts of the Privy Council*, x, 329.
[5] *Lancs. Quarter Sessions Records*, i, 101.

'Piping and dancing' in time of church services led to two indictments before the Hertfordshire Bench, which also received two presentments against fairs: part of Stortford fair was held in the churchyard, and St. Giles' Fair at Cheshunt was commonly kept on a Sunday. It was bad enough for many Englishmen to be prevented by justices and constables from indulging in most of their customary pastimes; but it was worse when their neighbours interfered. In Elizabeth's last year some Buntingford folk, doubtless kill-joy Puritans, cut down a maypole.[1]

The Wiltshire records contribute an interesting item. In 1581 a Londoner and two Oxfordshire men 'confessed that they used certain games called trolemadame and ryffling for dishes and platters in the county of Wilts., being unlawful and cozening games.'[2] The Elizabethan magistrates were not so harsh, after all, in their attempts to suppress games, for much unlawful play was gambling. To stop gaming, with its sister vice of cozening (cheating), the justices were showing paternal care to prevent the poor from losing what little money they had.

---

[1] *Herts. County Records*, i, 13, 18, 34.
[2] *Wiltshire County Records*, 70.

20

Poaching

Deer

'In every shire of England', wrote William Harrison in his *Description of England* (1577), 'there is plenty of parks . . . well near to two hundred . . . In Kent and Essex only, to the number of an hundred'.[1] John Norden, nine years later, declared in what is the shortest paragraph in his *Description of Essex*, 'It is full of parks'.[2] His manuscript maps of Essex certainly confirm this remark. In the Camden Society's reproduction 47 are seen, and 44 in the Essex Record Office version.[3] Twenty years before Norden wrote, there appeared George Turberville's *Noble Art of Venerie or Hunting*, setting out the elaborate ritual of the chase, with its own language mostly of French origin. Preservation of game, for sport and food, was a privilege, and a costly one. It required a park, which meant in law a large area of ground enclosed, generally with a paled fence, for the purpose of keeping beasts of the chase, and necessitated a keeper and his men, watching by day and night for those intent on poaching – a term used anachronistically in our account of Elizabethan life as it does not appear until the next reign. To all Elizabethans, except the poachers, it was always 'unlawful hunting'. It is with this aspect only that the records of Quarter Sessions and Assizes are concerned, and those for Essex yield by far the longest series of poaching pictures from Elizabethan criminal records.

In any discussion of the game laws, the Elizabethans, like their predecessors, made a distinction between forests, chases and parks. Hunting in forests was a royal prerogative; chases were open, while parks were enclosed. A chase, park or rabbit warren existed solely by crown grant or ancient prescription.

Harrison's strictures against parks are among his most severe. It was bad enough that corn and cattle, formerly to be seen within park circuits, were now mostly banned by their owners, and the whole area given over to game 'cherished for pleasure'; much worse in his view was the enlargement of parks by enclosure of land, even of commons. God had cursed

---

[1] Harrison, *Description of England*, 253. I have to thank Mr. G. C. S. Curtis, O.B.E., M.A., and Mr. James Wentworth Day for reading this chapter.

[2] Norden, *Speculi Britanniae Pars . . . Description of Essex, 1594* (Camden Society, 1840), 9.

[3] E.R.O. Publication No. 29. See endpapers of this book; F. G. Emmison and R. A. Skelton, 'The Description of Essex' (*Geographical Journal*, cxxiii).

England, he thought. He estimated that one-twentieth part of the realm was already 'employed upon deer and conies, these great and small games (for so most keepers call them)', for whose preservation so many families had been evicted. Thus Parson Harrison wrote in his chapter on 'Parks and Warrens'. And, later on, when he came to 'Savage Beasts and Vermins', his ire was again directed against the park-owning gentry, who in his opinion ought to practise with warlike arms rather than indulge in effeminate coursing of fallow deer and hares, though he accepted red deer as worthy of men's chase.[1] Most of the owners were justices of the peace, and in no other respect was this privileged and closely-knit society more concerned in trying to suppress an offence which affected their personal interests. To what extent their perennial battle against the ubiquitous poacher succeeded we shall see. In following the conflict we may be surprised to find some of those who invaded gentlemen's demesnes were themselves gentlemen. To cross a neighbour's boundary, even to jump his pale fence, in the excitement of the chase was understandable; but the sport of most of these gentlemen involved their killing and taking away the quarry. As will be clearly seen, 'gentlemen's son of worship' and yeomen poached because they enjoyed hunting and eating game. In the account that follows there is little to suggest that the poorer poachers were driven after disastrous harvests to seek animal protein where it could be found.

In our records many of the illegal hunting scenes are sketched only in outline, but others are portrayed with all the paraphernalia used in poachers' pursuits. Brought together, these details help in reconstructing a remarkably full picture of this aspect of Elizabethan disorder.[2] The depositions include a few in which the poachers and the keepers can be discerned even in the pale moonlight or near darkness in which so many of the expeditions took place.

Those who indulged in poaching, as we are told that Shakespeare did at Charlecote Park in 1585, knew what penalties awaited them, if caught; Shakespeare is said to have left Stratford to avoid prosecution. An Act of 33 Henry VIII, c.6 (1541), had prohibited anyone not having lands, etc., to the annual value of £100 (a very substantial property qualification) from keeping a 'gun, dag, pistol, crossbow, hagbut, demi-hake, or stonebow'. (A dag was another name for pistol, and a hagbut much the same as a harquebus, a demi-hake being shorter.) The legal phrase is 'handguns charged with hailshot'. Such was the law at the beginning of the reign. By 5 Eliz., c.21 (1562), the penalty was three months' imprisonment and a

[1] Harrison, *op. cit.*, 256, 327–9. But, for once, his conclusions are open to doubt. At this period, there is some evidence pointing to the reverse of enclosure. For instance, in Essex, Petre disparked part of Crondon Park (plate 20) and two Thaxted parks were wholly converted to arable in our period (K. C. Newton, *Thaxted in the Fourteenth Century*, E.R.O. Pubn. no. 33, 1960).

[2] For a slighter sketch of lawful hunting, see the chapter on Sports in Emmison, *Tudor Food and Pastimes* (1964).

fine amounting to treble damages, and the poacher was not to be
released until he had found sureties for abstaining from the offence for
seven years. But, in the few cases in which the Essex poaching records give
the punishment, the facts do not tally very closely with the statutes, as
will be seen. Whatever the sentence might be, adventurous spirits ever
liked to pit their ingenuity against that of the keeper, hoping, if he
appeared, to outwit him in a lucky foray; others, less courageous, trusted
that their noiseless bows and arrows and mute greyhounds would not
disturb the keeper. If caught, they were relatively lucky in the mildness of
the Tudor game laws, bearing in mind the ferocity of the old Forest Law
and the heavy punishments inflicted in the eighteenth and nineteenth
centuries.

Records of the chace use terms, now mostly archaic, which were familiar
to Shakespeare. They refer to pricket, sorrel and sore, all employed with
punning effect in *Love's Labour's Lost* and denoting a buck in its second,
third or fourth year; also lyams, which were mute and keen-scented,
leashed hounds, and rascal, a small deer with fewer than ten points. But
hearst, an adolescent stag or hind, which is found in a deposition of 1586,
is lacking in Shakespeare's works. Other terms will be explained where
they occur. Greyhounds figure in the majority of cases, and a bloodhound
in 1595. A crossbow (an ideal weapon for poaching) is mentioned several
times, and a longbow in 1581. But guns occur almost as frequently, from
1570 onwards. Fowling-pieces and birding-pieces were used in several
raids in the 1590s. Pikestaves, clubs and daggers were employed to dispatch
a wounded animal, and once, in 1587, a poacher is recorded as protected
in plate armour! Very large nets, known as toils or buckstalls, into which
deer were driven, are occasionally mentioned. The Act of 19 Henry VII,
c.11 (1503), refers to the great destruction of deer by this means, but our
cases do not suggest anything of this nature. There is, however, little doubt
that poachers whose sporting instincts were strongest preferred greyhounds. Certainly 'the course' – the spectacle of the deer running for life
with the swift dogs at its heels – was the motive for many of their expeditions. The fox was still regarded as vermin: to catch the red thief was
not a poaching offence.

We shall begin our account with big game, then continuing with small
game and fish, and each section will first narrate the incidents of which
more or less detailed depositions are preserved, followed by those recorded
only in the less informative indictments.

Few of the parks in Essex are absent from the chronicle, yet only a
small fraction of the poachers could have been caught, and the blanks in
the general scene portrayed in the court records may be filled in by the
reader's imagination. Poaching was a widespread feature in rural Essex,
and raids a regular menace to the larger landowners. Some nocturnal visitors
probably thieved almost with impunity, as one or two of the illuminating

letters received by the county justices reveal. Whereas the man or woman who stole anything worth over 12d. went to the gallows, unless the jury valued it under that sum or the accused was able to claim benefit of clergy, the most seasoned poacher never risked his neck unless he killed a keeper, as taking game was neither larceny nor a felony.

The chief foresters of the great Forest of Essex had their own districts or 'walks', a term which is stated to appear first about 1582.[1] A deposition of 1581 refers to one of these walks. William Symons, a drover of Waltham Abbey, said that on 'Friday was sennight' (a week before Friday), he bought cattle to sell at Epping, and happening into widow Archer's tavern he fell in company with Thomas Wheler of Epping and three local men, who 'made a motion to them all to go a-hunting into Sir Thomas Heneage's Walk, affirming that Rygsbye had a great herd of bucks and that they might hunt there'. They decided to go there three days later. On Sunday morning, somewhat early, he met Wheler in Long Mead near Copt Hall Park and warned him that Rygsbye watched his game with three or four of his neighbours. Wheler said he would warn the others. But on the morrow about 5 p.m. Wheler and his brother 'persuaded' (urged) him and a drover to go hunting with them to Nazeing Wood *alias* Greenmead, Mr. Grevyll's park. Both 'flatly denied' (refused), whereupon the Whelers departed about 6 p.m., saying that they would go, one having a longbow and arrows and the other a long piked staff.

On Friday before Shrove Sunday 1586 Arthur Nun, a servant of George Basford of New Hall, Boreham, esquire, with Charles Colt and John Harris, two of his 'fellows', went into Dwekes Park in the daytime, where they killed a doe, hid it in a heap of faggots, and the two fellows fetched it at night, 'whither he knoweth not but as he thinketh to Mr Basford his house'. Charles Colt of New Hall gentleman, 'Mr Basford his wife brother and servant' (i.e. brother-in-law and servant to Mr. Basford), confessed that after Christmas last he coursed a doe at his master's commandment with a white greyhound in Draynes Park 'that he keepeth'; the dog killed the deer; and 'the course was given to this examinate's brother by Mr Basford.' He further confessed that about Whitsuntide last his master had a black greyhound which he kept at the Lodge in the Red Deer Park. It broke loose and 'pulled down a black buck in the same park, and to the fall of the deer came Drayne, the keeper of the Great Park', and took the dog off the buck before his (Colt's) coming, but what became of the deer afterwards he does not know. He also confessed that, about Whitsuntide, with others of his fellows, he 'did strike a hearst with a gun at his master's commandment and afterwards they hunted her with their hounds but did not kill her.' On the same day the examining J.P., Eustace Clovile (of Clovile Hall, West Hanningfield), also found it necessary to bind Colt, with Basford

[1] W. R. Fisher, *The Forest of Essex* (1887), 145.

and Roger Barniston of Boreham esquire, to keep the peace towards
Ferdinand Stanton and Neville Good gentlemen. The case reached the
Privy Council in the following year. Beresford (as he was now spelt),
Colt and Harris, with two other men, had been summoned before the
Council. They were committed to the Marshalsea prison, to remain
there until the Countess of Sussex (the owner of the Hall) had accepted
their humble submission.[1] The two unnamed men escaped.

It was not long before Colt resumed his poaching activities and he was
caught a second time. Robert Jackson of Newport weaver and Colt, again
termed a gentleman, with six unknown persons, at 1 a.m. on a July
night in 1590, killed and carried off a pricket in Easton Park (in Little
Easton), the property of Edward Huberd. Here again Colt was not the
principal but had apparently been engaged by a group of young bloods,
'gentlemen's sons of worship, the most part of them'. This delightful
phrase with the rest of the story comes from Jackson's deposition, taken
down in October. Three of them had ridden to Dunmow the night before
and 'hosted at Bemyshes' there. One he thought was Heigham. Another
called himself Christopher Hatton, who was all apparelled in black silk
and had a gilt rapier hanging by his side. They were joined the next night
by three others, and in a wood near the park they met Jackson by
appointment, who had five greyhounds with him. He held their horses
while they took the dogs into the park. After they had 'killed and horsed
the deer' and given him 16d. for his pains, they all departed towards
Stortford. Jackson and Colt, on whose instructions he acted, were left to
bear the blame for the expedition. A true bill was found against Colt,
while Jackson was acquitted. The owner of the gilt rapier was the future
Sir Christopher, cousin and eventual heir of Lord Chancellor Hatton. His
home was Clay Hall, Barking. On succeeding to the Chancellor's estate in
the following year he moved to Northamptonshire. In 1589, it is related,
the judge attended a wedding, when he gaily divested himself of his gown,
saying, 'Lie thou there, Chancellor,' and joined the dancers.[2] It may be
that he used his influence to suppress any charge against his poaching cousin.

In 1581 Francis Harvey (of Cressing Temple) examined John Johnson,
a husbandman of Witham, who said that on the last day of May he
journeyed from the 'George' there at midnight with one Rooke Songer
and a brace of dogs to Creeksea Ferry, where they arrived very early in
the morning, going to one Anderkin's. An hour later they went on to
Burnham to one Evered's, where they stayed two hours, returning to
Anderkin's and dining there. He denied coursing or killing any deer in
Mr. Arthur Herris's grounds (Creeksea Place).

Four J.P.s dealt with a suspicious case in 1591, which had probably
arisen from idle chatter. 'Three years past he had a shoulder of venison
eaten at his house in Lent', deposed a Little Laver man, who added that

---

[1] *Acts of the Privy Council*, xv, 222, 224, 236.   [2] *Dict. Nat. Biog.*

'Parson Barfoote' (possibly George Barfoote or his successor Thomas Barfoote, rectors of Fyfield, 1578–1630), with Collins of Laver and his wife, were 'at the eating thereof', and that Thomas Glascocke of Dodding-hurst had sent him the venison. He also denied having killed any deer on the previous Friday night in Rookwood Hall Park (in Abbess Roothing, which belonged to the Brownes of Weald Hall, see p. 106). Peter Hurst, up for poaching again next year, and two others also denied having been in the park.

The next two stories relate to Horham Park and Bardfield Park in important estates fairly near each other on either side of Thaxted and belong to the years before and after the defeat of the Armada. The Queen had stayed a week in 1571 at Horham Hall, where she and Cecil trans-acted a lot of state business, and her entertainment there by Sir John Cutte probably included some hunting. Thomas Stebbinge, a tanner of Thaxted, said that on 10 October 1587 he and John Badcocke tailor and John Johnson *alias* Hubberd husbandman went into Horham Park about 2 a.m. in order 'if they might have made a fair course to their liking' with their black greyhound. But they did not course any deer because they found two men there, whose names he did not know, one of whom had a coat of plate and a long staff and led a dunnish, crop-eared dog, and the other 'went all in black' and had a crossbow under his arm and six arrows with forked arrowheads. The two groups had nothing to do with each other beyond exchanging 'God speed' or 'such like'. Badcocke and Hubberd deposed in similar vein, adding that they 'let go their dog' at a deer in the corner of the park, and that neither they nor the other two men, thought to be of Dunmow, killed any deer. All of which plea of unsuccessful poaching in Sir John Cutte's well-stocked park sounds some-what improbable.

Bardfield 'Great Park' was owned by Robert Wrothe, and as we shall see later was a favourite haunt of deer-stealers. John Sansom, a husband-man of Wethersfield, deposed that Henry Overed invited him a fortnight after Michaelmas (1589) to go hunting in Bardfield Park after they had supped at Titerell's alehouse in Wethersfield. Sansom said, 'How dare you so do?' Overed claimed that he had the consent of one of the keepers. But Sansom declared that he would not go for twenty nobles and utterly refused. He added that a servant of Josias Sansom told him three weeks later that, he, in company with five others, had coursed in the park with two greyhounds but killed nothing, and that his brother said that the servant and he would have hunted there a few nights before then, but 'the ground was then dangerous'. John Overed, a clothier of Shalford, said that he supped with his brother Henry, John Sansom, and others. They had with them a brace of greyhounds, and afterwards he went home. In parting company the others said that they 'would gladly have a course at deer that night, but where they did not make him privy'. The clothier asserted that his brother tarried at Titerell's alehouse all that night. In other words, a brace of denials.

Thus, honestly or falsely but in their own words, a few of the deer-stalkers told their stories to the examining magistrates, enabling us in turn to stalk behind the poachers. Here, in contrast, is the damning view of two J.P.s. The County Bench learned in 1595 about a particularly obnoxious, organised gang, intent on taking both deer and conies, in a letter from Sir John Smith and Arthur Herris, written at Tofts (in Little Baddow). It is a prize example of involved statement. The keepers of Humphrey Mildmay and of John Pascall (of Great Baddow) had reported deer and cony raids to their masters. The culprits were 'a company consociate together for such ill purposes, having had now of late (and whether of long time before or no we know not) a very suspicious resort' to the house of Ralph Some of Sandon, 'in such sort as the neighbours of late became very fearful lest they would attempt robbery or some other violence.' The two justices had also received complaints from Mr. Perryn, a gentleman, and Mr. Goddarde the minister there (Thomas Goddard, rector of Sandon, 1587–1601) as well as from other inhabitants and the two keepers, one of whom had been struck down in his warren at night. Further reports had come from many 'noblemen and men of worship' in Essex whose grounds had been 'greatly abused this year by these ill-disposed companions and their confederates.' John Hamond and Jonas Browning, 'men very notorious in this ill business, are known unto us not only to have been principal agents but from long time accustomed and (as it were) flesh bred in this kind of treachery, often remitted but never amended'. One of them the justices had arrested but he had been rescued and escaped ; a second man was not to be found. Three others had been bound over, 'supposed to be of this society.' The men named by the justices we shall meet more than once, especially Browning, an inveterate poacher – of deer, rabbits and fish, or anything that he could take.

Indictments for unlawful hunting in four of the royal parks and chases are found. Queen Elizabeth is known to have hunted in the Forest of Waltham, of which the present Epping Forest is the surviving major part, and to have built what is known as her Hunting Lodge, or open viewing-stand, at Chingford. But we are concerned only with those who had no right to enjoy the pleasures of the chase. In 1576 two men from Takeley and Hatfield Broad Oak killed a doe with a club and a gun in the Queen's park called Hallingbury Morley Park (in Great Hallingbury). Six years later two Chigwell men with bows and arrows killed two does in the Forest at Chigwell. In 1596 Thomas Crane of Navestock gentleman broke into the Queen's Havering Park and killed two male deer with a birding-piece. These matter-of-fact indictments are typical. Several poachers in the forest or chace of Lord Rich at Hatfield Broad Oak, originally royal demesne, were caught. In 1596 two Takeley men killed a pricket three days before Christmas, one of whom killed a doe there a week later; and in 1588 another doe was killed with a fowling-piece and carried off by a Lambourne fellow and Thomas Barfoote, a gentleman of London. The Forest of Waltham and Hatfield Chace were well stocked with red and fallow deer – the fattest, so Camden wrote, in all England.

The records of the Swainmote or Court of the Forest of Waltham add a little to the story of incessant poaching. A father and son named Dimsdale of Woodford were big offenders. One night in 1594 they were hunting in the forest with crossbows, while a companion 'fetched in the wanlace', that is, drove the deer towards them (p. 244). On another occasion they went to Chigwell Hills, where the father 'killed a hind at stalk.' A night expedition in the previous year when poachers were coursing deer in the forest had led to blows. The keeper's man charged them in God's and the Queen's name to stand, whereon he was 'very sore hurt with a bill' and attacked by their mastiff. At Collier Row, on the east fringe of the forest, four or five men from Anthony Cooke's house (Gidea Hall, Romford) not only killed a doe but also set upon the keeper's men, wounding them 'very sore.'[1]

Several parks lay within or close to the Forest of Waltham. John Hollye of Epping husbandman and Reginald Playle of Fyfield and Richard Ford of Harlow yeomen were up for suspicion of hunting in 1596 in Sir Edward Denny's park at Waltham Abbey. To the north of the Forest lay the park anciently (and still) known as Nazeing Park or Nazeing Wood. It belonged to Edward Greville and was the scene of four poaching excursions with greyhounds between 1589 and 1600. One party of three with others unnamed, using clubs, bows and arrows, killed seven does; another group of seven, including two gentlemen, all of Wormley (over the Hertfordshire bank of the River Lea), with others, hunted deer at night and assaulted two of Greville's servants, doubtless park-keepers, taking from them a couple of bloodhounds with collars and 'lymes'; a third raid, also at night, by an Epping man with others killed two bucks and a doe; and two Roydon labourers were charged with hunting there. On the same side of the Forest was Copt Hall Park, owned by Sir William Harvey and Mary his wife. It was entered twice in 1601 by Epping men, first by five husbandmen and a glover, who confessed to killing a buck; and a month later by a solitary poacher. The manor of Aldersbrook in Little Ilford, which was owned by Nicholas Fuller and also lay within the Forest, was the scene of a riot with night poaching in 1581 by four Leyton men. In this incident two men, probably keepers, were assaulted. Three gentlemen, Henry Young and Ambrose Barker of East Ham and William Waldegrave of Little Ilford, were among five sureties who stood bail for the offenders' appearance at the Sessions.

[1] W. R. Fisher, *The Forest of Essex* (1887), 210–11. The records quoted are in the Bodleian Library.

Sir William Petre, of Ingatestone Hall, Secretary to Henry VIII, Edward VI and Mary, had five Essex parks – at Ingatestone (later disparked), Crondon (which had been partially disparked in 1551, plate 20), East Horndon, Writtle, and the adjacent Horsefrith Park. Four years after his death in 1572 his son Sir John moved to Thorndon Hall, but his widow retained the Ingatestone and Writtle estates. Her deer-park at Crondon was raided twice. In 1572 that ne'er-do-well, Edward Cheveley *alias* Lacye, killed and carried away a doe. Six years later James Hanchett and Anthony Erington (or Herrington) of Stock gentlemen and three yeomen carried off two stags. The first two confessed. A like fate overtook a stag in Writtle Park in the same year, the four poachers including Edward Bugges of Harlow and Arthur Tappes of Blackmore gentlemen. These gentlemen's parishes, unlike abodes given in many assault indictments, are genuine. In 1582, a month before old Lady Petre's death, Edward Bell and Thomas Stanley of Margaretting 'farmingmen' and Francis Moncke of Buttsbury tiler were charged with killing deer by night. The park is not named but it must refer to Crondon or Writtle; and the same remark applies to another indictment for hunting in Sir John Petre's park eight years later.

William Heygham of Hatfield Peverel gentleman, with others unnamed, in 1583 entered the Queen's New Hall 'Little Park' in Boreham, 'shot' John Lacye the keeper with arrows, and took a buck. Henry VIII had purchased the manor in 1517 and it was to remain in the Crown's hands for another ten years. In 1573 it was acquired by Thomas Ratcliffe, Earl of Sussex, who was succeeded in 1583 by his brother Henry, the fourth Earl. Was the poacher a relation of one of 'gentlemen's sons' who indulged their sporting instincts in Easton Park in 1590? In 1587, two Terling men with dogs broke into the Dowager Countess of Sussex's preserves called New Hall Park or Red Deer Park and hunted a stag, which died three days later. These may be the two men who escaped, referred to without name, in the Privy Council case of this year already related. Next year four local men were charged with killing a deer in her park. In 1591 we have one of the fairly rare recognizances to commit no further poaching; this document refers to 'all his (the fourth earl's) game in all his parks in the county of Essex.' At the Midsummer Sessions 1594 the Court received indictments of four poachers in the same preserves: Robert Gynes of Great Leighs gentleman at night coursed with his greyhounds in New Hall Great Park belonging to Robert Earl of Sussex (who had succeeded Henry the year before); Edward Evered of Great Leighs miller hunted there in the daytime and killed a doe; a Great Leighs man, poaching there at night, wounded 'Adams the keeper'; and two Little Waltham yeomen paid a visit at night, killing a doe. In the last case three of them confessed; Richard Pateson of Little Waltham clerk (rector 1585–1616) was one of their sureties for appearance. The earl also lost three deer,

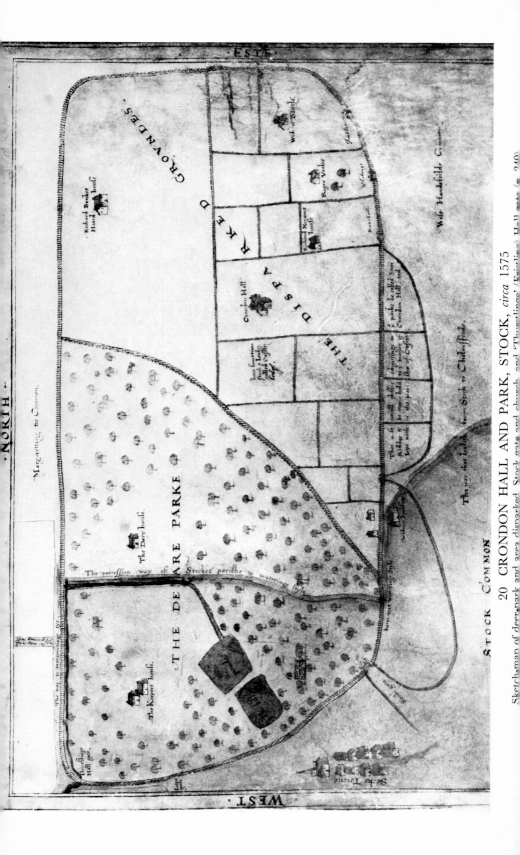

20 CRONDON HALL AND PARK, STOCK, *circa* 1575

Sketch-map of deer-park and area disparked. Stock gate and church, and 'Dwellinge' ('Friolinge') Hall gate (p. 249)

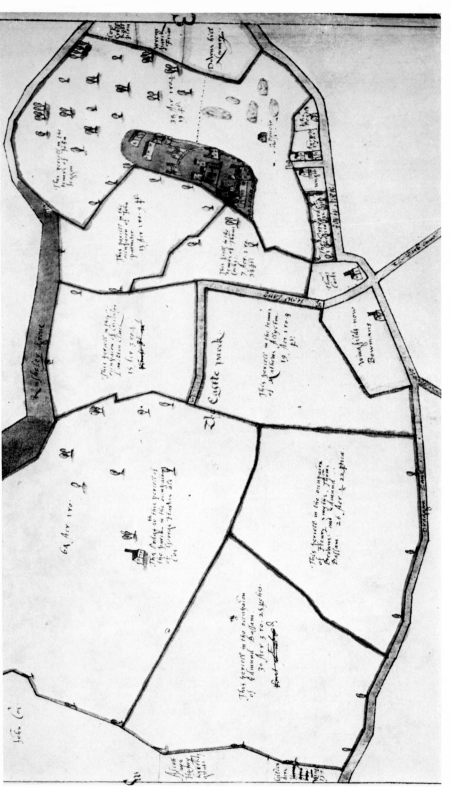

21 HEDINGHAM CASTLE AND PARK, 1592

Map showing the Norman castle keep, Bayly 'Strete', and 'Draggon Lane', and the long 'Rusheley grene' (p. 241).

killed in Henham Park in 1597 by men of the neighbourhood – a party of four including Richard Baron of Henham gentlemen in October and four others in December.

A midnight poaching foray in 1570 led to several South Weald and Navestock men being charged with chasing the deer in South Weald Park, stated to belong to Edmund Huddleston; also with netting 16 rabbits in his field there called Marlands. His wife was Dorothy daughter of Sir Anthony Browne of Weald Hall, Chief Justice and founder in 1557 of Brentwood School. In 1568 Huddleston and his wife had laid a memorial stone there which was re-discovered in 1870.[1] This case confirms that 'they lived apparently for some years with her father at South Weald Hall',[2] who had died three years earlier, and was succeeded by his great nephew and heir, Wistan Browne, but Browne made his home at Rookwood Hall in Abbess Roothing.

A good deal of poaching took place in the parks in North Essex. Twice, in 1573 and 1576, Edward Earl of Oxford's 'Great Park' at Hedingham Castle (plate 21) was raided by two men of Yeldham and Toppesfield who shot at the wild and fallow deer, and by five men of Gestingthorpe who killed a doe. The five confessed and were ordered to remain in prison for three months and afterwards to be bound over to be of good behaviour for seven years: the sole instance in which the sentence follows the Act of 1562. In 1576 a villager killed deer in the earl's Tilbury Park, a few miles to the north of Hedingham.

John Wentworth's park at Gosfield was poached in 1597 by five men including Henry Snellock and Francis Snellock gentlemen, all of Castle Hedingham, who killed two rascal deer. Next year Francis Snellock, described as a gentleman of Toppesfield, killed a spotted male deer at night in Little Sampford Park owned by Rooke Green. A year earlier Henry Snellock stood accused of attempted murder (p. 163). A few miles away at Great Bardfield lay another 'Great Park', belonging to the Wrothe family. In 1573 a buck and a sorrel were killed in Sir Thomas's park; and ten years afterwards a sore was taken in Robert's park, on both occasions by Wethersfield men. William Smyth junior, a gentleman of Shalford, killed a doe great with fawn worth 40s. a few months before other Wethersfield poachers made out that they had a barren night in Robert Wroth's Bardfield Great Park.

We conclude the catalogue of poaching expeditions in the northern half of the county with a minor miscellany. John Brooke of Witham innholder and Thomas Mathew of Chelmsford yeoman killed a buck in Bradwell Hall Park (near Coggeshall) in 1577. Nearby lay Sir Edmund Huddleston's Pattiswick Park, where a Bradwell man, with others unknown, hunted deer in 1599. In 1597 William Fytche, a mercer of Chelmsford hunted in the park of Sir William Waldegrave, unnamed but

[1] *Essex Review*, xv, 99.   [2] *Ibid.*

S

apparently Wormingford Park, his chief residence being Smallbridge, just over the Suffolk boundary. In 1593 an indictment was laid at the Assizes by way of an information against a Little Birch man for shooting at a buck with a fowling-piece. Exceptionally, it states that the poacher was unqualified, not having property worth £100. The informer claimed half the £10 penalty imposed by statute. The incident took place at Messing, which must have been at Bouchier's Hall or Messing Hall. A doe was killed in 1597 by three local men in (Great) Canfield Park belonging to John Wyseman. One night in 1601 Edward Heade and John Meade of Elmdon gentlemen, with others unknown, assaulted William Nicholls, keeper of William Wyseman's Broadoaks Park in Wimbish.

Several of the parks of the numerous branches of the Mildmay family got their quota of poaching. Jonas Browning of Maldon woollendraper entered Sir Thomas Mildmay's Terling Park, killing a white buck; and the same Browning and Robert Solme of Sandon poached in Humphrey Mildmay's Danbury Park, killing a sorrel; both incidents occurred in 1595. In 1593 three local men tried to kill deer in Terling Park; they also broke into closes of Lady Dorrell in Faulkbourne and of Emery Rochester esquire in Terling, to catch conies with dogs and nets. In 1600 a Faulkbourne yeoman killed two fawns with a net called a buckstall (p. 234) in the same park. It was the turn of Sir Thomas Mildmay's park at Moulsham by Chelmsford in 1601, when Richard Browne, an innholder of the town, shot a deer. Two years before this, Sir Thomas, standing at his park pale, had bought a pair of garters from Will Kemp, fellow actor with Shakespeare, during the journey to Norwich when he danced his famous jig.[1]

Hares

As far back as 1389 the Act of 13 Richard II, stat. 1, c.13 (1389), had declared that no artificer or labourer not having lands or tenements of the yearly value of 40s., nor any priest or clerk not having £10 yearly, might keep a greyhound or any other dog for hunting, nor use ferrets, hayes, nets, or other engines for taking or killing hares, conies or gentlemen's game, under pain of imprisonment for one year. A haye was a net, and cony was (and still is) the lawyer's term for a rabbit.

There is only one deposition about hunting hares, which were regarded, with deer, as common beasts of the chase. Examined by Sir Thomas Barrington in 1575, Thomas Robiaunte of High Easter yeoman said that he went with Thomas Hawkin of Good Easter and three other men to (Lord Rich's) Pleshey Park. There they hunted with Mr. Elkin, the park-keeper, until noon, killing a hare in Mr. Evered's ground (Richard Everard of Langleys in Great Waltham, an adjoining estate), and then

[1] *Will Kemp's Nine Daies' Wonder* (1599); see *Essex Review*, xii, 90–97.

went to one Knightbridge's for dinner. After hunting in the Old Park until 'night', they went again to Knightbridge's for supper. About 6 p.m. Hawkin and he returned homewards together part of the way, parting a quarter of a mile from his own house immediately after the bell had been rung at (Great) Waltham, 'which ordinarily is rung at 7 of the clock'. He got home between 7 and 8.

Poachers were rarely presented by the hundredal juries, but in 1577 a Bocking man was reported for finding, as he went homeward one winter day, the trace of a hare; 'he did course her but killed her not', so he was fined only 6d.

In 1567, three Wakes Colne men were prosecuted under the Act of 1389 for keeping hare-nets; next year a Woodham Walter tailor, for using hayes and hare-pipes (traps); in 1572 a Great Ilford man, not having lands worth 40s. a year, for keeping a greyhound bitch and two beagles (the latter, keen-scented small hounds, were of course specially bred for hunting hares); and ten years later a Bocking man, for keeping ferrets to catch hares and conies.

Conies

While Harrison gave a guess that there were two hundred parks in England, 'warrens of conies' he judged 'almost innumerable and daily like to increase.'[1] Anyone pursuing hares, conies, partridges or pheasants in a privileged warren was punishable by common law, although the warren might lie open. Skins of black rabbits were worth as much as their flesh; grey rabbits were less valuable. The London food market was eager for young rabbits. Of the cony-catcher's possessions – hayes and ferrets – the former figure in most of the poaching records. Such nets, stretched over rabbit-holes, were sometimes varied with pursenets, which were bag-shaped and corded at the mouth.

A deposition of 1580 introduces two rare words: 'jebots', or clamorous horn-notes blown to frighten game; 'muses', holes in a park-fence for rabbits to pass through; but 'withstall', apparently not defined by any lexicographers, seems to be another form of 'stale', to snare. It is not difficult to visualise this scene. Robert Fuller, a tanner of Stebbing, was in trouble for frequently ordering two of his servants to 'withstall and destroy the conies and game' of Henry Capell esquire in land called Gyffardes within his charter warren of Stebbing. The specific indictment was that on a Sunday in November they 'killed the game there with dogs, jebots and snares in stopping the muses in the pale, to the great hurt of the warren.' But, although Capell was the powerful squire of Rayne Hall and lord of the manor of Stebbing (and had been Sheriff in the previous year), the tanner stoutly resisted the charge, declaring that he leased

[1] Harrison, *Description of England*, 253–4.

the land, 'wherefore he thought he might have lawfully done it, and so intends still so to do'.

In 1578 the complaint of William Washer, rector of Upminster (1562–1609), led to indictments against two men of Upminster and Dagenham. Both confessed that a fortnight before Christmas, in the company of John Robson, a warrener to Mr. Latham (Nicholas Latham of Upminster), and another, they pitched a haye in Mr. Washer's meadow about 10 p.m. and caught three conies, and next morning about two hours before dawn they returned and took a black and grey cony, which 'John Warrener' carried to his master's house.

On 12 September 1582 Edward Ryche investigated two poaching affairs on Ingrave Common. William Pascall, servant to Geoffrey Lorken of East Horndon brickmaker, who had the property qualification to take conies (p. 242), admitted that, on Saturday 18 August between 1 and 2 a.m. he went with his master and Edmund Grantham of Ingrave brickmaker to Ingrave Common. There they met Sir John Petre's warrener, who, of course, questioned their being abroad at night. Pascall denied that they had a haye with them or that they were hunting, but Lorken made off and the others ran to their houses. Lorken said that they 'let fall their haye in the brakes' (thicket) and confessed to a couple of conies taken on the common. John Wells, servant to James Pattryke of Ingrave husbandman, deposed that, on Saturday 1 September also between 1 and 2 a.m., his master, a labourer, a 'strange man' with him named John, and he went to Ingrave Common and pitched a haye, taking four conies. Going further into the common they pitched again, when the warrener appeared and forbade them to hunt. His master, the labourer and the stranger fought with the warrener, whilst the servant took up the haye and ran to his master's house. He added that his master had a bow and arrows, and the others each a long staff. Pattryke confessed likewise, but said that he had a bearing bill (a long staff with a spearhead) and that the stranger had a bow and arrows. The Pattryke gang was charged with assaulting two of Sir John's servants. Pattryke was fined £10, the other two 13s. 4d. each.

From the examination by Anthony Maxey of three Great Leighs men in 1586 it appears that they were apprehended at night in Lord Rich's park at Little Leighs (Leighs Priory) with a mongrel dog, two pitchforks and a forest bill, having 'pitched their hayes and fetched in a wanlace' and taken one grey cony. ('To fetch a wanlace' was to form an intercepting group of men.) They also submitted that their master (not named) bade them take his dog and catch a couple of conies.

Two brothers, Thomas and Francis Monk, bricklayers of Stock, were caught in 1587 in Sir John Petre's warren at Ingatestone 'about Bartholomewtide' (24 August) before midnight. Thomas was examined on 11 September by Henry Gray (of Pyrgo Park near Romford) and said that they took seven conies but carried none away. Francis, examined on 27 February by Eustace Cloville (of West Hanningfield), confessed that they came to 'blows' with the warrener, leaving their haye behind, and that he had bought it for 3s. 4d. at Gravesend ten days before and kept it hidden in his mother's barn.

A complete denial was put in by a Pattiswick labourer when charged with hunting in Sir Edmund Huddleston's park there in December 1591. He stated that he possessed a haye of about twenty fathoms (120 feet) in length and a piece of another of three or four fathoms, which he had had for fifteen years, but had never used them. Two days before Christmas he came to Peter Warner's house in Pattiswick, and seeing a haye lying on his table asked to borrow it, saying he had conies in his yard, one of which he caught that same night, beating it out of his woodstack. The following evening Matthew Warner told him that his (the labourer's) house had been searched for nets, so he earnestly entreated Matthew to tarry a little until he could go home for Peter Warner's haye. The examination was taken before Huddleston himself.

Another member of the Solme or Some family of Sandon was charged also in 1595. This time it was Zachary, who, with the same Jonas Browning that killed a deer in Danbury Park, attacked John Pascall's warrener at Great Baddow and dispatched eight conies. The grand jury returned a true bill for Zachary but no true bill for Jonas.

Three Orsett men were examined by Thomas Kyghley in 1600 about a poaching expedition on an August Sunday. Robert Saunders confessed that he was in company with Thomas Newman and Charles Dawdry at a wedding there, with dancing until past midnight. Then they went into a stubble wheatfield in South Ockendon, where they had laid their haye the day before. The moon went down. About an hour afterwards they took up the haye and returned towards Ockendon Green, and in a nearby field, across a path at a long burrow, they took one black and one grey cony and no more. They had removed the haye out of the loft of Saunders' master, William Hurte of Orsett, 'without his privity.' Newman had one cony; the other he left in his master's kitchen. He also confessed that on another day he was hunting in the grounds of Robert Herd of Bowers Gifford about 10 p.m., where he met Thomas Heyes of Orsett with two of his servants poaching with two hayes. The others admitted that they hunted in Mr. Harlestone's warren before dawn.

Was Francis Harvey, J.P., of Cressing Temple, particularly mean in connection with his own man's alleged petty offence in 1583, or was his attitude typical of the landowners' obsession with the preservation of game, even small game? At any rate, he sent to the Court the confession, which he had taken in London, of Thomas Smythe, who had begged of his master a couple of conies. 'Being bolder than he ought', it runs, 'he took couple of conies, intending to give them to his friends at his coming to London ; and because his master stayed longer in the country than he thought, and the conies being stale, he desired Jesse Neale the cooper to sell them for him, who did at Braintree for 4s., and brought him money for them, wherewith he minded to buy other conies against his coming to London'. But, as, we shall see shortly, Harvey had particularly strong reasons for sternness.

Conflicting evidence was taken by Thomas Coleshill, J.P., who lived at Chigwell, about some alleged sales of conies from the Earl of Leicester's warren in Wanstead Park in 1580. John Tailor deposed that William Ware, Lord Leicester's warrener, asked him to sell 18 couple of conies. He sold 12 couples to Robert Raie for 12s., which he handed to Ware. Tailor, who was a walker (gamekeeper), having been appointed by Ware, received 6s. from Ware on the previous Saturday near 'my Lord's conduit at Wanstead' to the intent that he 'should get himself out of the country' (i.e. district) and remove himself to 'the backside of Leighton'. Raie denied having stolen any conies from Wanstead Park, asserting that he had bought 20 couples from Tailor, paying 12d. the couple. The warrener, also implicated, not only denied theft but stated that he had delivered seven or eight couple of conies to Tailor, which were served in 'my Lord's house'. Thomas Ware of Writtle gentleman was William's surety. No indictments are found in this and the previous case, both of which properly belong to the chapter on Larceny.

The remaining evidence about cony-taking comes from the barer indictments. In the winter of 1562–63 six raids were made in south-east Essex by a local gang. Their rascally leader, Edmund Cheveley *alias* Lacye, here described both as a yeoman and a labourer of Hadleigh, has already been met. With three or four mates he took eighteen dozen conies from Edmund Tyrell's manor of Beeches in Rawreth on 1 November, eighteen and five dozen there on 20 and 31 January, fifteen dozen from Robert Lawson *alias* Edmundes' land at Southchurch Hall on 2 November, sixteen dozen there on 22 January, sixteen conies from Richard Goslyng's land at Thundersley on 23 January, and sixteen from William Stephens' land at Benfleet on 24 January: a total of 896! Two of the men were fined 12d. each by Lord Rich, Edward Barrett, George Nycoll and Edmund Bockyng, J.P.s; the indictments against Cheveley and another were certified by Quarter Sessions into the Queen's Bench for trial at the Assizes.

Three days before Christmas 1562 Francis Chaunsey of Shenfield gentleman took conies with ferrets and pursenets (see p. 243) from the lands called Osgoods there belonging to Thomas Parker gentleman, and was fined 20d. In 1565 fifteen men, mostly of Great Warley, were charged with 'cony stealing' and bound over to appear by mutual recognizances, and Matthew Pery, a gentleman of that parish, was separately charged with shooting both with a crossbow and a handgun. Two years later a Margaretting man with his greyhounds broke into Christopher Harrys's grounds at 'Shenfeld' (now Killigrews, p. 18) and chased his conies with intent to kill them; fined 12d. John Bridges senior and junior, and John Simpson their servant, all grocers of Chelmsford, chased conies with sticks, nets and ferrets in Sir Thomas Mildmay's free warren at Moulsham at 9 p.m. on 10 September 1569. But when the case was heard at Quarter Sessions they claimed that the indictment was insufficient in law, and it was removed to the Assizes. In 1577 two Thaxted men went into Rooke Green's Little Sampford Park and took five conies with ferrets and purse-nets. A couple of Downham men in March and June 1580 were indicted for catching conies in two widows' warrens, Lady Petre's at Ingatestone and Margaret Ayloff's at South Hanningfield; a Lambourne man likewise in 1588 in the grounds of William Smith esquire at Theydon Mount (i.e. Hill Hall, p. 133); and two Barking men in 1591 in 'the cunniver' there (a reminder of the pronunciation of 'cony' and meaning a rabbit-warren) next to the house of William Nutbrowne, who was lord of the manor of Cockermouth in Dagenham.

In 1602 killing five conies with a haye one hundred yards long in a close at Faulkbourne involved four local poachers in assaulting two men, perhaps Faulkbourne Hall park-keepers. Seven others, including Henry Hobsone clerk (not the rector), testified against them.

How many of these poaching excursions led to bloody affrays one cannot say, but at least one incident had a fatal result, in the last week of the reign. Three Dunmow labourers, thwarted in their cony-hunt, attacked the Newton Hall Park keepers, one of whom died (p. 160). There was also the death caused by a Waltham Forest keeper's man investigating alleged deer-chasing by dogs (p. 153).

An unusual pair of indictments of 1563–64 reveals how John Patricke of Ingrave enclosed and obstructed 'a common orchard in an ancient lane called Chick House Garden' in Ingrave for the purpose of taking conies by stretching nets across the lane. With the same aim he also obstructed a common pathway there called Drugdells Lane, through which Richard Vicars and other inhabitants were accustomed to drive their cattle. He was fined 12d. for the first offence and 20d. for the second. Next year Drugdells Lane was still stopped up, and this time his purse was the lighter by 3s. 4d. And between these appearances before the County Bench this 'very troublesome and disorderly person' was the subject of a forthright complaint by his fellow parishioners (p. 140).

Eight further cases of cony-hunting yield nothing worthy of mention, except a recognizance of 1590 binding Richard Peverel of Rochford yeoman to answer for stealing conies, 'if in the meantime my Lady Rich (of Rochford Hall) do not release him', and an indictment of two men, who had fled after raiding the warren in Wanstead Park.

As a useful preliminary to catching rabbits a Henham carpenter in 1601 stole a ferret (2s. 6d.) from a stable at Chawreth Hall in Broxted owned by Robert Salmon, whose name helps to fill a gap in the lords of this manor. The case about the dispute in 1585 between Thomas Gent of Moyns Park in Steeple Bumpstead and Robert Kempe of Spains Hall in Finchingfield, who stoutly defended his warrener, declaring that his conies were 'a great part of my living', arose out of an alleged threat to beat the constables of Halstead, and has already been related (p. 111).

Pigeons, Pheasants and Partridges

To shoot at pigeons was an offence under the Act of 1541. It appears in several indictments, e.g. shooting three house-doves with a hand gun; and 'shooting twelve shots' with a fowling-piece and killing five ring-doves and eight more shots accounting for six doves at Radwinter in 1591.

Sir John Bramston has left an entertaining account of how his school-master at Blackmore, about 1630, encouraged his pupils to eke out their scanty rations by trapping his neighbours' doves.[1] Feathered creatures provided food but less sport than chasing conies. A foray in 1581 furnishes some interesting facts about the method by which the birds were caught. Fifty-nine pigeons caught at a single drawing of the net on one expedition shows how profitable this form of poaching could be. Unfortunately the depositions from which all this is taken are not matched by any others. Two servants were first examined. Margaret Ayers of Witham, until recently in the service of William Hutte of Braxted and William Hutte his late father for $3\frac{3}{4}$ years, said that William junior and his (male) servant Juny Wallygar and his kinsman John Hutte brought to the house two dead swans, which they baked and ate although in Lent. She had heard that Mr. Draper missed swans about that time. Juny and Leonard Skynner, another of Hutte's servants, also brought to the house four or five ducks, his master brought four, and John Hutte brought two 'betwixt Holamas (All Souls' Day) and Christmas last', which was about the time he was married. Further, she said, in the time of her 'old' master, William the son took now and then a few housedoves with a 'staynet', and in the week when she departed from her master, which was about Twelfth Day last, 'there was one great draught taken of doves', of which she was told by Elizabeth Crofte, who helped her to brew that day and also told her that some pies of the same pigeons still remained in the house. Gilbert Crakbone servant to Ellis Lurkyn of Great Braxted baker said that, when he was servant to William Hutte and aged fourteen his master said one day, 'In faith, Leonard, we had trim sport with long necks.' He also said that Leonard and Juny and John Hutte brought in eight ducks at various

[1] Bramston, *Autobiography* (Camden Soc., Old Series, vol. 32 (1845). I owe this reference to Mr. J. Holmes.

times, and that all three laid a staynet 'of set purpose' at Page's and took in one draught three score lacking one, then laid their net five times more, taking one, then twenty-five, then nine (one of which was a pied dove, which they knew to be Mr. Robert's), then ten, and at the last draught four. Most of them were carried to Coggeshall, and they would have drawn again, but their pulley broke. Then William and John Hutte, Juny and Leonard were examined. Not surprisingly, all denied everything, saving that John admitted he killed two ducks in the back river, which were his master's. The Huttes' activities were not legally poaching since their prey – swans, ducks and doves – were not wild birds.

Apart from two indictments for shooting at ducks, the only wildfowling incident, and not an illegal one, comes from a coroner's inquest (p. 160).

Two Acts, 11 Henry VII, c.17 (1495) and that of 1541, had dealt with the taking of pheasants and partridges by 'nets, snares or other engines'; the culprit to forfeit £10 (£5 to the prosecutor, £5 to the owner), a clear indication of the gravity of the offence in the landowning legislators' view.

Four depositions and a precious letter bear on partridge-taking. Examined in 1587, Edward Eastwood of Hockley said that between the Feasts of All Saints and Christmas last one John Foster, naming himself to be a servant to Lord Cobham (who incidentally was William Harrison's patron), came to an alehouse at Hockley for one or two weeks, taking partridges and other fowl in the parish. The deponent saw Foster driving a covey of partridges towards his net, catching five or six; Foster however, declared that he did so by virtue of Lord Rich's warrant. The witness also said that Foster took six partridges at Asheldham about New Year's Day, which he saw in a bag. And Richard Jewse of Hockley victualler deposed that Foster while in his alehouse had brought in amongst other fowl six dead partridges, which he said he took for Lord Rich.

Two Elsenham men in 1590 went into Thomas Crackbone's fields in the manor of Elsenham about 10 p.m. and netted eight partridges, which they left in a shed near Mr. John Wyberd's house at Takeley. They had fetched the sparrow net from his house, and had added insult to injury by borrowing Crackbone's horses. The indictment states that the partridges were caught in 'the pease field' belonging to Richard Barlee esquire without his leave. Barlee was one of the two examining J.P.s.

In 1578 Edward Tunbridge of Cressing yeoman took ten partridges with nets on the land of Francis Harvey called Westockes at Rivenhall. (Westock's Farm is in the adjoining parish of White Notley.) Taken before Harvey, he was bound by his own recognizance, with Nicholas Smythe of Fryerning gentleman as his surety, not to take any partridges or pheasants except in the grounds of Sir John Smythe of Baddow, 'in which he may at the pleasure of Sir John'. By good fortune the letter has been preserved which Harvey addressed to the Court on 3 October 1598 'at his house in Tolleshunt D'Arcy' (though he usually lived at his other home, Cressing Temple). Utterly exasperated by this incorrigible poacher of everything, who had little respect for one who was a J.P. for the county and had been an M.P. for Colchester, Harvey 'prays that he may continue to be bound with good sureties'. Then follows a catalogue of Tunbridge's poaching career. 'He hath for more than twenty years continually', Harvey declared, 'abused me and others, and yet (i.e. still) doth, in stealing my conies, robbing my fishponds, and taking my partridges and pheasants. He hath for stealing my conies procured some to come so far as Baddow, Danbury, Springfield and other towns in these parts, and that they all should meet at his house to steal Sir Edmund Huddleton's, Mistress Wilson's and Mr Babington's, mine, and divers other men's conies, and they were in my warren and Mistress Wilson's and stole some there by the confessions of sundry of the parties themselves before me. He has been indicted and sent to gaol and bound in at least four bonds in more than £100, and has not cared to forfeit any bonds, neither is he to be trusted of any words he speaks, for I charged him with causes which he most vehemently denied, yea, and desired to be damned both body and soul if he were guilty of the cause that he was charged with, and I do assure you I made him within less than a quarter of an hour after confess all to be true'. This was to the man's credit, the justice concluded, 'and I am forced to take this course, for my conies are stolen so that I have not any to serve my house, my ponds which I stored for the provision of my house are robbed, most of my partridges and especially in the ground near his house are taken this year, and pheasants he hath not left any, and except there be order taken he will abuse all these parts, for all gentlemen and others do much complain of him.'

To the list of inveterate poachers may be added one whose abode is not given. He confessed in 1592 to three excursions in which he had taken 11 partridges in Clay Hall grounds (in Ilford), which 'Mr. Pawle of the Chancery had of him' (?Sir George Paule, died 1637), 20 for Mr. Latham of Upminster, and six for Mr. Russell, purveyor for veal, all taken by daylight. He added that George Larder was always present at the taking of those which his master had. George Larder of Upminster husbandman had been bound in 1580 not to take pheasants or partridges. After two men had been charged as 'common takers of partridges' in October 1577, the justices tried to restrain them, as with Larder, by insisting on their binding themselves not to commit the same offence, and they had to renew their recognizances annually for the next three years. It is interesting to note that in the previous month the Council had sent out a letter to 'certain shires for the restraining of takers of partridges and pheasants', probably as a result of the bad harvest of that year.[1]

[1] *Acts of the Privy Council*, x, 39, 61.

In 1567 Anthony Caudell of Danbury yeoman was charged with killing a pheasant with a handgun on Strawberry Hill in East Hanning-field. He appeared by Richard Peyton, 'his attorney', and pleaded not guilty. John Sewting of Great Dunmow clothworker caught partridges with nets or snares in Lord Rich's manor of Felsted in 1574.

A unique entry is found in the Lexden hundred presentment to the Midsummer Sessions 1602. 'Sander' (Alexander) Harvy of Colchester and his brother Edward of Stanway 'took money of the country' (i.e. county) for the watching of the beacon at Stanway, but in the night, when they should have been on duty, they were taken with another Stanway man, 'a-killing of partridge in standing corn'; and 'this they used from time to time,' so clearly they often played truant.

Hawks

Two ancient Acts of Edward III concerning hawks were still in force. Not only was it a felony to steal a hawk, but also to conceal or 'embezzle' one that was lost: the finder's immediate duty was to take it to the Sheriff, who was to proclaim its discovery publicly in order to restore the hawk to its owner.

A serious charge of wounding a man in Norfolks Wood at Rivenhall, the property of John Stokes gentleman, was brought in 1575 against Thomas Beeson gentleman, George Tonbridge cook, both of Layer Marney, and William Salmon of Copford turner, who had carried away three sparrowhawks worth £3 belonging to Stokes by the order of Edward Beeson of Layer Marney gentleman. No sentence is noted. In the same year two men stole four sparrowhawks worth £4 from a Mountnessing wood.

On 4 July 1577 Lord Rich wrote from his home at Rochford Hall to the justices that 'there are divers persons bound by recognizance to appear for certain evil facts by them committed, both for unlawful hunting and for unlawful taking of hawks' (who were presumably due to appear at the Midsummer Sessions to be held that day), and because he was 'by other occasions restrained' from coming to Chelmsford to testify in these matters he asked the Court to bind them over to the following Sessions. (But the roll for Michaelmas is not extant.)

One Sunday in June 1585 a Great Baddow yeoman and two Margaret-ting husbandmen were accosted at 2 a.m. by Sir John Petre's keeper in Gyles Wood in West Horndon Park. Taken red-handed with no less than ten sparrowhawks (they must have broken into the hawks' mews), they put up a fight. One of them, at least, went to gaol. A month later Edward Bell of Margaretting was caught taking sparrowhawks in Pyrgo Park near Romford, the home of Henry Grey. Bell had been before the Court in 1582 (p. 240). Grey wrote from Pyrgo to the justices, requesting that, as he could not be present, the case might proceed against Bell with 'judgment as others had at the last Assizes for the like offences'. (But no such indictments appear on the Midsummer Assize file.)

In 1596 Matthew Goodeve of Great Waltham yeoman was indicted for stealing a hawk called tassel-gentle (a male peregrine falcon) belonging to Benjamin Gonson of Great Baddow esquire; but he had fled. Edward Luckyn of Roxwell yeoman in 1594 found a goshawk there belonging to Lord Morley (of Great Hallingbury), which was lost, and did not take it to Humphrey Mildmay the Sheriff according to the statute. And in 1602 a Little Baddow man was charged on suspicion of 'embezzling away' certain young hawks out of the demesne land of the same former Sheriff in Danbury.

Fish

The only form of poaching in which gentry and yeomen do not seem to have indulged was fishing. Several generations were to pass before Izaak Walton introduced the gentry to the joys of angling. Apart from the bald indictment in 1565 of a Great Bentley man for 'taking fish', having been committed by Lord Darcy of St. Osyth's Priory, the charges of illegal fishing are fairly specific. In June 1567 Thomas Blatche senior and junior of Great Waltham husbandmen were caught fishing in 'Much Waltham River', belonging to Lord Rich. Both were fined 12d. by Robert Kempe and Edmund Bocking. Nine days later, John Cortman senior, husbandman, and five labourers including two more Cortmans, all of Felsted, 'riotously diverted the course of Felsted River', also owned by Rich, into an adjoining field, thereby taking his fish : a crafty, but not unknown method. In the same year seven Sible Hedingham men, all termed 'websters', broke the flood gates of Alderford Mill there, belonging to John Grene, letting out the water and netting 100 'roaches' worth 40s. Each was fined 12d. by William Waldegrave, Kempe and Bocking. In 1578 two Maldon fishermen unlawfully fished at a weir there called 'Hellapolle Weir' or a flood weir, belonging to Brian Darcy of Tiptree (Priory) esquire, catching fish worth 10s. On several occasions in 1586 six Halstead men – three weavers, a baymaker, a kempster (woolcomber), and a glover – netted fish worth in all as much as £5 in the local streams of Arthur Breame (lord of the manor of Abels in Halstead).

The Queen's Bench indictments include a case which was initiated in the court baron of the manor of Heybridge in 1588, when the jurors presented four Maldon men – Thomas Brett yeoman, George Woodder weaver, William Tyler grocer, and Jonas Browninge woollendraper (this was the first of his run of poaching offences), for stealing nets and taking fish from the river at Heybridge belonging to the Dean and Chapter of St. Paul's, London (lords of the manor).

A midsummer night's dream of fishing was too vivid for the three Coggeshall watchmen appointed for duty by the two constables. On 28 June 1589 they deserted their watch. Joined by a fourth man, they dragged the stream and fishery of Richard Benyan of Coggeshall and caught fish worth 20s. The watchmen were fined 20s., 10s. and 6s. 8d. (according to the number in their nets?); the fourth apparently went free. In 1593 three Widford men were charged under the Act of 5 Elizabeth with netting 100 'carps' worth 20 marks in the ponds and weirs of Sir John Petre in Writtle. Two justices in 1583 bound over an unemployed weaver of Stebbing in the same way as the partridge-poacher was dealt with, 'not to fish hereafter any ponds of William Bendlowes of Bardfield Saling gentleman or the ponds of any other persons', and they also added a clause banning him from the parish.

In the autumn of 1579 the youths of Roydon indulged in a varied bout of poaching. Five of them, Stephen Leonard, Robert Spencer, John Claye, John Harris and Thomas Querne, were indicted for catching ten conies with dogs, nets and other instruments in the grounds of Richard Swyfte gentleman, contrary to the Act of Richard II. Depositions had been taken by James Altham. One by one, the constable brought them into the justice's hall or parlour, and he or his clerk wrote down what they said. He then apparently tried to get a composite story by calling them in a second time, and compiled a further account, under headings: 'Hunting conies, fishing, geese and ducks, stealing apples.' About Shrovetide three of the defendants went hunting with two mongrel dogs at 10 p.m. in Mr. Swyfte's grounds at Roydon and killed six conies on the green by the pond, in the 'stubbed field' and in the mead, which they divided among themselves and carried to John Finch's house and 'spent' them there; about Michaelmas Leonard, Spencer and Claye raided the same land and caught another cony; and about 'a sennight ago' Leonard, Spencer and Richard Maye, with four pursenets bought for 7d. killed another, which they handed to William Graygoose. Between Easter and Whitsuntide Leonard with Jonas Leonard and Thomas Leonard, Thomas Ward and George Young, went fishing at 10 p.m. in Christopher Ayston's ponds at Great Parndon, taking a casting-net. They caught some 'roaches and tenches', which they took to James Young's alehouse at Roydon and ate them there. Ayston, who was away from home, had given them leave to fish at night. As for the apples, Stephen and Thomas Leonard and John Hubberd confessed to having broken into Mr. Tuck's house. Stephen Leonard with another Roydon labourer was charged at the Assizes in 1582 with stealing six hats belonging to Squire Swyfte for which he was whipped. Swyfte, who belonged to an armigerous family, was the son of John Swyfte of Roydon, a Queen's Auditor.

There are a few indictments under the punitive legislation against the mere possession of poaching implements, e.g. in the 1560s three men for keeping ferrets and hayes. Keeping dogs is the subject of two indictments – a greyhound and two beagles; and a 'couple of greyhounds' and a 'grewhound' (a different word, the etymology and meaning of which is uncertain). In 1600 two Grays Thurrock men were indicted for keeping ferrets to catch conies, contrary to the Act of 13 Richard II, one of whom was Henry Barbor (the rector), 'being a spiritual man' (p. 242).

Four cases under the 1541 Act are found: Matthew Perry of Great Warley gentleman for using handgun and crossbow (and for taking conies) in 1565; three labourers for shooting with handguns in 1572; four East Donyland men including Robert Prowe gentleman (also for forcible disseisin of the manor house, p. 121) in 1582; and two East Tilbury men and a Hertfordshire man for shooting with a handgun at a rook on the highway at Epping in 1602.

Poaching was an offence which figures occasionally in manor courts, mostly for illegal fishing or for keeping greyhounds or pursenets. It was not an ecclesiastical offence, but hunting on a Sunday or holiday in time of church service led to a few presentments in the archdeacons' courts; one, for example, for hunting squirrels.

Remarkably little about illegal hunting is found in the surviving Elizabethan Quarter Sessions records of other counties. While the Essex records yield no actual indictment for 'hunting the Queen's deer', this specific charge is found in one of the two Middlesex deer-poaching cases – against a Tottenham butcher who had crossed the River Lea, doubtless to provide some venison from 'the Forest of Waltham' for his customers.[1] The other excursion was made by three local men into the royal Enfield Chase. During the whole reign the Middlesex justices dealt with only one cony-catcher and not a single poacher after partridge or pheasant, fowl or fish. Were Essex men particularly partial to poaching, or were the gamekeepers more skilled in looking after their masters' interests? Certainly this offence was a significant element of disorder in Elizabethan Essex. Lancashire and Worcestershire records each have a single indictment for tracing hares in the snow. The latter have a single charge of hunting and hawking with spaniels and hawks – offences not represented in Essex, also a case of deer-poaching in a park a day's march from Charlecote (fourteen years before Shakespeare's foray); but virtually nothing else. Nor are there more than occasional references in other county records before 1603, except in Staffordshire. The small selection of Kent Sessions records of crime has one poaching story of 1597, the

[1] *Middlesex County Records*, i, 269.

scene of which was Sissinghurst Park, the home from which Sir John Baker's son came to marry the step-daughter of Sir William Petre of Ingatestone. It tells of whistle-calls at dead of night when the master was asleep, of abandoning the loom for the case of crossbow arrows, and of hiding them for the next raid in a bush near the park pale.[1]

[1] *Kentish Sources : Crime and Punishment* (ed. E. Melling), vi, 39.

21

Larceny

The many kinds of larceny, like those of assault, were variously classified by legal writers at great length. We need only draw a few items from their text-books to explain points arising from our records. Larceny was primarily the theft of another's goods in his absence. It was grand larceny when the value of the goods was above 12d., and petty larceny if 12d. or below. The former was a felony punishable by hanging, except where benefit of clergy was obtained; for the latter, a misdemeanour, the guilty party got a whipping but forfeited his goods.

If two or more persons stole goods worth above 12d., both were charged with grand larceny. Besides simple larceny, thefts committed in certain circumstances were, as nowadays, known by different names. To break into and steal goods from a house constituted housebreaking if it occurred by day, and burglary if by night. But closebreaking (a man's field or garden was his 'close' in law) included both theft and trespass, the latter implying damage, however trifling, such as trampling down his grass.

How to deal logically with the vast number of cases of larceny, housebreaking, burglary, closebreaking and highway robbery, with all their incidental information about Elizabethan life, poses several problems. Taking these five categories in turn, the first three were sometimes accompanied by assault, occasionally by homicide or murder; and they have already been narrated under those crimes. Closebreaking ranged from driving away another man's cattle to aggravated cases of trespass such as unlawful dispossession, violent assault, or even riot: where nothing was stolen we have assigned such incidents to Trespass, Disseisin, Assault, or Riot, but there is much overlapping. Criminal encounters on the queen's highway were a special category in the eyes of the law, which differentiated between highway robbery with or without assault and highway assault without robbery. The latter is dealt with under Assault. Stealing of church goods was also a separate crime. Killing deer and smaller game and illegal fishing were never regarded by the lawyers as larceny, and will be described in the chapter on Poaching. Indictments for killing or taking away deer never use the word 'stole', but one of them, for 'hunting and killing a doe' in Canfield Park, has a related recognizance of the men 'suspected to have stolen' the doe.

Such, then, are the main 'vertical' divisions. Two of the most important aspects of these disorders are cattle-, sheep- and horse-stealing, and thefts connected with the cloth industry and other trades and crafts. Instead of describing each separately, the former under larceny and close-breaking, the latter under all five of the categories first mentioned, it was felt that their inter-relationship demanded 'horizontal' treatment in order to bring the evidence together and to avoid some tedious repetition. As a result, closebreaking has been whittled down to insignificant thefts of clothes from gardens, and a closebreaking 'vertical' section is not needed. It seemed equally logical to link all thefts by craftsmen and tradesmen of materials connected with their own business (pp. 296–301). Many indictments list clothes, household furniture and farming implements. Except for the few sample lists given in the chapter on the earliest records (pp. 8–10) these articles are not considered but will be dealt with in a later volume in relation to the mass of similar information in Wills.

The law demanded that the indictment for any offence should state the abode of the accused. If this was not known, the parish in which the offence was committed was inserted. This anomaly has misled some parish historians to appropriate such culprits as their own 'parishioners'. For example, the abode of a highwayman who had successfully operated in several places but was caught would appear as a different parish in each indictment. Only if his abode is not the same as the scene of the crime can one be certain that it is his home parish.

Any theft with violence was a robbery. Indictments for stealing 'forcibly' or with assault (but not in the highway) are few in comparison with those for highway robbery. There are only a dozen cases, none for more than a few pounds; for example, Thomas Sturley of Kirby gentleman in 1581 forcibly stole £3 belonging to Thomas Cookuc, but was acquitted. Several robbers, despite assault as well as theft, got off with a whipping when the value was under 12d. One, unluckily as he doubtless felt, found only 11d. inside a stolen purse. But he was caught, and the 1d. added for its value brought him dangerously near the gallows. The jury assessed the whole at 11d. Among the hundreds of charges, the goods were never valued at exactly 12d., the maximum limit for petty larceny. In a solitary instance, a man put the rope round the neck of his son, whom he prosecuted for stealing 20 marks from himself.

In a period long before facilities for banking cash were generally available, many gentlemen, merchants and tradesmen were obliged to keep large sums of money in their houses or to carry it about with them when attending market or on other business. As will be seen from the individual crimes recorded, the biggest plunder in Elizabethan Essex was taken by highway robbers and burglars. Among the indictments for grand larceny, the highest-value theft was committed by two men described as 'of Witham labourers'; one name is struck through because

T

the jury brought in 'no true bill' for him. The victim was Richard Southwell, who in 1593 lost his gold chain valued at £80 and £60 in money. The Southwells had owned several Essex manors, but now lived mostly in Norfolk. Thomas Tusser, the agricultural writer, had received their patronage. 'Not in prison; in the Counter at London' indicates that instead of being in the county gaol the other defendant was in one of the nine London prisons.

By far the most interesting haul, and almost as high in assessed value, deprived Jane Clovyle widow of much of her jewellery and fine linen. The accused were William Massey and Thomas Leighs, termed gentlemen of West Hanningfield; and the victim was evidently the widow of Eustace Clovyle of Clovile Hall in that parish, who had died in 1589. On 16 August 1593 they stole a gold chain (£60), another gold chain with a sweet pomander (£5), two unspecified jewels (£10), a damask tablecloth (£2), two towels (£1), three cambric sheets (£10), three lawn sheets (£10), six pillowbeers (£1), a square damask cloth wrought with a bone lace of gold and four tassels of pearl and gold (£5), and 'other parcels of linen' (£20). Such is the description in the Sessions roll. No note of the pleas or verdicts is added, but the case came up at the Lent Assizes. The indictment on the file differs in two respects: Leighs' name is absent, and the list ends with the same linen (valued at £6 13s. 4d.) but adds a bed valance of orange tawny velvet and damask fringed with silk and gold (£3), two unspecified books (4s.), and a horse (£2). Massey was found guilty for the 'goods' but not for the horse. Neither can be traced as local men.

The largest sum in cash alleged to have been stolen was £100 taken from a bag belonging to Roger Appleton esquire by a Chelmsford spinster, who was acquitted (1590). He was the son and heir apparent of the active Essex J.P., Henry Appleton of Jarvis Hall in South Benfleet. Next comes the theft at West Ham of a gold chain worth £90 belonging to Lionel Curion gentleman (1564). John Fyrmynge of West Thurrock miller and Henry Bowden of Aveley tailor took £70 from James Humfrey in an Aveley house (1598); and another £50 was stolen from him in 1601. Arthur Breame (lord of the two chief Halstead manors) was relieved of £54 in 1599. The theft of £50 from from John Levington's chest at Latton (1560) was noted earlier (p. 10). Elizabeth Starlynge spinster stole £53 from Mary Same widow, both of Castle Hedingham (1594), and William Melbrook of Little Easton yeoman took £46 10s. from Deodatus Throgmorton (1589). Thomas Ferne *alias* Lawrence, a clothier of Dedham, presumably a man of some substance, forcibly removed £46 from Thomas Allen (1580). There are five other thefts of more than £10, none of interest, except perhaps that of £19 from John Sammes of Wickham (Bishops, later of Langford Hall), gentleman, by a cook, possibly his own.

A very different charge was heard in 1575 against Thomas Rudyart of Little Hallingbury clerk, who stole at the rectory there a tablecloth and

seven books, viz. 'The Orations of Cicero' (worth 14d.), 'De Re Curiali of
Balthasar Castalio' (14d.), 'Epithita Ciceroniana' (6d.), 'De Anima of
Ludovicus Vives' (2s.), 'Marcell Palengenium latine' (12d.), 'Tonstall In
Ethicis Aristotelis' (8d.), and 'Virgil' (12d.), belonging to Babigia Hulck
widow. The Little Hallingbury clergy list is defective at this period, so it
may be that Hulck was the previous rector and was succeeded by Rudyart,
or he may have been a temporary curate. At any rate, he was found not
guilty. As it is not possible to identify the books as belonging to the
rector's library, it seems unnecessary to comment on these items. Two
more books appear in the section on Burglary (p. 267).

Cutting or picking a purse furtively out of a man's pocket ranked as
robbery. For example, at Belchamp St. Paul's in 1574 a leather purse
(4d.) containing £4 6s. 8d. was stolen secretly from the person of John
Smythe; and another leather purse (1d). with 10s. 8d. from the person
of John Copsey at Nether (Little) Yeldham. In 1602 a purse (6d.) with
4s. in it was lifted from the person of Alice wife of Edward Broane
at Braintree (to be hanged). A fuller record of a cutpurse in action is
the recognizance of Thomas Ansell of Billericay sawyer to prosecute a
Fingringhoe seafaringman for cutting the purse from his wife's girdle
combined with the sailor's indictment for assaulting her and secretly
taking from her person 1d. and three races (roots) of ginger, two thimbles
and certain clasps, being in her purse. He confessed only to petty larceny.
A Brentwood spinster who took a 'gold piece called an angel' and 30s.
in a purse belonging to Thomas Wright (probably of Kelvedon Hall) was
also a pickpocket, Walter Brumley, a Brentwood glover, being charged
as an accessory; and a Northamptonshire labourer and three Chelmsford
labourers and a woman, who took the purses of five men, gaining £3 6s. 2d.
in all. Cutpurses could not claim clergy if the sum was above 12d.

The everlasting struggle to defend the coastal and estuarial marshes
accounts for the alleged theft by three Barking fishermen in 1601 of four
piles of wood (12d.) 'fixed in the bank there to strengthen it against the
inundation of the Thames, whereby the bank was weakened'. They were
acquitted.

Among unusual articles stolen were 40 lb. of tallow (5s.) in 1590, two
title-deeds of a Colchester house taken from the owner's own chest in
1570, and 'divers deeds' in a 'portmanteau' in 1587 (a bag used when
travelling on horseback, first recorded in the *New English Dictionary* only
three years earlier). A 'masty (mastiff) mongrel dog' was valued as
high as 20s., and cost the thief his life.

It was a grave crime for a servant to steal or embezzle his master's or
mistress's property. For the first case there is a deposition taken before
Edward Rich, J.P. John Hamonde confessed that on Monday before
Whit Sunday 1572 he came to Billericay and offered his service to John
Daivy, a shoemaker there, who took him on trial. After a fortnight, he was

sent to his father at Hornchurch to find out if he would give consent to his son being apprenticed to Daivy for five years. He did not go, but tarried about and returned that night to the town, was taken up by the watchman, carried to his master's house, and sent to bed. An hour afterwards he went to his master's chamber, took a purse out of his hose, removed the money ('how much he knows not'), stole 59s. 6d. out of the till of a chest in the same chamber, and ran off to South Benfleet and thence over the river to Rochester, where he spent 20s. of it. There he was traced and brought back to Essex. He admitted all this 'in the presence of eight gentlemen.' His master was bound over to prosecute him at the next Assizes, but the file for that Assize is missing. On being examined in 1599 a St. Osyth husbandman's servant told a lame story. After cleaning some wheat for his master, he took half a bushel to a house. The man was not at home, and the wife, in bed after bearing a child the day before, refused to accept the wheat, saying that she would not meddle with it. But he left the corn in the buttery, claiming that his purpose was to sell it for his master, and not to steal it.

A maidservant of Henry Sepon of Shenfield was indicted for stealing a cassock (15s.), a hat (4s.) and three shirts (10s.), 'contrary to the faith and confidence placed in her by her master and contrary to the statute for servants embezzling their masters' property' (1565). Two servants of Edward Raynolds of Great Oakley gentleman, described as husbandmen and being in their master's house, stole £5 10s.; one guilty, the other acquitted (1560). John Grene of Maldon butcher, in service with Evan Pryce gentleman, stole a sword and shield and a pair of linen sheets from him at Tendring; not guilty (1565). The dwelling-house of John Fownhall, a miller of 'Easterford' (Kelvedon) was broken into in 1566 by his servant, who took £8 from his chest; guilty. A few clothes, a 'bow of ewe', and £3 4s. 8d. belonging to two people were stolen by another man in the house of his master, William Bonner of St. Lawrence; not in prison (1566). A Great Canfield spinster left the service of her master, William Tyler husbandman, without licence, stealing two petticoats, four kerchers, an apron, a shirt and a piece of bacon. Three weeks later, at Stock, she broke into John Martindale's house, stealing more clothes. She pleaded pregnancy at the next Assizes, but the file is incomplete (1569). The last three are, of course, housebreaking charges. Seven more dishonest servants were before the Courts for sums of money between £3 and £14; one, a maidservant, broke open a chest to find £10 in it, and on being declared guilty she also pleaded that she was pregnant; another stole some clothes, made the same plea but was found not pregnant. A young servant, in charge of his master's flock of 18 sheep, decamped with them to Romford, where he sold them in open market (p. 283).

Very few weapons appear in the indictments, probably because most were worn or carried by their owners. A 'fowling piece' was stolen in 1590 from John Payne's house at Ingatestone. Priced at 20s. (*sic*), the thief was found guilty only to the value of 10½d. and was whipped. Payne was not the Catholic martyr of Ingatestone Hall, who had been executed for high treason in 1582 (p. 52). Apart from this, the whole list only amounts to three swords, two daggers, a rapier, and several bows with arrows. No jewel-hilted swords! But the Lord Chancellor's young cousin wore a gilt rapier on his poaching excursion (p. 236).

22

Housebreaking

Some housebreakings were narrated from the earliest Sessions and Assize files for 1556–61 (pp. 3, 8–9). In later years a number of famous mansions and other large houses received unwelcome visits. On 30 September 1579 the 'house' of the Earl of Sussex at Boreham (New Hall) was broken into by John Crosfield 'of Boreham yeoman' (the parish may be fictitious), when Frances his countess and the household were in residence. He removed a gilt bowl (worth £4), a silver bowl (30s.), a silver combcase (£4), and two silver trencher plates (30s.). Found guilty, he was hanged. Housebreaking and burglary were committed when the owner or a member of the family was at home; otherwise, as already explained, it was larceny.

Breaking into the house of Thomas Smith esquire at Blackmore (Priory) in 1586 a Stock labourer carried away a salt-cellar (£4), a pepper-box (30s.), and a tankard (£4), all silver-gilt, two silver spoons (13s. 4d.), and 1½ lb. woollen yarn (18d.). He was found not guilty for the plate, but guilty for the yarn to the value of 10d. only. Eight years earlier he and another labourer had been acquitted on a charge of burgling another house in Blackmore.

Four men broke into the house of Anthony Browne esquire (Weald Hall) in December 1600. Their takings were two silk quilts (£5 each), a train for a canopy of watchet (light blue) silk (£5), an embroidered bed tester and valance (£10), five taffeta curtains (£5), four silk-fringed (table) carpets of green cloth (£4), a taffeta cushion (5s.), and a pillowbeer (5s.). All were at large. Were these rich bedroom furnishings their real objective? (See plate 23.)

Substantial sums in cash were removed from several yeomen's houses. That of Gregory Stone at Great Bromley was broken into in 1598, when £86 was taken by John Payne and Henry Sammes, two gentlemen of Kirby. From the house of Richard Brydges of Great Stambridge yeoman in 1576 was stolen £35 'in coin' (they are not named in this case), also a coral tipped with silver, a thimble, a pin, a spoon, a mermaid, and an aglet, all of silver, and some silk and linen. The first item was an ornamental piece of coral, perhaps a baby's teething-ring;[1] an aglet was a tag

---

[1] Cf. 'six pieces of coral worth 2s.' stolen in 1601 (*Middlesex County Records*, i, 266).

or pendant to a dress; and a 'mermaid of silver' was among the bequests in a Kent will of 1464. The thief, William Holder of Witham, was apprehended at Romford by Robert Brydges, taken by him to Richard Cooke (of Gidea Hall, Romford), J.P., who gaoled him evidently in the Liberty of Havering prison. There he hanged himself on the 'iron pin on the stocks'. All this is learned from the Liberty coroner's inquest at Romford. The suicide's possessions were his horse, sword and dagger, cloak and other apparel, some grain, and 12d. in his purse; and £12 12s. 10d. of the £35 was in the custody of Thomas Turke, chief constable of the liberty, and another 20s. with Thomas Hare butcher.

The house of Leonard Barker, rector of Stanford-le-Hope, was broken into by two local men in 1573 and nine bushels of rye (20s.) were taken. One was found guilty and pleaded benefit of clergy; the other was acquitted. This document supplies the name of a rector at a period when there is a gap in the clergy list. A pair of 'petty chapmen' (pedlars) from Sussex and London stole some clothes in 1579 from the house of Christopher Mercere clerk. Both were guilty but read their neck-verse. The victim was apparently a curate, Edward Nowell the vicar perhaps being an absentee.

Housebreakings accompanied by violence were apparently uncommon. Six men and women, mostly related, 'with others unknown', in 1597 assaulted William Maldon in his Great Baddow home, also his wife, two daughters or sisters, and a manservant. Not satisfied with collecting £40, they also took away the barley, pease and hay from his garden. A Billericay man and a Laindon woman attacked Thomas Felsted in his house at Laindon with a dagger and stole £25 and some linen. She was found guilty as an accessory before the fact, as well as the thief.

Some of the wares stolen in grocers' shops are listed in two indictments (see also p. 8). The man who stole Pleshey communion cup in 1591 (p. 278) had been busy in the previous year. From Richard Hesseldyne's shop in Ingatestone he removed 16 dozen bone-laces, 2 lb. of pepper, 4 lb. of ginger, 1 lb. of cinnamon, 20,000 pins, and 1,000 needles! These were valued (as a total) at £4. He confessed. Earlier in the same month he had stolen 'divers pieces of linen' (40s.) at Great Leighs, for which he was also convicted. A Chelmsford tailor broke into John Tennatt's shop there and got away with 2 lb. of sugar (3s. 4d.), 8 oz. of cinnamon (2s. 8d.), ½ lb. of nutmegs (3s.), and 4 oz. of cloves (2s.). But the jury assessed their total value at only 10d., so he was whipped. A Chelmsford shoemaker's shop was broken into in 1564 by a labourer, whose loot amounted to 57 pairs of shoes (53s. 4d.). Charges of housebreaking occasionally mention specific rooms, backhouses, milkhouses, or barns. Housebreaking cases at Chelmsford and Colchester in 1589 and 1570 include the only references to a gallery (an attic store-place) and to 'evidences or charters' (title deeds) removed from a chest.

An indictment of 1566 gives one of the longest list of named coins in our records (see also pp. 3 and 9). A Finchingfield husbandman broke into the 'premises' (a term rarely used) of William Mortimer at Toppesfield. In addition to carrying off various articles of linen valued at 61s. 4d., he took £6 and the following gold coins (their value is given in brackets): a 'portague' (£4), a double sovereign (20s.), forty-nine angelets (each 10s.), twelve single sovereigns (each 10s.), eight English crowns (5s. each), four French crowns (6s. each), all belonging to Mortimer, £4 10s. in a purse and a ryal (10s.), and 36s. 8d., belonging to his two daughters. His total bag was therefore valued at £55 12s. The case was transmitted from the county justices to the Assizes, at which he was found not guilty. While it is interesting to find a portague – the Portuguese great crusado, kept by some people as an heirloom and valued according to the decade between £3 5s. and £4 10s., coins of much greater interest are revealed in a document of 1575, when Jasper Brown, a Hadleigh blacksmith, raided the house of John Bonner, a Leigh mariner. He stole £10 2s., eight 'pieces of money called quarters of dollars and royals of plate' worth 6s. 8d., also a silver flute worth 33s. 4d., with which he may have whiled away his calmer hours afloat. A 'royal of plate' was the *real de plata*, the eighth part of a Spanish dollar, and the English name for 'pieces of eight', i.e., eight reals. Perhaps the sailor had taken part in one of the expeditions when English ships overhauled and robbed Spanish treasure-galleons upon the high seas. Leigh was a busy little port, at which a generation later Samuel Purchas, rector of Eastwood, collected stories of travels in distant lands, including those of his 'near neighbour' Andrew Battell of Leigh, who had been captured by the Portuguese on the coast of Brazil and shipped to the Congo, where he lived for many years.[1] The accused was found not guilty.

[1] Samuel Purchas, *Purchas his Pilgrimage* (1614), book 7, ch. 9.

23

Burglary

There is not much difference between the total numbers of indictments for burglary and housebreaking (see Appendix D, p. 316). The robberies of plate in each category indicate how large an amount of silver was possessed by the more substantial Elizabethans, as Harrison remarked more than once. Only those burglaries and housebreakings of interest are related; a few others are mentioned in the sections on Cloth and Food stolen (pp. 292–9).

The earliest, but incomplete, Sessions and Assize records (1556–61) disclose no less than twenty cases of burglary, including one mortal attack, two big hauls of money and three visits to clergymen's houses (pp. 9–10). The house of Clement Sisley of Barking, J.P., was raided on 5 January 1567 by a party armed with swords and dags (pistols). There were five of them, all Londoners including William Rogers gentleman, and they attacked his five servants, getting away with four silver and gilt spoons and a salt-cellar (worth £6) and £6 in cash. Two London watermen 'abetted' them in a way that is obvious. All seven confessed and were hanged. The case was heard at a special Assizes at Stratford on 9 January and again on 20 January, the only recorded adjournment.

In 1579 William Reynoldes shearman, Gabriel Manneringe and John Bere yeomen, all of Maldon, with daggers and other instruments broke open a chest in John Steven's inn there and took away £17 10s. and a gold ring (13s. 4d.). All were found guilty. From his will, proved in 1586, in which he calls himself John Steven *alias* Fawnce, we find that he owned the 'New Inn' in Maldon; incidentally, the first witness to the will was George Gifford (the town preacher, p. 53).[1] Steven did not live in the inn (he was a linen-draper), but that, too, was burgled three times earlier in the same month by another man, who stole 20s. from his tenant, 48s. and 'divers goods' from one guest, and £3 2s. and three rings (£5) from another guest. He also was convicted. A widow's house at South Benfleet was burgled in 1580 and she lost £25. Two Prittlewell labourers were involved; the verdict for the thief is not given, but the 'procurer and abettor' was acquitted. In 1585 a customer of John Lilley, the innkeeper of Terling, suffered the loss of his chest containing 10s., his hose, six pound weights, and a silver toothpick.

[1] Essex Record Office, D/ABW 336/34.

There are six other cases in which men committed a series of three or more burglaries. In 1566 a Laindon labourer always chose to burgle at 9.0 p.m., breaking into two houses there and another at Billericay belonging to Henry Theedam, a linendraper. The total takings were of little value and included 3 lb. of raisins (6d.) and 3 dozen points (tagged laces). On a November evening in 1567 two weavers of Writtle and Chignal St. James first stole four 'fishes called two warp of ling' (a warp meant four fish) (5s.) and two hens (12d.) belonging to Thomas Barker, a gentleman of Chignal, took some wheat and more fowls elsewhere in the parish, and then went 'as vagabonds' to a Writtle man's house at midnight, 'banged at the door and demanded that he should open it willingly or they would break it down and come in to look for certain sums of money that were in his keeping, unless he gave the money to them through the window'. At the same Assizes a fourth charge of robbing a man on the highway at Hornchurch produced a verdict of not guilty. A little later they went to the gallows. A mariner burgled three houses at Elmstead in 1570, removing a few clothes and a piece of ox hide. Later that year three Elsenham labourers took part in five burglaries, two at Clavering on 1 December, the rest at Berden, Great Hallingbury and Little Laver on 2, 18 and 20 December, collecting an assortment of clothes and linen, odd bits of food including three 'rounds of brawn' (4s. 4d.), and putting the women in two of the houses in fear of their lives. They were found guilty on all counts. In 1590 two Mundon men stole £10 and much cloth of various sorts (see Appendix B, p. 313) from the house of William Norris at Burnham, which suggests that he was a merchant or ship-owner whose house may have stood on the wharf. One was acquitted; the other had not been caught.

Perhaps the most remarkable discovery is the burglary that took place in December 1584 at the house of Philip Earl of Arundel at Romford. Anne, his countess, and 'her whole household' were in residence. The deed was perpetrated by Francis Morris *alias* Sames of London cook, Stephen Prentice of Romford blacksmith, and Robert Robynson of London yeoman. They concentrated solely on the great store of valuable plate, comprising a parcel-gilt basin and ewer (valued at £23), fifteen 'argent parcel gilt' trencher plates (£34), fifteen silver spoons (£6 10s.), a gilt salt with a cover (£6 10s.), three silver wine pots (£20), a great silver beer pot (£12), three silver bowls (£15), five silver jugs (£26), and five silver salts (£15), all belonging to the earl: a total valuation of £158. Morris confessed, and was 'remanded without judgement', but the others had not been caught. The part played by Prentice was doubtless a vital one. Where was the earl's house? One or two substantial Elizabethan houses were still standing in Romford until last century, but no association with the Fitzalans or the Howards Earls of Arundel is found. A tenuous link with Pyrgo in Havering is provided by a brief reference to the death in 1580 of Philip's predecessor, Henry the 12th Earl, in a short history of Pyrgo,[1] but this mansion belonged to the Greys.

It is possible, however, that ascription of the earl's ownership of the burgled house is a legal fiction, and that the countess was only staying there temporarily. Philip was the eldest son of Thomas Howard, the fourth Duke of Norfolk, and was known by the courtesy title of Earl of Surrey. He succeeded to the earldom of Arundel in 1580. His marriage to Anne Dacre took place in 1571, when they were both fourteen. The countess openly professed Romanism in 1582 and was committed to the custody of Sir Thomas Shirley in Sussex. Soon afterwards Philip came under suspicion and the Queen placed him under house arrest in London. Three months before the burglary he himself adopted the Old Faith, and in April 1585 he attempted to flee from England, was captured, and sent to the Tower. On 7 July 1585 Anne gave birth to Thomas, the future second earl who was to be renowned as an art collector, at Finchingfield parsonage. The Howards' right of patronage of the benefice had been passed to the Kempes of Spains Hall, Finchingfield (p. 110), who were tenants of the rectory manor. Shortly after her son's birth Anne returned to London, on Elizabeth's orders. This stormy period of Anne's life has already been told in some detail,[2] but nothing has previously been known of the burglary. It would seem that she had left London to escape the Queen's displeasure, and that her sojourn at Romford was perhaps only a short one during her journey towards Finchingfield, thirty miles beyond. She was particularly unfortunate with her plate and jewels. Soon after Philip's committal to the Tower, her London house was searched; her goods, even her coach, were seized; and she was forced to sell her jewels to pay her remaining servants' wages.

Two burglaries mention books. In 1591, the owner and his servants being in the house, a Chelsea labourer stole from George White of Hutton (Hall) 'Le historie des gueres d'Italie' (so the scribe has it) valued at 16d. as well as a carpet worth 20s. Ten years later an Earls Colne carpenter broke into the house of Thomas Sandford gentleman (perhaps Brome House[3]) shortly before midnight, 'put him in bodily fear', and took £15 from a chest, a musket worth 16s., and 'Eliottes Dictionary' valued at 20s.; and, the indictment adds, Walter Newman of Earls Colne mason, before the felony, was 'consulted' by the burglar. It is surprising that the thieves bothered to take a French book and Sir Thomas Elyot's Latin-English *Dictionary* (1538). White, at any rate, would have had only three more years to use it. A brass inscription in the church commemorates

[1] M. Browne, *Yearly Records of Pyrgo Park* with lineage of its Ancient Families (1889). I owe this reference to the Borough Librarian of Havering.

[2] Eliza Vaughan, 'The Birthplace of Thomas Howard, Earl of Arundel' (*Essex Review*, xxxi, 225–36), quoting partly from Mary Hervey, *Life of Thomas Howard, Earl of Arundel* (1920).

[3] Morant, *History of Essex*, ii, 223.

him. He was a Catholic and mentions Sir John Petre as his especial friend in his interesting will.

Had a burglary at Walthamstow in 1597 occurred thirty years earlier, one of England's most distinguished scholars might have been deprived of some of his treasured books. For two of her girlhood years the future Queen was tutored by Roger Ascham, who after 1564 apparently lived at Salisbury Hall in Walthamstow (p. 103). His second son Thomas was posthumously born in 1569. Roger's widow, Margaret, married Thomas Rampston (p. 109) later in that year. Litigation which broke out in 1594 shows that Thomas Ascham was still then living at Walthamstow, and the burglary three years later extends this date, though it is not certain that it took place at Salisbury Hall.[1] The burglars were two labourers of Leytonstone and Chelmsford, who were charged with stealing a trunk (20d.), a silk 'rash' (smooth silk) gown and a white hat (2s.) from Thomas Ascham's house. Two more labourers of Chelmsford and Walthamstow were indicted for receiving. 'No true bill' for the receivers; the others were hanged.

A Londoner burgled the house of George Wythers of Witham gentleman in 1588, stealing a silver cup worth £3 6s. 8d. A local man unlawfully received it. What relationship, if any, he had with his namesake, rector of Danbury and archdeacon of Colchester, is not known. In the same year Thomas Markaunt, a gentleman of Great Holland, fared badly. When his wife Jane was at home he was robbed by three Great Oakley and Ramsey labourers of £140, two gold rings (£6) and a silver salt cellar (£3), all found in his chest. Two of them paid a second visit five months later, when the owner was there, but then they only took 17s., a hat and a piece of Milan fustian from a coffer. All three were hanged.

In 1597 the house of Christopher Burford at Laindon was burgled by a man who removed £53, a double-gilt salt (£6), a silver tun (small drinking vessel) parcel-gilt, a jug trimmed with silver (each worth £3), and a dozen spoons (£6 8s. 4d.). He confessed and was hanged.

Was a raid planned in 1600 because an old Essex J.P. was known to be on his deathbed? A rich haul at any rate was achieved by seven Londoners. The victim was Edward Riche of Horndon-on-the-Hill esquire, he and Joan his wife and all their household being at home. These burglars also confined themselves mostly to the plate and jewellery. They took 3 parcel-gilt goblets (£10), an all-gilt standing cup (£6), an all-gilt standing salt (£6), a parcel-gilt salt (£6), a third gilt salt (£3), an all-gilt trencher salt (£1), 2 gilt-silver jugs (£10), 2 silver tuns (£4), an all-gilt cup (£3), a silver cup (30s.), 8 silver and gilt spoons (30s.), 13 silver spoons (£3), a gold chain (£10), 4 gold rings (£3), and 4 more gold rings with precious stones (value illegible); also £60 in cash. All the accused were at large. The

---

[1] Information about the two Thomases kindly supplied by the Borough Librarian and Curator of Waltham Forest and the Editor of *V.C.H., Essex*.

house of John Butler esquire (J.P., of Thoby Priory) in Mountnessing was burgled in the same year, he and his household being there, by two Margaretting women who were charged with stealing shirts and linen valued at £9 13s. 4d. Both were acquitted.

A burglary at James Wilkinson's house in Braintree in 1597 led to his losing two cups, one worth as much as £8 (probably all gilt, the adjective being illegible), the other worth 20s. His will, proved two years afterwards, shows that he was innkeeper of the 'George'. The names of the thieves were Edward Stranguyshe and John Mychell, and Edward Buncheley and John Hammersley were procurers and receivers. They were all gentlemen of Braintree, except Hammersley who was a blacksmith. One February night in the same year two Purfleet watermen left their river and sallied inland breaking into a house at Shenfield. Their booty amounted to £7 and some cloth (50s.). They were hanged, but the receiver, another waterman, was acquitted.

A labourer and two spinsters of Chelmsford, at monthly intervals in 1598, committed two burglaries and a housebreaking there and at Orsett, getting away with a variety of kitchen articles and some food. Another Chelmsford labourer incited and abetted them on each occasion. The thieves were all found guilty of felony but not of burglary; the labourer read, but the women could not read and were hanged. The accessory was found not guilty and was bound over to good behaviour. Also in 1598 an Inworth carpenter burgled Woodham Mortimer rectory. Nicholas Johnson (1568–1611) lost a lot of clothes, pewter and kitchen implements (worth 59s. 8d. in all), and 'a great rib of beef' (3s. 4d.), and the thief lost his life. A labourer in April and May 1601 committed two burglaries at Fordham and West Bergholt, stealing some clothes and kitchen implements, also three acts of larceny there and at Earls Colne, taking 18 sheep and a horse, for which he was hanged.

In 1601 two labourers and a woman burgled the house of Thomas Plumbe junior at Belchamp Walter and stole a silver goblet (20s.), 2 stone pots tipped with silver, and other articles. The men were at large; the woman, found guilty of felony but not of burglary, was remanded for pregnancy. Ten days later one of the labourers and the woman burgled the house of George Harlackenden gentleman and stole six silver spoons (18s.): similar verdict and judgement. At the same Assizes two husbandmen of Great Baddow and Springfield burgled the house of Humphrey Baldwyn gentleman, taking four bushels of wheat. They were also charged with putting his servants in fear of their lives, but were acquitted despite the testimony of five men including the servants. The juries dealt with four further burglars. In two cases they were hanged; in the others, acquitted.

Another series of planned excursions, mostly to one house, took place in 1589. In November John Springfield of Chelmsford bricklayer, John Norton carpenter and Jonas Standishe haberdasher, both of Springfield,

broke into William Doggett's house at Wickford, taking 26 cheeses (30s.).
In December the first two and Thomas Crosse of Widford glazier again
entered the same house, taking three women's gowns, three women's
petticoats, a cloak, a coverlet, a blanket, eleven ells of blanketing and
eight pieces of linen, worth £6. Two days earlier the same pair, with
John Glascocke labourer and Richard Brainwood innholder, both of
Chelmsford, broke into the outside kitchen of Francis Bowsey at Chignal
St. James, running off with five cocks and two hens (6s.) and 30 lb. butter,
thirty cheeses and two sacks (40s. in all). The result: Springfield not
guilty of the first charge but guilty of the others, to be hanged; Norton
and Standishe not in gaol; Crosse and Glascocke guilty of felony but not
of burglary, read; Brainwood not guilty.

Two interesting features are exhibited in cases which came before
Quarter Sessions in 1581. John Pepper of Hatfield Peverel was indicted
for breaking into the house of Bridget Wood at Little Baddow 'with intent
to rob', stealing her purse with 7d. in it. The jurors were confronted with
a problem. 'We find as follows', they returned, 'that John Pepper did
break a hole in a wall in the night time, and so put his hand into the
house, the said Bridget being in the house, and so took hold of the purse
being about her, and pulled her with the hold he had of the purse into the
wall and by violence took away her purse; and whether he be guilty of
burglary we know not, therefore we desire the help of the Court, and if the
Court do think that the said breaking of the hole and pulling away the
purse be burglary, then we find him guilty of the burglary also; if not,
we find him not guilty of the burglary but guilty of the felonious taking
of the purse and money.' The justices were equally uncertain. So he was
sent back to gaol until the next gaol delivery. The case then came up at the
Assizes, but we are left in the dark about the final result. At the same
Sessions Pepper had been tried for a separate and straightforward theft
for which he was acquitted. The other burglary, itself of no intrinsic
interest, produced a verdict of guilty. 'Upon this he said he was a clerk
and sought benefit of clergy, but because upon inspection of his left
thumb it appeared plainly to the Court that benefit of clergy had been
elsewhere allowed him and that he had been branded on the left thumb
with the letter T, therefore the Court replied that benefit of clergy should
not be allowed him.' But, as related in the next paragraph, a statute
passed six years earlier would in any case have deprived him of claiming
clergy. The justices ordered the prosecutor to 'produce a record testifying
that he (the burglar) had elsewhere had benefit of clergy.' In the meantime, back to gaol. In 1597 Thomas Clarke, a Great Bardfield husbandman, was sent to the gallows for burglary involving only 12d. in money.

Thomas Quilter, a Writtle blacksmith, turned burglar in 1600, when
he broke into Geoffrey Beckett's windmill there, his servant Thomas Luckyn
being in the mill, but he stole a mere bushel of wheat (5s.) belonging

to Jerome Weston esquire (J.P., of Skreens manor-house in Roxwell). He was found guilty of the second charge, and read, but acquitted of burglary, probably because benefit of clergy had been taken away for burglary by the Act of 18 Elizabeth, c.7 (1575). Doubtless the same reason led a jury in 1575 to devalue 13½ yards of hair cloth burgled at Shalford from 8s. 8d. to 10d., for which the defendant got off with a whipping.

When drawing indictments for burglary, it was occasionally necessary to give the hour as well as the date to ensure that the felony had been committed in the hours of darkness : between 4 and 5 p.m. (9 January), about 7 p.m. (30 October), 5 a.m. (25 May), about the fourth hour of the day (18 May), and twice 'at dawn' are the six examples of the practice. Burglary was in fact defined as taking place 'between the sun-setting and the sun-rising.'

Very occasionally a house was burgled without anything being stolen but the occupant being 'put in fear of his life'. This offence ranked merely as trespass, not felony. In most cases 'with intent to despoil his goods' was included in the charge but the verdict was 'not guilty.' Exceptionally, however, a Feering labourer who broke into a house in the parish at midnight with that intention was hanged in 1597. A more violent incident in 1587 involved Charles Adsley, a Bocking clothier, two Great Waltham husbandmen, with many unknown persons. They broke into the house of Henry Purkas and assaulted him, his wife and five others (perhaps servants), with intent to despoil them. The grand jury's verdict was *ignoramus* for one; the clothier and the third man had fled, but the latter was found not guilty.

Elizabethan Essex houses were mostly timber-framed, the interstices between the studs being usually filled with wattle and daubed clay. Breaking through such walls, as we have seen, was an alternative to breaking windows or forcing locks. The mysterious remarks about the walls at Master John's, Mountnessing (p. 96), may have been made after such a forcible entry. A suspected sheep-stealer in Kent, on whom the constable descended during a search, 'tumbled out of his bed', and broke *out* through the wall, 'being a simple cottage.'[1]

---

[1] *Kentish Sources : Crime and Punishment*, 37.

24

Highway Robbery

Every schoolboy knows of the exploits of Dick Turpin, born in 1706 and bred in an Essex alehouse. It is common knowledge, too, that many roads in England in Turpin's century and later were infested by hundreds of other highwaymen. But, as with some other aspects of social history, many writers have bewailed the dearth of accurate facts about highway robbery in earlier periods. For the latter half of the sixteenth century the Essex records go some way towards filling this gap although it is unfortunate that only one deposition about highway robberies is preserved. The reader will find none of our desperadoes' exploits narrated in detail.

What were the biggest hauls and what was the booty? Which highways were frequented by robbers? Is there evidence of gangs or of several attacks by the same men? Were any gentlemen involved as highwaymen? Did they wound their victims? How many of the villains were local men or foreigners to Essex? With over sixty recorded incidents an attempt may be made to answer some of these questions. These have all been analysed in Appendix A (p. 308), and only cases of interest are now described. The table shows that money and goods valued at £1,000 were plundered by those highwaymen who were charged.

The biggest plunder taken by convicted highway robbers in Elizabethan Essex was collected at Corringham on two days in October 1575, when a pair of robbers, Reynold Peckham and Henry Iseley, both given as gentlemen, 'with cudgels, swords and fists', assaulted five men. From John Wakeman they took £180 in money, from Thomas Lynsey £115, from John Kinge £60, two gold rings worth £4, and his horse worth £4, and from James Drake £38 and a gold ring worth 13s. 4d. On one of these days, at noon and in the same parish, they also robbed William Jeffrey of Rawreth of £24 belonging to Edward Bartlett of Hockley. The total valuation was £425 13s. 4d. In the attacks on Wakeman and Jeffrey they were joined by Thomas Tysdale yeoman, but by the time the case had reached the Essex Assizes he had been hanged after trial at the Kent Assizes four days earlier. Peckham and Iseley are termed 'of Corringham'. Both men belonged to well-established Kent families,[1] and the evidence suggests that they had come over Tilbury ferry from Kent. Through Corringham ran the highway between Leigh, then a prosperous little port, and London.

[1] Inf. kindly given by Dr. F. Hull, County Archivist of Kent, and Dr. P. Clark.

The next highest sum stolen was in 1599, when John Smyth, described as of Feering gentleman but probably again a mere 'legal' appellation, was indicted for highway robbery, taking £140 in a 'wallet' (traveller's bag) from the person of Thomas Whitefield belonging to his companion Thomas Rochester and £5 18s. belonging to Whitefield. This presumably took place at Feering, on the Great Essex Road from London to Colchester.

In 1585 Richard Banckes was robbed of his gold chain worth £30, and on another day Thomas Crysall was assaulted by the same man, intending to rob him. As the assailant is described in the first indictment as of Chishall and in the second as of Stanway, the encounters evidently occurred in these parishes, the latter being on the same London road. He was 'not in prison' at the time of his trial.

An indictment of 1567 is less terse. Two named men, 'with others unknown', jumped out from the roadside at Brentwood on Christopher Rudding about 4.0 a.m. one November day as he was riding towards London. They bound him with two sacks, then threw him violently into the roadside ditch, having robbed him of £29 17s. 6d. Both were found not guilty. In 1571 a Londoner, either alone or with a confederate, lurked near the same highway at Great Ilford and Stratford. In three successive months Robert Glover of Navestock husbandman, William Good of Hornchurch wharfinger (the parish runs down to the Thames), and Richard Bronner of London poulterer were robbed of £5, £16 and £1 respectively. On the same thoroughfare, on the further side of Chelmsford at Springfield, a man was relieved of £29 in 1580. Seven men of Chelmsford and Little Waltham assaulted four travellers there in 1596, robbing one of £28 but the others only of small sums. An eighth man, a Chelmsford labourer, was also charged with inciting and procuring the gang to commit the felony. This time the defendants definitely belonged to several neighbouring parishes. Four of them were butchers and one a cutler. Two were hanged; two remanded to prison; the rest were at large.

One of the two London–Cambridge roads lay through Waltham Forest, in which robbers waited for their prey. A gang from London made up of four butchers and a tanner, perhaps frustrated in an intended cattle-stealing expedition, lay hiding at Snaresbrook (in the parish of Wanstead) 'in the Forest of Waltham' in March 1587. They attacked Robert Dawes, taking 45s. and his horse and saddle worth £6. They were all found guilty; they had fled, but during the three months before the Assizes two had been caught and were in Newgate gaol. John Clarke of Chingford robbed an unknown man there of £3 10s.; two Chingford labourers robbed a woman of 6s. at Walthamstow (acquitted); and a man robbed another at Woodford of his cloak and hat worth 14s. and 12s. cash; all these incidents probably took place in the Forest. A robbery in the parish of Waltham Abbey in 1597 by a sailor may also have been in the Forest; he appropriated 39s. 7d. and 8d. from two men. George Wood husbandman

U

and Thomas Garnet gentleman were accused in 1600 of robbing Henry Field at Walthamstow of his cloak worth 10s. and 12s. in money. The jury returned 'no true bill' for Garnet, and Field's case went to the Lent Assizes, when he was at large, but at the Summer Assizes he was acquitted. Two mariners, nominally of Ingatestone, a few days before Christmas 1587 robbed a man there of 24s. 8d., his cloak worth 26s. 8d. and his knife ; and another there of 4s. and his knife ; they then escaped. This pair and the culprit of 1597 may have been discharged seamen.

Other roadside woods also hid theives, such as John Pudney of Wickham (Bishops) labourer, who robbed John Maldon of 14s. in 'Poddes Wood' by the highway at Messing. (The Maldon–Colchester road still runs, dark and narrow between two woods here, one of which is the large and ancient Pod's Wood, a name first found as far back as 1289 ; in the last War it hid ammunition dumps.) The incident took place in November 1595, and on New Year's Day 1596 Thomas Ive esquire (perhaps of East Donyland) had written to John Sammes, J.P., asking him to warn Quarter Sessions that Pudney had been convicted, with others, of highway robbery in Norfolk, so that if acquitted by the Essex court he should be re-committed to prison to receive the verdict for the Norfolk indictment. In the meantime the deputy of the Clerk of the Peace for Norfolk had notified his Essex counterpart of the indictment of John Pudney and Thomas Fuller, both of Great Henny, at the Norfolk Quarter Sessions in May 1594 before Sir John Paston and other justices for robbery ; they had failed to appear at four sessions and at the fifth they were duly outlawed, having forfeited the huge sum of £400. Since then Fuller had also forfeited another £40 for failing to appear at the West Suffolk Quarter Sessions at Bury. In 1598 a labourer of High Easter not only assaulted Hugh Northedge in Park Lane there (thus named in 1351 and still so called), robbing him of 11s. and his hat, but also burgled William Serredge's house, stealing two flitches of bacon, another hat, and odds and ends (guilty, hanged).

At Ridgewell (on the Colchester–Cambridge road) John Loker *alias* Riddesdale junior of Finchingfield linendraper was relieved in 1602 of £29 9s. 8d. and his mount. The indictment gives 'both at large'. The victim's deposition reveals that he was travelling to 'St. Edmundsbury', when he was set upon by two men, one of whom he knew – Richard Deane, born in Moulton in Norfolk, aged about 28.

In 1585 Thomas Turke of Romford gentleman, sometimes in company with a Brentwood labourer and two others, committed three robberies on roads at Great and Little Waltham and Great Leighs, collecting a total of £27 16s. Turke was pardoned by the general royal pardon of February 1586. Surprisingly, he seems to be identical with the chief constable of the Queen's Liberty of Havering-atte-Bower some years earlier (p. 263).

In 1568 a London tailor robbed a man of £4 at Saffron Walden ; and in 1599 Henry Payne of Aldham gentleman assaulted a man at Henham (on the Stortford–Walden road), taking £5 (acquitted). At Gestingthorpe two men were attacked in 1597 by a pair of highwaymen, one losing £10, his cloak and sword, the other 2s. 4d. (both were hanged) ; and in 1596 at Lawling (in Latchingdon) three Blackmore men stole £10 5s. 3d. (two hanged, the third at large).

Only in three instances is personal injury recorded. On 31 October 1579 two Dartford (Kent) men were at Sible Hedingham. Two charges were preferred against them, for stealing a horse worth £8 belonging to Elizeus Hartop esquire, and for 'intending to murder and despoil Roger Aglande and Roland Grene, following them thence to Stifford, and by the bridge there assaulting them with swords and daggers, wounding and illtreating them.' Here is a case for which some depositions are sadly needed. If the indictment is correct the miscreants caught up with their victims only after a pursuit across Essex from north to south, nearly forty miles. Two coopers and a joiner of Thorpe-le-Soken wounded a man, taking his purse with 2s. and a gold ring worth 10s. (the joiner was not guilty, the coopers had fled). In 1601 four Woodford men were indicted at the Assizes for wounding two men at Epping, but not of robbing (both acquitted). But at the previous Quarter Sessions the justices had received a letter from Francis Gaudy, an Essex J.P., who was also a justice of the Queen's Bench, written from Serjeants' Inn and stating that the two victims had declared that they had been violently attacked and robbed of 47s., and because it appeared to him to be 'very foul and fit to be strictly examined' he advised that the defendants be bound over to the Assizes. Epping also was one of the parishes that included part of Waltham Forest.

Occasionally the reward was trifling for the risk of swinging. A Heybridge tinker and a Maldon weaver at about 4 a.m. on a winter's night only gained 7s. after assaulting a man at Purleigh (one guilty, the other acquitted) ; a man merely got a hat after cudgelling John Coxe clerk (not the rector) at Runwell ; and at Hatfield (more likely Hatfield Peverel on the London–Colchester road than Hatfield Broad Oak) three men beat and wounded their victim, but their share-out was only 5d. each. Even worse was the princely 2d. with a pair of gloves worth 3d. appropriated by three Essex men at Great Baddow (on the Maldon road) ; the first was also convicted of cattle-stealing and housebreaking and was hanged, but the others had escaped.

Of the robberies which took place on the Essex roads during our period the scoundrels were indicted in 65 cases. How many people were robbed without the rascals being charged must, of course, be a matter of pure speculation. A number between five and ten times greater is perhaps a fair estimate. In addition there are two indictments for robbery on or near a footpath. The first is most exceptional because it occurred twelve years before the case came before the Assizes. Late one evening, eight months before Elizabeth became queen, a Witham man assaulted and wounded a Braintree glover on the head on a path from Cressing to Witham, robbing him of £6 13s. 4d. and a Witham butcher of £8 18s. 4d. (guilty). In the other case (1596) the grand jury considered a charge against Richard Denham of North Fambridge yeoman for assaulting John Tabor one summer afternoon on a common footway at Stow Maries and for robbing him of 3s. 4d. Their verdict was a true bill for the battery, no true bill for the felony.

It is interesting to find that the Thames was regarded as a highway. In 1594 the justices apparently had some doubt about an indictment. 'We do find', a paper document on the Assize file begins, but it is not clear whether 'we' were the justices in Quarter Sessions who sent the case to the Assizes or the Assize justices. Four men one night had entered a hoy (a small boat) in the river at Purfleet, 'being a common highway for passage for boats and hoys and other vessels with their carriages (i.e. goods) upon the Thames.' The hoy was about twenty-five rods from the shore and about twenty rods from the main channel towards the Essex side. With a fowling piece they assaulted a man in the hoy, stealing his gun and 24s. in money. 'If this be felony and robbery', the jurors opined, 'then we find them guilty, but if it be not felony or robbery then we find them not guilty.'

It would seem that a presentment in 1591 refers to trees behind which robbers could lurk. Between Dunmow and Little Canfield, on the highway to Bishop's Stortford (Stane Street) 'certain trees are standing, to the great danger of those that travel that way, for there hath been an attempt given in that place.'

While most highway robbers' objectives were money, rings and jewellery, it is not surprising to find that the chief industrial products of Essex and East Anglia were sometimes equally attractive to the thief, who could probably sell or use textile goods as readily as jewellery. Some of the travellers carrying cloth were perhaps merchants or clothiers, while others were presumably their servants. Five robberies involved textiles. In 1577 Anthony Mychell of London gentleman and John Smythe *alias* Gamwell and Walter Cooke of Brentwood yeomen assaulted Thomas Paynter and Michael Strutt there. They stole £49 in cash and five yards of bays (worth 15s.) and a green broadcloth (£6) belonging to Alice Parkin widow and took both their horses. Smythe confessed; the others escaped. On the highway at Springfield two pieces of linen cloth worth 20 marks were forcibly taken by a man, who also escaped (1588). Three Hertford men attacked one carrying 'divers parcels of taffeties' belonging to another and worth £10, which they appropriated. The theft took place at the Four Want Way (the Essex term for crossroads) in Great Parndon in 1590. On the same Hertford–Harlow road three years afterwards three men took a well-laden horse with its pack of linen worth as much as £40 and 30s. in money, again apparently from a servant. Two men and a woman were also charged with receiving. All the defendants were of Clavering, three of the men apparently of the same family of Barly. The robbers were all found guilty, but one was at large; two of the receivers were acquitted; the woman was convicted and claimed pregnancy. At Harlow, which could mean either the same road or the London–Harlow–Cambridge road, six ells of holland cloth (12s.) were taken in 1598; and at Latton, which also might be either road, the same robber assaulted another man, but again collected little booty.

William Harrison has two passages in which he writes of ostlers and other inn servants being in league with highwaymen, to whom they passed useful information about wayfarers' baggage and routes.[1] For obvious reasons, such informers would usually escape detection, and the Assize records yield virtually nothing to confirm Harrison's remarks. Of the two thefts by ostlers, the first as well as the second may have been cases of simple larceny. In 1566 a Chelmsford ostler was charged with aiding and abetting a fellow townsman of stealing 3s. from a man's purse at Moulsham; both were acquitted. Two years later two ostlers were found guilty of stealing £26 from their master, Richard Rodes, innholder of Kelvedon.

No Elizabethan Dick Turpin's exploits seem to be chronicled in other county records, but Ludovick Grevill, Sir William Petre's son-in-law, was reported to the Privy Council as a notorious highwayman and his end was tragic.[2] Indicted at the Warwickshire Assizes in 1589 he bravely endured the *peine forte et dure* to avoid his estate being forfeited. Twelve years earlier the Council had dealt with a highway robbery between Coventry and Birmingham by '11 lewd persons upon 4 yeomen of Kent, from whom they took the value of £200, and after escaped, notwithstanding hue and cry presently made after them, not as yet heard of.' Sir John Throgmorton was enjoined to convene local J.P.s to enquire into it.[3] And doubtless in Essex, too, many highway robberies never reached the Courts because the result of hue and cry after such ruffians was 'not as yet heard of.'

---

[1] Harrison, *Description of England*, 238, 398–9.
[2] *Acts of the Privy Council*, xii, 30; Emmison, *Tudor Secretary*, 287.
[3] *Ibid.*, x, 47.

25

Church Thefts

As in other centuries parish church possessions, even lead roofing, were sometimes the thieves' objective. A communion cup (53s. 4d.) and another cup (10s.) were stolen at Wickham St. Paul's about 11 p.m. in 1579, and a communion cup (£3) at Margaret Roothing in 1587 (plate 24). The church was burgled by two men in the former case, a churchwarden's house by a single thief in the latter. The accused in each case were hanged. Both communion cups must have been recovered, as each parish still possesses a cup dated 1562. It was during 1562–64 that many of the then surviving pre-Reformation or Marian chalices were sold and exchanged for 'decent' cups, in accordance with Archbishop Parker's wishes. The cost of the new communion cup of Great Dunmow is given in the churchwardens' book as £6 7s., and the rather exact valuation (53s. 4d.) of the Wickham cup was doubtless taken from the wardens' accounts. Also about 11 p.m. on the same 24 September the two men went off with some bed linen, table linen, a doublet and a pair of 'gaskins' (breeches), worth £4 8s. 4d. in all, belonging to one of the churchwardens. Did they find a key of the church in his house and then proceed to the church? The indictment definitely states that they broke into the church.

The man who broke into a house, probably a warden's at Pleshey, and took a communion cup (£4) in 1591, also removed domestic silver and £30 in money. The cup now in use is modern.[1] In 1567 the belfry of East Donyland church was forcibly entered by Richard Edwards of Colchester 'kember' (comber) and John George of Lavenham (Suffolk) butcher, who took a bell valued at £6. They were found not guilty.

Four sheets of lead worth £3, presumably stripped from the roof, were taken from Wennington church in 1568. Until very recently the tiny village consisted only of the manor-house and a few cottages. The culprit was pilloried. No further lead hauls are recorded until the end of the reign. In 1601 'two hundred fothers' worth 26s. 8d. were stolen from Feering church; nobody was arrested. (A fother of lead was about 20 cwt., but it seems to denote a theft of 2 cwt.)[2] Next year a bricklayer stole 40 lb. of lead (3s.) from Debden church; he was acquitted.

---

[1] W. J. Pressey (ed.), *The Church Plate of Essex* (1926), 229, 148, which records many thefts but not these.

[2] *Middlesex County Records*, i, 242 ('six hundred pounds weight of sheet lead' stolen in 1599 and valued at £3 6s. 8d.).

Feering church had been raided eight years earlier, when the parish armour was removed. The thief stole four calivers (40s.), four (powder) flasks and touch boxes (13s. 4d.), five swords (16s. 8d.), a dagger and a belt (2s). Proved guilty, he was found to have 'read before' (the brand-mark on his hand would have revealed his having previously claimed benefit of clergy), so he was undoubtedly hanged. To have carried off ten weapons including the calivers (light muskets), apparently unaided, suggests that he had broken into the church after dark. Every parish became responsible for providing arms by the Act of 4 & 5 Philip and Mary, c.2 (1557), and a few later lists of armour stored in churches survive in parish archives.[1]

The incomplete Middlesex records contain no Elizabethan indictments for thefts of church goods, but three of Mary's time illustrate the obligation to buy new chalices, vestments and the like to replace those which parishes had sold under Edward VI. In these incidents, churchwardens of two Buckinghamshire and one Essex parishes were evidently relieved of such plate and altar linen on their homeward journeys. At High Holborn on 27 August 1555 the two wardens of Arkesden lost their newly acquired red silk cope (36s. 8d.), altar-cloth (12d.), alb (6s. 8d.), and amice (hood) (2s.), all of linen, corporas cloth (on which the bread and wine were placed in the mass) (5s.), and sacring bell (2d.). The thief was Simon Cosyn of Saffron Walden, who must have known of their visit.[2] Three discharged soldiers, who had landed at Dover a few days before Christmas 1596, broke into Charing church at night, 'saying there was good hope to find some plate and other good things there,' but all they found were service books.[3]

---

[1] See F.G. Emmison, *Catalogue of Essex Parish Records* (Essex Record Office, 2nd edn., 1966), 17.
[2] *Middlesex County Records*, i, 24 (also preface, p. 1).
[3] *Kentish Sources : Crime and Punishment*, 38.

26

Livestock and Cloth

Cattle

In many parts of Essex, especially the east and north-east, wide stretches of common or heath afforded free grazing to thousands of animals. In the east and south-east lay the coastal marshlands and in the south-west the royal Forest of Waltham. Essex had been largely enclosed, much of it at an early date when woodland was cleared. But the Saxon open-field system had been implanted over much of north-west Essex, and this area extended also along the northern and western boundaries and towards the centre. Most of these common fields remained open until the parliamentary enclosure period of about 1760–1860. After harvest the stripholders exercised their grazing rights over the stubble when the open fields virtually became big commons. In the same way the common meadows were open after haymaking. As in most of the other counties except in the narrow sunken lanes of Devon and Cornwall, some of the roadside verges were grazed. It was not easy for the owners to guard their sheep, horses and cattle effectively in any of these areas of common, even where common rights were restricted by the manorial court. How rife was livestock-stealing under such conditions? And were animals also stolen in large numbers from the small enclosed fields? It is possible to give some sort of answer as far as Essex was affected.

Only twelve indictments, in addition to giving the parish, specifically name a heath, common or open meadow where the theft took place. Fairmead in Waltham Forest, was mentioned earlier (p. 10). During our period, the vast Tiptree Heath, which stretched into seven parishes, must have tempted many thieves. Convicted, at any rate, were five men at various times, who drove from the heath 20 steers, 3 heifers, 1 cow, 19 sheep, and 3 ewes in all. One man stole 11 sheep and 10 lambs on Bicknacre Common in Woodham Ferrers from three owners; a cow was stolen from Danbury Common; and 13 ewes and 6 lambs at Chigwell Row, which lay on the east side of Waltham Forest. Two oxen from a common meadow called East Mead in Stanford Rivers, four oxen from Cow Mead in West Ham marshes, and six sheep from a Wix common are among the other examples. But although a few justices or justices' clerks thus gratuitously specified the place where the crime was committed, it was not legally necessary. It may therefore perhaps be assumed that the majority of the animals stolen in parishes having large commons, heaths or long roadside greens were in fact driven away from these open spaces.

The first indictment in the earliest Elizabethan Assize file records that William Crowche of Tolleshunt Knights, a husbandman, on 27 November 1558, stole 17 sheep (worth 40s.) belonging to Robert Wade, 8 sheep (20s.) from Nicholas Cowey, 6 sheep (16s.) from an unknown woman, 3 sheep (6s.) from Thomas Osborne, and 2 sheep from William Symnell, all at Great Birch (the big Layer Breton Heath extended into Birch parish). On 22 November he had also stolen 4 sheep (10s.) and 5 sheep (12s.) belonging to two men at Little Totham (an arm of Tiptree Heath lay in the parish); and on 9 December he broke into a close at Rettendon, fifteen miles away, and stole 20 ewes and 6 wethers (3s. 4d. each). He was hanged. The first indictment in the last file lay against a Great Baddow labourer for stealing a roan mare (£3) and a bay mare (£2) belonging to William Peachie at Woodham Ferrers (which included Bicknacre Common as well as two creekside fen commons). At the same Assizes (1602) two labourers who had taken three lambs on four separate days from three men confessed and were condemned to the gallows. Between these dates, a span of 45 years, the Assize and Sessions records contain scores of indictments for stealing horses, cattle and sheep. (See Appendix D, p. 316.) Prices increase somewhat, as would be expected, in the later years of the century, when we find sheep valued at around 5s. each and cows about £3, but prices of horses varied within wide limits.

Which of the two sets of figures of cattle-stealing is the more remarkable – the grand total, or the highest total of a single raid or series of raids? To be able to ascertain, by tedious examination of both series of indictments, that men were charged with stealing 2,834 sheep and lambs, 660 oxen, cows and calves, and 289 horses from their lawful owners in Essex during 1558–1603 is a result, for what it is worth, that could not be worked out for any other county. But individual cases probably give an equally impressive picture of the constant menace that deprived so many farmers, husbandmen and cottagers of part or the whole of their stock and of their main livelihood.

There were many audacious raids, especially of course on flocks of sheep. Perhaps the most daring was Crowche's taking, single-handed, 71 sheep in 1558. An Aveley collarmaker stole 36 sheep there in 1569. On an April day in 1582 a Westminster smith and a Greenstead-juxta-Ongar labourer stole two flocks each of forty sheep at West Hanningfield, and three weeks later £20 in cash from a man at Great Leighs. Next month a South Ockendon labourer stole 40 sheep at 'Horndon'. An Ilford shoemaker stole 39 sheep from two fellow-townsmen in 1590. Two men of Wimbish and Wendon were charged in 1601 on five separate indictments with taking 85 animals: on 1 June 22 wethers and 24 wethers and a ram at Wickham Bonhunt; on 27 July, 15 sheep from each of two owners at Littlebury; on 1 November, a ewe and 5 white rams and 2 white wethers from two owners at Newport. One of the thieves, a shepherd, read and was branded; the other, perhaps his master, had fled. In 1585 a Latchingdon husbandman broke into a field 25 miles away at Margaret Roothing, where he stole 37 sheep and 25 lambs. A Prittlewell labourer in 1591 stole 28 sheep and 26 lambs at North Fambridge Hall belonging to James Osborne, lord of the manor, a relation of the Sir Peter who married Dorothy Temple of the well-known love-letters a generation later.

A small gang of four husbandmen and a labourer of Kelvedon and adjacent parishes, all together, as a pair or individually, were indicted at Quarter Sessions on no less than eight charges of sheep-stealing, seven in May and June and the last in November 1602, at Kelvedon, Great Wigborough, Layer Marney, Virley and Cressing. Between them they accounted for 52 ewes, 1 wether and 30 lambs.

A Danbury labourer took 44 sheep from seven men, some on 6 December at Ramsden Crays, the rest on 14 December at Great Baddow (1569). A Walden labourer collected 22 sheep from five owners in a single day (1570); also on one day a Waltham Abbey labourer stole 30 in six incidents. A Roydon labourer took 20 sheep there and another 18 at Waltham (Abbey) a few weeks later (1582). Four Mistley men were raided by a Lawford labourer, whose combined haul was 16 ewes, 18 wethers, 1 ram and 13 lambs (1601). On five days in the same month another labourer not only stole 18 sheep but also burgled two houses. Four men of Hazeleigh and Purleigh, adjacent villages, lost between 21 sheep and 8 lambs (1591). A West Mersea husbandman stole 24 sheep and 13 lambs there belonging to Robert Crane gentleman (1588). A field in the demesne of the 'manor or farm of Fanton Hall' in North Benfleet belonging to Robert Drywood was entered and 18 ewes stolen (1568), and another at Warley Hall in Great Warley belonging to Henry Baker when 20 lambs were stolen (1571).

Two excursions are recorded as taking place at night: at Wimbish in 1567, when a Hatfield Broad Oak husbandman took 37 sheep; and at Barking in the previous year, when a local labourer made four raids, stealing two ewes each time. A unique indictment in 1575 tells of the act of a lad, two days before he became 21, who defrauded his master, William Higham of Hazeleigh, by driving 18 wethers thence all the way to Romford, where he sold them in open market to various unknown persons.

Only once is violence recorded in a sheep-stealing case. In 1566 Thomas Farnam (or Vernam) took 33 sheep at Heydon belonging to John Cheyney esquire, Sheriff of Buckinghamshire, but fearing arrest he abandoned them within the manor, owned by Elizabeth Asplond widow, and absconded.[1] The flock thereby became in law 'goods waived' and

---

[1] According to Morant (*History of Essex*, i, 601–2), Robert Aspland had alienated the manor to George Gille in 1563.

William Barlee of Heydon gentleman, her 'servant' (probably steward of the manor), seized them. One sheep died, but a few weeks later the remainder were taken by the hundredal bailiff and delivered to Cheyne's servant, before Farnam was attainted for felony. Farnam is given as of Earls Colne labourer otherwise Farnam *alias* Hogherd of Marsworth (Bucks.), and not being captured was in due course outlawed.

Occasionally the indictment specify hoggerels (sheep of the second or third year) and theaves (probably ewes of the first or second year). A Great Totham husbandman got away with 28 wethers, ewes, hoggerels and theaves in 1572 : three sorties in neighbouring parishes. Not un-naturally, round figures are given for some flocks stolen : 20 at Langford, 20 at Chelmsford, 20 at Willingale, 25 at Stapleford Abbots, 25 at Epping, 30 at Castle Hedingham. But most flock-owners alleged that they were able to give precise numbers; and more exact figures of over 20 are recorded at Easterford, Great Wigborough, Little Stambridge, Elmdon, Inworth, Chelmsford, and Wethersfield.

A sheep-stealing indictment of 1585 is of interest because it explains why Richard Harrison, rector of Beaumont, who was instituted in 1566, was deprived in 1586, though later restored to his benefice at an unstated date.[1] A 'clerk' and a labourer, both of this parish and bearing this name, stole an ewe at Moze. The case went from Quarter Sessions to the Assizes, but neither defendant was 'in prison'. Another clerical sheep-stealer was Edward Fenton (or Fynton) of Ugley. In 1569 he took two ewes from a field at Chickney, when a true bill was found; and, a month later, one ewe from a field at 'Pottivers End' (probably Patmore End). He was bound in his own recognizance of £20 to appear at the Assizes. There is a hiatus in the clergy list for Ugley at this period, and it is not known whether he was vicar or curate.

John Gyll of Ugley husbandman in 1597 confessed that he last served with John Sabyn of Stortford (Herts.), husbandman, and had since been at his fathers at Ugley. Coming from Stortford with his brother Anthony, they espied sheep in Edward Hamond's field at Bentfield (in Stansted Mountfitchet). That night they carried away one of the sheep to their fathers where they dressed, boiled and ate it, and they had no other company. Anthony said that they ate a quarter of the sheep that night, and next day they boiled the rest and they with their father and mother ate it. Both denied that their parents were privy to the stealing or knew whence they had it.

The chronicle of stealing oxen and cows is much the same. Occasionally they are identified by colour : 14 cows (5 dun-coloured, 5 red, 4 black), stolen by two gentlemen, John Wyggmore of Harwich and Thomas Barney of London in 1560; or 8 oxen (4 'brinded' or brindled, i.e.

[1] Newcourt, ii, 41.

brown with streaks, 3 black and 1 red) taken from Crondon Park near Stock in 1588. Cases in which ten or more were stolen involved a Chadwell labourer (1582), 8 cows and 2 calves on five days in three neighbouring parishes but he managed to read his neck-verse; Robert Downinge of Heybridge butcher (1586), 7 heifers and 7 steers from two persons there on successive days; an Ardleigh labourer (1592), 22 heifers at Boxted; two labourers (1587), 14 steers at Oakley; and Henry Jepson of Billericay blacksmith and James Slack of Great Easton husbandman (1600), 14 steers from three persons at Billericay.

A butcher and a labourer stole an ox (£3) and a runt from Richard Archer's field at Theydon Garnon in 1568. The labourer was acquitted, but the butcher stood mute, and he was pressed to death (see p. 149). Four steers were stolen in 1573 by a labourer of Ugley from a field called Rickling Brome belonging to Thomas Newman gentleman. It was he, according to Morant, who built Newman Hall in Quendon which was much later replaced by the present Quendon Hall; he also owned half the manor of Rickling. A ram (5s.) was stolen in 1597 from 'Lyttles' in Springfield, the home of John Pinchon gentleman, who was the father of William Pynchon, the founder of Springfield, Massachusetts (1636). In 1576 a Pleshey man stole 4 'milch bullocks', a steer and a bull at Brentwood belonging to Edmund Rendisshe of Girton (Cambs.) gentleman; and a London pinner at Boreham took 6 'northern bullocks', a bull and 3 young steers. The sole reference to Horsey, which belonged to the parish of Kirby, occurs in connection with the stealing of two cows from the island by a Kirby weaver in 1586.

The values placed on the bovine animals is fairly consistent. Oxen were worth about £3–£5 6s. 8d., bulls 30–40s., bullocks 30s., steers 25–40s., northern bullocks 30s., northern steers 60s., heifers 20–35s., cows 30s. As with other animals, all these thefts were presumably furtive affairs, and a few night raiders were prosecuted. A Stondon Massey butcher one midnight in 1590 stole two calves, one 'frosty-coloured', from the rectory garden or glebe of Lewis Bynner at Kelvedon Hatch. In contrast, three clothworkers of Sturmer and Kersey (Suffolk), with four others unknown, drove away 13 cows and 17 runts worth £10 in all, after attacking their owner.

The loss by Geoffrey Nightingale, an interesting personality (see plate 25), of some farmstock has given us a letter from him, dated 7 January 1591, from his Newport home (Pond Cross). 'Of late,' he wrote to Robert Clarke, Baron of the Exchequer and one of the principal J.P.s, 'I was robbed at Newport of three milch bullocks, and, with much sending about, the thief is taken and committed to the gaol in Essex. Myself and one of my men are bounden before Sir Thomas Lucas to prosecute suit against him the next General Sessions holden in Essex, but now I understand it is your pleasure to deliver the gaol at this Quarter Sessions, where by reason of some earnest business already appointed for the trial of a copy-hold title I cannot be there present to give evidence against my prisoner, yet notwithstanding I have sent my man, who can give as full evidence as I can do. The prisoner's name is Andrew Howe. Sir Thomas Lucas has the examination, which he has promised to bring or send to the Quarter Sessions, wherein he has fully confessed the matter and also the stealing of eight other bullocks of certain persons dwelling about the Rodings, for which he had this trial this day twelve months at the Quarter Sessions at Chelmsford, and there was then burnt in the hand and so delivered, and the Clerk of the Peace has the record there now to show you. Now what favour this man deserveth, I refer the same to your good considerations. Besides this, I have understood now at Newport very lately that Andrew Howe, about six years since, committed a rape upon a young maiden, and for that she fled and could never be heard of until this day. Laying these his often offences together, whether he deserveth to be cut off or not, I refer the same to your worship.' The scoundrel had indeed been indicted a year earlier for stealing nine beasts, when be confessed and read. The new charge was heard at the Lent Assizes; confessing again, he must have been hanged.

Geoffrey Nightingale is honoured in Essex history as having influenced his friend, Joyce Frankland, a widow of Rye House in Stansted Abbotts (Herts.) and daughter of a London goldsmith, to found a free grammar school in Newport. This she did under her will (1587) and Newport Grammar School started in the upper storey of the Guildhall. The fine brass (1608) to the memory of Geoffrey and his wife is preserved in the church tower.[1]

Pigs, being mostly shut in, were not so easily stolen, and there are only twenty cases. A Great Warley sawyer in 1569 stole 6 pigs from two men in Crondon Park; a Hitchin (Herts.) butcher at Epping, 13 pigs and a boar belonging to another Herts. man; three Cambridge labourers, 9 hogs at Ridgewell; and two Fobbing labourers, a total of 14 pigs from four owners at Bulmer in the opposite corner of the county. Values lay between 4s. and 10s. for pigs and hogs, and 13s. 4d. for boars. But a Lindsell labourer who had broken into the property of Thomas Young, a gentleman of Hockley, many miles away, and stolen six pigs, was saved from swinging by their being grossly undervalued at 11d.

From our analysis on which this pedestrian account has been based there emerge no less than forty-six butcher-thieves. The earliest case (1564) is fairly typical. William Smyther butcher and Thomas Nycholl labourer, both of Chelmsford, broke into a close at Steeple, 20 miles away, stealing 17 wethers. At the Lent Assizes 1567 William Newman butcher was not only indicted for stealing two oxen and four cows, total value

---

[1] For the founding of the school and the brass, see *Essex Review*, xv, 73–82 ; ix, 89 (plate).

£9 6s. 8d., at Blackmore belonging to four men, but also for 19 sheep at Chigwell Row. These numerous butchers did not concentrate on one kind of meat. The indictments range over oxen, bullocks, cows, heifers, rams, sheep, lambs, pigs, with an average of two or three animals taken by each thief. The number of cases certainly show an increase during the last decade of the reign, the period of distress through bad harvests. In about one-fourth of the cases two men were involved, presumably to drive the animals away, and the pair was either the butcher with a labourer to help or more often both were butchers, perhaps master and journeyman. In three cattle-stealing raids made in the Spring of 1597 by five men, two of whom were locals and two were butchers of West Thurrock, they collected from Great Wigborough and the neighbourhood 56 sheep, 2 oxen and a horse.

Approximately one in every four butchers was acquitted, one in four read and was branded, and a few fled; the rest were found guilty and with few exceptions were hanged. One butcher who stole 4 ewes worth 6s. and confessed was hanged (1597), but another who stole 3 sheep and also confessed was whipped because they were valued at only 10d. Two butchers stole unspecified carcases worth 40s., a calf's carcase (20s.), and three sides of beef (£5). One was acquitted; the other was at large.

Horses

Horse-stealing was as common a crime as cattle-stealing. A few indictments will show something of this prevalent plague. In 1589 two Blackmore men, Charles Smyth *alias* Parker gentleman (son of Thomas Smyth of Blackmore Priory?) and Henry Daniell yeoman, stole a gelding at Writtle; both fled. Horse-thieving cases were very numerous in 1596. Three labourers of Stapleford Abbots took two mares and a nag from their three owners, but were acquitted. George Bascoe of Battersea (Surrey) and Richard Wyldinge of Stratford (in West Ham), both wheelwrights, on 17, 18 and 26 February 1596, at Epping and Waltham Abbey, stole three mares and a gelding, two of them belonging to Francis Stacye gentleman; and on 26 February at Epping three cows; both were hanged. So was another thief, although it was a 'flea-bitten grey horse' worth only 16s. William Rycard of Little Ilford clerk (rector, 1555–83) lost his mare (£5) in 1572. In 1579 Richard Kynge, Keeper of Colchester Castle Gaol, suffered a double indignity in having two horses (20 marks) and a gelding (£8) stolen from him by three of his prisoners, who escaped with the mounts they had so usefully acquired.

The indictments yield a few scraps of evidence about 'professional' horse-thieves. William Runwell, between 2 July and 9 September 1596, appropriated ten horses (£28) from eight owners, including Henry Lord Windsor; five of these thefts took place at Widford and two at 'Hanningfield.' Three men were hanged in 1588 for stealing five geldings (£60) at

Saffron Walden from Thomas Sutton esquire, but not on the annual fair-day. Sutton was later to become the richest commoner in England and the founder of the Charterhouse. He had strong links with Essex, including Ashdon and Littlebury. In 1572 John Hayward, sometimes in company with one or two other men, on three days took five horses and a sheep from six owners, two of whom were unknown, at Salcott, Great Totham, Maldon and Witham. In the following year he pilfered some clothes and purses at Southminster and Bradwell-juxta-Mare. Found guilty, he claimed benefit of clergy. In 1574 he was at the Assizes again for breaking into a field of John Byrcheley gentleman at East Hanningfield and stole a horse (£5). This time he apparently refused at first to plead and was sentenced to the *peine forte et dure* (p. 149) but seems then to have pleaded guilty, and was hanged. The two Dartford horse-thieves who were charged with attempted murder have already been mentioned (p. 275).

The description in 1578 of the clothes of a man wanted for stealing a horse from John Flower and John Godfrey of Stapleford Abbots may be compared with that of a modern police statement: 'a canvas doublet cut, without coat or cloak, and gascoynes (breeches) of blue and nether-stocks (stockings) of the same colour'. The story set out in the depositions taken before Richard Cooke and Henry Archer is a long and complicated one, and it is not clear whether an arrest had been effected. It centres around a 'waived' mare, that is, one which had been abandoned by the thief. The man, said Flower, came into his yard about sun-setting, asking him for lodging, and he directed him towards Havering. A little before night he sent a maidservant of his to Havering for drink, and as it was late and she had not returned his wife sent his man-servant to meet her on the way homewards, and they returned together. He added that there was a gap in the hedge of the field where the waived horse was found and spoke to his man about mending it; but the old saddle also found in the field had been left there by his servant's negligence.

Godfrey said that a fellow apparelled as described overtook him on the way on this side of Harlow. They rode in company for half a mile, when the 'suspect' enquired the distance to London, to which he replied, 'Sixteen miles'. The suspect said that his master was in London and had willed him to lead up his mare, but being weary he rode on her, and his master would there buy a saddle and bridle for her; and so he 'overrode' Godfrey. Richard Owler of Navestock, servant to William Browne, said that the suspect overtook him in the highway not far from 'Hell Hall' (Hill Hall in Theydon Mount), and asked the way to Stapleford. 'Which Stapleford?' Owler demanded, the reply being 'Where Mr. Flower the embroiderer dwells'; so he directed him thither, the suspect riding away fast. Thomas Hoskyns of Stapleford, servant to Flower, confirmed that his mistress sent him to meet her maid, that he met her 'at the park', and after coming home he carried his master's mare to the pasture, his master going and returning with him. They had gone outwards by the common to 'Boylands Oak' (shown on Chapman and André's Map of Essex, 1777, as 'Boiling Oak' : at the edge of an arm of Hainault Forest). But they did not go into the close where the 'waived mare' was put, nor into the next close where the mare was driven through. He did not see it until it was brought home to his master's house next morning by the constable of Stapleford, and he saw no such person as that described by his master. Hoskyns, however, was called in again, when he confessed that his master and he were in the close where the mare was put and had spoken to him about mending the gap.

Mary Awgor, servant to Flower, confirmed that she had been sent to Havering, and on her outward journey near Boyland's Oak she saw a tall fellow in a doublet and a bluish pair of hose with a black hat, who was looking about. William Durrant, servant to Godfrey, said that he saw a mare which was stolen, but by whom he does not know, and he heard Flower and Hoskyns talking in a close where the waived mare was put, and Hoskyns said, 'The sweat should be washed off' ; it was late in the evening and 'something dark.' A later incident centres round the oak.

Flower's recognizance terms him both as 'of London, merchant-tailor' and 'of Stapleford Abbots, broiderer'.

Another long story of a stolen horse, taken down before Sir Thomas Lodge in the following year, is told in the examination of William Clements, a collier (charcoal-burner) of Romford, who was accused of receiving it, and of William Gresham, a clothworker of London, charged with stealing it. Clements, who had been arrested for lying at Plaistow (a hamlet in West Ham) four or five days suspiciously and was required to explain, as he had a house of his own so near, said that he brought a load of coals thither and sold them, but being indebted to many men he dared not return home for fear of arrest. He met Gresham last Michaelmas, when he lay at the sign of the Greyhound at Romford for a week, who showed him a horse there at grass, which he afterwards bought in Smith-field (Market) for £3 1s. 4d. He owed Gresham 8s., part of the £3 1s. 4d., and Gresham did not demand it until 'Sunday was sevennight', when he paid him 4s. and still owed 4s. Gresham, asked where and when he 'wrought' last, said that he had not worked in his own occupation since Michaelmas because he had been a prisoner in the Marshalsea, whence he was delivered on bail on Saturday last sevennight. His imprisonment was for buying a horse at Gravesend, which he sold at Smithfield to whom he knew not. Questioned how he obtained the horse sold to Clements, he said he had him of his brother Edward Gresham and kept him at Romford, intending to have ridden him to Bolton in Lancashire where he was born, but for want of money he was 'urged' to sell it to Clements. It is interesting to find that two more 'colliers', Thomas Stoddard and William Watnall, both of Abridge (in Lambourne), were

22 ALEHOUSE-KEEPER'S BOND, 1586

Recognizance of Thomas Harles (£10) and his two sureties (£5 each), all of Little Hallingbury, taken before John Wyseman and Edward Hubberd, J.P.s, to 'kepe a Com[m]on Alehouse or Tiplinge house.'

23 WEALD HALL, SOUTH WEALD

Built probably *circa* 1540–50, enlarged *circa* 1560–70, and demolished 1950 (p. 262).

sureties for Clements' appearance. The numerous Tudor wills of colliers testify to the importance of the charcoal-burning industry.[1]

That infamous character, Edmund Chevely, who features more than once in Elizabethan Essex crime, on Wednesday after St. Peter's Day 1583 met his friend Roger Prickett of Moulsham and said, 'Thou canst help a friend of mine to a piece of venison against St. Peter's Day and he will content thee for thy pains'. Having agreed to do what he could, Prickett was promised 'a horse, a sack and a sheet to bring it in and money in his purse to spend'. Chevely carried him to a Horndon man, bidding him to 'let this good fellow have his horse, a sack and a sheet and some money to bear his charge', promising the lender a piece of flesh. Next morning Prickett was duly furnished with a black mare, saddle and bridle, a pair of boots, a sack, a sheet, spurs and cloak, with 12d., and rode to Pleshey where he spent the night. Next day he rode to one Bat Grene's, as bidden, to borrow his crossbow, but it had been lent to a man at Abridge, where he sought him in vain, obliging Prickett to try to find him at the 'Three Nuns' without Aldgate, where he lay the night, spending 6d. for his supper and a groat for his horse. But the Abridge man was not there, and the mare needed two shoes, so he sold his boots and spurs to the smith for 2s. 6d. and then went to Stratford Langthorne (in West Ham) to find one Crompton 'to see if he could help him to a piece of flesh'. Failing again, he rode to Chigwell Row, once more in vain, so returned to London and 'inned at the sign of the George at Whitechapel', remaining in London for two days, then returning to borrow some money from Crompton and offering the mare for sale. But Crompton had no money and said he would find a chapman to buy the mare. Back again to London to his inn for six days, when he went once more to Stratford, where he eventually agreed to sell his mare to a furrier for 33s. 4d., taking 12d. earnest money. He 'conditioned' to deliver the animal four days later in Smithfield. The furrier came to the 'George' and paid him 10s. before they went to the market, where they entered the mare in the toll book and he was paid the balance. Three days later he met Chevely in London, lying in the same inn as Chevely, and two days afterwards they went to 'Stratford of the Bow', where he confessed that he had only 6s. 8d., asking Chevely to take it to the Horndon man until he could pay the rest. Chevely said he would talk with him to see if he would agree to 'a twelvemonth day of payment' (deferred payment) of the money for which Prickett had sold the mare. In the end the wretched man never got the piece of venison and was of course arrested for horse-stealing.

A 'notable horse-stealer' was the subject of a letter of January 1591 sent by Israel Amyce, J.P., lord of the manor of Tilbury Hall, from his house at Tilbury-juxta-Clare to Robert Clarke, who occasionally presided

[1] Emmison (ed.), *Wills at Chelmsford*, i (index), and *Tudor Food*, 64–66; *V.C.H. Essex*, ii, 447–50.

W

at Quarter Sessions. 'Whereas a gaol delivery has been appointed by you', he wrote, 'where one John Browne *alias* Marshe is to appear among other prisoners, for a felony committed in October last, for which he cannot have his due trial because one Mr. Chapman (who stands bound to prosecute him) is at this present in Wales and does not return until Candlemas, therefore I thought it good to advertise you to the end the prisoner may be reprieved, being supposed to be as strong a thief as ever appeared before you, and he has been (as I am credibly informed) twice or thrice before this time in our gaol, and he has confessed unto me that he was in Bury gaol (Suffolk) at the last Assizes there and received his trial there for four sheep, also he is vehemently suspected in these parts to be a notable horse-stealer, the truth whereof, as also of divers others of his foul misdemeanours, I doubt not will be manifested before you at the next Assizes.' A John Marshe butcher, with Hugh Wrighte of Stoke-by-Clare (Suffolk), was indicted at the Lent Assizes for stealing three sheep and a cow from two persons and was found guilty (Wrighte had not been caught), but nothing about horse-stealing is found, though it was Allen Chapman who lost the cow.

On being questioned by Anthony Cooke, J.P., a servant of Richard Godfrey of Doddinghurst yeoman, deposed that about 4 a.m. one December morning in 1592 his master had ordered him and Peter Hurst to go to Boyland's Oak in Stapleford Abbots in order to see if any cattle were in his four closes there, and if so to drive them to the pound. Finding none, he asked a man if there were any deer abroad, adding that he had company with dogs below in the woods; but he now denied having either. They went down to the woods to await the master who had promised to meet them there. Questioned why his master should meet them so early in the morning, he gave a lame explanation, but admitted that he was weaponed with a long bill and a dagger and Hurst with a long pikestaff and a dagger. The constable, being suspicious, enjoined them to go with him to a justice of the peace, but they refused until the master should come. Hurst stated that, about sun-setting the day before, Godfrey asked him to go with his servant next morning to Boyland's Oak, but he denied their having any dogs.

A majority of the horse-stealers who were arrested were found guilty, and in most cases their indictments are marked 'Sus :' (to be hanged). One saved his neck by being drafted 'into the Queen's service' (army or navy). But a significant percentage were recorded as 'at large' or 'escaped'. Little light is shed on the question of disposal of the horses, if not kept by the thieves for their own use. Occasionally an accessory or receiver was also indicted, but usually acquitted; if guilty, he also was hanged, as benefit of clergy could not be claimed by a horse-stealer or his accessory.

Harrison has some sharp remarks about horse-stealers and dishonest horse-dealers. 'One of this company', he wrote, referring to an arrested thief, 'was beforetime reputed for a very honest and wealthy townsman. It was his custom to say, if any man hucked hard with him about the price of a gelding, "So God help me, gentleman or sir, either he did cost me so much, or else, by Jesus, I stole him". Which talk was plain enough, and yet such was his estimation that each believed the first part of his tale and made no account of the latter, which was the truer indeed.'[1] The poorer, roguish horse-thieves were called 'priggers of prancers' in the Elizabethan vagabonds' cant.[2] And in another chapter he opines that 'there is no greater deceit used anywhere than among our horsekeepers, horsecorsers (horse dealers), and hostlers'.[3] A few receivers of stolen horses were charged at the same time as the principals. Two men stole the horse of Thomas Howell clerk at Paglesham in 1596 (he was rector 1578–99). It was received by Richard Reade of High Laver yeoman, who was at large. Two dishonest innkeepers, both of Rayleigh, were indicted. In 1601 John Morecocke stole a horse and remained at large. And in the previous year an Epping joiner was hanged for a similar crime, and John Norcott, the other innkeeper, charged as receiver, had also absconded. In 1597 Edward Haddesley of Takeley yeoman was indicted for a stolen horse, and Edward Thursby of Bocking gentleman for receiving it there, but he was pardoned by the general pardon of that year. This is of more than usual interest, as Thursby was the first of the family to live at Dorewards Hall, Bocking. 'It seems probable', according to a well-known local authority, 'that he built the present house.'[4] In the previous year Sir Thomas Lucas of St. John's, Colchester, J.P., took the trouble to write to the Court testifying to his good opinion of an alehouse-keeper at Ford Street in Aldham, suspected of having had dealings with a horse-stealer ('a most bad fellow'), whose implication of the other man, he urged, should be rejected as worthless.

To what extent do some of the cattle-raids and horse-stealings by strangers ('furriners' in customary Essex language) represent deliberate plans? Some have been noticed in this section and in Chapter 24. It seems probable that thefts which took place in the towns include cases of this kind. Others who belonged to neighbouring or more distant counties are found, such as a Bedfordshire baker who stole two horses at Newport and a Kent rippier (one who carried fish inland to sell) who took a horse from an unknown person at Chelmsford. Newport's market and especially its Cold Fair in November were noted for horse-dealing, and the horses referred to were stolen at fair-time. A horse probably taken at Thremhall Fair (1556) was mentioned earlier (p. 2). Long before *The Vicar of Wakefield* was written, dishonest horse-dealers haunted fairs. But the evidence is

[1] Harrison, *Description of England*, 307–09.
[2] *Ibid.*, 184, quoting from Harman's *Caveat or Warning for Common Cursitors* (1566).
[3] *Ibid.*, 307.
[4] A. Hills, 'Inlaid Coat of Arms' (of Thursby and others in the house) (*Essex Review*, xli, 201).

slight, and other foreigners committed their felonies elsewhere: a
Leicestershire yeoman, 5 sheep in a field at High Easter; two glovers of
Gloucestershire and Westminster, 4 cows at Great Baddow; a Lambeth
labourer, 18 sheep at Corringham. As already explained, the indictments,
however, are misleading in so far as Elizabethan lawyers had not yet
coined the phrase 'of no fixed abode' and were obliged to give a precise
place. This led them, where the accused's parish was not known, to
insert as the abode the name of the parish where the offence was committed. For example, John Bell was given four different Essex abodes
corresponding with the parishes in each of which he stole a horse. As
likely as not, he lived nowhere in the county. Much the same applies to
two men who acquired four horses and three cows in four expeditions
near Waltham Forest, though in the first indictment one of the men was
ascribed to Battersea, which was probably correct. And the drover who
was found guilty of stealing four cows at Woodham Ferrers, although
nominally a parishioner, probably plied his business over a wide area. So
that the number of animal thieves who did not belong to the county is
certainly somewhat larger than is stated in the indictments.

A few thieves of course acquired whatever animals they could find. In
1593 a Belchamp St. Paul's labourer stole 40 sheep, 3 heifers and 2 horses
from five men: four thefts there, the fifth at Ridgewell. A Doddinghurst
labourer took 16 sheep at Great Hallingbury and 3 steers at Matching.
Another labourer went off with 7 lambs at Rettendon and a horse and 11
lambs at South Hanningfield. He confessed for the lambs, and his plea of
not guilty for the horse was accepted, but it made no difference, as he was
hanged for the rest.

A single indictment for stealing a 'tame goat' (13s. 4d.), belonging to
William Ayloffe of Great Braxted esquire, is found in 1602, but the man
was acquitted.

Cattle-stealers do not seem to have infested other counties whose
Elizabethan records have been published as much as Essex, but so
few have survived that it would be futile to draw any conclusions. In
Middlesex, only nine indictments were laid. But in that county horse-
stealing was rife throughout the period. A certain Henry Bowyer was
charged on no less than ten indictments for this crime in 1600 'in and
about London', but did not favour Essex with any visits. And another
flea-bitten horse figures in the same records.[1]

Food

Elizabethan poultry raids, unlike those in our time, were small affairs.
A Birdbrook carpenter on Christmas Day 1587 prowled around that parish

---

[1] *Middlesex County Records*, i, 261, 210, and index under 'Sheep-stealing', 'Horse-
stealing'.

and the next, collecting from three places 2 capons, 8 hens and a goose; 2 capons, 10 hens and 2 geese; and 15 hens. (Guilty; read as a clerk.) A cooper, a tanner, a tailor and a labourer, or three or two of them, between 13 January and 12 February 1597, made six excursions in the villages around Chelmsford, their home district. Their total bag was 2 cocks, 8 cockerels, 11 capons, 29 hens, and 15 ducks; also 2 hives of bees (20s.). (The tanner was acquitted; the rest were branded on confessing and reading.) Three similar searches in the Dunmow area by two local men yielded 19 pullets, 16 chickens and 4 capons (one not guilty, the other branded); and four around Arkesden, also by two locals, 7 capons, 5 hens and 5 ducks, as well as 4 lambs (both confessed and were hanged). A Finchingfield labourer who stole 15 pullets was dead before his case came up; and a Stock weaver remained at large after running off with 30 fowls. Earlier in the century, 'turkey' meant guinea-fowl, but nearer the end it is more likely to bear its current meaning. It is mentioned in several documents, for example, 2 turkey-hens (2s.) and 1 turkey-cock (12d.) stolen from Edward Bugge gentleman by two Harlow men there. One of them, a 'poulter' (the Tudor form of poulterer), was whipped on being found guilty for 10d. only. The other, a glover, stole further poultry from Bugge, who was thus visited three times at quarterly intervals, and from John Collen gentleman at High Laver (confessed and read). A second 'poulter' who went off with 38 hens (20s.) in two raids at Little Maplestead also managed to read his neck-verse. If we except these two traders, the aim of some of the thieves was probably to provide for their hungry families; and it is noticeable that nearly all poultry snatching took place in the last decade of the reign – a period of famine and high prices. Several cases in our account of poaching rightly fall here.

We now leave the thefts mostly for gain and come to petty thieving mostly for food and nearly all in that same decade. Despite their strident objection to being approached, a gaggle of geese, or a single goose, appears in a score of indictments; but ducks only in three. There is clear evidence of under-valuation, not only by the juries but even in the indictments. Twelve geese worth 6d. (confessed for petty larceny) and seven at 11d. (not guilty) may be set against one at 10d. (fled), two at 12d. (fled), and five at 12d. stolen by a poulterer (not guilty). Three labourers who took two geese (2s.) and five ducks (2s.) belonging to Philip Morris of Dunmow gentleman got away with a whipping because the verdict was 'guilty to the value of 10d. only.' So did a Barking labourer, when his theft of three geese (3s.) was treated by the jury as only petty larceny. In contrast, when reduction to under a shilling would have been patently unreasonable, we find twelve geese valued at 7s. 6d.

The forty thieves of grain nearly all took small amounts – a few bushels of wheat or barley. Corn prices are well known, and there was of course a marked rise in the years of disastrous harvests. Wheat went up from about

2s. to 5s. and barley from 1s. 8d. to 3s. 4d. a bushel; oats (2s. in 1577) and rye (3s. 4d. in 1596) occur rarely in the records. Malt was about 2s. 3d. a bushel, and a bushel of tares was valued at 12d. But under-valuing by the jury resulted once in only 11d. (and therefore petty larceny) for one bushel of wheat (5d.) and two bushels of rye (6d.), and on several occasions juries reduced the value to 10d. (once from 4s.). Most of the other verdicts for grain thefts were 'not guilty'.

Out of the very large number of indictments for larceny, food, apart from cheese, was involved only a dozen times. Appropriately, in the county in which the famous Dunmow flitch of bacon custom originated, we find 4 flitches of bacon (5s.); a piece of bacon (10d.); another flitch (5s.) and 19 pairs of 'puddings' (3s.); 'three pieces of pig's meat called two flitches and a half of bacon' (12d.); and '3 pieces of bacon called 2 flitches and 1 gammon' (10s.); two firkins of butter (20s.); 80 lb. of butter (20s.); 20 lb. of butter (6s. 8d.) and 4 pieces of pork (12d.). Only twice does bread occur: a penny loaf and a piece of beef; and two brown loaves (8d.). In 1597 three labourers of West Bergholt went off with half a mutton (6d.), 10 lb. of suet (3s. 4d.), a neat's tongue (4d.), and 4 cheeses (2s.).

But hunger could not have accounted for the felony committed by Edward Lorken of Mountnessing yeoman in 1586. Burgling the house of William Brook at Danbury, he broke down the kitchen wall (probably separated from the house itself) and went off with 5 geese (5s.), 5 fat capons (7s.), 10 fat pullets (8s.), a bacon flitch (3s. 4d.), a loin of pork (10d.), a breast of pork (6d.), a roll of pork (6d.), 8 chine pieces of two hogs with 3 smaller pieces of pork (3s. 4d.), and 2 double ribs of beef (3s.).

This laconic account of stolen food is relieved by the case of a clerical thief. In 1595 Reginald Medcalfe, vicar of Elmstead (1588–?), was before the justices on the double charge of stealing there on successive days 12 cheeses (10s.) from Henry Wayte and one cheese from John Kempe. Lionel Foster, rector of Little Tey (1588–97), stood bail for him, and his bishop wrote from London interceding earnestly on his behalf. 'I do hear of a very notable and lewd practice of two men called Wayte and Kempe, parishioners of Elmstead, who have preferred indictments against the said vicar for felony in taking certain cheeses, a thing so improbable in itself and savouring strongly of practice (underhand scheming) against the poor minister and conspiracy, that I hope of yourselves you will have that Christian regard of his cause and his enemies' maliciousness.' The bishop, who had addressed his letter to Sir Thomas Mildmay and Sir John Petre and the other county justices, continued, 'Nevertheless I do heartily pray you that if his bond be to appear at the General Assizes there to answer it, that he be not pressed to answer it at the Quarter Sessions but that he may keep that time of trial (if it must needs come to that issue) and be not otherwise by your wisdoms ordered, and that you would stead (help) the

poor man in justice against the malice of his accusers. It were very hard,'
he concluded, 'if it may be discerned that their proceeding is pretended
and evidently savoureth of practice, that a man of that calling should be
put to so public a reproach as to stand upon deliberation and trial of his
life, especially when the wound he shall receive, whatsoever it be, shall
be made upon the Gospel of God, whereof he is a minister.' The upshot
unfortunately is not recorded, nor is anything else known about Medcalfe.

Cheeses figure in eighteen of the thirty thefts of food. Five labourers and
a yeoman, all stated to be of Great Easton, stole 9 cheeses (12s.) belonging
to a parishioner; one labourer was found not guilty, the others were at
large (1573). An Inworth bricklayer, a Kelvedon husbandman, and two
Coggeshall glovers, at night stole 24 cheeses (50s.) at Little Totham; no
true bill for the glovers, the others acquitted (1587). Three Prittlewell and
Southchurch labourers took 9 cheeses (10s.); all acquitted (1597). The
only women caught, all spinsters, were two of Steeple and Southminster,
the first for taking 37 cheeses (30s.) belonging to her master, the second
for receiving them; one of Epping, who admitted stealing cheese (2d.)
and 1 lb. of bread (1d.), and she was whipped; and one of Langford, for
stealing six cheeses (20d.). In the remaining twelve cases, one or two men,
mostly labourers, were tried for stealing between two and twenty-one
cheeses. The price range was between 6d. and 2s. 1d. per cheese. One
pair among them also took 5 lb. of butter (15d.), 4 loaves of bread (9d.),
and 3 hens; another, 6 lb. of butter (2s.); another, from Francis Harvey
esquire (a J.P.), 2 firkins of butter (not guilty); another, 10 lb. of butter
(16d.) and a bowl of grease (2d.).

None of these entries tells us anything about the size or weight of the
cheese. We know of course that the Essex cheeses were probably the giants
of England: 'cheeses of an extraordinary bigness' made from ewes' milk
in the marsh pastures of south-east Essex were commented upon by Camden
and Norden. And Skelton, a little earlier, had not been complimentary:

> A cantle of Essex cheese
> was well a foot thick
> Full of maggots quick:
> It was huge and great
> And might strong meat
> For the devil to eat,
> It was tart and punicate.

Much about the making and consumption of Essex cheese can be gathered
from the detailed account-books of Sir William Petre of Ingatestone Hall.[1]

Honey, the popular sweetener, does not appear, but a 'hive of bees'
figures twice in indictments, in one of which the bee-hive was valued as
highly as 20s. (1601).

[1] Emmison, *Tudor Food and Pastimes*, 38–9, 68–9.

A unique indictment was that laid against a High Easter woman for milking two cows. She apparently sold the four quarts (8d.) to a neighbour, and later fled to escape arrest.

Cloth

Although much has been written about the North Essex woollen industry, there is still no authoritative published history of this extremely important aspect of the economic and social life of the county.[1] While Colchester was the main hub of the Essex cloth trade, other centres were at Braintree and Bocking, Coggeshall and Halstead, with Dedham, West Bergholt, Boxted and Langham to the north of Colchester. Our Essex records are of much interest in giving a mass of detail about the heterogeneous kinds of cloth, with the values placed on the stolen goods, throughout the Elizabethan period. The extraordinary variety of the finished materials ranges from the ancient native broadcloth to the 'new draperies', the manufacture of which was brought to England by the Flemings (called 'Dutch' by Essex folk). They settled in Colchester in 1573, establishing the trade in 'bays and says', as well as 'perpetuanas' and 'several sorts of stuffs (which I neither can nor do desire to name)', as Dr. Fuller of Waltham Abbey was to refer to these foreign textiles nearly a century later. Even then, apparently, much of the nomenclature, imported by the Flemings, remained strange to Englishmen. They are all brought together, old and new, in Appendix B (p. 311), which incorporates the evidence from simple larceny, housebreaking, burglary and highway robbery.

The 'prices' given in the indictments appear to be fairly reliable. There is of course a marked increase on the whole in the later years. In contrast the prices in the earlier years are about 25–50 per cent. higher than those in the personal account-books of Sir William Petre, which have been analysed for the period 1544–61.[2] The textiles include both the better-quality goods such as the fine, plain-weave broadcloth, the inexpensive mixtures of woollen and linen yarn such as fustian, lockram, kersey, fri(e)ze and russet, and coarse materials such as sowtage (canvas). Cotton was probably the cheap woollen cloth made in Wales and the North with a long nap like the original cotton imported by the piece from India. Some varieties of the

[1] A good account of the Essex manufacture is in *V.C.H., Essex*, ii, 380–404. For another account based on more recent research, see J. E. Pilgrim, 'The Cloth Industries of Essex and Suffolk' (unpublished London M.A. thesis, 1939, and 'The Rise of the "New Draperies" in Essex' (*Univ. of Birmingham Hist. Journal*, 1959, 36–59)), to whom I am much obliged for help in this section.

[2] About 800 entries relating to cloth and materials, edited by myself, will probably be published as *Costume, 1544–61: from the Petre Accounts* by Phillimore in 1971. A few are quoted in C. W. and P. Cunnington, *Handbook of English Costume in the Sixteenth Century* (1954), which has a valuable 'Glossary of Materials'.

new draperies appear and become more frequent in the later years. Among them are carrel, rash, grograine and perpetuanas, the last probably from Norwich, though some seem to have been made at Sudbury. Mockado (1568) was probably manufactured at Norwich, but the bays (1577) were almost certainly made at Colchester. Both references belong to the early period of the Flemish immigration. It is difficult to know whether the fabrics with European names, such as 'osnabrig' and 'holmes' (from Osnabrück and Ulm in Germany), 'gentish' (Ghent in Flanders), were imported or of home manufacture resembling their originals. The range of colours is surprisingly wide.

The same records also reveal something of the extent to which those engaged in the woollen industry and trades were involved in theft and embezzlement of the goods of their fellows – goods at various stages of their manufacture or temporarily in their custody in one of the stages between the raw material and the finished product. Weavers, for instance, stole wool and yarn, fullers and millers dishonestly appropriated unfulled cloth, and tailors stole the finished cloth. Some of the large quantities stolen must have been taken from clothiers' premises. Their temptations were different from those of other thieves. At a rough estimate, about one-half of the thefts of textile goods were committed by persons engaged in their manufacture or sale. As most of the poor made nearly all their own clothes, they, too, sometimes stole the materials; and of course in a good many housebreakings and burglaries the thieves took whatever they could find, including cloth.

Beginning with the raw material there is first the unique indictment of 1598, for stealing 'the wool shorn from two sheep', valued at 2s. to which a Great Clacton labourer confessed. Thefts of wool were a common feature of larceny cases, ranging from the 17 lb. stolen at Borley Hall in 1556 to the 14 lb. taken by a Haverhill (Essex) weaver in 1602 belonging to another person, perhaps his customer. In 1601–02 five Coggeshall men were in trouble in their own town. Stephen Royse weaver and John Cooper fuller stole 36 lb. wool (30s.) belonging to Thomas Shortland there. Jeremy Tyler weaver and John Pearson fuller were also charged as receivers. Royse was branded – Pearson acquitted, but the others were at large. John Browning fuller stole 5 lb. 'hemp wool' belonging to John Clemens; acquitted. At Rainham (possibly at the Thames-side wharf) two West Ham persons stole 60 lb. wool (£3), also 8 cheeses; the man had confessed but had died in gaol when the case came up and the spinster was acquitted.

The theft in 1597 of 47 lb. wool from Henry Ingram by Joseph Collyn, a glover of Gosfield, who was branded, suggests that he produced his wares from knitted wool, instead of leather, the commoner material. Two terms apparently unrecorded by lexicographers occur. Among various articles stolen was a 'packlane' (Latin, *laneus*, wool) containing 36 lb. of azure-coloured wool (1579) ; and a Coggeshall weaver stole some wool called a 'bay chain' (1591), two Halstead weavers also being charged as receivers.

The spun wool became yarn, which was usually wound on a wheel into skeins of fixed lengths in readiness for weaving. In two burglaries in 1591–93 three Halstead weavers got away with 10 skeins of warp, 7 of coarse yarn, 5 of middle yarn, an ell of coarse cloth, and a great quantity of linen ; and a weaver and two fullers of Coggeshall with an unspecified amount of wool and woollen skeins. Four skeins of 'Dutch work' yarn stolen by a Markshall spinster led to a whipping. A dishonest Maldon weaver was indicted in 1590 for 'deceitfully selling' 46 lb. of woollen yarn (30s.) which had been delivered to him by a St. Lawrence man to be made into three 'coverlets of weaver's craft'.

The streams of North Essex abounded with fulling mills. A Bocking weaver stole a broadcloth from John Little's mill at Brundon on the Stour in 1578. William Longthorpe *alias* Stanley and Thomas Longe, both millers of Liston, also on the Stour, stole 8½ yards of medley-coloured cloth and 14 yards of grey russet belonging to three men there, and a piece of russet from a fourth belonging to a Foxearth man ; the former was found not guilty, the latter was at large. The Stisted miller, George Cackbread, in 1591 stole 'divers parcels of linen' (£4) after breaking into the house of Sarah Wilson widow called The Gatehouse in Bocking. The mill of Thomas Barton of Mucking, on the Thames marshes, who stole three pieces of cloth belonging to his master Richard Cheeseman in 1572, was one of the many fulling mills, which were concentrated in the north.

After the woven cloth had been milled by the fuller, it was stretched on a tainter (or tenter), being held firm by tenter-hooks, thus drying out evenly and without shrinking. Two Kelvedon fullers, Robert Allygant and John Ower, in 1568 saw a 'sorting cloth' (applied to Somerset cloth in the *New English Dictionary*'s earliest reference, 1593) containing six yards of broadcloth 'hanging over the tainter' in Richard Skynner's field at Braintree and took it ; the first was found guilty, the second was at large. Four days afterwards, one of them, this time called a shearman, also stole elsewhere in Braintree seven yards of russet woollen cloth, and on the same day, if the record is correct, three lengths of cloth at Heybridge, fifteen miles away. A Cressing fuller filched a 'piece of bays' at Bocking. Instead of cloth, John Larke, a Coggeshall fuller, stole from an unnamed dyer there in 1593 '16 wooden bars and rails called a tainter' and from a widow four iron tainter keys.

An indictment of 1590 tells of a Coggeshall weaver who stole ten yards of coarse white cloth belonging to Edward Warner clothier and of a Hatfield Peverel weaver who received it. As much as fifty yards of cloth worth £10 was stolen at Earls Colne by a weaver and a carpenter ; but weavers' pilferings were mostly for smaller lengths. A Braintree labourer and a Kirby weaver were each indicted for an alleged theft from Henry Appleton, J.P., in 1585 and 1590 respectively, but it is interesting to note that neither was found guilty. Two burglaries which yielded 16 ells and 24 yards of various qualities were typical of tailors' depredations. The theft of five sorts of cloth from a Braintree booth on 21 September 1566 is found to coincide in date with its annual fair; the booth, curiously enough, was that of a London salter.

The examples which have been selected show how some employees and a few employers stole, pilfered and embezzled. But when it is remembered that a large percentage of the population was connected directly or indirectly with the woollen industry and its ancillary trades and occupations the court cases are not numerous enough to indicate any large-scale dishonesty. There is well-known evidence from other sources that the 'Dutch' settlers were particularly honest.

As with other trades, some indictments against clothiers and weavers for working without having served an apprenticeship occur. Trade offences will probably be dealt with in Volume 3 under Work. In 1599 Quarter Sessions ordered that 'the matter in variance between the clothiers and weavers of Bocking and Braintree' be referred to six justices among their number in order to settle the controversy. No details are vouchsafed. This is the only allusion in Elizabeth's time to the ancient rivalry between the twin clothing-towns – a rivalry which was to continue for many years. The Sessions rolls of the next century disclose the existence of a customary annual fight between the youth of Braintree and Bocking!

Parallel material in the published Quarter Sessions records of other counties is quite meagre. In the Worcestershire records, 1591–1603, only two indictments for thefts of cloth appear, despite the fairly important cloth industry in that county. There is, however, a little comparative evidence for Middlesex, but it had virtually no cloth-manufacturing.

Leather

Elizabethan clothing made use of a great deal of leather, and the very large number of tanners and tawers (who whitened the skins) bears witness to the importance of the industry, especially in Colchester.[1] As with cloth, some of the men in the leather and tailoring crafts and trades were involved in stealing skins and hides. Their values vary within a wide range (see Appendix C).

[1] The index of trades in *Wills at Chelmsford, 1400–1619*, ed. F. G. Emmison (Brit. Rec. Soc., vol. 78) reveals wills of 136 tanners, curriers and tawers and one pointer; many people of course made no will. Detailed regulations for the craftsmen at Colchester are given in *V.C.H. Essex*, ii, 459.

Typical thefts of hides were committed by Thomas Coxe of Harlow (1580), Edward Challys of Steeple Bumpstead, glovers, John Marshe of Stebbing (1586), Richard Ward of Great Yeldham (1566), John Lorkin and Thomas Carton, both of Walden (1589), and Andrew Horsenayle of Langford (1600), tanners, and Matthew Coxe of Brentwood leather-seller (1587). Richard Warner pointer (maker of points or laces for fastening clothes) stole from Richard Maslyn glover, both of Brentwood (1567), 2 buckskins, 8 sheepskins, a doeskin, and a calfskin; a Stortford (Herts.) glover also took buckskins and doeskins from Stephen Nightingale and Robert Harvye of Newport glovers (1582) ; and Clement Bale currier and Roger Ogesdon, both of Witham, broke into John Garret's tan-house at Boreham, making away with two hides (1588). At Vange in 1572 three men stole 30 'fells called lambskins' worth as much as £19.

There are a few thefts of horse-hair, which was used for stuffing cushions and other articles. A Great Bardfield labourer burgled a Sampford stable in 1571, taking 'mane-hairs' and 'tail-hairs' of eleven horses (2s. 6d.), and two years later stole 'tail-hair and mane-hair' from six horses (4s. 8d.) in two adjacent villages. Having claimed benefit of clergy for the first offence, he was found guilty again and was probably hanged. Robert Usher, the miller of Beeleigh near Maldon, in 1580 stole a variety of articles including 25 'asses' flock' (3s. 4d.), which presumably was also to be used as a stuffing material.

Other Goods

The records afford some evidence of thefts by other craftsmen and tradesmen. Thomas Jarvis, a Walden pewterer, purloined 13 pewter platters and a pewter dish. A few travelling tinkers succumbed to running off with metalware, doubtless handed to them for repair, such as brass kettles and a pewter chamberpot. Two tinkers broke into a kitchen at North Fambridge in 1590 and took away a 'furnace' (probably a big cauldron) worth 10s. Another pair of tinkers in 1562 stole 19 brass kettles weighing a hundredweight and worth £16 13s. 4d., a brass cauldron (16s.) and two brass pots (40s.), evidence of the high price of such large brass implements. They belonged to a London pewterer, and were appropriated at Braintree on 21 September, which was its annual fair-day.[1] Despite the remarkable increase in glazed windows in place of lattices in Harrison's time,[2] only one glazier, Nicholas Adyen of Mersea, appears, and all he stole was a pack of glass worth 3d.

A ray of light is shed on the important West Ham starch-making industry by the indictment in 1600 of John Tapp and Benjamin Baynarde, described (perhaps fictitiously) as gentlemen of that town, who stole

[1] Harrison, *Description of England*, 396.   [2] *Ibid.*, 197–99.

2,000 lb. of starch made from wheat and afterwards sold it to 'divers of
the Queen's loyal subjects'. They were at large when the case came up
at the Assizes. The next document on the file is a unique presentment of
all persons who had made starch in Essex since the publication of a royal
proclamation for their suppression. The list contains no less than thirty
persons, including three women, all of West Ham, with the weight of
starch in each case. This will be dealt with in a later volume on Home
and Work. In Essex, with its long coastline and numerous creeks pene-
trating deeply inland, one might have expected to find a fair number of
boat-stealers brought to book, for the craft would be readily recognizable
if the owners were smart enough to trace them before the thieves removed
any marks of identification. But there are only two indictments. A
Salcott sailor in 1574 stole a 'little boat' (£6) ; and in 1599 two Prittlewell mariners, who took a wherry (16s.) with its two oars (4s.), were
found guilty for the oars only and were whipped.

Agricultural implements left lying in the fields or hedges or in unlocked
barns must have been a constant temptation to the poorer farmworkers
having a little land, despite the weight of some of them. In this context
an extremely rare word is found three times : 'cronge' is defined as a
handle, but its exact meaning is not clear. Plough chains (2s.), an iron
cronge (4d.), and a coulter (8d.) were taken by an Ashdon husbandman
at Radwinter from one man, and similar implements (but no cronge)
and a mattock (6d.) from another (1592). Another iron cronge (11d.)
was stolen by a Great Maplestead labourer (1597). In 1594 a Colne
Engaine labourer stole a winch for a grindstone (6d.), 20 iron harrow
tines (teeth) and 20 iron cart nails (6s. 8d.), 12 horseshoes (3s.), 3 locks
(18d.), 3 'great hinges for a door' (5s.), and 'divers other parcels of iron'
(20s.), apparently from the smithy. He confessed to the felony, and 'had
had the book before', so he must have been hanged. A carpenter and
another labourer of the same village were also indicted for receiving,
but *Ignoramus* was returned by the grand jury. The reverse occurred at
Ashdon, when Robert Fromant and Thomas Fromant, the Hadstock
blacksmiths, stole 'a plough team and lez cronge', foot chain, coulter,
plough ear, and hook, and a week later similar items except the last two
from another man (1601). This looks like embezzlement of property in
their hands, as with the proverbially dishonest millers.

Among other goods stolen were of course large quantities of clothes,
bed-linen and table-linen, furniture, and kitchen utensils. It has not been
possible, within the authorised length of the book, to deal with these
articles. A recent work made good use of the typescript calendar of the
Essex Sessions records and a number of items about clothes from this
source are specifically quoted.[1] The account-books of Sir William Petre,
Secretary of State, of Ingatestone Hall, 1544–62, are exceptionally rich in

[1] C. W. and P. Cunnington, *Handbook of English Costume in the Sixteenth Century* (1954).

entries relating to the clothes of himself and his family, servants' liveries, jewellery and other accessories, and this material will appear in the near future.[1] Wills are a much better source for clothes, furniture and household articles than criminal records, and it is probable that a later volume of *Elizabethan Life* will be based on the collection of over 10,000 Essex wills.

Unlike so many of the crimes and offences for which the published Elizabethan Sessions records of other counties add relatively little to our account of Elizabethan disorder, larceny with housebreaking and burglary is well documented.[2]

Young Thieves

Children under the age of fourteen years were not punishable for theft. Thomas Sharpe of Chelmsford was found guilty of burglary. He had stolen 13s. from Henry Lennard's house. The Court scribe laconically noted, 'A boy of 8 years.' Richard Cracknell's house at (Great) Braxted was burgled by Thomas Toyse, who lived in the parish. He took a shirt, a hat, and 18s. in money. The county justices passed his case to the Assizes. Found guilty, he was remanded without judgement 'because he is a boy.' Fyndern Catesbye of Layer Marney stole a cloak, a woman's kirtle, a sheet, and some linen, worth 31s. 4d. in all. Having confessed, he was only whipped, 'because he is a boy.' Rachel Brackley of Prittlewell spinster stole a woman's gown worth 30s. and a kercher worth 20d. belonging to William Keeler of that parish. Five months later she stole a 'neckenger' (12d.), an apron (6d.), and 5s. in money from another Prittlewell man, William Dayes. She was found guilty on both charges and was remanded without judgement because she was only eleven years old.

---

[1] See p. 296, n.2, also next footnote.
[2] The index to *Middlesex County Records*, vol. i, under 'Apparel' is useful.

27

Treasure Trove

The taking away of hidden treasure was not a felony and was punished by fine and imprisonment. A royal licence was required for 'digging for treasure trove', and such licences are occasionally recorded in the State Papers and Patent Rolls. Two cases of illegal searches occur in the Sessions records, but no resulting indictments are preserved. The first, in 1591, is a recognizance for the appearance of John Warner of Great Waltham husbandman, charged with being 'one of the company of certain persons who of late have frequented the town of Witham pretending to have a commission to dig for treasure.'

Rumours of a stranger seen digging led to his being suspected of searching for hidden treasure. So Roger Harlackenden, J.P., summoned him for interrogation. Henry Wright of Pillerton (Warws.) clerk, according to his deposition, had been a student at Oxford, then a curate at Pillerton for five years, and was a practitioner in physic. Meeting one Shaa, a Cambridge fisherman, at Banbury Fair on St. Luke's Day last, he told him he lacked a benefice. Shaa recommended him to go to one Mr. Beriffe of Aldham, who would help him in that way. He therefore came to Essex. Beriffe 'set one Mr. Banbridge, a minister about Colchester' (apparently William Banbridge, vicar of Tolleshunt Major, 1581–91, when he resigned), 'on work to procure him a living'; and one Turner, the defendant's uncle, also told him that Browne, the governor of the Coggeshall house of correction, had undertaken to prefer him to a living. It then came to his knowledge that Thomas Turner of Earls Colne was a near kinsman of his, and he had since often stayed with him, practising physic, and 'had divers cures thereabouts' during his abode with Turner. William Turner of Halstead, who, he said, was his uncle, often visited him at Earls Colne. Coming to the point, Wright said that he had 'been in the lane where the digging was to look for herbs divers times', and once Thomas Turner was with him, but he had 'never heard of the digging until this morning as he was coming hither'. He finished by saying that 'one Neale hath a commission to dig for money at such places and that if he knew of it he would quickly be there to look for it.' Thomas Turner, also examined, said that Wright was his first cousin and by profession a physician, and had stayed with him for the last three weeks, never going out in the night-time. On Saturday last they went together to the place 'that is now digged, to look for herbs', but never otherwise.

Harlackenden endorsed the deposition with a memorandum to the effect that, while Wright was staying at Earls Colne, complaint had been made to him (the justice) about 'certain digging of ground in the night-time for money, as was supposed', and Wright being a stranger was suspected to have done it. The J.P. found 'much contrariety' in the two deponents' statements. He had ascertained that Shaa was 'a man of passing lewd behaviour', and he also considered that Wright's preferment to a cure depended on persons who had no means to advance him. 'Therefore', he concluded, 'I do in my poor opinion think him to be a man very suspicious, and so leave him to your good considerations.' What those considerations were are not in the Court's records. Harlackenden had taken recognizances for the two men's appearance, but Wright's two sureties, Thomas Turner and Robert Beriffe, both described as weavers of Earls Colne, defaulted, so Harlackenden sent Wright to gaol 'till further order be taken by Mr. Towse', J.P. (who lived at Bassingbourne Hall in Takeley).[1]

---

[1] The Librarian, Royal College of Physicians, kindly searched his records but found no reference to Wright.

24 COMMUNION CUPS
Both dated 1562, both stolen (in 1579 and 1587)

Wickham St. Paul's : broad band of foliated
strapwork, much restored, with later stem.

Margaret Roothing : conventional strapwork,
with narrow bands of decorative mouldings.

(See p. 278.)

HERE LYETH BVRYED THE BODY OF KATHERINE NIGHTINGALE,
WIFE TO GEFFERYE NIGHTINGALE ESQVIRE, WHO HAD ISSVE
BETWENE THE 7 CHILDREN THOMAS, HENRY. WILLIAM, MARYE,
ANNE, IHONE AND ELIZABETH. SHE DEPARTED THIS LIFE $\stackrel{E}{Y}$ 9TH
OF NOVEMBER IN THE 54 YEARE OF HER AGE, AND IN $\stackrel{E}{Y}$ YEA-
RE OF OVR LORD 1608. A GRAVE AND MODEST MATRON SHEE
WAS LOVEINGE & FAYTHFVLL TO HER HVSBANDE, CAREFVLL &
TENDER OVER HER CHILDREN, KINDE TO HER FREENDES, CVRTE-
OVS TO ALL, HELPEFVLL TO $\stackrel{E}{Y}$ POORE, HVRTFVLL TO NONE, HER
SORROWFVLL SVRVIVING HVSBANDE HATH CAVSED TO BE MADE
THIS DVRABLE MONVMENT AS A SADD MEMORIALL OF HIS GRE-
ATE LOSSE & HER WORTHE.

25 BRASS OF GEOFFREY NIGHTINGALE AND HIS WIFE,
NEWPORT CHURCH, 1608

(See p. 284.)

28

Contempt

While the records disclose no instance of anyone rash enough to assault a judge or a justice of the peace, there are a few cases of contempt in speech to justices or in refusal to execute parochial duties. A small part of the Suffolk town of Haverhill lay in Essex. What certain townsmen of the Essex end had done (or, more likely, not done, perhaps by disobeying a summons to appear) is not stated, but a stern letter was written by Lord Rich in his own hand in 1570 to the constables of the Essex 'hamlet' ordering them to summon five men to answer for their contempt before the Assize justices at the next gaol delivery, 'and at their utmost peril not to fail.'

To offer contemptuous words to an examining magistrate in his home was tantamount to exhibiting stupidity, or 'stomach' (p. 110). In the charge against Mr. Kempe's warrener the owners of Moyns and Spains Halls expressed conflicting opinions (p. 109). The only similar case is not so colourful. A Great Parndon husbandman was bound over in 1576 for contempt committed against James Altham in the J.P.'s own house (Mark Hall in Latton). At the same Sessions the constables of Rayleigh were each fined 20s. because they were unable to 'gainsay their contempt' to the satisfaction of the Court for refusing to receive certain rogues sent by the constables of Billericay on the warrant of Mr. Appleton, J.P. Ten years later a Lambourne tailor was enjoined to answer for his contempt at the gaol delivery. In 1600 a Boxted constable ordered by Edward Grimston, J.P., to arrest a villager charged with lewd behaviour with a woman, told the man who brought the warrant that he would not execute it, 'not for ten warrants.' One witness declared that she heard him say that there were better men than Mr. Grimston, and another testified that the constable said to the messenger, 'Do it yourself, and I will aid you.' In the same year John Frize, a yeoman of Great Braxted, was committed by the Commissioners for the Subsidy without bail 'for certain contempts'. This is learned from his recognizance taken before the Earl of Sussex, K.G., and Sir Thomas Mildmay, Custos Rotulorum. The County Bench deputed two of their number to settle the matter.

The Statute of Winchester (13 Edward I, 1285) laid down the general obligation to keep watch from sunset to sunrise. It enjoined the watchmen 'to arrest all strangers until morning, when enquiry should be made.'

x

Three months before Elizabeth's accession the Privy Council had asked the Earl of Oxford to order 'divers villages appointed to the watching of the Blockhouse of West Tilbury' to continue to be responsible for their normal 'town watches and beacon watches.'[1] This small fort put up by Henry VIII on the north bank of the Thames estuary for the defence of London was considerably enlarged in 1672 when the beautiful Water Gate of Tilbury Fort was built.

In 1569 Witham hundred jurors reported, 'The constables of Terling present that Dame Agnes Lady Browne' and five named men, 'being commanded by the constables to keep watch, utterly refused, but will watch at their own pleasure, by what right we know not, but pray reformation for the better service of the Queen's Majesty and the more aid and strength of our parish.' Two of the men were also presented for refusing to bear their charges for the Queen's service, meaning the army or the navy, and one of them again at the following Sessions for refusing to perform watch duty. It is rare to find a parish appointing six persons and equally rare to see a woman appointed. Three watchmen who absconded to raid a private fishery were mentioned earlier (p. 253). Six Great Dunmow men had been warned to watch by 'the constable's deputy, the constable being sick.' Said one of them, 'I know better when to watch than the constable knoweth when to warn me'; and of the others, some said they would not come and some would watch at another time, 'and so make the constable stay up, waiting for them till 10 or 11 o'clock at night, and then must go hire their watchmen.' Two Hatfield Broad Oak men were presented in 1583 for not keeping watch from Ascension Day until 1 July, and two of Earls Colne in 1592 for the same offence and for not appointing any of the inhabitants to watch.

Three presentments against constables for failing in their hue and cry duty are found. In 1574 it was the constable of White Notley whose mare was stolen, but, having 'made hue and cry to Black Notley', his counterpart there neglected to take it up. Ten years later there was a robbery at Goldhanger, the constable of which carried out his job, 'until he came to one Wilkinson, constable of Layer-de-la-Haye, and charged him to make the said hue and cry unto the next constable, but he answered that he needed not to make it forth without a justice's warrant.' Goldhanger and Layer-de-la-Haye are separated by six other parishes, and it is not clear why the Goldhanger constable's pursuit did not end at his own boundary. The third prosecution is a reminder that separate constables were appointed for certain hamlets which were either populous, distant from the main town or village, or lay in a different hundred from the remainder of the parish. Such a hamlet was Audley End (in Saffron Walden), which took its name from Sir Thomas Audley to whom Henry VIII had granted

[1] *Acts of the Privy Council*, vi, 390.

Walden Abbey in 1538 and still survives as an 'end' opposite the mansion formerly known as Audley House. In 1602 a yeoman and a tiler of Audley End stood bail for their neighbour, a tailor, who as constable of Audley End had 'most obstinately and contemptuously' refused to execute many warrants, hues and cries, 'and others'.

A few years earlier Shakespeare had immortalized such Dogberries, who mostly received rather than gave such contempt (p. 176) ; but contempt was a serious offence, as it generally implied refusal to obey a J.P.'s warrant, even if only that of Justice Shallow. If, to Shakespeare, Sir Thomas Lucy was the Justice Shallow of his own county, can we discover his Essex counterpart? The reader may recall the two cases of contempt exhibited against Robert, the third Lord Rich, in 1582 and 1592 (p. 67). Was he 'a cipher' in the eyes of the County Bench as well as in those of the vicar of Felsted? It is more fitting, however, to end this account of Disorder in Essex, against which the justices of the peace strove, with the tribute rightly paid to them by Dr. Samaha (p. 322) :

> These unpaid, and to a large extent unnoticed, men who spent so much of their time in the dull and often unprofitable business of administering their county are truly unsung heroes of English history.

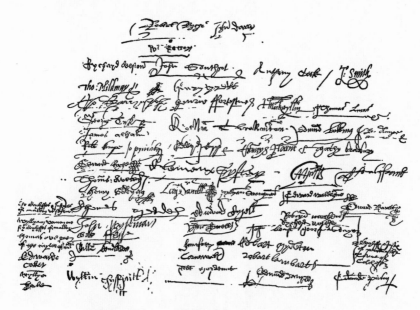

ESSEX JUSTICES OF THE PEACE, 1569

Signatures at a Special Sessions at Chelmsford for subscribing obedience to the Act of Uniformity. First line : Robert (Lord) Ryche, John (Lord) Darcy. Second line : (Sir) William Petre.

Appendix A
Highway Robberies

† = accessory or receiver   (n.) g. = (not) guilty   conf. = confessed   l. = labourer   y. = yeoman   hus. = husbandman   p. = prison

Date of robbery	Parish in which robbery committed	Victim(s) No.	Victim(s) Abode, etc.	Robber(s) No.	Robber(s) Abode, etc.	Verdict or sentence	Stolen Money	Other goods
Mar. 1558	Cressing (footpath)	1; 1	Braintree glover; Witham butcher	1 } 1 }	Witham y.	g.; g.	£6 13 4; £8 18 4	
Aug. 1567	Warley	1		2	Chipping Ongar tailor; Warley —	1 g.; 2 not in p.	£6 3 10	
Sep. 1567	Hornchurch	1	(unknown)	2	1 Chignal St. James hus.; 2 Writtle weaver	n.g.	1 10	
Nov. 1567	Brentwood	1		2	+ others unknown	n.g.	£29 17 6	
Sep. 1568	Walden	1		1	London tailor	g.	£4	
Dec. 1569	Purleigh	1		2	Heybridge tinker, Maldon weaver	1 g.; 2 n.g.	7 0	
Apr. 1571	Gt. Ilford	1	Navestock hus.	2	London y.	g.	£5 0 0	
May 1571	Gt. Ilford	1	Hornchurch wharfinger	1	London y.	g.	£16 0 0	
Jun. 1571	Stratford (in West Ham)	1	London poulterer	2	1 London y.; 2 Redbourn, Herts., cobbler	1 n.g.; 2 not in p.	£1 0 0	
Oct. 1572	Chingford	1	(unknown)	1		n.g.	£3 10 0	
Feb. 1573	Hatfield (?Peverel)	1		3		g.	1 3	
Oct. 1575	Corringham	1; 1; 1; 1		} 3		1, 2 sentence not stated; 3 hanged at Kent Assizes	£60 0 0; £38 0 0; £115 0 0; £180 0 0	horse £4, 2 gold rings £4
Dec. 1576	Manuden	1		2			£24 0 0	gold ring 13s. 4d.
— 1577	Kelvedon and Ilford	1 at each		—		g.	£2 0 0; —	
Sep. 1577	Brentwood	2		3	1 London gent.; 2, 3 Brentwood y.	1, 3 not in p.; 2 conf.	£49 0 0	2 horses £6, 5 yards of bays 15s., a green broadcloth £6, hat 2s.
Jul. 1578	Runwell	1	(to be despoiled)	1		n.g.		
Oct. 1579	Sible Hedingham	1		2	Dartford, Kent, y.	g.		

Date of robbery	Parish in which robbery committed	Victim(s) No.	Abode, etc.	Robber(s) No.	Abode, etc.	Verdict or sentence	Stolen Money	Other goods
Sep. 1580	Chadwell (in Dagenham)	1		3		1 g.; 2, 3 deleted	10 0	
Nov. 1580	Springfield	1		1		g.	£29 0 0	
Aug. 1584	Lt. Thurrock	1	(gent's servant)	1		g.	5 0	
Feb. 1585	Gt. Waltham	1		5	1 Romford gent.; 2 Brentwood l.; 3–5 unnamed	1 g.; 3–5 —	£10 0 0	
Feb. 1585	Lt. Waltham	1					£16 10 0	
Feb. 1585	Gt. Leighs	1					£1 6 0	
Oct. 1585	Chishall	1				not in p.		
Dec. 1585	Stanway	1	(to be robbed)			n.g.	—	
June 1586	Potter Street in Harlow	1		2	Takeley l.	not in p.	£2 10 0	gold chain £30
Mar. 1587	Lexden	1		2	Aldham l.	g.	£1 13 6	
Mar. 1587	Snaresbrook (in Wanstead)	1		5	1, 2, 3, 5 London butchers; 4 London tanner	1, 2, 4, 5 g.; 4 not in p.	£2 5 0	horse £6
Mar. 1587	Hornchurch	1		1	l.	g.	£1 10 0	hat 2s.
Dec. 1587	Ingatestone	1		2	mariners	g., not in p.	£1 4 8	cloak 26s. 8d., knife 4d.
Oct. 1587	Springfield	1		1	Fen Ditton, Cambs., l.	not in p.	4 0	knife 4d.
May 1588	Chrishall	1		3	1,2 Chelmsford; 3 Rettendon l.	in Cambridge gaol	2 8	2 pieces of cloth (£13 6 8)
Mar. 1589	Gt. Baddow	1		3	1 joiner; 2, 3 coopers	1 g.; 2, 3 not in p.	2 2	2 pairs of gloves 3d.
Jan. 1589	Thorpe	1		1	Chelmsford hus.	1 g.; 2, 3 not in p.	2 0	gold ring 10s.
Oct. 1589	West Ham	1		2	1 Coggeshall, 2 Braintree y.	g.	6 0	
Jan. 1590	Wickham Bishops	1		3	1–3 Hertford l.	1 conf.; 2 n.g.	£2 6 4	many parcels of silk taffeta £10
Nov. 1590	Four Want Way in Gt. Parndon	1		1	Quendon l.	1 n.g.; 2, 3 not in p.		
Nov. 1590	Newport	1		3	1–3 Clavering yeomen	not in prison	1 0	cloak 5s.
Feb. 1593	Netteswell	1		3†	4–6 do. yeomen and spinster	1 not in p.; 2–5 g.; 6 pregnant	£1 10 0	pack of cloth £40, horse £3
Feb. 1594	Epping	1		2	1 Epping l.; 2 Epping cook	g.	£2 9 2	
Aug. 1594	Purfleet (in West Thurrock) (river)	1		3		1–3 g.	£1 4 0	fowling piece 20s.
Dec. 1594	Braintree	1		1+1†	1 Finchingfield tailor; 2 Braintree l.	not in p.	18 0	

Date of robbery	Parish in which robbery committed	Victim(s) No.	Abode, etc.	Robber(s) No.	Abode, etc.	Verdict or sentence	Stolen Money	Other goods
Nov. 1595	Pod's Wood in Messing	1		2	Gt. Henny y.	outlawed for robbery in Norfolk	14 0	
Mar. 1596	Springfield	4		7+1†	1, 2 Lt. Waltham l. and butcher; 4–8 Chelmsford butchers (3), tailor and cutler	1–4 g. (2 hanged, 2 remanded to p.) ; 5–7 at large	£28 0 0 / 10 0 / 3 10	
Aug. 1596	Ardleigh	1	(unknown)	2		acq.	12 8	
— 1596	Stow Maries (footpath)	1		1	North Fambridge	g. for assault only	3 4	
Dec. 1596	Lawling	1		3	Blackmore tailor, hus. and shoemaker	1 at large ; 2,3 hanged	£10 5 3	
Apr. 1597	Waltham Abbey	1		1		hanged	£1 0 0	
Apr. 1597	Waltham Abbey	2		1	sailor	at large	£1 19 7 / 8	
Apr. 1597	Rame Acre in Gestingthorpe	1 }		2		hanged	£10 0 0	cloak 10s., sword 4s.
May 1597	Do.	1 }					2 4	
Dec. 1597	Park Lane in High Easter	1		3	1,2 Danbury ; 3 Gt. Easton	1,2 at large ; 3 hanged	11 0	hat 2s.
Feb. 1598	Harlow	1 }		1+2†	1 High Laver l. ; 2, 3 Magdalen, man and wife	1 hanged	3 0	6 ells holland 12s.
Feb. 1598	Latton	1 }		1	High Laver		6 0	cloak 3s., sword 12d.
Aug. 1599	Walthamstow	1		2	Chingford l.	acq.	1 0	
Sep. 1599	Maldon	1		1		acq.		
— 1599	Feering (?)	3		1	gent.	—	£145 18 0	
Nov. 1599	Henham	1		1	Aldham gent.	acq.	£5 0 0	
Nov. 1600	Walthamstow	2		2		1 g.; 2 no true bill	12 0	cloak 10s.
Jan. 1601	Epping	2		4	1–4 Woodford l.	acq.	£2 7 0	
Aug. 1602	Ridgewell	1	Finchingfield draper	2	1 Norfolk ; 2 —	at large	£29 9 8	horse £6

Money	£863 16 11
Goods	£135 3 7
Total	£999 0 6

Appendix B

Textile Goods Stolen

This table has been compiled from all cases of simple larceny, housebreaking, burglary and highway robbery of cloth, etc., but not clothes. Lines without a year belong to the same case as the dated line above.

The scores of indictments for stealing *clothes* contain similar information, e.g. 'doublet of black russet', 'French russet cloak'. These have not been included in the table, but may be considered under Costume when Wills are dealt with in Volume 3 of *Elizabethan Life*.

The English ell was 45 inches in length, the Dutch or Flemish ell 27 inches; the nail was 2¼ inches. Pieces were not of fixed length.

As 'holland' and 'kersey' were always written without an initial capital, 'manchester', 'gentish', 'milan' and 'hamborow', etc., have been treated similarly. The best explanation of the terms used is the 'Glossary of Materials' in C. W. and P. Cunnington, *Handbook of English Costume in the 17th Century* (1955).

Date	Quantity	Quality	Value		
1558	2 ells	white damask		13	3
1558	2 yards	red woollen cloth		6	8
1559	3 yards	white frize		4	0
	2 pieces (4 yards)	cloth called housewife's russet		5	0
	1 piece	sarcenet cloth		1	0
1560	16 ells	canvas		19	4
	1 ell	calico		2	0
	1 yard	holland		2	8
1563	20 pieces	woollen cloth	£3	0	0
1563	2 ells	kersey		5	4
1564	4 yards	kersey		10	0
	2 yards	frize		2	0
1565	1 piece (7 ells)	sheep's russet (2s. ell)		4	0
	1 piece (9 ells)	grey manchester frize (12d. ell)		9	0
	4 ells	coarse white cloth (1s. 8d. ell)		6	8
1566	21 pieces	cloth	5	0	0
1566	1 ell	broad blue cloth		12	0
	5 ells	white holmes fustian		5	4
	8 ells	russet woollen cloth	1	19	4
	2 ells	white linen		2	8
	1 ell	tawny frizado		4	8
1566	6½ ells	whited canvas		7	7
1566	10 ells	linen called gentish cloth		15	0
	2 ells	fine holland		11	0
	3 ells	lockram		3	9
	2½ ells	canvas		2	0
	8½ yards	fustian		7	1
1566	2 half ells	fringe holland	—	—	
1567	3 yards	broad woollen cloth		15	0
1567	4½ yards	three-quarter cloth		3	0
1567	2¼ yards	new colour kentish broadcloth	£1	0	0
	1½ yards	sheep's colour broadcloth		12	0
	1¾ yards	orange tawney kersey		6	0
1568	7 yards	red mockado		9	4
	2 yards	azure broadcloth		14	6
	4 yards	devonshire kersey		10	0
	6 yards	fustian		4	6
	5 yards	puke cloth	£2	10	0
1568	1 sorting cloth (6 yards)	broadcloth	£1	0	0

Date	Quantity	Quality	£	s	d
1568	1 length (7 yards)	russet cloth		14	0
1570	2 ells	lockram		1	8
1570	3 ells	canvas		2	6
1570	20 pieces	linen cloth	£2	0	0
1571	5 pieces	white cloth	£20	0	0
1572	28 ells	linen cloth	£2	10	0
	1 piece	housewife's cloth		13	4
1572	2 pieces	velvet		13	4
1572	1 yard	buckram		1	0
1573	3 yards	russet cloth		5	6
	3 yards	woollen cloth		2	8
1574	2 ells	kersey		5	0
1574	13½ yards	hair cloth		8	8
1576	13 yards	red mockado		13	0
1577	4 yards	kersey		13	4
1577	18 ells	linen		13	4
1577	2¼ yards	rat colour broadcloth		—	
	3¼ yards	black bays		7	7
	¾ yard	red mockado		1	4
	12 yards	grey frize		16	4
1577	5 yards	bays		15	0
	one	green broadcloth	£6	0	0
1578	12 ells	hamborow cloth		10	0
	6 ells	fine canvas		12	0
	3 remnants	brown holland	£1	6	0
	10 ells	whited canvas		12	6
1579	8½ yards	medley (colour) woollen cloth		17	0
	14 yards	grey russet	£1	5	4
1579	4 yards	russet cloth		13	4
	2 yards	broadcloth		6	8
	3 yards	white frize		5	0
1579	13½ yards	stammel cloth	£6	15	0
1579	6 yards	woollen cloth		15	0
1579	2¾ ells	brown blue cloth	£1	13	4
1580	1 piece	durance		1	0
1580	18 yards	flaxen cloth		12	0
1580	27 yards	flaxen cloth	£1	10	0
1580	18 yards	linen cloth		18	0
1581	3 yards	russet		4	0
1581	4 ells	russet colour cloth	£1	4	8
1581	32 yards	white frize	£2	0	0
	6 yards	black frize		10	0
	12 yards	white cotton		9	0
	9 yards	white kersey		18	0
1581	12 yards	white frize		15	0
	4 yards	grey broadcloth	£1	2	0
	3 yards	linen		3	0
	¾ yard	white canvas		2	0
1581	1 ell	fine osnabrig			8
1581	2 yards	kersey		—	—
1581	12 yards	russet	£1	7	0
	1½ yards	broad silk russet		13	6
1584	1 piece	frizado		7	0
1584	2 pieces	frizado		15	0
1584	1 piece	russet cloth		10	0
1585	1 piece	azure colour cloth	£1	0	0
1585	27 yards	russet cloth	£2	10	0
1585	20 yards	sowtage		5	0
1586	3¾ yards	grey frize		4	0
	2½ yards	green cloth		5	0
	2½ yards	white cotton		2	0
1586	1 piece	bays	£2	0	0
1586	½ ell	lockram			8
1586	4 yards	russet cloth		12	4

Date	Quantity	Quality	Value		
1586	8 pieces	holland cloth	£10	0	0
	7 pieces	canvas	£5	0	0
1587	14 pieces	holland cloth	£24	0	0
	2 ells	dutch fustian		6	0
1587	remnants	woollen cloth	£1	0	0
1588	1 piece	violet cloth		16	0
	1 piece	yellow cotton		17	0
	1 piece	red cloth		18	0
	1 piece	white frize		2	0
	1 piece	green cotton		5	0
	1 piece	blue cloth		15	0
	1 piece	red cotton		1	3
1588	2 pieces	cloth	£13	6	8
1588	divers parcels	woollen cloth	£15	0	0
1588	15 yards	red and green medley colour broadcloth	—	—	
	6 yards	pheasant colour broadcloth	—	—	
	3¾ yards	cloth rash	—	—	
1588	2 pieces	cloth	£13	6	8
1589	1 piece	milan fustian		10	0
1589	2½ yards	red cloth		3	0
	3¾ yards	russet cloth		4	0
1589	11 ells	blanketing	—	—	
	8 pieces	linen	—	—	
1589	2 yards	blue cloth		13	4
1590	1 piece (10 yards)	russet cloth		10	0
1590	15 yards	white sacking		12	0
	15 yards	straw colour sacking		12	0
	15 yards	ditto red striped		12	0
	3 yards	orange tawny carrel		5	0
	6 yards	'leven' black taffeta		10	0
	2 yards	'leven' blue taffeta		3	4
	12 yards	crane colour taffeta		9	0
	5 yards	black rash		7	0
	7 ells	holland	£2	7	0
	1 parcel	the gathering		2	0
1590	14 yards	violet and grain cloth	£7	0	0
1590	2 pieces of rolls	holland	£12	0	0
1590	10 yards	coarse white cloth		10	0
1590	3¾ yards	housewife's white woollen cloth		6	0
1590	divers pieces	silk taffetas	£10	0	0
1591	1 yard	broadcloth		3	4
1591	1 ell	coarse cloth		1	0
	divers parcels	linen	£4	0	0
1592	3 pieces	fustian		4	0
	12 yards	holland	£2	0	0
	many pieces	fringe and lace	£1	0	0
1592	10 yards	white twill		14	0
1592	7 yards	cotton		7	0
1593	9 yards	wadmol		9	0
	9 yards	osnabrig	—	—	
1593	2 yards	holland		5	0
	6 ells	osnabrig		4	0
1593	1 pack	linen cloth	£40	0	0
1593	5 yards	white frize		6	8
	6¼ yards	russet cloth		14	10
1593	1 yard	russet		2	0
	1½ yards	cotton		1	0
1593	4 yards	woollen cloth		10	0
1593	2 yards	cotton		1	0
1594	50 yards	woollen cloth	£10	0	0
1596	6 yards	blue cloth		6	0
1596	18 yards	hempen cloth		10	0
1596	6 yards	kersey	£1	0	0
1596	16 yards	bays		8	0

Date	Quantity	Quality	Value		
1597	9 yards	peach colour pennistone	£1	10	0
	8 yards	sage colour kersey	£1	12	0
	3 yards	ash colour bays		7	0
	3½ yards	milan fustian		10	0
	3 yards	hamborow fustian		2	6
	4¼ yards	russet cloth		15	0
	1½ yards	blue cloth		12	0
1597	10 yards	canvas		5	0
1597	6 yards	frize		6	0
	4 yards	hempen cloth		4	0
	4 yards	fine canvas		10	0
	3 yards	hamborow whited cloth		4	0
	19 yards	brown hempen cloth		10	0
1597	23 yards	white cloth	£3	6	0
1597	9 yards	broad azure cloth	£2	0	0
1597	30 ells	flaxen cloth	£1	10	0
1598	6 ells	holland		12	0
1600	11 yards	canvas		2	8
	3 yards	fringe		2	0
	5 yards	white russet cloth		12	4
	4 yards	white frize		6	8
1600	12 ells	woollen cloth	£1	0	0
1600	8 yards	white flannel			11
1600	3 yards	white russet cloth		1	6
1600	¾ yard	broadcloth		2	0
	3¼ yards	fustian		6	0
1600	3 nails	silk grograine		2	0
1600	¾ yard	broadcloth		2	0
	3¼ yards	fustian		6	0
1601	2 yards	perpetuana		3	4
	1 piece	cipres			6
1601	100 yards	hempen cloth	£2	11	4
1601	2½ yards	linen cloth		5	0
1601	10 yards	russet cloth	£2	10	0
	6 yards	white cotton		6	0
1602	2 pieces	white fustian	£1	12	8
	1 piece	white osnabrig	£1	1	0
	1 piece	green kersey		8	4
	1 piece	white frize		4	6

Appendix C

Leather, etc. Stolen

Date	Quantity	Value		
1563	4 curried (dressed) calfskins		4	0
1566	2 white leather hides (pelts)		6	0
1567	2 buckskins		6	0
	8 sheepskins		2	8
	1 calfskin			6
	1 doeskin		1	4
1570	a piece of ox hide		2	0
1572	30 fells called lambskins	£19	0	0
1573	1 bend (thin strip) of leather		2	0
	2 half crops of leather		1	8
1574	1 raw hide		2	0
1579	6 buckskins	£1	0	0
1580	13 skins	£1	0	0
1582	buckskins and doeskins		—	—
1583	2 lambskins and 1 sheepskin			10
1584	7 buckskins and doeskins, 12 calfskins,			
	12 sheepskins and lambskins	£2	0	0
1586	2 buckskins		8	0
1586	23 sheepskins		5	0
1586	2 raw cow hides		10	0
	3 sheepskins		1	0
1587	1 steer hide		4	0
1587	3 dozen lambskins		6	8
1588	2 hides		12	0
1589	6 wool fells		6	0
	1 cow hide		6	8
1589	1 cow hide		10	0
1591	4 cow hides	£1	6	8
	3 doeskins		8	0
1594	1 steer hide		7	0
1597	2 sheep carcases		16	0
1598	2 sheepskins		1	4
1600	2 tanned cow hides	£1	0	0
	2 cow hides	£1	0	0
	11 calf skins		10	0
1602	9 sheepskins		10	0

Appendix D
Theft in Essex, 1558–1603
(*Larceny, Housebreaking, Burglary, Closebreaking, Highway Robbery, Assault*)

The tables, which incorporate the information in Assize, Quarter Sessions and Queen's Bench records, give the amounts of cash and the value of the livestock and goods stolen, the number of cattle and horses, and the number of 'cases'. Where an indictment includes items of more than one kind (e.g. food, clothes), each is counted separately, but indictments transferred from Q.S. to Assizes are not counted twice, and trespass cases are ignored. Some Sessions rolls and Assize files are lost : to estimate the total values for the 45 years, had both series been perfect, add 10 per cent. ; but the enhanced number of 'cases' probably represents the number of individual indictments in both Courts during the reign. A few indictments do not allow precise analysis, and most figures should therefore be taken as approximate. Figures for 'food' exclude lambs, etc., stolen.

Livestock	*Larceny*		*Closebreaking*		*Highway Robbery*		*Total*	
	cases	*animals*	*cases*	*animals*	*cases*	*animals*	*cases*	*animals*
sheep, wethers, rams, lambs	201	2,301	41	533			251	2,834
		£503		*£38*				*£541*
cows, heifers, oxen, steers, bulls, bullocks, calves	102	558	36	102			138	660
		£802		*£79*				*£881*
pigs, hogs	6	69	6	6			12	75
		£30		*£2*				*£32*
horses, geldings, mares, foals	98	244	19	39	5	6	122	289
		£707		*£95*		*£25*		*£827*
	417	3,172	102	680	5	6	524	3858
		£2,042		*£214*		*£25*		*£2,281*

	Larceny	*House-breaking*	*Burglary*	*Close-breaking*	*Highway robbery*	*Assault*	*Total*
	cases	*cases*	*cases*	*cases*	*cases*	*cases*	*cases*
	value	*value*	*value*	*value*	*value*	*value*	*value*
Money, including named coins	101	68	34	4	61	2	270
	£1,068	*£320*	*£396*	*£14*	*£864*	*£30*	*£2,692*
Plate, gold, etc. articles, jewellery	22	19	22		14		77
	£210	*£70*	*£330*		*£35*		*£645*
Clothes, bed- and table-linen, wool, cloth, leather	315	115	90	24	8		552
	£467	*£173*	*£186*	*£6*	*£74*		*£906*
Household, kitchen articles	41	6	5				52
	£52	*£7*	*£5*				*£64*
Grain	27	5	4	4			40
	£10	*£9*	*£2*	*£2*			*£23*
Food, including poultry	53	13	13				79
	£38	*£18*	*£10*				*£66*
Miscellaneous goods	22	5	6	1	1		35
	£41	*£12*	*£13*	*£2*	*£1*		*£69*
Church goods	7		1				8
	£21		*£3*				*£24*
cases	588	231	175	33	84	2	1,113
value	*£1,907*	*£609*	*£945*	*£24*	*£974*	*£30*	*£4,489*

Livestock cases 524
Livestock value £2,281

Total cases 1,637
Total value £6,770

Appendix E

Crime and Punishment in Elizabethan Essex

CONTRIBUTED BY J. SAMAHA[1]

The tables are based on cases for four types of felony – public (witch-craft); private, against the body only (murder, homicide, and rape); private, against the body and goods (burglary, robbery, forcible entry to commit felony); private felony, against the goods only (larceny). The records of these felonies are found mainly in the Assize files. In addition, indictments removed from Quarter Sessions by writ of *certiorari* for trial at Assizes, records of gaol delivery, coroners' inquests, and occasionally jury presentments, all in Queen's Bench records, produce evidence. Quarter Sessions rolls do not ordinarily yield evidence of felony unless they were held in conjunction with a gaol delivery. They are, of course, the only real evidence of almost all criminal offences prior to indictment. For those Sessions which also delivered the gaol in Colchester Castle there are the invaluable recognizances to appear and give evidence, only a few of which remain for indictments of felony at Assizes.

The choice of the years (1559–60, 1570–71, 1580–81, 1588–89, 1601–2) needs explanation. At first an attempt was made to tabulate the data for the whole reign. After analysing 2,500 cases from the beginning, middle and closing years and all cases from 1571 to 1603 in Chelmsford and Lexden hundreds, it was clear that it was unnecessary to collect every case. Several considerations determined the choice of the two-year periods. It was necessary, *inter alia*, to take years with almost complete records.

Certain important omissions must also be noted. No cases from Star Chamber appear in these samples. They would surely augment the number of cases for riot, but would not affect any of the felonies here since that court had no power over life or limb. Neither did the writer consult the ecclesiastical court records, which include many cases for witchcraft, though the trend in the cases would probably not be altered.[2] Finally, these tables show no pardons issued out of Chancery or otherwise, unless they are recorded in the Assize files or Quarter Sessions rolls.

It is also important to point out that trends are only general. Variations occur within any court term and even within a year. To even this out, two-year totals were used. Cases from Lexden hundred showed an obstinate refusal to fit into anything but the most erratic patterns. Further work in this densely-populated, wool-producing urban area must be done to explain this striking exception. These are important limitations on the conclusions to be drawn from the evidence. But they do not vitiate the most striking feature of all these records – that of steady and inexorable growth, both in the sheer numbers of documents and in cases of both felony and misdemeanour.

[1] Somewhat condensed by myself from Dr. Samaha's MS.—F.G.E.
[2] See A. Macfarlane, *Witchcraft in Tudor and Stuart England* (1970), based largely on Essex records but not published until after Dr. Samaha had completed his work.

TABLE 1 FELONIES BY TOTALS AND PERCENTAGES

	1559–1560 no.	%	1570–1571 no.	%	1580–1581 no.	%	1588–1589 no.	%	1601–1602 no.	%
Public Felony										
Witchcraft	1	1.1	11	7.1	14	9.0	29	11.0	16	5.0
Private Felony Against the Body Only										
Murder and Homicide	2	2.3	10	6.5	20	12.0	22	8.0	17	6.0
Rape and Buggery	6	6.3	1	0.6	1	1.0	4	2.0	7	2.3
Private Felony Against the Body and Goods										
Burglary	22	25.0	25	16.1	18	11.0	27	10.0	33	11.0
Robbery	6	6.8	10	6.5	8	5.0	8	3.0	4	1.0
Forcible Entry	–	–	–	–	2	1.0	–	–	7	2.3
Private Felony Against the Goods Only										
Horse	15	17.0	11	7.1	20	12.0	26	10.0	19	6.0
Livestock	20	22.7	42	27.1	11	7.0	76	29.0	93	31.0
Food	1	1.1	4	2.6	2	1.0	14	5.0	21	7.0
Chattels	15	17.0	36	23.2	59	36.0	50	19.0	81	27.0
Chattels over £5	–	–	5	3.2	7	5.0	7	3.0	4	1.3
TOTALS	88	99.8	155	100.0	162	100.0	258	100.0	302	99.9

TABLE 2 FELONIES ACCORDING TO FREQUENCY

	1559–1560		1570–1571		1580–1581		1588–1589		1601–1602
1	Burglary	1	Theft–livestock	1	Theft–chattels	1	Theft–livestock	1	Theft–livestock
2	Theft–livestock	2	Theft–chattels	2–3	Homicide	2	Theft–chattels	2	Theft–chattels
3–4	Theft–horses	3	Burglary	2–3	Theft–horses	3	Witchcraft	3	Burglary
3–4	Theft–chattels	4–5	Witchcraft	4	Burglary	4	Burglary	4	Theft–food
5–6	Rape, etc.	4–5	Theft–horses	5	Witchcraft	5	Theft–horses	5	Theft–horses
5–6	Robbery	6–7	Homicide	6	Theft–livestock	6	Homicide	6	Homicide
7	Homicide	6–7	Robbery	7	Robbery	7	Theft–food	7	Witchcraft
8–9	Theft–food	8	Theft–over £5	8	Theft–over £5	8	Rape, etc.	8–9	Forcible entry
8–9	Witchcraft	9	Theft–food	9–10	Forcible entry	9	Robbery	8–9	Rape
10–11	Theft–chattels	10	Rape, etc.	9–10	Theft–food	10	Theft–chattels	10	Robbery
	over £5	11	Forcible entry	11	Rape, etc.	11	Theft–over £5	11	Theft–chattels over £5
							Forcible entry		

TABLE 3 SENTENCES, ETC. BY TOTALS AND PERCENTAGES

	1559–1560 no.	%	1570–1571 no.	%	1580–1581 no.	%	1588–1589 no.	%	1601–1602 no.	%
Hanged	17	19.3	49	31.6	36	21.2	54	20.0	50	15.3
Fined	–	–	–	–	–	–	–	–	3	0.9
Whipped	–	–	–	–	13	7.6	13	4.9	18	5.5
Pardoned	1	1.1	6	3.9	11	6.5	3	1.1	2	0.6
Clergy claimed	13	14.8	49	31.6	45	26.5	64	23.7	54	16.6
Pregnancy claimed	3	3.4	4	2.6	9	5.3	19	7.0	12	3.7
At large	21	23.9	5	3.2	15	8.2	31	11.4	80	17.2
Died in prison	–	–	1	0.6	–	–	–	–	3	0.9
Acquitted	33	37.5	41	26.5	41	24.1	81	30.0	95	29.1
Imprisoned	–	–	–	–	–	–	–	–	9	2.8

TABLE 4 SENTENCES ETC. ACCORDING TO FREQUENCY

1559–1560		1570–1571		1580–1581		1588–1589		1601–1602	
Acquit	33	Clergy	49	Clergy	45	Acquit	81	Acquit	95
At large	21	Hang	49	Acquit	41	Clergy	64	At large	80
Hang	17	Acquit	41	Hang	36	Hang	54	Clergy	54
Clergy	13	Pardon	6	At large	15	At large	31	Hang	50
Pregnancy	3	At large	5	Whip	13	Pregnancy	19	Whip	18
Pardon	1	Pregnancy	4	Pardon	11	Whip	13	Pregnancy	12
Whip	0	Dead	1	Pregnancy	9	Pardon	3	Prison	9
Fine	0	Fine	0	Fine	9	Fine	0	Fine	3
Dead	0	Whip	0	Dead	0	Dead	0	Whip	3
								Pardon	2

Totals

Acquit	291	Whip	44
Clergy	225	Prison	9
Hang	206	Dead	4
At large	152	Fine	3
Pregnancy	47	TOTAL	995

TABLE 5 HANGING SENTENCES ACCORDING TO FREQUENCY

1559–1560		1570–1571		1580–1581		1588–1589		1601–1602	
Theft–livestock	8	Burglary	16	Burglary	8	Burglary	16	Burglary	14
Burglary	4	Theft–livestock	12	Theft–horses	8	Witchcraft	14	Witchcraft	12
Theft–horses	3	Witchcraft	6	Witchcraft	4	Theft–horses	12	Theft–livestock	10
Theft–over £5	2	Theft–horses	4	Homicide	4	Homicide	4	Theft–horses	6
TOTAL	17	Theft–chattels	4	Robbery	3	Robbery	2	Homicide	2
		Robbery	3	Theft–chattels	3	Theft–livestock	2	Forcible entry	2
		Homicide	3	Rape, etc.	2	Theft–food	2	Theft–property	2
		Theft–over £5	1	Forcible entry	1	Theft–over £5	2	Theft–food	1
		TOTAL	49	Theft–livestock	1	TOTAL	54	Theft–over £5	1
				Theft–food	1			TOTAL	50
				Theft–over £5	1				
				TOTAL	36				

TABLE 6   HANGING SENTENCES ACCORDING TO PERCENTAGES

(This table shows what percentage of those convicted of each offence received a sentence of hanging)

1559–1560	%	*1570–1571*	%	*1580–1581*	%	*1588–1589*	%	*1601–1602*	%
Theft–livestock	40	Burglary	64	Rape	100	Burglary	59	Witchcraft	75
Theft–horses	20	Witchcraft	54	Theft–food	50	Witchcraft	48	Burglary	42
Burglary	18	Theft–horses	36	Forcible entry	50	Theft–horses	46	Theft–horses	31
Theft–chattels	13	Homicide	30	Burglary	44	Robbery	25	Forcible entry	28
		Robbery	30	Theft–horses	40	Homicide	18	Theft–over £5	25
		Theft–livestock	28	Robbery	37	Theft–food	14	Homicide	12
		Theft–over £5	20	Witchcraft	29	Theft–chattels	4	Theft–livestock	11
		Theft–chattels	11	Homicide	20	Theft livestock	3	Theft–food	5
				Theft–over £5	14			Theft–chattels	2
				Theft–livestock	9				
				Theft–chattels	5				

Appendix F

CONTRIBUTED BY J. SAMAHA[1]

For most counties it is extremely difficult, if not impossible, to compile adequate lists of justices of the peace for the Elizabethan period. Only a small number of commissions of the peace survive, a few of which were copied on to the *dorse* of the Patent Rolls. The list of names from one of these copies is reproduced in Table 4. Lists like this one have serious limitations. Since so few are extant it is impossible to uncover trends in the membership of the commission during the period. Furthermore, since only names appear they tell nothing of the extent of activity of the justices. Indeed, any attempt to use these lists for that purpose would definitely be misleading. A glance at Table 4 shows why. Only a small number of those named in the commission took an active part in the county's judicial administration.

Another source, the calendars of the justices of the peace in the Assize files, are preserved for Essex. Few counties are thus fortunate. These calendars are contemporary documents that the Clerk of the Peace drew up for the Clerk of Assize and handed them over shortly before the Assize opened. The Clerk of Assize used them as an attendance roster and put some revealing notes on them. The names of the justices who were ill, excused for other reasons, or dead were also noted; and from 1575 those who were present at the Assizes. Fines for those absent and unexcused were also noted. These calendars form an almost unbroken series and since the Assize Clerk annotated them they are specially important. From them it is possible to compile complete and current lists of the names of justices. They are thus more valuable than the few commissions on the Patent Rolls. It is also impossible to determine attendance at Assizes from the Assize Clerk's notes on the calendars. They do not, however, state whether and to what extent the justices were active at their own Quarter Sessions. Justices who often attended Assizes may have attended Quarter Sessions rarely. For example, Christopher Chibborne, easily the hardest-working justice in Elizabethan Essex, rarely attended Assizes. There is, however, for Essex another source by which to measure the extent of the justices' activity. The Sessions rolls include an almost complete set of rosters of justices who attended Sessions. Such lists for other counties during this period are almost non-existent. Unlike the later lists for Somerset which Professor Barnes found inaccurate[2] and a few other incomplete lists which give a few names followed by a tantalising 'and others', the Essex rosters are both accurate and complete.

The names in Table 1 and the attendance figures in Tables 1 and 2 are derived from these rosters. Though no better source for measuring a justice's activity exists, it has some limitations. The rosters include only justices who attended Quarter Sessions. Since the tables derive from them and since all justices in the commissions did not attend Quarter Sessions, it follows that some justices in the commission will not appear in Table 1, which, in fact, should be termed more accurately a table of *active* justices. Furthermore, attendance at Sessions did not always indicate which justices were most active. Sometimes between sessions an individual justice took many recognizances either for good behaviour or to

---

[1] Somewhat condensed by myself from Dr. Samaha's MS.—F.G.E.
[2] T. Barnes, *Somerset 1629–1640*, chapter 3 (Cambridge, U.S.A., 1961).

keep the peace, committed many suspected felons to the Colchester Castle gaol to await trial, quelled affrays, and together with a fellow justice tried cases of forcible entry, and yet did not attend the Session following. This is not common, but it happened occasionally.

All information on the justices' university background is based on Venn's *Alumni Cantabrigienses* and Foster's *Alumni Oxonienses*. Similarly, the information concerning their professional background included in Table 1 and summarised in Table 3 is based on the registers of admissions to the various Inns of Court. Again, information was included only when it seemed certain that justices with the same names were identical. Because of this restriction on entries it is fair to assume that these lists and the summaries based on them represent an absolute minimum.

Despite the limitations, the tables provide some interesting biographical information about a socially significant segment of Essex society. But they do more. Taken together with the tables in Appendix E they demonstrate some important developments. The growth in numbers of justices of the peace, in the number of sessions they attended, and in the average attendance at Quarter Sessions parallels the increase in the Court's business. The increasing percentage of those who attended university (usually Cambridge) points to a better-educated group of individuals. At the same time that their education improved, their professional training, however, declined. This decline should be compared with Professor Gleason's findings in the few counties which he studied.[1]

Together, these appendices and tables tell an interesting and important story. In Elizabethan Essex a growing number of more active, better educated and truly amateur men in the county were devoting their time to coping with the problem that a steadily increasing load of work was creating. They were, for the most part, purely local men who did not cast their ambition beyond their own county. These unpaid, and to a large extent unnoticed, men who spent so much time in the dull and often unprofitable business of administering their county are truly unsung heroes of English history.

TABLE 1

Names, status, education and professional training, years attended Quarter Sessions and number of sessions attended.

	Status	University	Legal background	Quarter Sessions	Sessions attended
Abell, John	gent.			1573–1575	3
Altham, James	gent.		Gray's Inn	1564–1581	11
Amys, Israel	gent.	Camb. (St. John's) B.A., M.A.	Middle Temple	1586–1589	4
Amys, Roger	gent.			1564–1569	4
Appleton, Hen.	gent.			1574–1588	14
Archer, Hen.	gent.			1575–1585	11
Ayloff, Wm.	gent.		Lincoln's Inn (Justice, Queen's Bench)	1562–1590	7
Ayloff, Wm. of St. Osyth	gent.			1590–1603	20
Barlie, Rich.	gent.			1586–1590	9
Barrett, Edw.	gent.	Oxford	Lincoln's Inn	1566–1580	5
Barrington, Frs.	knight	Camb. M.A., 1580		1586–1603	25
Barrington, Tho.	gent.		Gray's Inn	1564–1580	17

[1] J. Gleason, *The Justices of the Peace in England, 1558–1640* (Oxford, 1969).

	Status	University	Legal background	Quarter Sessions	Sessions attended
Beckingham, Tho.					
	gent.			1603	1
Bendishe, Tho.	gent.	Camb. (Peterhouse)	Middle Temple	1589–1599	6
Bendlowes, Wm.	gent.	Camb. (St. John's)	Lincoln's Inn (barrister serjeant)	1562–1564	4
Bocking, Edmund	gent.			1563–1576	16
Bradbury, Matth.	knight			1563–1582	16
Browne, Anthony			Justice (Queen's Bench)	1563–1564	2
Browne, Wistan	gent.			1578–1580	3
Bury, Edw.	gent.			1563–1569	5
Butler, Edw.	gent.			1602	1
Butler, John	gent.			1582–1601	21
Capell, Gamaliel	gent.			1599–1603	10
Capell, Hen.	gent.			1576–1581	6
Cardynall, Wm.	gent.	Camb. (St. John's)	Gray's Inn (bencher reader)	1562–1584	9
Cheshall, Wm.	gent.			1563–1564	2
Chibborne, Christr.					
	gent.			1575–1602	36
Clarke, Rob.	knight		Baron of Exchequer	1582–1595	20
Clovile, Eustace	gent.			1582–1589	22
Cole, Nich.	gent.			1602	1
Colshill, Tho.	gent.			1583	1
Cooke, Anthony	gent.	Camb.	Gray's Inn	1563–1564	2
Darcy, Brian	gent.		Lincoln's Inn	1582	2
Darcy, John	baron		Middle Temple	1564–1588	15
Darcy, Rich.	gent.			1562	1
Darcy, Tho.	knight		Lincoln's Inn	1583–1593	2
Darrell, Geo.	gent.			1577–1581	3
Deane, Wm.	gent.			1582	2
Eliott, Edw.	gent.	Camb. (Christ's) B.A., M.A.	priest	1586–1595	18
Fortescue, Hen.	gent.			1568–1575	8
Franke, Rich.	gent.			1591–1602	9
Franke, Rob.	gent.			1598	1
Franke, Tho.	knight			1566–1574	10
Gaines, John				1595	1
Gardner, Tho.	gent.	Camb. (Peterhouse) B.A.	priest	1600–1603	3
Gente, Tho.	knight	Camb.	Middle Temple (barrister, Baron of Exchr.)	1572–1591	27
Golding, Hen.	gent.		Gray's Inn	1566–1576	10
Golding, Tho.	gent.	Camb. (Gonville)	Middle Temple	1566–1569	2
Graye, Hen.	knight		Gray's Inn	1573–1589	12
Grimston, Edw.	gent.	Camb. (Christ's), age 13	Gray's Inn (Master of Chancery)	1591–1602	6
Hadley, Geo.	gent.			1564	1
Hall, Rob.	gent.			1579	1
Harlackendon, Rog.					
	gent.	Camb. (Magdalene)		1593–1601	7
Harleston, John	gent.			1600	1
Harrys, Arthur	gent.		Lincoln's Inn	1572–1595	19
Harrys, Tho.	gent.		Lincoln's Inn	1593–1603	5
Harrys, Vincent	gent.			1571–1572	4
Harrys, Wm.	gent.			1600	1
Harvey, Frs.	gent.		Gray's Inn	1569–1598	16
Harvey, Geo.	gent.			1590–1593	3
Heygate, Reg.	gent.	Camb.	Gray's Inn	1571–1576	8
Higham, Wm.	gent.		Inner Temple	1585–1598	7
Hubbard, Edw.	gent.			1582–1598	15
Huddleston, Edmund					
	knight			1581–1588	5

	Status	University	Legal background	Quarter Sessions	Sessions attended
Isaake, Edw.	gent.		Gray's Inn	1566–1568	2
Ive, John	gent.			1594–1597	2
Josselyn, John	gent.			1599–1600	3
Kempe, Rob.	gent.		Lincoln's Inn	1564–1569	9
Kighley, Tho.	gent.	Camb. (Trinity)		1600–1603	10
Killingworth, John					
	gent.			1603	1
Leigh, Rob.	gent.		Gray's Inn	1588–1603	12
Lucas, Tho.	knight	Camb. (Trinity)	Gray's Inn	1564–1599	13
Mackwilliam, Hen.					
	gent.			1569–1577	3
Mackwilliam, Wm.					
	gent.			1574	1
Maxye, Anthony	gent.	Camb. (Corpus)		1580–1591	25
Maxye, Hen.	gent.	Camb. (Queen's)		1598–1603	8
Maynard, Hen.	gent.			1599–1603	7
Meade, Tho.	gent.	Camb. (Christ's)	Middle Temple (serjeant)	1568–1595	14
Medley, Hen.	gent.	Camb. (Magdalene)	Middle Temple	1573–1577	5
Mildmay, Hen.	gent.	Camb. (Christ's)	Gray's Inn	1581–1600	43
Mildmay, Hum.	gent.	Camb. (Peterhouse)	Gray's Inn	1591–1599	5
Mildmay, Tho.	knight	Camb. (Christ's)	Lincoln's Inn (Custos rotulorum)	1569–1603	92
Mildmay, Tho. of Barnes	knight			1586–1603	50
Mildmay, Walter	knight	Camb. (Christ's)	Gray's Inn	1575–1589	16
Mordaunt, John	knight		Middle Temple	1564–1568	4
Morley, Edw.	baron			1585	1
Morrice, James	gent.		Middle Temple (reader, barrister, Atty. Court of Wards)	1573–1593	22
Nicolls, Geo.	gent.			1562–1583	20
Nicolls, Tho.	knight			1566	1
Nightingale, Geof.					
	gent.	Camb. (Christ's)	Gray's Inn	1595–1602	11
Paschall, Andrew	gent.	Oxford (Exeter)		1587–1602	50
Petre, John	knight		Middle Temple	1573–1603	67
Petre, Wm.	knight	Oxford (Exeter)	Oxford, D.C.L. (Custos rotulorum)	1564	1
Pinchon, John	gent.	Oxford	Inner Temple	1568–1573	11
Powell, Steven	gent.	Oxford, B.A., M.A.	Middle Temple	1597–1598	2
Pyrton, Edmund	gent.			1574–1588	6
Rawlens, Tho.	gent.		Inner Temple	1600–1601	4
Raynsford, Rich.	gent.			1594–1601	3
Riche, Edw.	gent.			1562–1598	35
Riche, Rich.	baron			1564	1
Riche, Rob. I	baron			1567–1581	24
Riche, Rob. II	baron		Gray's Inn	1582–1603	21
Riche, Rob.	gent.		Inner Temple	1601–1603	4
Saltonstall, Rich.	gent.			1602	1
Sammes, John	gent.	Camb. (Emmanuel)	Lincoln's Inn	1595–1601	16
Sandell, Leon.	gent.			1569–1570	3
Smythe, John	knight			1584–1596	11
Smythe, Wm.	gent.	Camb. (St. John's)	Lincoln's Inn	1591–1603	23
Sisley, Clement	gent.			1566	1
Smythe, Tho.	knight	Camb. (Queen's), M.A., B.A.	Padua, LL.D.	1562–1570	6
Southerton, Geo.	gent.			1591–1593	4
Stannap, Edw.	gent.			1589	1
Stern, John	bishop	Camb. (Trinity), Colchester M.A., B.D., D.D.		1594–1603	13
Sulyard, Edw.	gent.		Lincoln's Inn	1579–1601	14
Sussex, Rob.	earl			1595–1601	3
Tabor, Wm.	gent.		Doctor of Divinity	1599–1601	4

	Status	University	Legal background	Quarter Sessions 1574–1582	Sessions attended 4
Taye, Tho.	gent.			1574–1582	4
Throgmorton, Kenelm					
	gent.			1562–1579	8
Towse, Wm.	gent.		merchant	1592–1603	25
Tuke, Geo.	gent.			1562–1572	2
Tuke, Peter	gent.			1591–1603	16
Turner, Edw.	gent.	Camb. (Emmanuel)	priest	1598–1603	11
Turner, John	gent.			1574	2
Twedye, Rich.	gent.			1572–1590	4
Tyndall, John	gent.	Camb. (Gonville)	Lincoln's Inn (barrister)	1593–1598	6
Waldegrave, Edw.					
	gent.	Camb. (Peterhouse)	Gray's Inn	1600–1601	6
Waldegrave, Tho.					
	gent.			1577–1602	8
Waldegrave, Wm.					
	gent.		Lincoln's Inn	1568–1571	3
Warryn, Rich.	gent.			1593–1596	7
Wentworth, John	gent.		Lincoln's Inn	1584–1585	2
Wentworth, Reg.	gent.			1580	1
West, Richard	gent.		Justice of Queen's Bench	1564	1
Weston, Jerome	gent.			1586–1603	29
Whetstone, Bernard					
	gent.			1589–1598	8
Wilson, Jerome	gent.			1586	1
Wiseman, John	gent.	Oxford (Queen's)	Inner Temple	1582–1590	9
Wiseman, Ralph	gent.			1598–1603	13
Wiseman, Wm.	gent.	Camb. (Peterhouse)	Lincoln's Inn	1592–1602	14
Wrothe, Rob.	gent.	Camb. (St. John's)		1580–1595	7

TABLE 2

Attendance of Justices at Quarter Sessions

(These figures are based on the available attendance figures from the Sessions rolls. The number beside the years shows the total number of rosters available for the ten-year period).

No. of J.P.s 1562–1571 (22 rosters)	No. of sessions attended	Average attendance
44	166	8.0
1572–1581 (35)		
38	331	9.4
1582–1591 (37)		
61	384	10.3
1592–1601 (37)		
66	496	13.4

TABLE 3

Justices' Education and Profession

Year	New J.P.s	University No.	%	Inn of Court No.	%
1562–1571	44	11	25	21	47
1572–1581	26	6	23	10	38
1582–1591	33	9	27	13	39
1592–1601	33	11	33	9	27

TABLE 4

Essex Commission of the Peace (11 February 1562)
(P.R.O. Calendar of Patent Rolls, 4 Eliz., Part X, no. 935)

*Nicholas Bacon
*William, Marquis of Winchester
*Henry, Earl of Arundel
*John, Earl of Oxford
*Thomas, Earl of Sussex
*Edward, Bishop of London
*Henry, Lord Morley
*Richard, Lord Rich
*John, Lord Darcy
*Henry, Lord Hundson
John, Lord Graye
*William Petre, knight
*Ranolf Chomley, serjeant
*Gilbert Gerrarde, Attorney General
*†Anthony Browne, Judge of Common Pleas
*Richard Weston, Judge of Common Pleas
*Robert Riche
*†Anthony Cooke
*John Wentworth
*Thomas Wrothe
Francis Jobson
*†Thomas Smythe, knight
Peter Mewtas

Thomas Josselyn
*†William Bendlowes, serjeant
*†Thomas Mildmay
*Thomas Powle
*George Medley
*Richard Cooke
†Kenelm Throgmorton
†William Ayloff
†William Cardynell
Edward Barrett
†Edward Bury
*John Tonworth
*George Hadley
*†George Nicolls
*†Edmund Bocking
Clement Sisley
George Christmas
Henry Golding
Edmund Daniel
†Matthew Bradburie
†Edward Riche
Roger Amys

TABLE 5

Calendar of Justices of the Peace (4 July 1560)
(P.R.O. Essex Assize File, 35/2/5, no. 16)

(I have added this list, as it pre-dates the commission of 1562. Essex had the highest number of J.P.s in Elizabeth's early years, Kent ranking second—F.G.E.).

Nich. Bacon, Keeper of the Great Seal, Wm. Marquis of Winchester, Treasurer, Henry Lord Arundell, Steward of the Queen's Household, John Earl of Oxford, Lord Chancellor, Thos. Earl of Sussex, Henry Lord Morley, Rich. Lord Riche, John Lord Darcye of Chiche, Henry Lord Hunsdon, John Lord Greye, Wm. Petre knight, Ralph Cholmeley, serjeant-at-law, Gilbert Gerrarde, Attorney-General, Rob. Ryche and Hum. Browne, knights, Anth. Browne and Rich. Weston, Justices of the Common Pleas, Anth. Cooke, John Wentworth, Tho. Wrothe, Edw. Walgrave, Wm. Fytzwilliam, Peter Mewtas, Frs. Jobson, Tho. Smythe, Tho. Josselyn and Tho. Golding, all knights, Wm. Bendlowes, serjeant-at-law, ‡Tho. Myldmay, Kenelm Throkmorton, Tho. Powle, Geo. Medley, Rich. Cooke, Tho. Averey, Wm. Aylyff, Edw. Barrett, ‡Henry Fortescue, ‡Edw. Berye, John Tomworth, Geo. Hadley, Geo. Nicols, Edw. Pyrton, Geo. Tuke, Wm. Cardinall, Tho. Latham, Wm. Chysull, Geo. Christmas, John Danyell, Tho. Smyth, Tho. Francke, Henry Goldyng, ‡Edm. Bocking, Matth. Bradberye, Edw. Walgrave, Edm. Danyell, Frs. Wyatt, ‡Hum. Cornwall, Edw. Riche, ‡Wm. Strangman, and Roger Amyce, all esquires.

* J.P.s who were made of the *quorum*.
† J.P.s who appeared at Quarter Sessions at least once within two years of appointment.
‡ J.P.s who attended at Midsummer Quarter Sessions, 27 June, 1560.

Index of Subjects

Index of Persons and Places

z